The Great Collection of
The Lives of the Saints

The Great Collection of The Lives of the Saints

Volume VII: March

Translated from the Slavonic edition
published by the Christian Printshop
of the Transfiguration Almshouse
in Moscow in the year 1914
from the original compiled by
SAINT DEMETRIUS OF ROSTOV
and published in Kiev

First English Edition
Translated by Father Thomas Marretta

Chrysostom Press
P.O. Box 536
House Springs, Missouri 63051
2008

Casebound ISBN 978-1-889814-10-0

Printed with the blessing of
His Grace ALYPY
Archbishop of Chicago and Mid-America
The Russian Orthodox Church Outside Russia

Library of Congress Cataloging in Publication Data
Demetrius, of Rostov, Saint, 1651-1709
   The Great Collection of the lives of the saints / first English edition translated by
Thomas Marretta.
   p. cm.
   "Translated from the Slavonic edition published by Christian Printshop of the
Transfiguration Almshouse in Moscow in the year 1914 from the original compiled
by Saint Demetrius of Rostov and published in Kiev."
   Includes indexes.
   Contents: — v. 2. October
   ISBN 0-9635183-8-0. — ISBN 0-9635183-9-9 (pbk.)
   1. Christian saints — Biography — Early works to 1800. 2. Church year sermons
— Early works to 1800. 3. Orthodox Ea stern Church — Sermons — Early works to
1800. 4. Sermons, English — Early works to 1800. 5. Christian Saints — Biography
— Sermons — Early works to 1800. I. Marretta, Thomas, 1954-
   BX393.D46 1995
   281.9'092'2 — dc20
   [B]   95-39035
                                                                                              CIP

Table of Contents

TABLE OF CONTENTS

To the Pious Reader

$\mathcal{I}$n these volumes of the present collection we offer to English-speaking Orthodox Christians the first set in any modern Western language of full-length accounts of the struggles and martyrdoms of the most eminent saints to cover the entire course of the year.

Our devout forebears in the faith had as their daily reading not newspapers and novels but the Holy Gospels, the Psalter, the Book of Hours, and the Lives of the saints. Nourished constantly by these, their souls were filled with ineffable delight and spiritual yearning, and they lived not for this fallen world but in expectation of the eternal kingdom. It is our hope that these volumes will likewise ever be in the hands of the Christians of our time.

Blessed is he who is able, every day, to read the Life of the saint whom the Church commemorates: such a man in some measure lives on earth the festive life celebrated by the inhabitants of heaven. For those yet unable to observe this custom, the present collection offers the possibility of at least reading beforehand of the saints and feasts they will hear praised at Vespers and Matins on those days when services are held in their parish churches.

The reader of the Lives of the saints should not expect to find in them the characteristics of a contemporary biography any more than one who regards a holy icon should expect to see a naturalistic portrait. Concentrating on what is of spiritual significance, the hagiographer produces a verbal image that enables us to gaze upon God's favorites through the light of the unwaning Sun of righteousness, Christ our Lord. By the use of certain conventions, of predetermined phrases and formulae, hagiography creates a particular atmosphere, a particular rhythm, as it were, which elevates us from earth to heaven, just as do the Church's other sacred arts, iconography, hymnography, and so forth.

The unbeliever, reading the Lives of the saints, may react skeptically to the miracles and numerous vicious torments described therein, but the faithful are reminded of our Saviour's words: *Verily, verily, I say unto you, He that believeth on Me, the works that I do shall he do also; and greater works than these shall he do; because I go unto My Father.*[1] Indeed, we should understand that any recounting of the marvellous works and sufferings of the saints is likely to be, if anything, incomplete.

Saint Demetrius of Rostov himself relates an incident that illustrates this truth very clearly. "One night in 1685, during the Nativity Fast," writes the holy hierarch, "I lay down to rest without undressing about an hour or so before Matins, having finished recording the account of the passion of the holy martyr Orestes who is commemorated on the tenth day of November. And in a vision during sleep I beheld the holy martyr Orestes, his face full of joy, who addressed to me the following words: 'I endured more torments for Christ than those you have recorded.'

"Having said this, he uncovered his shoulders and revealed to me a great wound on his left side, which penetrated to his bowels, and he said, 'Here they ran me through with a sword.' Then, baring his right arm to the elbow, he showed me a wound directly opposite the elbow and said, 'Here you can see how they cut through my sinews.' Likewise, baring his left arm, he disclosed a similar wound, saying, 'Here they also cut through the tendons.' And stooping down, he uncovered his legs and showed me wounds on his knees, saying, 'They cut through here with a wheel.' Finally, standing erect, he looked me in the face and concluded, 'Do you see? I endured more for Christ than you have recorded!'

"Not daring to say anything in contradiction to this, I remained silent."

The Lives of the saints are a true continuation of the Acts of the Apostles, a fulfillment of Christ's promise to be with us *always, even unto the end of the world,*[2] and proof of the Apostle Paul's assertion that Jesus Christ is *the same yesterday, today, and forever.*[3] They are the confirmation of all the holy and eternal dogmatic truths of the Orthodox faith, of the ethical theology of the Church, of the might of the precious and life-giving Cross, and of the entire economy of our salvation. In them the power of our risen Lord over sin, suffering, and death is abundantly

[1]John, ch. 14   [2]Matt., ch. 28   [3]Heb., ch. 13

demonstrated, and the soul hungering and thirsting for righteousness finds everything necessary for satisfaction.

May all who read these Lives be stirred up to obey the
charge given us by the holy Apostle: *Be ye imitators of me, even as
I also am of Christ,*[4] and may they strive to emulate the struggles
of the saints to the measure of their strength. May they also not
forget to pray for those who labored and sacrificed to make
these texts available to them.

---

[4]I Cor., ch. 11

The Teachers, Historians, and Chroniclers from whose works this book was compiled are as follows:

Ambrose, Bishop of Milan
Andrew, Bishop of Crete
Basil the Great, Archbishop of Caesarea in Cappadocia
Cheromenus, disciple of the holy hieromartyr Nicon
Cyril, monk of Jerusalem
Daniel, monk of Raithu
Dionysius the Areopagite
Ephraim the Syrian
Epiphanius, Bishop of Cyprus
Evodius, Bishop of Caesarea
Evodius Synchorus
Evodus, an apostle of the Seventy, Bishop of Antioch
George Kedrinus, the Greek historian
Germanus, Patriarch of Constantinople
Gregory the Dialogist, Pope of Rome
Gregory, disciple of Saint Basil the New
Gregory of Nyssa
Jerome the presbyter, teacher of Orthodoxy
John Chrysostom
John of Damascus
John Moschus
Leo the Grammarian
Macarius, Metropolitan of Moscow and All Russia
Nicephorus Callistus, surnamed Xanthopoulus
Nicephorus Gregoras
Proclus, Patriarch of Constantinople
Sophronius, Patriarch of Jerusalem
Sozomen, the ecclesiastical historian
Symeon Logothetes
Symeon Metaphrastes
Synchronius, monk of Sinai
Theodore the Studite
Theodoretus, Bishop of Cyrrhus
Varinus and his brother Armenius, authors of the Life of Saints
    Chrysanthus and Daria

Many other ecclesiastical books and many other trustworthy Lives of the saints have been consulted in the compilation of this book, as well as the Old Testament and the New, Prologues, Synaxaria, Menaia, *The Spiritual Meadow*, *The Martyrologium* (the ancient Acts of the Martyrs), *The Patericon of the Caves* (compiled by Nestor the Chronicler; Symeon, Bishop of Vladimir and Suzdal; and Polycarp, archimandrite of the Kiev Caves), other Paterica, and the manuscript versions of the Lives of the saints available to us. *Wherefore, seeing we also are compassed about with so great a cloud of witnesses, let us lay aside every weight, and the sin which doth so easily beset us, and let us run with patience the race that is set before us*, writes the holy Apostle Paul in the twelfth chapter of the Epistle to the Hebrews. Again in the same epistle, in the thirteenth chapter he writes, *Remember your instructors, who have spoken unto you the word of God: and considering the end of their conversation, imitate their faith*. And again, in the fifteenth chapter of the Epistle to the Romans: *For whatsoever things were written aforetime were written for our instruction, that we through patience and comfort of the Scriptures might have hope. If in the mouth of two or three witnesses every word may be established*, as the Creator has Himself said, how much more likely it is, that every word written herein is true, considering that so many witnesses testify to the veracity of these accounts?

 える ‪える‬

"The lives and praises of the saints are like the stars in brilliance. Because of their number, we do not know the names of all the saints; still, they amaze us by their radiant majesty, as do the stars, which while fixed in their position in the heavens, illumine all that is below, being seen by the Indians, yet not concealed from the Scythians, shining upon the land and guiding by their light those at sea. Similarly, the radiance of the saints, though their relics be entombed in sepulchers, is not bounded by the ends of this earth here below. Therefore, we marvel at their lives and are amazed at how God has glorified them that please Him."[1]

---

[1]Saint Symeon Metaphrastes, from the Life of Saint Xenia, January 24

Concerning the Month of March

This month, called *Martius* by the Romans, was the first in the Hebrew year from remotest antiquity. After the Jews returned from captivity, they named it Nisan. Regarding this month, the Lord spoke unto Moses and Aaron in the land of Egypt, saying, "It *shall be unto you the beginning of months: it shall be the first month of the year to you.*"[1] During this month God made the visible creation and its master Adam, the first man, for whose sake He *planted a garden eastward in Eden.*[2] To Adam He gave dominion over all the earth, with its beasts wild and tame, creeping things, and *the fish of the sea and the fowl of the air.*[3]

In this month the Lord commanded the Israelites to celebrate Pascha in Egypt and then, *with a strong hand and a lofty arm, led forth Israel out of the midst of them, divided the Red Sea into parts, and overthrew Pharaoh and his host.*[4]

In this month the Only-begotten Son of God came down to earth, without ceasing to be God. The archangel announced the Holy Spirit's overshadowing of the most pure, Ever-virgin Mary; and the co-eternal Word of the Father took up His dwelling in the womb of the immaculate child of God.

---

[1]Ex., Ch. 12   [2]Gen., Ch. 2
[3]Gen., Ch. 1   [4]Ps. 135

In this month Christ our Pascha was sacrificed for us. Having voluntarily suffered on the Cross, undergone burial as mortal, and risen in glory as God immortal, He Who brought Israel out of Egypt loosed from the bonds of Hades Adam, the whole choir of holy forefathers, and every righteous soul. So doing, He drowned the infernal pharaoh in the Red Sea of the cruel passions. During this month when the new light of our salvation shone, Adam and Eve were renewed and inherited a paradise better than that of old. During this month hell was harrowed, heaven opened, death put to death, life bestowed upon all, corruption abolished, and our tainted nature clothed with incorruption. The human race escaped slavery to sin and was granted freedom and the Kingdom of heaven.

In the beginning, it was in this month that visible light was created, and it was also during this month that the perfect light of the holy faith shone forth at the end of the ages; wherefore, this is the first of months, the beginning of the year. On its first day began the solar and lunar cycles, as well as the sequence of weeks, leap years, solstices, and equinoxes. When calculating the number of years since the creation, it is more accurate to begin with this month than with September. The word "September" is derived from the Latin *septem*, meaning "seven"; and September is the seventh month of the year, whereas March is the first after the creation of the world. In September begins the cycle of indictions established by Augustus, first Emperor of Rome and the entire known world, during the twelfth year of his reign, thirty years before the Nativity of Christ; therefore, the Homily on the Beginning of the Indiction is the first item in the September volume of the present menologion.[5] Neither Augustus nor any of the ancient idolatrous peoples knew the true God, Fashioner of creation, or anything about the world's beginning, or about Adam, the first man. Imagining that the universe is uncreated and beginningless, they did not reckon time from its inception, but from various important events. Some calculated from the establishment of kingdoms and monarchies, such as the Assyrian, Median, or Persian. The ancient Greeks reckoned from the first Panhellenic Olympian Games, a vile festival

---

[5]That is, St. Demetrius' *Great Collection of the Lives of the Saints* (Tr.)

involving athletic contests and horse-races. Roman chronology began with the founding of the city of Rome. Other nations used other systems. The cycle of indictions was unknown prior to Augustus' time, and as originally introduced had no connection to the creation of the world. We no longer use the indiction of Augustus, but that of Constantine the Great, first Christian emperor. After defeating the persecutor Maxentius and delivering the Roman Empire from tyranny, Saint Constantine granted the Christians freedom of worship. He abolished Augustus' indiction and inaugurated his own, which the holy fathers at the First Ecumenical Council decreed be celebrated as the onset of liberty for the Church.

While the passage of years since the creation of the world is calculated beginning with March, the indiction established by Saint Constantine in these latter times to celebrate the joyous deliverance of the Church from persecution begins in September. On the seventh day of creation, in March, God rested from His works, and in the Old Testament He commanded the people to keep feast in the seventh month. During Old Testament times a second new year's celebration was held in September, according to the divine ordinance written in the books of Moses, because of the reckoning of the year of jubilee[6] and not because the world was created in that month. The Hebrews had two chronological cycles, one connected with the year of jubile and beginning in September, and the other connected with the creation of the world and beginning in March. Now, in the New Testament era of grace, we still thankfully commemorate the creation of the world in March, and we also observe Constantine's indiction, celebrating God's renewal of mankind through the freedom granted to the Church. Beyond this, during September, the seventh month after March, we commemorate the entrance into the synagogue of Him Who rested on the seventh day after creating the world. There He read the Scripture concerning Himself, which tells how the Holy Spirit, Who bestows gifts sevenfold upon us, sent Him *to preach the acceptable year of the Lord*,[7] that is, the renewal of the world originally fashioned in March.

---

[6]Lev., Ch. 25   [7]Is., Ch. 61; Luke, Ch. 4

The First Day
of the Month of March

The Life and Passion of the
Holy Monastic Martyr Eudocia

During the reign of Trajan, a young woman named Eudocia lived in Heliopolis, a city of Coele-Syria, in what later became the province of Phoenicia Libanensis. She was a Samaritan and a servant of the devil, his dwelling and tool. Her exceptional beauty entrapped many and led them to perdition, allowing her to amass a huge fortune by sinful means. No artist could capture her loveliness, which was so renowned that young noblemen and magistrates from faraway provinces came to Heliopolis for the sole purpose of seeing Eudocia and enjoying her favors.

Over time Eudocia accumulated almost as much gold as was stored in the Emperor's coffers, but her heart became hard as stone and her soul gravely ill due to her shameful way of life. No power except God's could heal such a hopeless sinner. And so it was that the Good Shepherd, Who searches for the lost sheep, stretched out a helping hand; the Creator remembered His creature, defiled by the devil, and vouchsafed renewal to her. The true Householder took thought for the fruit of the vineyard and rescued it from the thief; the Master of the celestial treasury snatched the lost drachma from the mud and deposited it on high. The Guardian of the bounty reserved for the righteous made the lost Samaritan woman heiress of His perfect hope: He put the devil to shame and transformed the swine wallowing in filth into an immaculate lamb. The cauldron of degradation became a vessel of purity; the pit of iniquity, a limpid spring; the stinking abyss of corruption, an alabaster jar brimming with fragrant myrrh. As a result, she who slew the souls of many would lead to salvation many more. Lo, this is the story of how Eudocia turned to God:

A devout ascetic named Germanus was returning to his monastery from a pilgrimage. On the way, he stopped for the night in Heliopolis in the home of a Christian who lived near the city gates. The dwelling of Germanus' host abutted Eudocia's mansion. After resting briefly, the monk rose, according to his custom, and chanted the psalms. He completed his rule, then sat and for a long time read a book telling about God's Dread Judgment, and about how *the righteous shall shine forth like the sun in the Kingdom*[1] of heaven, whereas sinners shall be cast into unquenchable fire and mercilessly tortured unto the ages. Providence ordained that Eudocia was alone that night in her room, separated from the monk only by a thin wall. As soon as he began reading, she woke and lay silently on her bed until he finished. She heard everything, because the monk read loudly. Smitten by compunction, Eudocia remained awake all night, in fear pondering her sins, God's awesome judgement, and the unbearable torments awaiting sinners. Divine grace roused her to repentance, and at dawn she sent for the monk. She asked him, "What sort of person are you and where are you from? Tell me about your beliefs and way of life. I was listening to your strange and terrifying reading last night and was extremely disturbed. Never have I heard anything like it. If it is true that sinners are bound for eternal fire, who can be saved?"

"You have never heard about God's Dread Judgment? What religion do you profess?" inquired the blessed Germanus.

"I am a Samaritan," replied the woman, "and was born in Samaria. I am extremely rich and was troubled most by the passage threatening the wealthy with unquenchable flames. Never have I heard anything like that read from our books, and it frightens me."

"My lady, are you married?" asked blessed Germanus. "How did you become so wealthy?"

"I have no lawful husband, but many admirers. They have made me rich," admitted the woman.

---

[1] Matt., Ch.13

"My Master Christ is truth itself, so I enjoin you to tell me truthfully: are you willing to become poor, in order to save your soul and live happily unto the ages? Or would you prefer to burn with your money and possessions in eternal fire?" Germanus asked.

"Far better that I inherit everlasting life stripped of possessions than to perish for all eternity with my wealth," Eudocia replied. "Still, I wonder why the rich must be punished after they die. Is your God so implacably cruel that He must consume with fire all who have money?"

"God neither hates the prosperous nor forbids the acquisition of wealth," said Germanus. "It is ill-gotten gain that He condemns, and wasting money on pleasures and sinful desires. If a man earns money in a lawful way and spends it virtuously, he is blameless and righteous before God. If, however, his fortune was gotten by immoral or dishonest means, by theft or exploitation, and he hoards it, neither showing compassion on the poor and beggars, nor clothing the naked, nor feeding the hungry, he will be tortured mercilessly."

"Do you think my wealth iniquitous?" asked Eudocia.

"Very much so!" exclaimed Germanus. "You obtained it by the sin most offensive to God."

"I have clothed many naked people, satisfied the hungry, and given away a considerable amount of gold directly to those in need," protested the woman. "How could my riches be evil?"

"My lady, hearken carefully," said Germanus. "Everyone prefers to bathe in clean springs rather than foul, stinking water. Do you really think that, failing to wash in the bath of God's compassion, you can, by a few acts of charity, be cleansed of the filthiness that clings to you as you wallow in the swamp of sin? As though by a mighty wave, the unrepentant are swept from the slough of iniquity to the abyss of pitch and brimstone, burning with the Lord's wrath. Your great wealth is an abomination before the mighty Master and eternal Judge. Already He has consigned it to the flames, as the wages of adultery and fornication. It does you no good at all to set aside for the needy a little portion of your riches. Your reward for small kindnesses is consumed in the fire with your countless vices; their fragrance is overwhelmed by the fetor of transgressions. As long as you willingly defile yourself, you cannot become a recipient of grace. Until you rid yourself of the stench of sin, wash yourself with tears of repentance, and adorn yourself with good deeds, God will not vouchsafe you His mercy. A person who walks barefoot in briars is pierced by many thorns. Although he may remove some, more remain embedded in his soles to torment him. By giving occasional alms to the poor, you may extract a few thorns of sin; but what does that matter, if most are still embedded in your conscience to fuel your fiery torment? God, the dread and righteous Judge, is wroth and threatens you with the everlasting tortures He has prepared for the unrepentant. But if you heed me, you can save yourself and inherit eternal joy."

Eudocia begged, "Servant of the living God, remain a bit longer and tell me more about how I may render myself worthy of divine compassion. I wish to expend my wealth in a manner that will lead to my salvation. You said that the Lord is pleased when we give alms as we should. There is no reason why I cannot trade some of my possessions to escape the miseries you say God will inflict on those whom He hates. Lo, Reverend Father, I have many slaves. If you can persuade your God to accept my gift and grant me salvation, I will send them to you bearing gold, silver, and other treasures."

"Do not reason concerning God as though He were a man," warned Germanus. "Do not imagine that He has any need of the worthless things people value so highly. The King Who is incomparably richer than all earthly rulers willingly impoverished Himself in order to gain us, that is, to purchase our eternal salvation. Therefore, daughter, distribute your possessions among the poor and the ill, for God loves them and counts gifts to them as gifts to Himself. In exchange for temporal wealth given to the poor, He bestows *a treasure in the heavens that faileth not.*[2] Do this, daughter; then come to the holy and saving font and wash away the grime of your sins. You will emerge from the waters of Baptism completely cleansed, born again through the grace of the Holy Spirit, and receive an inheritance in the realm of incorruptible, eternal light. In that land there is no darkness

---

[2] Luke, Ch.12

or night, no sorrow or grief. You will be a holy lamb, grazing in the celestial pastures of Jesus Christ our Redeemer. If you wish to be saved, do as I advise, daughter, and you will enjoy blessedness unto the ages."

Eudocia said, "If the words you read had not stamped themselves upon my mind, I would not have bid you come, Reverend Father. Take as much gold from me as you wish, but remain here, instructing me in virtue and the Christian faith. After I have given away my money and possessions, and settled my affairs, I will follow wherever you lead."

The blessed Germanus answered, "Your salvation suffices me; I do not require your gold. I must return to my monastery, but more important is leading the lost sheep back to Christ's fold. For a few days I will remain, to assist your conversion to God. Now, do as I say: summon a Christian presbyter. Have him catechize and baptize you according to the accepted order. Holy Baptism is the beginning, the starting-point of salvation. Afterwards, every God-pleasing endeavor follows in sequence."

Eudocia ordered one of her most trusted slaves to go to the Christian church and bring back a presbyter. The servant was told not to reveal who required the presbyter or for what purpose. When the priest arrived, Eudocia fell prostrate before him, kissed his feet, and begged, "My lord, sit with me for an hour and explain your faith. I want to become a Christian."

The presbyter inquired, "What is your religion at present?"

"I am a Samaritan and, I am ashamed to say, a woman of ill repute, a bottomless pit of vice," confessed Eudocia. "I have heard that unrepentant sinners who do not become Christians are tortured by inextinguishable fire, and I decided I must convert."

The presbyter said, "If you were once an abyss of sin, become henceforth a haven of salvation. If you were storm-tossed, enter the calm harbor. If you were being swallowed by turbulent waters, seek now the dew that drops from heaven. If you were drowning, find the skilled Pilot who can safely guide you to the port where immense wealth is stored. Make haste and become heiress to the treasures there. Give your temporal riches to the poor and free yourself from the grief of sin. So doing, you will escape the darkness and unquenchable flames awaiting the unrepentant."

"Is it true that your God shows no mercy to sinners?" asked Eudocia, beating her breast and weeping.

The presbyter replied, "When they are baptized, the Lord pardons repentant sinners every trespass they committed in a state of unbelief. There is no forgiveness, however, for those who remain in their sins and fail to repent. Such wretches are tortured without mercy."

"Tell me, presbyter: do you think that the blessings of heaven are preferable to those on earth?" asked Eudocia. "Here we enjoy gold, silver, jewels, entertainments, and delights of every sort. There is an abundance of fish and fowl, other foods, and wine. What is there in heaven better than this?"

"If you do not tear away your mind from the deception of this world and learn to disdain temporal pleasures, you will never behold eternal life or know its ineffable felicity," the presbyter warned. "If you wish to inherit the celestial bounty, forget the pride and delights of the present existence."

"My lord, may I never prefer what quickly passes away to the blessings of life everlasting!" cried Eudocia. "But when I accept the Christian faith, how can I be certain I will indeed attain eternal life? Where is the proof? How will I know that your God truly has forgiven my countless sins? What if I distribute all my riches (which would keep me in comfort until the day I die), and fail to receive what you describe? Who then would be in a worse plight than I, left without refuge in time of trouble? If in my distress I appeal to those whom I have seduced, they may shun me. I need stronger assurance of your fair promises and your God's compassion. If I am completely convinced, I will boldly give away all my possessions, go wherever you direct, and labor for the one God the rest of my life. As I was once an example of dissipation, so will I become a model of repentance. Do not be dismayed, Father, at my uncertainty: I have never before heard anything like Christian teaching. In our books and the Samaritan religion, in which I was reared, there is nothing comparable."

The presbyter said calmly, "Do not be troubled, Eudocia. Do not allow your thoughts to waiver or be tossed about. It is the devil's words you are speaking. Satan is the author of evil, the enemy of our salvation, a foul spirit. He is alarmed that you may enter Christ's service and is sowing doubts and misfounded fears in your heart. His hope is to divert you from the path of righteousness and return you to a life of sin. Through love of the world and love of the flesh he is trailing you, and plotting your death and destruction. This is his sole and secret purpose: to corrupt men and drag them from the path to salvation, so they will share the ever-burning punishment awaiting him. But our God, of Whose goodness, infinite mercy, and love for mankind you seek assurance, is eager to receive sinners in His fatherly embrace, forgive their transgressions, and grant them everlasting life. Of this you will be convinced if you lift your mind from earth to heaven, abandon temporal cares, and meditate on eternity. To attain steadfast faith you must offer the Lord concentrated, humble prayer. When the soul is reconciled with God and divine light shines in it, the Lord reveals to it higher truth, whereby a man clearly perceives the vanity of the present fleeting existence, and the glory of the world to come: he realizes how merciful is God and how measureless His compassion. If you wish to be saved, heed my words. Lay aside your costly robes, dress in your worst garments, and lock yourself in a room for seven days. Spend the time recollecting your sins, weeping, and repenting for your offences before God the Creator. Fast and pray, that our Lord Jesus Christ may enlighten you and show you how to please Him. The time will not be wasted. Our Master is gracious and infinitely kind: with open arms He accepts those who turn to Him. He always welcomes the repentance of a sinner."

Eudocia agreed to the presbyter's suggestions; therefore the priest rose and bade her farewell with these comforting, prophetic words: "Christ God justified a publican and had mercy on a sinful woman who bathed His feet with tears. May He justify and have mercy on you, and glorify your name throughout the earth."

As soon as the presbyter left, the blessed Eudocia called for one of her handmaids and instructed her, "If anyone comes here, wishing to enjoy commerce with me, do not let him know that I am at home. None of the servants are to reveal anything about my doings or whereabouts. Have them say that I went to a distant village and will tarry there. Give strict orders to the doorkeeper to let in no one. The slaves, including the cooks, may rest from all their duties. Keep the main gates to the property locked until further notice. In general, do everything possible to make it seem I am away."

Then Eudocia asked blessed Germanus, "Father, why do you monks dwell in the wilderness and deprive yourselves of the pleasures of human companionship? Do you find it more enjoyable there?"

"No, daughter, nothing of the sort," said Germanus. "Our sole purpose in fleeing cities and worldly pleasures is to escape vanity and pride, and to put to death the passions more easily by means of hunger, thirst, toil, nakedness, and lack of the necessities of life. Everything you enjoy is absent in the desert. We are distant from opportunities for sin. He who lives in the city easily falls, conquered by the weakness of nature, led astray by the devil, enticed by handsome faces or lascivious conversations, ever beguiled by unclean thoughts that debase the soul. The portal of heaven is closed to the defiled soul until it is cleansed by repentance. Heaven is the throne of timeless light, of true joy and enduring bliss. In heaven, there is neither sin, nor sorrow, nor grief. It is for the sake of the Kingdom that we make our abode in the wastelands. Our goal is to escape sin throughout our days and cleanse ourselves of past transgressions by means of the harsh desert life, thereby opening the way to the blessedness beyond. All our efforts are devoted to keeping our bodies unsullied by evil deeds and our minds untainted by wicked thoughts: to avoiding rancor, guile, hypocrisy, grumbling, swearing, jealousy, and anger. This way, we become like the angels, as Christ Himself assures us in the Gospel. However rich a person may be, however tirelessly he may accumulate money, he comes no closer to the Heavenly Kingdom, for wealth is like a corpse in a grave, powerless to help anyone. If we long for pardon of trespasses, let us tread the way of the Lord's commandments until the day we die. Let us walk in righteousness and truth and rend our hearts from sympathy for sin, just as we rend a garment; let us cry unceasingly to God. Thus we shall be purged of the stench of sin, concerning which David says, *My bruises are become noisome and corrupt in the face of my folly.*[3] David also teaches us to

---

[3] Ps. 37

chant in prayer the Lord's words, saying, *How sweet to my palate are Thy sayings! More sweet than honey to my mouth.*[4] The Lord's words are more delightful than the costliest food or wine and fortify the soul more than any meal can strengthen the body. It is written: *Wine maketh glad the heart of man, and bread strengtheneth man's heart.*[5] Wine and bread symbolize the commandments of our Lord Jesus Christ, which truly nourish the human soul. If a man diligently exercises himself in the commandments, they gladden and strengthen him, purify him from defilement, and justify him before the Lord. Therefore, lay aside your splendid robes and clothe yourself in humble attire. Turn the powers of your soul to repentance and virtue, and water the earth with tears, that you may reap a harvest of joy in heaven. Weep until you extinguish the furnace of sin, and the Lord will vouchsafe you consolation, permitting you to enter into the felicity of the righteous. Lament your transgressions, which the devil sweetened for you, and an angel will draw near and intercede for your salvation. Let tears run from your eyes, and you will dry up the stinking bog of depravity, in which you were long mired. You were held fast by the author of evil; henceforth, enjoy the bounties of paradise. Bring to despair him who deceived you by means of pleasure and burdened you with the yoke of sin. Always work eagerly to please God. A bee collects nectar to make honey, and you should multiply your righteous deeds in order to acquire virtue. Thus you will become a daughter of the unwaning light."

These words sank deep into Eudocia's heart, which was predisposed to accept them by what Germanus had said earlier. Moved to contrition for her sins, Eudocia threw herself at the elder's feet, crying, "O man of God, finish well what you have begun. Present me untainted before the Lord. I do not wish to be a laughingstock to those who would lead me astray, but to reach the end of the course and attain the felicity you attest. Do not withdraw hand and brush from the panel until you have completed depicting Christ in me."

"Abide in the fear of the Lord, daughter, and remain in your room," Germanus advised. "Weep and pray constantly until

---

[4]Ps. 118   [5]Ps. 103

God cleanses all your sins and grants you perfect assurance of His mercy. Our Lord Jesus Christ is compassionate and will not tarry in sending His grace to comfort you." Upon this, the blessed Germanus prayed for her, traced the sign of the Cross over her, and locked her in a room, promising to remain in Heliopolis for a week.

Eudocia spent seven days praying and fasting; then the blessed Germanus released her from confinement. Seeing that she was pale and thin, wore a humble expression, and looked quite different than before, the elder took her hand and bade her sit. He sat beside her and inquired, "Daughter, what were you thinking about for the seven days? What was revealed to you? Did you see anything unusual?"

"I will explain everything, Reverend Father," she answered. "I prayed the whole week long, as you instructed me. Last night, while weeping for my sins and praying, I lay prostrate with arms outstretched so that my body formed a cross. Suddenly a light more brilliant than sunbeams shone upon me. When I rose, there stood before me an awesome, radiant youth, whose garments were whiter than snow. He took me by the right hand, lifted me through the air, set me upon a cloud, and escorted me to heaven. At its entrance I beheld an even more wondrous, overpowering light and an innumerable multitude of men clothed in white. They were laughing with one another and were indescribably joyous. Seeing me approach, they greeted me as a sister. The men surrounded me and were leading me toward that incomparable light when a horrible specter appeared, black as soot or charcoal or pitch. The dreadful being stared menacingly at me, gnashed its teeth, and savagely attempted to snatch me out of the hands of my guides. 'Are you letting her enter the Kingdom of heaven!' it screeched. 'Why then do I waste time on earth, leading people into temptation? This harlot has corrupted the whole world, fornicating with countless men. For some time I have devoted all my cunning and power to ensuring her success. So many wealthy noblemen enjoyed and enriched her that she has as much gold and silver as the imperial treasury. She is my emblem of victory, the undefeatable weapon with which I smite those who have fallen away from God and into my nets. Are you so enraged with me, O chief commander of God's hosts, that you intend to cast me down and let me be trampled by her? Has the vicious revenge you daily exact on me failed to quench your wrath? Why must you abduct the slave I purchased at such a high price? Is nothing of mine safe from theft? I fear you will snatch away all the evildoers remaining in my grasp and present them to God, saying that they are worthy of the Kingdom of heaven. Vain are my labors, vain is my fretting! Why are you so merciless? Calm yourself, loosen my bonds, and you will see how, in a *twinkling of an eye*,[6] I blot out the human race from the earth. I was hurled down from heaven on account of a single act of disobedience; you wish to lead into the celestial kingdom the worst sinners, who mock God and have brazenly incited His anger for many years. Why not simply assemble at once all the sordid scoundrels in the world and present them to God? I should cease squandering effort and immediately withdraw to the murky abyss where everlasting torments await me.'

"My escorts glared at the raving imp and smiled lovingly at me. Then a voice sounded from the light, saying, 'It has pleased God to show compassion on the children of men, so that repentant sinners may find a place in the bosom of Abraham.' The voice commanded my guide, 'Michael, fulfiller of My covenant, return this woman to her dwelling below. I will be with her as she contests for Me.'

"The angel took me back to my room, saying, 'Peace be with you, handmaiden of God Eudocia. Take courage and be strong. The Lord's grace will protect you wherever you go.'

"Reassured by this, I asked, 'Who are you, my lord? Vouchsafe me a word about faith in the true God and explain how I may attain life everlasting.'

"'I am a prince of God's angels,' he replied, 'and am charged with caring for penitent sinners and leading them to the blessed life that never ends. *There is great joy in heaven in the presence of the angels over one sinner that*[7] flees the darkness of iniquity and arrives at the pure light of repentance. As the Father of all, God desires the salvation of the human soul, which He fashioned in the beginning according to His own likeness with His immacu-

---

[6]I Cor., Ch. 15   [7]Luke, Ch. 15

late hands. His servants the angels rejoice when they see a man's soul adorned with righteousness and worshipping the eternal Father. If a soul forsakes the gloom of sin, turns to the living God, and cleaves without reservation to the Father of all children of the light, the angels greet it as a sister.' So saying, he traced a cross over me. I made a prostration before him, and he departed for heaven."

At this the blessed Germanus said to Eudocia, "Henceforth, daughter, never doubt that the true God in heaven awaits repentant sinners and leads them to the everlasting light wherein He reigns, surrounded by royal servitors, the holy angels. You beheld the angels in celestial light, as well as the majestic, unending glory of our Lord Jesus Christ. You learned how quick is God to show compassion and forgive sins, how quick to bestow His grace on those who desire to be reconciled with Him. You saw the splendid palace in which He dwells and understood how dim, how weak is the visible light of this world when compared to the divine effulgence. Now tell me what else you learned."

Determined to serve the one God and King of glory with her whole heart, the blessed Eudocia declared, "I saw the glittering gates of heaven and confess that only the celestial King can save sinners!"

"Prepare yourself, daughter, to labor fervently for God," Germanus urged. "Make certain that your fruits of repentance outweigh the sins of your past life. Offer the immortal and eternal God an acceptable sacrifice; that is, tears and sighs. Do not desist from lamentation until you have been purged of every stain and presented to Christ as a spotless bride. Be done with pride and the soul-destroying, unbridled lusts of youth, that Christ the Lord may remit your debt of sin. Slip loose of the heavy harness of slavery to iniquity, laid upon you by the devil, and put on the blessed and easy yoke of life-bestowing repentance. So doing, you will be freed from sin and become a friend of the holy angels and all the righteous. Be strong in the true faith, keep yourself chaste, and do not violate your conscience. Tell the devil to his face, 'I have nothing more to do with you, or you with me. I have found my true Master and submitted to Him forever. I have torn off the rags of vile, gloomy, ruinous carnal love and put on the new, radiant, incorruptible vesture of righteousness. I have been touched by the grace of God, which has initiated me into eternal salvation. Nothing ties me to the earth: neither yearning for riches, nor love of worldly pleasures, which I have learned are fleeting and valueless. I strive to attain heavenly blessings alone. Be satisfied with what is your own, devil. Begone, you alien, deceptive spirit: robber, and slave of eternal darkness!'"

Emboldened, Eudocia inquired, "Reverend Father, what would you have me do next?"

"You must be marked with the emblem of faith, Holy Baptism, which will preserve you from harm until the end of your life," replied the holy monk. "As for me, I must return to my monastery, but will be back, if the Lord permits."

"Do not abandon me, my lord!" Eudocia pleaded. "Do not leave before I am perfectly converted to God and receive the fullness of grace, lest the ancient deceiver, seeing me forsaken and helpless, entice me back to harlotry."

The blessed Germanus assured her, "Your sacred hope and the fervent desire for a better life which God Himself granted you will preserve you from the nets of the foe. Abide a little longer in humble prayer, confessing your sins and preparing for Baptism. I will return soon and trust that you will be leading a godly life, assisted by the Holy Spirit." With this, the blessed elder committed her to the Lord's care and departed.

For several days the blessed Eudocia continued to fast, subsisting on bread, oil, and water. She wept and prayed day and night. Then she went to the Bishop of the town, who baptized her in the name of the holy and consubstantial Trinity. A few more days passed, and she sent a petition to the Bishop, in which she enumerated all her possessions and requested that he accept them on behalf of Christ. The Bishop summoned the blessed Eudocia and asked, "Did you, daughter, write this to me, a sinner?"

"I did, Your Grace," she responded, "and now I repeat my request that the steward of the Church accept my gift and divide it among paupers, orphans, widows, and other needy persons however you think best. I have come to understand that my wealth is tainted, because I acquired it by sinful means."

The Bishop (whose name was Theodotus) perceived Eudocia's pure faith in God and love for Him. Foreseeing with his inner eyes her future way of life, he said, "Pray for me, sister in the Lord. You have been deemed worthy to be called a bride of Christ, since you have learned to hate carnal lust and to love chastity. Having renounced fornication, you strive for virginal purity; having renounced the vain world, you wish to sell *all that you have and buy* the heavenly *pearl;*[8] having lived a short time in sin, you have attained by repentance life eternal and celestial; having death before your eyes, you have won immortality; having led many to perdition, you shall regenerate many in Christ. You have divested yourself of the rags of gloomy darkness and been clothed in the garb of the light of faith. You are indeed worthy to be called Christ's bride. Your name, Eudocia, means 'good pleasure,' and the Lord is well-pleased with you, because you have renounced commerce with men enslaved to the passions, and preferred the love of angelic choirs. Again I beg you, handmaiden and friend of God: pray for me and remember me in the Heavenly Kingdom." The Bishop wept as he said this and much else in a similar vein. Afterwards, he ordered his deacon, "Bring here at once the steward of the Church." When the steward arrived, Theodotus told him, "You are a devout man, charged with care for many souls. I now entrust to you this handmaiden of God, who is determined to struggle for virtue. Guide her to salvation and, by the hands of the poor, present to God whatever she gives you."

The steward was a presbyter, a blameless virgin who, upon the decease of his parents, had donated his entire inheritance to the Holy Church of God and devoted himself to the Lord's service. He went with Eudocia to her house, and Eudocia assembled her chief servants. "Each of you is to bring here everything I have entrusted to your safekeeping," the blessed one commanded. The servants brought the following: twenty thousand pounds of gold,[9] uncountable fine vessels and plates of every kind, numberless jewels and enormous pearls, 275 chests of

---

[8]Matt., Ch. 13
[9]A Roman pound is approximately equal to three-quarters of an English pound. (Tr.)

silk garments, 410 chests of white linen, 160 chests of gold-embroidered clothing, 152 chests of apparel decorated with jewels and gold embroidery, 123 large chests of everyday clothes of various kinds, 250,000 gold coins, twenty chests of perfumes and sweet spices, thirty-three chests of genuine Indian myrrh, eight thousand pounds of silver, 132 pounds of gold-embroidered silk curtains, seventy pounds of plain silk curtains, and innumerable garments and other items of lesser value. Besides her movable wealth, Eudocia possessed real property: land, villages, and entire rural districts which produced a yearly income of as much as 802,000 denarii.[10] After turning everything over to the holy presbyter and steward of the church's hostel, the blessed one assembled all her manservants and maidservants. She divided among them two thousand gold pieces, as well as vessels of every sort, curtains, expensive beds, gilded furniture, and whatever was of value in her mansion, except for what was stored in the trunks. Then, giving each one a kiss, she announced, "I release you from temporal servitude and urge you to liberate yourselves from slavery to the devil. You truly will be free if you hearken unto me and are united to Christ the true God, Who will grant you the everlasting liberty of children of God and number you among His spiritual warriors."

Next Eudocia declared to the presbyter, "It is time, my lord, for you to take what has been entrusted to you and dispose of it as you think best. I must devote myself to finding the Master Who is in search of me."

Amazed by the blessed one's unexpected repentance, rich offering, and fervent zeal for God, the presbyter exclaimed, "You are blessed, Eudocia, and have rendered yourself worthy to enter Christ's bridal chamber with the virgins! You have understood how to gain admittance into that blessed chamber and, not wishing to remain outside, vigilantly keep watch for the Bridegroom's coming. Your lamp is full of oil, and darkness will never again enshroud you. May God always help you advance in virtue. As one deserving to be numbered among the saints, remember to pray for me, a sinner."

---

[10]The Slavonic text does not actually specify the denomination of this income. (Tr.)

Shortly afterwards, the venerable Germanus was apprised of everything by the grace of the Holy Spirit. Returning to Heliopolis, he confirmed that the blessed Eudocia had given all her possessions to God, freed her slaves, and embraced spiritual and material poverty for Christ's sake; whereupon, he took her to a convent under his direction in the desert, not far from the monastery where he lived. There he made her a nun, and she devoted herself to monastic labors and struggles, toiling for God day and night. Seventy brethren had their dwelling in the blessed Germanus' coenobium and thirty nuns in Saint Eudocia's convent.

Thirteen months later Charitina, superior of the convent and a woman of holy life, reposed in the Lord. Under her direction Eudocia had achieved remarkable progress. She read through Sacred Scripture from beginning to end once and, guided by the Holy Spirit, attained a profound understanding of it. She also memorized the Psalter. Since no one in the community could equal her for asceticism, the sisters unanimously chose her as the new abbess. God did not tarry in confirming with a miracle her worthiness and His approval of the election, as our story will tell.

One of Eudocia's former lovers, an extremely wealthy young man named Philostratus, was unable to forget the intimacy with the saint he once enjoyed and, spurred by the devil, began pondering how to lure her back to a life of fornication. Every day the fire of lust burned hotter in him, and after a considerable time he devised a plan. Dressed in the habit, he took as much gold as he could carry and walked to Eudocia's convent, certain that money would buy success. At his knock, the portress opened the little window in the door and asked, "How can I help you, sir?"

"I am a sinner," he replied, "and have come to request prayers and a blessing."

"Brother," said the gatekeeper, "men are forbidden entry to this place. Go a little further and you will reach the monastery of Father Germanus. The monks will pray for you and bless you. Do not trouble us again, for I cannot admit you." So saying, the portress shut the window.

Frustrated and perturbed, but still burning with desire for Eudocia, Philostratus went to Germanus' monastery. He found the blessed Germanus reading by the monastery gates and humbly prostrated himself before the elder. The venerable one prayed for the visitor according to monastic custom, blessed him, and said, "Sit, brother, and tell me where you are from and the name of your monastery."

"Father, I am an only child and my parents recently passed away," responded Philostratus. "I did not want to marry, but preferred to labor for God as a monk; therefore, I put on these robes and am searching for a place to carry out my intention under an experienced guide. When I heard about your godly life, Reverend Father, I undertook the long journey here, hoping that, if I threw myself at your feet, you would accept me as a penitent into the monastery."

The blessed Germanus studied the man's face and eyes and could tell that he was under the dominion of the passions. "The monastic life is extremely arduous, my son. I am uncertain whether you are capable of it," he said. "We elderly monks can hardly withstand the grievous carnal temptations which the devil brings upon us. You are still a young man, aflame with sensual desires. How will you master the foe?"

"Father! Are there not many examples of young people who have embraced a life of virtue and conquered their lusts?" objected Philostratus. "I know about Eudocia, abbess of your convent. She is renowned for holiness, despite her youth and former dissipation. With your guidance, she vanquished the flesh and became steadfast in asceticism. Father, I will not hide the fact that her example deeply inspired me. Recalling her love-liness, her wealth, the luxury in which she lived, and how she suddenly decided to follow Christ on the narrow, difficult path, I was filled with desire to emulate her. If out of love for Christ she, a frail woman, could renounce the world and mortify her desires, then certainly I, a man, can do the same. Oh, if only I could see her just once! Her teaching would doubtless enkindle such zeal for God in my heart that I would have strength to overcome every demonic temptation for the rest of my life."

The Lord's servant Germanus was swayed to take the lie for truth and was persuaded that the young man sincerely wished to labor for God. "Since it was Eudocia's example that inspired you to virtue," said the elder, "I will allow you to speak with her." Then Germanus summoned an aged, respected monk who frequently took incense and other necessities to the convent. He instructed him, "The next time you go to the women's monastery, permit this brother to accompany you. He would like to see the handmaiden of God Eudocia, benefit from her discourse, and emulate her godly life."

By and by the monk had reason to visit the convent and took the young brother with him, as the abbot had commanded. Like a wolf in sheep's clothing, Philostratus entered the women's community clad in monastic garb. Seeing Christ's bride, Saint Eudocia, he marvelled at her humble appearance, poverty, and emaciated figure. Her complexion was sallow, her eyes were fixed upon the ground, her lips were silent, her habit was ragged, and her bed was a straw mat covered with sackcloth. When no one else was standing nearby, Philostratus took advantage of his opportunity and said, "What is the meaning of this, Eudocia? Who took you from your palace, fit for a queen, from your riches and pleasures, and brought you to this miserable place? Who removed you from the city, where you paraded before the crowd in gorgeous apparel and enjoyed universal admiration and praise for your marvellous beauty? What scoundrel deprived you of the fine things in life and reduced you to utmost poverty and degradation? All of Heliopolis is searching for you; everyone's eyes yearn for you; the very walls of your mansion weep for you. I have been sent by the whole city to entreat you to return and assuage the people's grief. Give heed to me, my lady, and abandon this pigsty; this hunger; these stinking rags; this rough, hard bed. Come back to your mansion and the pleasures you once enjoyed. You have lavished your wealth on others, but we will enrich you again. Why doubt my words? Why delay? Everyone loves you and wishes you well. Why are you your own enemy and torturer? Are you not ashamed to hide such beauty in a nun's habit? What a waste to destroy with constant weeping eyes radiant as the sun! What gain can there be in emaciating such a young, voluptuous body; in tormenting oneself with hunger, thirst, and other austerities? Where now are the perfumes that made fragrant the city that took you for a goddess? You have voluntarily exchanged those marvellous scents for the stench of a contemptible, poverty-stricken existence. Who led you astray, what vain hope enticed you to forsake riches beyond enumeration, which only promised to increase with time? What other wealthy person has given away everything as you have? We know where to find your former possessions and can easily recover them for you, if only you come back with me to the city, my lady Eudocia. I have more than enough money to arrange for proper transportation. When we get back to Heliopolis, everything that was yours will be retrieved."

While Philostratus babbled, Eudocia glared at him until she could no longer restrain herself. "May the God of vengeance silence you!" she said. "May the righteous Judge, our Lord Jesus Christ, Whose servant I am, prohibit your departure, for you came here, son of the devil, with a wicked intent." So saying, she blew on his face, and the wretched false-monk dropped to the floor dead.

The sisters were standing too far away to hear the conversation, but they saw Eudocia blow on Philostratus. At first the nuns were astonished at the power of divine grace working in the saint and horrified by Philostratus' sudden death; then they became afraid that the pagans, who hated the Christians and their monasteries, would learn what had happened. Although terrified that the authorities would conduct an investigation and commit their monastery to flames, they dared not question Eudocia directly, but discussed the matter in private. One of them suggested, "We should say nothing to the abbess for now: it is already evening. Let us pray tonight and perhaps the Lord will reveal why the monk died and what we should do."

Just before the Midnight Office, the Lord appeared in a dream to the venerable one, saying, "Rise, Eudocia, and glorify your God. Prostrate yourself beside the corpse of your tempter, sent here by the devil; pray to Me, and I will raise him. He will acknowledge Me, the God Whom you worship, and extol the power of My grace, which abounds in you." Saint Eudocia immediately awoke, prayed for a long time to the Master, and raised the dead man, who seemed merely to have been asleep. Philostratus confessed the true God, Who had shown mercy on him, and threw himself at the blessed one's feet, crying, "I beg you, holy Eudocia, handmaiden of the one God: accept my repentance! My wicked, obscene words have grieved you, but forgive me. Now I know what a compassionate and mighty Master you serve."

"Depart in peace," Eudocia bade him. "Do not forget how kindly God has dealt with you, and do not wander from the true path of holy faith, which you promise to tread."

About that time slanderous reports concerning Eudocia reached King Aurelian, ruler of the land.[11] A number of the saint's most eminent former lovers wrote the King alleging that Eudocia had taken with her into the desert much gold due as taxes. They requested a guard and permission to arrest the saint for accepting the Galilean faith, proscribed by the emperors: that is, for believing in Christ. The gold they promised to secure for the royal treasury. Hearing about the gold, Aurelian was easily persuaded to do their bidding. He summoned one of his officers, by rank a count, and ordered him to arrest Eudocia and bring her and the gold to him. With three hundred soldiers under his command, the officer set out for Eudocia's convent. Before their arrival, the Lord appeared in a dream to Eudocia, saying, "The King is wroth with you, but do not fear, for I am at your side."

It was evening when the officer and troops caught sight of the convent walls. They stopped to await nightfall and divided into groups in order to surround the monastery in the dark. However, when they attempted to approach the convent, God's invisible hand stopped them in their tracks. At daybreak the Lord's might was still thwarting their advance. Thus it continued for three days and nights, and they were reduced to despair. Then an enormous, horrible serpent attacked them, and they threw down their weapons and fled. Although the soldiers escaped the monster's jaws, they were struck down by its poisonous breath.[12] Some died immediately; others stumbled on a short distance, and then collapsed. Only the Count and three of his men returned unharmed to the King. Aurelian was furious and asked his nobles, "What should we do to this witch, whose sorcery has brought about the death of so many troops? What do you counsel? We cannot leave her unpunished."

---

[11]Not the Roman Emperor, but a subordinate
[12]The ancients believed that the breath of a serpent, as well as the bite, could be lethal. In this case, however, as well as that of Zeno, related below, supernatural forces were clearly involved. (Tr.)

When the others had spoken, the King's son proposed, "I will take an entire army to that brothel, level it, and bring Eudocia here."

Everyone agreed to this, and the next day the Prince and his soldiers left. Dusk found them near a village ruled by Aurelian, and the Prince decided it would be a convenient place to spend the night. At that moment, however, Providence intervened. A reckless youth, the Prince jumped off his horse and shattered his leg. Soldiers carried him to a bed, but his condition became critical and at midnight he died. The troops returned to the King, bearing the corpse. Aurelian collapsed and lay senseless; meanwhile, the citizens congregated and mourned for the Prince and the King, whose life was imperiled by grief. While matters were in this state, Philostratus stepped forward and declared to the King's advisors that Eudocia was God's handmaiden and that because a celestial power protected her, she could not be harmed. "The King's only hope of again seeing his son alive is to plead with Eudocia to entreat her God to raise the dead," explained Philostratus. "I know by experience the might of her prayer and the compassion of her God."

This heartened the King, who questioned Philostratus about what had occurred to him. He believed Philostratus' story; wrote a humble, respectful letter to the saint; and sent his tribune Babylas to deliver it. Saint Eudocia greeted Babylas with a prostration and asked, "Why is the King sending a letter to me, a poor, wretched sinner?"

While Eudocia was reading the letter, the tribune retired to a guest room, where a book lay open. His eyes fell upon the words, "*Blessed are they that search out* Thy *testimonies,*[13] O Lord." After reading the entire psalm, the tribune laid his head on the book and fell asleep. A radiant youth appeared to him in a dream, touched his side with a staff, and ordered, "Rise, Babylas, the dead man is waiting for you."

Babylas awoke terrified, related the dream to the blessed Eudocia, and requested her permission to leave. Eudocia summoned the nuns and announced, "Sisters and mothers, the King has written a letter to my lowliness. How shall I respond?"

---

[13]Ps. 118

As with one voice all replied, "The grace of the Holy Spirit will guide you. Write to the King whatever is pleasing to God."

The blessed one prayed for a long time, then wrote the following:

"It is not clear, Your Majesty, why you have written to me, an insignificant woman. I am a wretched sinner, and my conscience is so burdened by countless transgressions that I dare not entreat Christ God to have mercy on you and restore life to your son. I can only put my trust in the renowned compassion and might of my Lord, and hope that if you believe wholeheartedly and undoubtingly in Him as the true God Who raises the dead, He will manifest to you and your son His extreme benevolence. It is pointless for a man to call upon God's holy and dread name and make request of Him unless he believes with a pure heart; therefore, have sincere faith in Him, and you shall behold the matchless power of the immortal God, be deemed worthy of His beneficence, and enjoy His blessing."

After inscribing three crosses on its seal, Eudocia handed the letter to Babylas and dismissed him. Upon return to the palace, the tribune did not immediately give the letter to the King, but first placed it on the Prince's chest. Babylas shouted the name of Christ; and straightway the dead youth stirred, opened his eyes and spoke, and arose hale and whole, as though he had been asleep. Everyone was amazed and terrified by the glorious miracle. "Great is the God of Eudocia the Christian!" exclaimed Aurelian. "Holy art thou, O God of the Christians; rightly do the people turn to Thee. Thou art the one true God, and those that believe in Thee hold the true faith. I beg Thee to accept me, for I too confess Thy name."

The Bishop of the city baptized the King, his wife, his son who was raised from the dead, and his daughter, whose name was Gelasia. Aurelian gave abundant alms to the poor and presented a large quantity of gold to the blessed Eudocia so that she could build a church. He himself erected a church on the site of Eudocia's mansion and often wrote to the saint, requesting her holy prayers. Not long after his conversion, the King reposed, having attained a profound understanding of the faith and performed many good deeds. He was followed to the grave by his wife. His son was made a deacon and, when the Bishop of

Heliopolis died, was consecrated as his successor. Acknowledging the vanity of the world and eschewing marriage, Gelasia also dedicated her life to the Lord's service. Two of her eunuchs escorted her to Saint Eudocia's convent, where she lived out her days, laboring fervently for God and pleasing Him greatly.

Meanwhile, in their eagerness to bring about the perdition of souls, the wicked, God-hating heathen began persecuting those who secretly toiled for the Lord. Heliopolis was now administered by Governor Diogenes, a fanatical worshipper of false gods, who employed every cruelty against those who rejected idolatry. Earlier, he had hoped to win Gelasia's hand, and Aurelian had encouraged his aspiration. After his Baptism, however, the King rebuffed Diogenes, since he refused to marry his daughter to an unbeliever. When her father died, Gelasia, afraid that Diogenes would force the wedding, straightway entered the monastery of the venerable Eudocia. Rumor soon had it that Eudocia was hiding the maiden, so Diogenes sent fifty soldiers to arrest the saint as a Christian and bring her to Heliopolis for interrogation. During the night, while the troops were approaching the convent, the Lord appeared to the blessed one and said, "Eudocia, My daughter, watch, and be steadfast in the faith. The time is at hand for you to confess My name and manifest My glory. The contest awaits you. Savage men like wild beasts will pounce on you, but do not be troubled or afraid. I am with you: a sure Guide and strong Helper in every difficulty and trial."

As the vision ended, the soldiers reached the convent and scaled its walls. The Holy Spirit informed Eudocia of their entrance, and the saint went out to meet them. "What do you want?" she asked. "For whom are you searching?"

The troops laid hold of her and demanded that she betray Eudocia. The saint promised to deliver Eudocia if they would release her for a little while. They agreed, and immediately she went to the church, entered the altar, and removed from the tabernacle a portion of the immaculate, life-giving Mysteries of Christ, hiding it in her bosom. Then she returned to the soldiers and declared, "I am Eudocia. Take me to your master."

The soldiers left in the middle of the night with the blessed one. It was moonless and pitch black, but a holy youth appeared with a torch and lit the path for Eudocia. He was an angel, and only the venerable one could see him or the light. The soldiers wanted to put Eudocia on a donkey, but she refused, saying, "*Some trust in chariots, and some in horses,*[14] but I trust in Christ my God and shall walk."

The Governor commanded that the holy abbess be taken directly to prison. After three days he called for her guard and asked, "Has the witch been given anything to eat?"

"I swear to Your Excellency that no one has given her food or drink," replied the guard. "But every time I look in her cell, she is lying on the floor with arms outstretched − praying to her God, it seems."

"Today I shall be occupied with other matters, but will deal with her tomorrow," said the Governor.

On the fourth day Governor Diogenes sat upon his judgment seat and commanded that Eudocia be brought to him. Seeing that the godly one was clad in lowly apparel and that her appearance was humble and her gaze fixed to the ground, the Governor ordered his servants to uncover her head. For a long time Diogenes was silenced by the ineffable beauty and dignity of Eudocia's face, and he marveled at how divine grace flashed like lightning upon the saint's features. Finally, wavering in his determination to put Eudocia to death, he exclaimed to his advisors, "By my god, the sun! It is a pity to destroy such radiant loveliness. I am at a loss what to do."

One of the judges said, "Does Your Excellency think the witch's beauty is natural? Is he ignorant of the power of the black art? If Eudocia is deprived of sorcerous powers, she will appear as the hag she is."

"Tell us your name," the Governor ordered the blessed one. "What is your lineage? What sort of life do you lead?"

The saint made the sign of the Cross and answered, "I am called Eudocia, and of my lineage and way of life there is no need to speak. One thing alone should you know, that I am a Christian. In His ineffable compassion, the Creator of all has permitted me, the unworthy, to be called His handmaiden. Therefore, O Governor, waste no more time, but deal with me as with other Christians. Judge me, torture me as much as you like,

---

[14]Ps. 19

and put me to death. I trust that Christ, my true God, will not forsake me."

"A long-winded reply to simple questions," remarked the Governor. "Do you intend to hold forth when we tear away your flesh? Explain to me clearly why you hate the gods. Why did you forsake the city and flee to the desert with money due the public treasury?"

The saint replied, "I am a free woman and go wherever I wish. What law prohibits the free-born from changing their abode? As for the gold, let me confront my accusers, and the truth will become apparent. Do you really take me for a thief?"

Lengthy disputation followed, and the saint proved unshakeable in conviction and invincible in debate. Afterwards, the Governor ordered her suspended from a tree, stripped to the waist, and flogged mercilessly by four soldiers. When the soldiers tore open her robe, the immaculate, life-giving Body of Christ, which Eudocia had taken from the convent, fell to the ground. Servants picked it up and showed it to the Governor. No sooner had Diogenes taken it into hand to examine it than the spotless Body of the Master shot into flames, incinerating the tyrant's lackeys and scorching the Governor's left arm to the shoulder. Writhing in pain, Diogenes shouted to the sun, which he regarded as a god, "O lord sun, heal me, and I will straightway deliver the witch to fire! I know that I am being punished for my slowness in destroying her."

Suddenly a thunderbolt of fire fell out of heaven, killing Diogenes. His corpse resembled a charred log, and everyone was gripped by terror. One of the soldiers beheld a radiant angel standing beside the martyr, whispering consolation and covering her nakedness with a shroud whiter than snow. The soldier drew near Eudocia and said, "I believe in your God. Accept me, a penitent, O handmaiden of the living God."

"May the grace of a true conversion be with you, child," replied the blessed one. "It is plain that you want to be born again and enter a new life. If you wish to be saved, be done with idolatry."

The soldier begged, "Handmaiden of the Lord, have mercy on the Governor and entreat your God to return him to life. If you do, many will believe in the true God." So saying, he cut down Eudocia from the tree.

The holy martyr prostrated herself and prayed for a long time. Then she rose and shouted, "O Lord Jesus Christ, Who knowest men's secrets and in Thy wisdom didst create all things, Thy will is omnipotent! Restore to life all those who were burned to death, that many believers may be confirmed in the holy faith and that the heathen may turn to Thee, the living God, and glorify Thy most holy name unto ages of ages." After this she lifted up each corpse, saying, "In the name of the Lord Jesus Christ, Who rose from the dead, return to life." One by one the dead stirred as if from sleep.

While everyone was still marvelling at the ineffable and glorious miracles, a shout and sobs were heard. Word was brought to Count Diodorus, who was present with the troops, that his wife Firmina had been poisoned in her bath by charcoal fumes. Diodorus ripped his cloak in half and, grief-stricken, ran lamenting to his wife's body. He was followed by an enormous crowd and Governor Diogenes. When he saw Firmina's corpse, Diodorus rushed back to Saint Eudocia and declared, "I truly believe that your God is infinitely greater and more powerful than any pagan deity! If you wish to strengthen my weak, unfledged faith, come raise my wife from the dead. I will abandon doubt and believe in your God."

"It is not for your sake alone that the Lord, in His boundless compassion, intends to reveal His will," Eudocia responded, "but for the sake of all who wish to enter His Kingdom. May God help us. Let us go to your wife."

On the way Eudocia and Diodorus, who were accompanied by a huge crowd, encountered Firmina's remains being carried away on a bier. The saint ordered the bearers to halt. After weeping and praying for a long time, she took the corpse by the hand and cried, "O great and eternal God, Lord Jesus Christ, Thou art the Word of the Father and raisest the dead! Be pleased, I supplicate Thee, to edify the multitude by working a mighty wonder. Command Firmina to return to life and grant her the spirit of repentance, that she may cleave to Thee, God eternal and immortal."

No sooner had Eudocia spoken the word than Firmina rose from her bier. As with one voice, everyone shouted, "Great is the God of Eudocia! True and righteous is the God of the Christians!

We beg you, handmaiden of the living God, to save us, for we believe in the Lord."

Diodorus was overjoyed by the miracle and cast himself at the saint's feet, pleading, "Maiden of God, make me a Christian! Now I truly know how great is the God you serve." Diogenes and Diodorus, their households, and many other people were baptized in the name of the Father, Son, and Holy Spirit. All remained devoted to the faith until the end of their days.

Eudocia took up residence in Diodorus' house and taught the word of God to the newly illumined Christians. One day a youth named Zeno was working in a garden near the Count's home and at noon lay down to rest. He fell asleep and was killed by the poisonous breath of a serpent. Learning that the boy was the only child of a widow and that his mother was weeping inconsolably, Christ's lamb Eudocia told Diodorus, "Let us console the grieving woman, and we shall see the marvellous compassion of our God." Eudocia and Diodorus found the corpse black and swollen from the snake's venom. The saint said to Diodorus, "The time has come for you to show your faith in God. Lift up your inner eyes to heaven, pray, and raise the boy."

"My lady, I am but a beginner!" protested Diodorus. "I am still blind to the vision of God, O handmaiden of the Lord."

The saint responded, "I believe without doubt that my God hearkens unto repentant sinners and grants their petitions. Earnestly entreat the almighty Lord, and He will reveal His mercy."

Diodorus bowed his head, beat his breast and, with tears in his eyes, shouted so that all could hear, "O Lord God, Thou hast deigned to call me, the unworthy sinner, to holy faith in Thee and didst send Thy handmaiden to serve as the intermediary of my salvation! Thou knowest my sincere, undoubting hope in Thee. For the sake of Thy glory, raise this child who was killed by a serpent, that he and all men may glorify Thy most holy name unto the ages." Then Diodorus commanded the dead boy, "Zeno, in the name of Jesus Christ, Who was crucified under Pontius Pilate: arise!"

The youth stood up and his flesh regained its natural color. Seeing that he was free of all ill-effect of the venom, everyone glorified God, the Creator of heaven and earth, and believed in Him. When the crowd began to disperse, Eudocia, the Redeemer's holy lamb, shouted, "Wait, brethren! Christ our Saviour soon will be glorified again." The people remained nearby, Eudocia prayed, and forthwith the serpent slithered out, hissing horribly. As though burned by supernatural fire, it flung itself about and writhed in torment. Finally, it disintegrated. All the pagans who saw this went, with their wives and children, to the Bishop of Heliopolis and requested Holy Baptism.

Not many days later the venerable Eudocia retired to the convent and resumed her monastic labors. She would visit the city from time to time to confirm the Christians in the faith and lead the heathen to Christ God. Fifty-six years after her Baptism, Saint Eudocia was martyred. Following the death of Diogenes, a brute named Vicentius became governor. When this enemy of the Christians heard about the godly Eudocia, he sent troops to the convent to decapitate her. It was the first day of March when Saint Eudocia was beheaded for our Lord Jesus Christ, to Whom be glory, with the Father and the Holy Spirit, now and ever and unto the ages of ages. Amen.

ક⁂ક⁂

Let not the reader or hearer doubt that in antiquity a prostitute could become extremely wealthy. The Greeks were worshippers of idols and ignorant of the true God, and regarded harlotry as worthy of esteem. One of the most highly revered of their vain deities was Aphrodite, patroness of whores. Ancient historians record numerous examples of wealthy Greek harlots. For example, when Alexander the Great destroyed the walls of the renowned city of Thebes, Phrina, a harlot from Athens, offered to build new ramparts, more powerful than the old. She required only that the following be inscribed on the fortifications: "What Alexander destroyed, Phrina the courtesan rebuilt." Laisa, a harlot of Corinth, was so rich and famous that all of Greece, it is written, was spellbound by her. Thais, another Athenian whore, was so beautiful, respected, and wealthy that Ptolemy, first King of Egypt after Alexander the Great, was not ashamed to marry her. Rodope, a Thracian prostitute living in

Egypt, built for herself a pyramid rivalling those erected by the pharaohs. Eudocia equalled these earlier Greek harlots in renown and wealth, but when the blessed one forsook the world, she gave away all that she owned and became poor in spirit. Pleasing God by repentance, she was numbered with the holy virgins and became a companion of the angels and heiress to the eternal riches that *eye hath not seen*.[15]

❦❦❦

According to the Moscow and Kiev registers of saints, Eudocia was baptized in the year 5,604 from the creation of the world,[16] during the reign of Trajan, and was martyred in the year 5,660.[17] If this chronology is correct, the Emperor actually ruling at the time of Eudocia's Baptism was Domitian. He was succeeded by Nerva, Trajan, Hadrian, and Antoninus, in that order. Saint Eudocia would have suffered in the thirteenth year of Antoninus' reign.

❦❦❦

On this same day we commemorate the passion of the holy martyrs Nestor and Tribimius of Perga in Pamphylia. After they had endured grievous torments for Christ, their heads were severed by knives. We also commemorate the holy martyr Antonina of Nicaea in Bithynia. She suffered for Christ during the reign of Diocletian and Maximian. Angels came to her rescue while she was under torture. After every torment had failed, she was put in a sack and drowned in Lake Ascania.

On this same day we commemorate the holy martyrs Marcellus and Anthony, who were burned alive for Christ, and the holy virgin Domnina of Syria. Theodoritus, Bishop of Cyrene, writes about Saint Domnina in the thirteenth chapter of his book *Philotheos*.[18]

---

[15]I Cor., Ch. 2
[16]The year 96 after the Incarnation of Christ
[17]The year 152 after the Incarnation of Christ
[18]Commonly rendered as *The Religious History, Ascetic Life,* or *A History of Monks of Syria* (Tr.)

The Second Day of the Month of March

The Passion of the Holy Hieromartyr Theodotus, Bishop of Cyrene

The holy hieromartyr Theodotus was born in Galatia and became Bishop of Cyrene, a town on the island of Cyprus. His parents, who were Christians, provided him a good education, and from an early age he distinguished himself by wisdom and virtue. Theodotus went to Cyprus and taught the heathen to abandon the deception of idolatry and to believe in Christ as the true God. His preaching of the word of God converted many from pagan impiety to the path of salvation, on account of which he was chosen Bishop of Cyrene.

In those days the ungodly Licinius was emperor and Prince Sabinus was Governor of Cyprus. A persecution of the Christians was raging, and the saint, hoping to suffer for the Lord, fearlessly engaged the unbelievers in public debate. When Sabinus learned that Theodotus was reviling pagan error and openly declaring Christ to be God, he ordered the blessed one seized and brought to him for interrogation. The Lord's hierarch heard about the command and did not wait for it to be carried out, but presented himself to the Governor and announced, "Lo, I am he whom you seek. Neither did I hide, nor was I brought by force, but have come of my own choice to proclaim the truth of Christ my God, which should not be concealed. I intend to expose the whole falsity and weakness of your religion, which should not take long, since you heathen are nothing more than frightened toads. A single Christian has thrown a whole city full of un-believers and an entire army into panic. One servant of Christ is enough to disarm the whole diabolical host of pagan gods."

Unwilling to listen to any more of this, the Governor ordered Theodotus flogged mercilessly with leather straps. While being thrashed, the saint repeated David's words: *The sinners wrought upon my back, they lengthened out their iniquity.*[1]

When the servants' work was done, the Governor said, "Behold the result of your impudence and vaunting!"

"If your inner eyes could see, you would understand the true result of my bravery, which you call impudence," replied the martyr. "However, you are blind and cannot know the blessings that await me. But ponder this: because my spiritual gaze is fixed on the celestial reward given to Christ's martyrs, I do not feel torments. In me divine joy prevails over all physical pain."

"Empty are your boasts, Theodotus," said the Governor. "You may deceive the onlookers, but not me. When I am finished, you will eagerly confess the might of our gods."

"Test your ingenuity; try on me every torment you know," retorted the saint. "You will learn the strength of Christ's soldier. We shall see who prevails: the torturers or the tortured."

"Surely you are aware that the imperial decree permits me to mangle and destroy you," said the Governor.

"The God Whom I serve has made me mightier than emperors or princes. This is why I address you as though you were a slave or a worthless captive," said Theodotus. "I am not afraid of torture, because I have the help of God, Who has taught us to regard all things temporal as of no more value than hay or chaff or dung. Do not imagine that you will cow me by threats. You boast that you can destroy my body, but highway robbers can

[1]Ps. 128

do the same. Your sword gives you license to disregard justice, making you a tyrant, so you forgive adulterers and murderers, and the punishments these deserve you employ against blameless and devout men."

The infuriated Governor commanded that Theodotus be suspended naked from a tree and that his sides be scraped. Christ's sufferer endured bravely and prayed, "O Lord Jesus Christ, Creator of all things visible and invisible, Vanquisher of death and Conqueror of Hades, while on the Cross Thou didst destroy the principalities and powers of the underworld and condemn the ruler of this age. Thou didst bestow celestial power upon Thy holy apostles, preserving them from temptation; Thou didst grant young David victory over Goliath the giant; Thou didst bedew the Babylonian furnace, so that its flames could not harm Thy holy youths. Do Thou strengthen me as I endure torments. Thou knowest men's weakness; Thou knowest that we are more fragile than the most delicate flowers. Glorify Thy name, O Lord, and make me resolute. Crush the power of those who have risen up against Thy sacred flock, and the whole world shall know that Thou alone art God Most High, Who givest courage and endurance to all that hope in Thee." While the saint prayed, the persecutor's servants tore flesh from his bones.

After some time the Governor had Theodotus cut down from the tree and sent to prison. As the saint was being led through the streets, he shouted for all to hear, "Let everyone who witnesses my passion understand my hope! Christ God recompenses the martyrs for their sufferings and I await my reward. If an earthly ruler decorates troops who fight bravely and compensates them with gifts when they are wounded, then certainly the eternal Sovereign and Judge of the contest will bestow upon His soldiers and champions honor now and a place in the Kingdom of heaven at the resurrection. Even the bones of the martyrs are venerated as a token of their future glory, for the Orthodox regard these relics as more precious than any earthly treasure. Such reverence reflects the esteem in which the souls of the martyrs are held by God and His angels on high." The saint continued in this vein until he reached the dungeon.

Five days passed before Theodotus was again presented to the Governor. "I do not think you need to be tortured a second time," remarked Sabinus. "The severity of the torments already inflicted doubtless has made you eager to avoid a repetition and to worship our gods. Now hearken attentively to what I say lest, remaining unsubmissive, you force me to employ even harsher punishments."

Saint Theodotus asked, "Is it possible, thrice-wretched beast, that you still do not understand? Even if you shatter my bones and strip them of flesh, I cannot be broken. I am ready to endure any torture you devise, because I wish to reach the finish-line and obtain the garland of righteousness from my Lord Jesus Christ."

"Do not dishonor this tribunal by mentioning the Crucified One!" shouted the Governor.

"Fool, you are a vessel of every sort of impurity," replied Saint Theodotus. "When I say the most holy name of Christ, you undergo inner torment, become agitated, and blaspheme. It is you who defile this tribunal, by mentioning the vile heathen gods. The demons you worship were similarly tormented when they beheld Christ in the flesh. They wailed, *What have we to do with Thee, Jesus, Thou Son of God?*[2] It is no wonder you cannot bear the sound of Christ's name. You are akin to the demons, which you serve, as did your ancestors."

The Governor said, "I thought that torture would make you compliant and favorable to offers of clemency. Instead, you have become even more arrogant, argumentative, and eager to suffer for Christ. You leave me no choice but to punish you again and prove that your hope in Christ is ill-founded. You are destroying yourself for the sake of a deceiver."

"If I were to suffer for a mere man, I would be as wretched as you godless pagans," said Theodotus, "and would have no hope for the life to come. I can endure your brutality only because my gaze is fixed on the Kingdom of heaven, where Christ the true God rewards us more richly than we deserve. Having Christ's assistance and expecting eternal blessings, I shall prevail over whatever torments you devise. Behold how

---

[2]Matt., ch. 8

Christ helps me, and understand that my confidence in Him is boundless. His divine hand protects me, so that I do not fear your cruelty. My flesh may be corruptible and subject to pain, but it matters not, since my mind is fixed upon God."

Presently Sabinus ordered a gridiron brought and had the martyr stretched out upon it. Beneath the couch, brushwood and kindling were ignited. Amazed by the passion-bearer's endurance, the Governor marvelled, "How can you Christians be so indifferent to pain? How can you have compassion for your fellow-men when you are so merciless to yourselves? What can anyone expect from stony-hearted people like you?"

"You know nothing about love for others, yet discourse on compassion," said the saint. "By condemning me to die, you allow me to take leave of this temporal life and attain the Kingdom of heaven. You make me your debtor. Torment me savagely, so that I may win the crown of righteousness yonder. Torture me to death, so that I may prove myself a perfect sufferer for Christ, the Ruler of the contest, and bring joy to the choirs of holy angels."

"I will happily devise grim torments certain to make you a perfect sufferer," the Governor sneered.

Christ's martyr exclaimed, "Oh, if only you knew the benevolence of the God in Whom I trust! As recompense for my brief distress, He will vouchsafe me life everlasting. If you knew the Lord's mercy, you would be as eager to suffer for Him as I; but your heart is hardened and you do not look for life beyond the grave, because you worship demons. Therefore, you have surrendered yourself to the vanity of this world, preferring the temporal to the eternal."

Shaken by these words, Sabinus admitted, "I was told that you are an ignoramus, but clearly, you are an extremely wise man."

"It is Christ Who speaks through me," said Theodotus; "as such, no orator can best me in debate. I am indeed unlearned, as you were told, but the grace of Christ is with me. It instructs me what to say, strengthens me in suffering, and eases the pain of my wounds."

"I do not intend to show you clemency," the Governor reminded Theodotus.

"Do as you wish," answered the saint. "I am ready."

At this Sabinus ordered his soldiers to drive nails into the martyr's feet and to force Theodotus to walk. While the troops were hammering, the saint raised his hands and prayed, "I thank Thee, O Lord Jesus Christ, for allowing me, the unworthy, to share in Thy Passion! How is it that I, an outcast, have gained access to heaven while still in this world? I thank Thee also, O my Saviour, for delivering me from those who seek my life. May Thy name be glorified in me, O Master Christ. Son of God, Thou art my life, and to die for Thee is much gain. I beg Thee to aid all who suffer for Thy name's sake. Be their helper and calm the storm buffeting Thy Holy Church, that Thy people may extol Thee in peace unto the ages." Then he addressed the Christians standing nearby: "My contest has almost ended, and Jesus Christ is about to bestow on me a crown, the emblem of right-eousness. He was crucified for me, and I have surrendered my flesh to wounding for Him. He died to deliver me from corrup-tion, and I am about to die, that I may become worthy of His Kingdom. How wondrous is the grace of Christ! In exchange for brief torments endured for Him, my Lord grants ineffable, unending, incomparable blessings. *The sufferings of this present time are not worthy to be compared with the glory which shall be revealed in us.*"[3]

Then the soldiers forced Saint Theodotus to walk through the streets with the nails piercing his feet. Witnessing his patience and hearing him thank the Lord, numerous heathen believed in Christ, publicly mocked the idols, and reviled the persecutor. When he learned that the people were glorifying the name of Christ, Prince Sabinus ordered the saint returned to the dungeon. "The sorcerer must not be allowed to deceive the rabble," he muttered. Although he took counsel with his advisors as to how the saint should be executed, the Governor did not put Theodotus to death. Instead, Sabinus allowed the martyr to languish in prison, where his wounds began to fester. The Orthodox Christians who visited Theodotus wiped away the pus with clean handkerchiefs.

---

[3]Rom., ch. 8

Before too long, Constantine the Great defeated Maxentius by the power of the Cross, ended the persecution, and granted the Christians freedom of worship. When Saint Theodotus learned that those held in bonds for Christ's sake were to be released, he was very downcast, because he wished to die in torment for the Saviour. After being let out of prison, he returned to Cyrene and fulfilled his episcopal duties for two years, then reposed in peace. Christ the Lord, Who honors His champions with everlasting glory, bestowed on him a double crown, for his service as a bishop and his sufferings as a martyr. May we be deemed worthy of similar glory, through the prayers of the holy hieromartyr Theodotus and the grace of our Lord Jesus Christ, unto Whom, with the Father and the Holy Spirit, is due praise forever. Amen.

❦❦❦❦

On this same day we commemorate the holy martyr Troadius, a youth of Neocaesarea. While on a remote mountain in hiding from the persecutors, Saint Gregory of Neocaesarea miraculously beheld Troadius' passion. One day, as he was offering up his usual prayers to God, the holy hierarch became greatly troubled. He fell into a stupor and stood motionless for a long time without uttering a word. At first his face wore a sad expression; then it became radiant and joyful. With a mighty voice he gave thanks to God, chanting this hymn of victory: *Blessed be the Lord Who hath not given us to be a prey to their teeth.*[4] The saint's deacon asked, "Why this change in you, Father? Earlier you seemed troubled, but now you are jubilant."

"Child, I have seen a wondrous vision," answered the saint. "A young boy entered into combat with a powerful devil, overcame it, and threw it to the ground." Since the deacon did not understand what this meant, Gregory continued, "A short time ago the Christian youth Troadius was taken to the persecutor's tribunal. He endured many grievous tortures for Christ and has departed to heaven in triumph. At first I was troubled, fearing he would falter and renounce Christ, but now I rejoice, having

---

[4]Ps. 123

seen him complete the contest of martyrdom." The deacon marvelled at how the saint could see things far away as though they were nearby.

On this same day we commemorate the 440 saints martyred in Italy by the Lombards. In the twenty-seventh and twenty-eighth chapters of *The Dialogues*, Saint Gregory, Pope of Rome, writes the following about them:

"Approximately fifteen years ago, as we were told by eyewitnesses, the Lombards attacking the Roman domains seized forty peasants and tried to compel them to eat flesh that had been offered to idols. When our people refused to taste the defiled meat, the Lombards threatened to kill them. In spite of this, the peasants remained true to their faith. They chose eternal life in preference to this transitory existence and so met death together. There can be no doubt that they are martyrs for the truth, since they chose death by the sword rather than to offend the Creator by eating flesh sacrificed to idols.

"During those days the Lombards were holding captive another four hundred persons and sacrificed the head of a goat to the devil. The barbarians dashed about braying lewd songs and grovelling to the goat's head. They attempted to force the prisoners to do the same, but without exception the Christians refused to obey the loathsome command, choosing through death the way to endless life. Always having bowed their heads in adoration before the Creator, they would not do the same before a creature. Their enraged captors hacked to pieces everyone who had mocked the idolatrous rites."

On this same day we commemorate the holy virgin Eulalia of Sicily. She was beheaded for Christ by her own brother and thus gained entrance into the bridal chamber of the Saviour.

On this same day we commemorate our holy monastic father Agathon, desert-dweller of Scete in Egypt. While dying, he remained for three days with his eyes wide open, looking up. The brethren asked, "Abba Agathon, what do you see?"

"I am standing before the judgment seat of Christ," he said.

"Are you afraid?" they asked.

The venerable Agathon answered, "I have done my best to keep the Lord's commandments, but I am a man. How do I know whether my life is acceptable to God?"

The brethren said, "Do you not have confidence in all the good deeds you have done for God?"

"I shall have no confidence until I meet God," he replied. "The Lord's judgements are not the same as man's." So saying, he reposed.

On this same day we commemorate our father among the saints Arsenius, Bishop of Tver. His Life may be found in *The Prologue*.

The Third Day of the Month of March

The Passion of the Holy Martyrs Eutropius, Cleonicus, and Basiliscus

Ꭿfter the holy great-martyr Theodore Tyron[1] was put to death in the town of Amaseia, his companions in suffering, fellow-soldiers, and beloved friends Eutropius and Cleonicus and his nephew Basiliscus remained imprisoned for Christ. A wrathful God had made an end of Governor Publius, Saint Theodore's tormentor, but the persecutor was replaced by another savage atheist, the Phrygian Asclepiodotus. Having received authority from the Emperor Maximian to torture and destroy all Christians who failed to sacrifice to idols, Governor Asclepiodotus raised havoc with the faithful.

One day, Asclepiodotus, surrounded by his counsellors, was sitting upon his tribunal and ordered Eulasius the archivist to read the records of the provincial court. Hearing the account of Theodore Tyron's sufferings, he marvelled at the saint's endurance and asked Eulasius, "What became of Theodore's companions, mentioned in the narrative?"

"They remain in prison with other criminals," replied Eulasius.

Gazing at the burnt-out shell of the temple of vile Juno,[2] mother of the gods, which was visible from the judgment seat,

---

[1]Commemorated on February 17

[2]Saint Theodore Tyron burned down the temple of the Phrygian goddess Cybele in Amaseia. This goddess was identified by the Greeks with Rhea, wife of Cronus, and by the Romans with Ops, wife of Saturn. The text here mistakenly has the temple dedicated to Juno, Jupiter's wife. (Tr.)

and imagining the great-martyr's acts of defiance, the Governor roared in anguish like a lion. Without delay he dispatched soldiers to the prison to fetch the holy martyrs Eutropius, Cleonicus, and Basiliscus. Now Eutropius and Cleonicus were brothers, born in Cappadocia, while Basiliscus, Saint Theodore's nephew, was a native of Amaseia; however, all three were called brothers because of their mutual love.

Entering the dungeon, the soldiers said to the guard, "Give us Theodore's friends."

The guard announced to the saints, "Rise: your hour has come. The Governor is waiting for you. Remember me as you confess the Lord." This the guard said because he had observed the martyrs praying constantly and knew the wonders worked by their entreaties. He had seen the saints bathed in celestial light and the prison doors time and again miraculously thrown open; therefore, he understood that the Lord was with the holy sufferers. The martyrs were eager to contest, but the other prisoners were grieved to be separated from them. Saint Eutropius encouraged his fellow prisoners, "Do not weep, brethren, for we shall see one another again. Pray our Lord Jesus Christ to permit us to complete the course of suffering for Him. May demonic paganism be stamped out and the earth filled with the Lord's grace!"

As the martyrs were leaving, Saint Eutropius sang, *Behold now, what is so good or so joyous as for brethren to dwell together in unity?*[3]

From heaven a voice rang out in reply, "I will not separate you from your brethren, but will take you to Saint Theodore and to repose in the bosom of the patriarchs amid the land of the living."

Asclepiodotus was astonished at the radiant faces of the holy martyrs, and especially the face of Eutropius, who was wise and comely beyond the wont of men. "You have languished underground for a long time. Why such a cheerful air?" the Governor began.

The blessed Eutropius replied, "Truly, O Governor, Christ visits us with His grace every day; therefore, the word of

---

[3]Ps. 132

Scripture is fulfilled in us: *When the heart rejoiceth, the countenance is cheerful.*"[4]

"What is your name?" asked the Governor.

"My chief name is 'Christian,'" declared the saint. "But the name my parents gave me is Eutropius."

Imagining that the Lord's favorite could be won over by flattery, the Governor said, "I see that, besides being a handsome man, you are well-bred. Doubtless you were early initiated into the mysteries of philosophy."

"The Lord Jesus Christ initiated me into spiritual wisdom. I trust that He will enable me to respond wisely to you," the martyr said.

"Heed me, Eutropius, and persuade your companions to submit to the imperial decree and sacrifice to the gods," advised the Governor. "For my part, I will write to the emperors requesting that you be made military commander of the province. You will hold the rank of prince and become a wealthy man, thus learning by experience how beneficial it is to obey the rulers and submit to their edicts. If, however, you fail to comply, I shall cut your flesh to shreds and throw it to the dogs. Your bones will be cast into fire and their ashes scattered on a river. Do not imagine that the Christians will be allowed to anoint your corpse with myrrh as a sacred treasure. Submit, and offer oblations to the gods, or at least say before the people that you will sacrifice. Everyone is awaiting your decision. Do not turn away from the gods those who would render them their due; do not make yourself an object of scorn to those who will watch you and your companions undergo hideous, shameful tortures."

"Enough of this nonsense, son of the devil, inheritor of Gehenna!" the saint exclaimed. "Cease your attempts to lead astray the Lord's servants, O foe of God, stranger to eternal blessings and the bounty of paradise, captive of nethermost Hades. Stop your yelping, pustulous, stinking cur. O hinderer of those wishing to do good deeds, teacher of evil and godlessness, wicked deceiver, no words can do justice to your iniquity. You promise fleeting honor and wealth, which we must all leave behind. Of what value to me are these things, the root of every

---

[4]Prov., Ch. 15

soul-destroying passion: of vainglory, fornication, theft, and murder? What good did riches and repute do for Prince Publius, Saint Theodore's murderer? Publius' body now rots in the earth, and his soul burns in hell, fuel for the black fire of the underworld and food for the worm that never sleeps. Know, impious wretch and malefactor, that God's wrath will soon overtake you. Threaten torture, the sword, fire, or wild beasts; but do not imagine, fool, that you intimidate me. No torment can compel me to sacrifice. My fondest desire is to suffer for Christ God, the riches, boast, strength, and glory of the faithful. Neither my brethren nor I will forsake the Lord. We are eager to die for our Saviour, the Author of life, the invincible Commander, and the Deliverer of those in distress. He will surely rescue us from your clutches."

Hearing this, the Governor flew into a fury and ordered the saint beaten upon the mouth. "Knave, you were brought here to offer oblations to the gods, not to revile me!" he raged. The servants' hands withered when they struck the martyr, and at the sight of this, the notaries recording the proceedings were overcome by terror and flung away their pens. It was a Christian onlooker who completed the task of setting down for posterity everything that happened. Meanwhile, the Governor asked the martyr, "Do you intend to worship the gods and live? If you refuse to sacrifice, I shall destroy you at once."

Saint Eutropius answered, "I will never worship inanimate gods. If you adore them, you are as lifeless as they. I worship the true God and offer Him the sacrifice of praise, the fruit of my lips. Christ says through the blessed David, *'The idols of the nations are of silver and gold, the works of the hands of men. They have a mouth, but shall not speak; eyes have they, and shall not see.*[5] *They have hands, feet, and other bodily members, but all are lifeless. Let those that make them become like unto them, and all that put their trust in them.'* You are blind and deaf and wish me to share your plight, but I will never renounce my Lord Jesus Christ."

The Governor asked Saints Cleonicus and Basiliscus, "What do you say? Will you save your lives by sacrificing to the gods, or will you remain unsubmissive like Eutropius and undergo the same tortures as he?"

---

[5]Ps. 113

"The faith of our brother Eutropius is founded upon the rock which is Jesus Christ. We believe in the Father, Son, and Holy Spirit and will suffer for Christ with Eutropius. The devil cannot separate us, for Christ has united us in love and the holy faith. Three-ply rope is hard to break; and we three, being one in faith and love, are like the Most Holy Trinity in that we cannot be sundered. We shall endure every torment you devise and thereby glorify our Lord Jesus Christ, your enemy," declared Saints Cleonicus and Basiliscus.

At the Governor's orders, four soldiers stretched out the martyrs and mercilessly scourged them until the ground was red with gore. The passionbearers entreated the Lord's assistance and bravely endured the lash, Christ's power aiding them so effectually that it seemed they were not suffering at all. Saint Eutropius prayed thus:

"O God Almighty, good and merciful! Disdain us not, Master, Who savest the righteous and raisest up sinners, Who convertest the impious and settest aright the froward, Who deliverest the wise and correctest the foolish. Thou didst bind the devil and loose man. Thou art the helper of those in bonds and the rescuer of those in torments, the fount of goodness and the Saviour of our souls. O Thou Who permittest sufferings to befall us and grantest us the courage to endure tortures, enable us to bear this flogging, that we may gain the perfect crown of martyrdom. Rescue us as Thou didst rescue Thy servant Theodore. Reveal the devil's plottings, and Thy mercy and all-powerful aid; for Thou alone art our King, Jesus Christ, and Thee alone do we worship, glorifying Thee with the Father and the Holy Spirit forever."

As soon as Saints Cleonicus and Basiliscus said the "Amen," a fearful earthquake shook the tribunal. Though exhausted from wielding the whip, the terrified soldiers raced away like frightened rabbits. Meanwhile the martyrs, bearing no trace of their stripes, were loosed by an invisible hand; and the Lord, His angels, and Saint Theodore appeared. Eutropius cried, "I praise Thee, O Christ my Master, for hearkening unto me so quickly! *And whence is this to me, that my Lord should come to me?*"[6]

---

[6]Luke, Ch. 1

Then he asked Cleonicus and Basiliscus, "Do you see our King Jesus Christ standing before us in glory?"

They replied, "We do."

"Brother Eutropius," Saint Theodore said, "your prayer has been heard and the Saviour has come to help you and reveal the glory you shall enjoy in eternity."

After this, the Lord Himself declared, "While they were flogging you, I was nearby and saw your patience. Since you bravely endured, I shall help you complete the contest and will write your names in the Book of life." With these words the Saviour and Saint Theodore disappeared.

Meanwhile, the soldiers charged with torturing the martyrs implored Asclepiodotus, "Master, relieve us of our duty. We are afraid to inflict further harm on these men!"

Pointing at the saints, Asclepiodotus cried, "The prisoners are wizards and have frightened my troops with hexes!"

Many of the onlookers had been deemed worthy to see the vision, and they shouted, "We also beheld Christ, the King of the Christians, and Theodore, who was put to death recently, as well as a choir of angels singing. They were neither illusions, nor phantoms created by a spell!"

"I saw and heard nothing," scowled the Governor.

"You have spoken truly," agreed Eutropius. "You could not see the divine vision or hear the celestial voices, because the prince of this world has blinded your inner eyes. You are like the people of whom Isaiah said, *Their ears are heavy and their eyes shut.*"[7]

Realizing that the crowd was turning against him, Asclepiodotus ordered the saints bound and sent back to prison. Those in the dungeon rejoiced at their return, and Christ's sufferers chanted, *Our help is in the name of the Lord, Who hath made heaven and the earth.*[8]

That evening, while dining with his advisers, the Governor admitted, "I am uncertain what to do with those men. The whole city is in tumult because of them. What do you suggest?"

---

[7]Is., Ch. 6   [8]Ps. 123

One of the nobles advised, "Execute them without delay, or everyone will follow them and forsake the gods. Especially, silence that long-winded Eutropius."

"To my appeals and threats Eutropius replies by reviling the gods and the Emperor," frowned Asclepiodotus. "I will give him one more chance to worship our deities. If he submits, his life will be spared; if he remains defiant, I shall put him to death. Either way, we shall win back the mob for the compassionate gods." So saying, the Governor commanded his guards to fetch Eutropius.

When the saint arrived, Asclepiodotus asked him, "Would you be pleased if I personally escorted you to the temple of our gods and watched as you sacrifice to them?"

"As the Lord my God lives," exclaimed Eutropius, "I will never renounce the Christian faith, which is founded upon the unshakeable rock of truth!"

The Governor invited Eutropius to join him at table, but the martyr declined. The others urged, "Eat with us, Eutropius. Obey the Governor."

The saint replied, "I am Christ's servant. I will not eat with defiled men. David the holy prophet says, *Blessed is the man that hath not walked in the counsel of the ungodly, nor sat in the seat of the pestilent,*[9] and, *I have not sat with the council of vanity, nor shall I go in with them that transgress the law.*[10] And the Prophet Isaiah writes, *Depart ye from their midst, go ye out from thence, saith the Lord. Touch no unclean thing of theirs, and I will receive you.*[11] The Scriptures teach that the friend of holy men himself is hallowed, while the companion of the godless shares their sin."

"At first I thought you were well-bred, but now I realize what a boor you are," said the Governor.

Eutropius responded, "Not ill-breeding, but resolve to keep God's commandments prevents me from sharing your meal. I am far more zealous to fulfill the statutes of my Master, the immortal King of heaven, than you are to carry out the orders of earthly emperors."

"Come with me tomorrow morning and offer oblations, so

---

[9]Ps. 1   [10]Ps. 25
[11]Is., Ch. 52; II Cor., Ch. 6

that the people will know that you do not reject the gods. Your friends need not be present," said the Governor.

"Impious man, why do you so desire that I lead astray Christ's flock?" asked Eutropius. "I will never do as you wish, for my Lord says, *Whoso shall offend one of these little ones which believe in Me, it were better for him that a millstone were hanged about his neck, and that he were drowned in the depth of the sea.*[12] He also teaches, *No man can serve two masters.*[13] *What communion, then, hath light with darkness? And what agreement hath the temple of God with idols?*"[14]

Next the Governor had servants bring gold, expensive robes, and 150 pounds of silver. He said, "I swear by the gods and the invincible emperors to give you all this, if only you say tomorrow before the crowd, 'I submit to the Governor.' Afterwards, pray to your own God, if you wish. You may still have the gifts."

Eutropius exclaimed, "Wicked deceiver and cunning serpent! You will never lead me astray, for I am always mindful of the words of Scripture: *What is a man profited, if he shall gain the whole world, and lose his own soul? Or what shall a man give in exchange for his soul?*[15] Your brother Judas, that lover of money, slew his own soul, and you shall perish with him. Why are you so hesitant to put us to death? By now you should understand that nothing can *separate us from the love of Christ.*"[16]

For hours Asclepiodotus argued with the saint and attempted to win him over by blandishment. Eutropius never wavered in his confession of Christ, but constantly heaped insults on the Governor and his gods. Finally, the cock crowed and, as everyone was exhausted and wanted to sleep, Asclepiodotus told the servants, "Take Eutropius back to prison and fetter him and his friends. There is no reasoning with him: he is incorrigible."

As the martyr was being led away, he shouted to the Governor, "The ground of your soul is property of the devil, and he scatters on it evil seed. Wheat cannot grow on such poor soil as your heart; therefore, you will never bring forth a harvest of righteousness. I say to you: be forewarned. The

---

[12]Matt., Ch. 18   [13]Matt., Ch. 6   [14]II Cor., Ch. 6
[15]Matt., Ch. 16   [16]Rom., Ch. 8

reaper will soon mow you down and cast your weeds and thorns into fire." Entering the dungeon, Eutropius found Cleonicus and Basiliscus on bended knees. They had been praying for him since evening.

Asclepiodotus decided that the next day the whole city would offer oblations to the gods. After dawn heralds summoned everyone to bring sacrifices to the temple of Artemis. When the people had assembled, Asclepiodotus came to the shrine and had the holy martyrs Eutropius, Cleonicus, and Basiliscus brought to him. Some of the idolaters offered incense to their deities, others offered animals. The Governor said, "Eutropius, you and your brethren should also sacrifice to the gods and avoid a cruel death."

Instead of replying, Eutropius and his friends said this prayer:

"O Lord God Almighty, eternal, perfect, and unchanging, Who dwellest on high and art glorified here below, Thou didst establish the heavens and make firm the foundations of the earth; Thou didst uplift the mountains and number the stars, giving each its name. Thou dost wondrously illumine us from the celestial realm. O Thou Who once delivered the Three Children from the Babylonian furnace, saved Daniel from the jaws of lions, rescued Thy handmaiden Susanna from death, preserved Saint Thecla from destruction by fire and wild beasts, and stood beside Saint Theodore during his passion, be with us now. Reveal Thy power and bring to nought all the devices of the heathen. Grant that on this site the Christians may offer unbloody sacrifices to Thee, the true God; for Thou art the Father of our Lord Jesus Christ, and unto Thee, with Thine Only-begotten Son and Thy Holy Spirit, is due glory, now and ever and unto the ages of ages. Amen."

No sooner had the saints completed the prayer than thunder roared and the earth quaked. The temple tottered, and the Governor and the crowd fled in panic. Then the idol of Artemis came crashing to the ground, and a voice louder than the earthquake sounded from heaven, saying, "Your prayer has been heard. On this site the Christians shall build a church." Hearing this promise, the saints rejoiced in the Lord.

After the tremors had ceased and the panic subsided, Asclepiodotus returned to the judgment seat. Gnashing his teeth, he ordered pitch and brimstone heated in three kettles, then had posts set in the ground and the martyrs stand naked between them. Each passion-bearer was commanded to stretch out his arms, one of which was nailed and tied to the post on his left, the other to that on his right. When the cauldrons had reached a furious boil, Cleonicus said to Saint Eutropius, "Pray to the Lord, brother: we are about to undergo a fearful torment."

All three saints prayed, "O Lord Jesus Christ, come now to our assistance. Reveal Thy might, for we are weak. Strengthen us to endure this torture."

Servants brought the seething cauldrons, holding them carefully by the handles. The blessed Eutropius told them, "May the Lord *return* your *toil upon* your *own head.*"[17]

Suddenly, the power of God loosed the saints' hands. The martyrs snatched the kettles and harmlessly poured out the liquid on one another's backs. The pitch flowed like water onto the marble floor and spattered the servants, burning their flesh to the bone. Ascribing the wonder to Christian sorcery, the outwitted Governor commanded other servants to rake the martyrs' flesh with iron claws, then rub mustard and salt into their wounds. The saints endured both torments bravely. Eutropius taunted the persecutor, "Impious man, castaway from God's glory, you must devise worse barbarities, so that we may be rewarded with more splendid crowns by our Master." Infuriated by this mockery, Asclepiodotus ordered the servants to double their efforts. "Rid yourself of us quickly, godless one!" the saints jeered. "We certainly desire to be rid of you and behold the face of our Lord Jesus Christ."

Only at sunset did the Governor return his victims to the dungeon, where they were loaded with shackles. In their cell, the saints prayed, "O Lord Jesus Christ, forsake us not until we escape the tempest of suffering and the clutches of the merciless Governor. May we attain the calm harbor where there is neither sickness, nor sorrow, nor sighing."

At midnight, while the martyrs were sending up entreaties

---

[17]Ps. 7

to Christ, the Lord appeared to them, saying, "Because you are giving your lives for Me, you shall certainly inherit My eternal Kingdom with the saints." The Saviour's visitation comforted the martyrs and greatly strengthened their faith.

In the morning Asclepiodotus returned to the judgment seat. The saints were brought to him, and he asked, "Have you come to your senses? Are you prepared to worship the gods and sacrifice to them, or will you perish wretchedly?"

"How many times must we repeat ourselves, benighted, blind, senseless murderer!" Saint Eutropius marvelled. "We will neither worship deaf and dumb statues, nor offer them oblations."

Hearing this, the Governor pronounced the following sentence: "Because Eutropius, teacher of sorcerers, and Cleonicus, his disciple, profess the Christian faith and refuse to obey the edicts of the immortal emperors, we justly decree that they be crucified. Basiliscus, however, is to be imprisoned in the common dungeon."

"Let me die with my friends!" cried Basiliscus. "We want to enter Christ's presence together."

"Never," the Governor smiled. "The gods have inspired my decision. You made a pact to die together, and I will see it broken."

"You are truly more vicious than any wild animal, to sunder our splendid company, united by unbreakable bonds of faith and love," declared Eutropius. "Your wicked schemes will come to nought and divine retribution will soon overtake you. You cannot stop the buds of grace from quickly blossoming here, producing abundant fruit for the churches of God."

Saints Eutropius and Cleonicus were then taken out of the town to the place of execution, where crosses had been prepared for them. The holy martyrs were accompanied by all the citizens, Christian and pagan. Seeing the crosses, the passion-bearers prayed, "O Lord Jesus Christ our God, we glorify and thank Thee for deeming us worthy of dying, as Thou didst, by crucifixion. Vouchsafe us crowns of righteousness so that, having shared Thy sufferings, we may be glorified with Thee in Thy Kingdom. On behalf of Thy Holy Church we entreat Thee: calm the tempest besetting Thy servants, humble the heathen, and grant peace to the race of Christians."

Before the saints could finish the prayer, soldiers began nailing them to the crosses. A voice from heaven called Christ's witnesses to eternal rest, and the holy martyrs Eutropius and Cleonicus breathed their last words: "*Into Thy hands*, O Master, we *commend* our spirits."[18] The saints were put to death on the third day of March. Two pious citizens of Amaseia, Conitus and Velonicus, persuaded the Governor to give them the martyrs' bodies. Velonicus anointed Saint Eutropius' corpse with myrrh and buried it in his village, two miles from the town. Conitus gave Saint Cleonicus' remains an honorable burial in the hamlet of Kyme. Numerous miracles occurred at both martyrs' graves, unto the glory of God.

As Saint Eutropius had foretold, Asclepiodotus' miserable death followed soon, and it was the latter's successor who beheaded Saint Basiliscus. The holy martyr Basiliscus was executed on May 22 and thus is commemorated twice yearly, alone on that day and with his brethren on this, unto the glory of Christ our God, Who is ever praised with the Father and the Holy Spirit. Amen.

ঀঀঀঀ

According to *The Prologue*, the holy hieromartyr Theodoritus, presbyter of Antioch, is commemorated both on March 3 and March 8. In *The Prologue*, his synaxarion is printed under March 8, but only a notice of his commemoration under March 3. According to his synaxarion, the saint was put to death on March 8.

ঀঀঀঀ

On this same day Saints Zeno and Zoilus reposed in peace. I could find no account of their lives.

On this same day we commemorate the holy virgin Piamon of Egypt. She led a God-pleasing life and was granted the gift of prophecy. Palladius writes about her in *The Lausiac History*.

---

[18]Luke, Ch. 23

The Fourth Day of the Month of March

The Life of Our Holy Monastic Father Gerasimus of the Jordan[1]

The great ascetic Gerasimus was born in the province of Lycia. From childhood he nurtured within himself the fear of God, and after receiving the tonsure retired to the Thebaid, in the Egyptian desert. He lived there for some time, engaged in God-pleasing spiritual struggles, but eventually he returned to Lycia. He again left his homeland at the end of the reign of Theodosius the Lesser, now settling in the Palestinian wilderness near the Jordan River, where he shone like a star with virtue and built a monastery.

After the saint had taken up his abode in Palestine, the Fourth Ecumenical Synod was held at Chalcedon. Marcian and Pulcheria were the rulers at that time. The holy fathers of the council anathematized the impious Dioscorus, Patriarch of Alexandria, and Archimandrite Eutyches for teaching that Christ the Lord has but a single nature.[2] Afterwards, heretics revolted against the council's authority, maintaining that the synod had denied the true faith and affirmed the errors of Nestorius. Prominent among the miscreants was Theodosius, a false monk, sorcerer, and disciple of the doctrines of Eutyches.

---

[1]From the Lives of Saints Euthymius the Great and Cyriacus, and from *The Spiritual Meadow*

[2]Dioscorus and Eutyches were the originators of the heresy of Monophysitism, which rejects the Orthodox teaching that Christ has two distinct natures: one human, one divine. (Tr.)

Arriving in Jerusalem, he threw all of Palestine into confusion, leading astray not only the simple, but holy people as well. He even succeeded in corrupting the widow of the Emperor Theodosius the Lesser, Eudocia, who was residing in Jerusalem. With her assistance and that of the Palestinian monks he had led into delusion, the warlock drove the blessed Juvenal, Patriarch of Jerusalem, from his throne and occupied it himself. To escape persecution at the hands of the false patriarch, the Orthodox fled to the uttermost parts of the desert. First to depart was Euthymius the Great, and he was followed by many holy fathers.

At that time God permitted Saint Gerasimus to fall into heresy, but the Lord's favorite soon repented. In the Life of our venerable father Euthymius, Cyril of Jerusalem[3] writes, "There was an anchorite named Gerasimus who came to dwell in the wilderness west of the Jordan after passing through all the trials of monastic life and conquering the evil spirits in his homeland of Lycia. Despite his subjugation of invisible demons, he was fooled by visible demons, the heretics, and accepted the pernicious opinions of Eutyches. Hearing about Euthymius' virtue, which was universally acclaimed, Gerasimus visited the saint in the desert of Rouba. He was greatly edified by Euthymius' sweet discourses about Orthodoxy, remained with the man of God for a time, and returned to the true faith, sincerely repenting for his dalliance with heresy."

Before too long the Most Holy Juvenal regained his throne. A decree arrived from the devout Emperor Marcian, commanding that the false-patriarch Theodosius stand trial and be punished for his misdeeds, but the imposter escaped to a dismal corner of the wilds of Sinai. The light of Orthodoxy again shone brightly in Jerusalem and throughout Palestine, and many who had fallen into error corrected themselves. Among the repentant was Empress Eudocia, who returned to the bosom of the Orthodox Church.

Saint Gerasimus' monastery was about four miles from Jerusalem and less than a quarter of a mile from the Jordan.[4]

---

[3]Cyril of Scythopolis (Tr.)
[4]In actuality, both distances are considerably longer. (Tr.)

Here the godly one received novices, but experienced disciples were provided cells in the desert. No less than seventy anchorites were under the saint's direction. Gerasimus gave them the following rule. Five days a week they spent in their cells, maintaining silence and doing handiwork. For food they had a few rusks and dates brought from the monastery; for drink, water. No cooked food was allowed and it was forbidden to build a fire, lest any of the brethren be tempted to prepare a proper meal. On Saturday and Sunday everyone went to the monastery, assembled in church for the Divine Liturgy, and partook of the most pure, life-giving Mysteries of Christ. After the service, the monks repaired to the refectory and partook of cooked food and a little wine, unto the glory of God. The fathers presented to the elder the handiwork they had made during the week, and on Sunday afternoon departed for their cells in the wilderness, taking bread, dates, and a vessel of water, as well as palm branches for weaving baskets. So extreme were their non-acquisitiveness and poverty that for possessions they had nothing but a single threadbare robe, a rush sleeping mat, and a waterpot. The monks were under orders from Abba Gerasimus to leave open the door to their cell when they were absent so that anyone who wished could take whatever was there. The brethren led a truly apostolic life, being *of one heart and of one soul.*[5] No one *said* that *aught of the things which he possessed was his own; but they had all things common.* Once it happened that desert-dwellers begged the venerable Gerasimus' permission to burn a candle for reading at night and to light a fire for boiling water. The saint responded, "If you want fire in your cell, return to the monastery and live with the novices. As long as I am the elder, no anchorite will build a fire or burn a candle." Hearing about the austere rule of Gerasimus' disciples, the inhabitants of Jericho began visiting the monastery every Saturday and Sunday, bringing large quantities of food and wine, and necessities of every kind. The venerable Gerasimus' own asceticism was so harsh he did not eat during Holy and Great Lent. Until the bright day of Christ's Resurrection he sustained body and soul by the divine Mysteries alone.

---

[5]Acts, Ch. 4

One of the saint's disciples was the blessed Cyriacus. In the Life of Saint Cyriacus, it is written: "The venerable Euthymius received the newcomer Cyriacus, foreseeing the gifts of God that would be revealed in him. After a short time Euthymius clothed Cyriacus in the schema. Because the great Theoctistus had already gone to the Lord, he sent the newly tonsured monk to Saint Gerasimus, who had his abode near the Jordan. Seeing that Cyriacus was young, Gerasimus told him to live in the coenobium and toil in obedience.

"Cyriacus readily undertook every labor. During the day he worked for the monastery, while at night he stood at prayer. He slept very little, ate only bread, and drank only water. Every other day he observed a total fast. Seeing such rigorous abstinence in one so young, Abba Gerasimus marveled, and came to love Cyriacus greatly.

"It was Saint Gerasimus' habit during Great Lent to retire to Rouba, a place deep in the wilderness, where the venerable Euthymius had stayed for a long time. Since Gerasimus loved the blessed Cyriacus for his severe way of life, he took him along. While they stayed at Rouba, Cyriacus partook of the Holy Mysteries from Gerasimus' hands every Sunday. They abode in stillness until Palm Sunday, when they returned to the monastery, their souls much profited.

"Not long afterwards, our holy father Euthymius reposed. The venerable Gerasimus was in his cell when he saw God's angels joyfully ascending to heaven with Saint Euthymius' soul. Taking Cyriacus, he hurried to the lavra of Euthymius and found that the saint had fallen asleep in the Lord. He buried Euthymius' remains, then returned to his cell with his beloved disciple Cyriacus."

Gerasimus, the Lord's favorite, was served by an irrational beast which acted as though it were a rational being. In *The Spiritual Meadow*, John Eucrates and Sophronius the Sophist write the following: "We visited the lavra of Abba Gerasimus, which is about a mile from the Jordan. The monks there told us that, one day, while walking through the desert, Saint Gerasimus came upon a lion roaring in pain. A thorn was imbedded in its paw, which was swollen and full of pus. Unable to express its plea in words, the lion wore a humble, downcast expression, making plain its desire that the elder heal it. Seeing the beast in such distress, the old man lanced the paw and removed the thorn and pus. After cleaning the wound, he bound it with his handkerchief and dismissed the animal, but the lion would not leave. Like a disciple, it followed Gerasimus wherever he went. Amazed by the lion's gentle disposition, Gerasimus fed it bread and boiled vegetables.

"The fathers of the lavra used an ass to fetch water from the Jordan, and the elder gave the lion the task of taking it to pasture on the riverbank. One day, while the donkey was grazing, the lion wandered off a short distance and fell asleep in the sun. An Arab with his camels came by, and took the unattended donkey. Upon awakening, the lion searched for the ass, and not finding it, returned despondent to Abba Gerasimus at the lavra. The elder thought the lion had eaten the donkey and asked, 'Where is the ass?' As though it were a man, the beast stood silent, hanging its head. 'Have you eaten it?' the elder demanded. 'Blessed be God! You shall remain here and do the donkey's work.' After this the lion, loaded with saddlebags, would bring water in four skins from the Jordan to the monastery at the elder's command. This continued until one day a soldier came to ask the elder's prayers. Seeing the lion carrying water and hearing the explanation, he took pity on the beast and gave the fathers three pieces of gold to purchase another ass. In this way the lion was relieved of his duty.

"Some time later the Arab merchant who had taken the first donkey was traveling to the holy city of Jerusalem with a caravan to sell grain. The donkey was among the pack animals. Upon crossing the Jordan, the merchant found himself face to face with the lion. Catching sight of the ass, the lion roared and sprang, and everyone fled in terror. The lion took the donkey's rein in its mouth, as it had always done in the past, and led away the ass and the three camels tied behind it, all loaded with wheat. Roaring with delight at having found its charge, it presented the animals to the elder, who smiled and admitted to the brethren, 'We scolded the lion in vain, thinking he had eaten the donkey.' The saint named the lion 'Jordan.' For five years the beast lived at the lavra and received its food from him, never leaving his side.

"When Abba Gerasimus' soul departed to the Lord and his holy body was buried by the fathers, the lion was nowhere in the lavra. Later, it came looking for its elder. Abba Sabbatius, Saint Gerasimus' disciple, told the beast, 'Jordan, our elder has left us orphans. He has departed to the Lord. Now come, have some food.' No matter what Sabbatius offered, the lion would not eat; instead, it looked about for the elder, roaring mournfully. Abba Sabbatius and the fathers gently stroked its mane, repeating, 'The elder has gone to the Lord; he has left us,' but they could not calm the animal. The more they tried to comfort it, the louder it roared, expressing by its sounds and appearance, and especially by its eyes, grief at being separated from the elder. Finally Abba Sabbatius said, 'If you do not believe us, we will show you where the elder rests.'

"Taking the lion, the monks went to the grave, which was five paces from the church.[6] Abba Sabbatius told the animal, 'See, this is where our abba lies.' So saying, he prostrated himself and wept over the elder's remains. Suddenly the lion began beating its head on the ground and roaring in misery, then fell dead upon the grave. This occurred not because the beast had a rational soul, but because the Lord wished to glorify our holy father Gerasimus in death as during his lifetime. God also wished to show how submissive were the animals to Adam before he disobeyed the commandment and was driven out of paradise."

This makes it clear how greatly the venerable Gerasimus pleased the Lord, for Whom he labored fervently from his youth. Having attained ripe old age, Abba Gerasimus joined God in the eternal Kingdom. There he dwells with the saints, glorifying Father, Son, and Holy Spirit unto the ages. Amen.

೬ಿ೬ಿಿ೬ಿ೬

It is written in *The Prologue* that our holy father Gerasimus lived during the reign of Constantine Pogonatos, grandson of Heraclius; but according to the Life of Saint Euthymius the

---

[6]According to the Greek text of *The Spiritual Meadow*, the distance was about a half a mile. (Tr.)

Great, the venerable Gerasimus lived at the time of the Fourth Ecumenical Synod, held at Chalcedon during the reign of Marcian, more than two hundred years earlier. Marcian died in the year 457 after the Nativity of Christ, while Constantine Pogonatos came to the throne in the year 668.[7] The Moscow and Kiev registers of saints mention the year 7508 from the creation of the world[8] in connection with Saint Gerasimus, but this cannot be the year of the venerable one's death. It is possible that Saint Gerasimus was born then. The ruler at that time was Theodosius, Marcian's predecessor on the throne.[9] As mentioned in his Life, Saint Gerasimus came to Palestine from Lycia after the death of Theodosius the Lesser, at the beginning of the reign of Marcian, in the year 450 after the Nativity of Christ. He lived in Palestine during the reigns of Marcian, Leo the Great, Leo the Lesser, and Zeno. His repose occurred in the second year of Zeno's reign, during the thirteenth indiction, 475 years after the Nativity of Christ and 192 years before Constantine Pogonatos ascended the throne.[10]

---

[7]668 was the year of Pogonatos' death, not the year his reign began. (Tr.)

[8]The year 399/400 from the Nativity of Christ (Tr.)

[9]In the year 7508 the Emperor was not Theodosius (the Lesser), but his father Arcadius. (Tr.)

[10]Actually, 166 years before Constantine Pogonatos ascended the throne. (Tr.)

On the Same Day

The Passion of the Holy Martyr Paul, His Sister Juliana, and Those with Them[1]

$\mathcal{T}$ he Roman Emperor Aurelian published a decree throughout his domains commanding all Christians to offer oblations to the gods. Whoever refused was to be put to death by means of brutal tortures. On the way to Assyria, the tyrant stopped in Ptolemais, intending to compel the local Christians to sacrifice. Seeing Aurelian enter the town, the blessed Paul traced the sign of the Cross on his face and told his sister Juliana, "Take courage: the Christians are about to undergo a grievous trial."

The Emperor noticed that Paul had crossed himself and commanded that he be seized and held in fetters until morning. Shortly after dawn the ruler ordered his throne placed in the arena, where it could be seen by everyone, then seated himself and called for the blessed one. When the saint was presented, Aurelian asked him, "Wretch, how is it that yesterday you dared trace the Christian symbol on your face when you caught sight of me entering the city? Are you ignorant of the imperial decree against the Christians?"

"I have heard about your edict, but it is impossible to intimidate Christians into renouncing the true God or keeping silence about Christ, the Son of God," replied Paul. "Your tortures are fleeting and cannot terrify or truly harm those who fear the Lord. The torments that follow God's impartial judgment, however, are unending, as is the glory which the Lord confers upon Christians. Who then would be so foolish as to forsake the living God and worship deaf, dumb idols, especially when our Saviour Jesus Christ says in the Gospel, *Whosoever shall deny Me before men, him will I also deny before My Father Which is in heaven?*"[2]

"I have shown extreme patience, listening to you rant," Aurelian said. "Now sacrifice to the gods, unless you wish to perish in agony."

---

[1]From Metaphrastes and *The Great Collection of Readings*
[2]Matt., Ch. 10

The blessed Paul answered, "The only God I know is our Lord Jesus Christ. From childhood I have served Him with a pure heart."

Aurelian ordered his soldiers, "Suspend this knave and torture him until Christ comes and delivers him."

The executioners stripped the martyr naked, suspended him from a tree, and began their cruel work. Paul cried out, "O Lord Jesus Christ, true Son of God the true Father! Neither angels, archangels, thrones, dominions, principalities, virtues, powers, cherubim, nor seraphim can comprehend the manner of Thy generation, which is known only to Thy Father. Help me, Thy slave, a lowly outcast, and deliver me from Aurelian's clutches." Without delay the Lord Jesus Christ eased Paul's sufferings.

Meanwhile, Christ's bride, Saint Juliana, seeing Paul being tortured, approached the tribunal and shouted, "Persecutor, why are you abusing my brother? He has done no evil!"

Aurelian told his servants, "Uncover that woman's head and pummel her face so that she will learn to address me more respectfully. As for her impious brother, show him no mercy, for he still thinks that Christ is his helper and shield."

The blessed Juliana laughed defiantly, "I am amazed, O Emperor, at your lunacy. Do you not know that Christ eases the pain of His sufferers, who with faith call on Him?"

Aurelian said to his lackeys, "This woman is mad," then told Juliana, "Worship the gods; otherwise, you will die at my hands."

Saint Juliana responded, "I fear neither tortures nor threats, for the God of heaven can deliver us from your grasp. Do your worst, godless man, and you will see how the Lord Jesus Christ succors me."

"You are a beautiful woman," leered the Emperor, "and I do not want to disfigure you. I beg you to submit and sacrifice to the gods. If you do so, I will take you as my lawful wife and share the throne with you. Your brother will be recompensed for his sufferings and honored with a lofty rank."

The blessed Juliana lifted her eyes to heaven, traced the sign of the Cross on her face, and laughed. "Why do you mock my kindness?" demanded Aurelian.

"I am not mocking your supposed kindness, but laughing

from joy," said Juliana. "With my inner eyes I see the celestial Bridegroom. He is *comely in beauty more than the sons of men*[3] and desires the salvation of all. Sitting on His holy throne, He urges me to suffering. You, however, are a garrulous, deceptive, despicable wretch. You call yourself emperor, but are a slave to idols made of wood and stone."

His wrath enflamed, Aurelian commanded the executioners, "Suspend the wench and torment her cruelly. She must learn to respect the imperial tribunal."

As Juliana's torture began, Saint Paul reminded his sister, "Do not fear the tyrant's threats or brutality. After a little suffering here, we shall enjoy eternal rest with Christ."

Aurelian urged the soldiers, "Torture her mercilessly! She must be humbled and brought to her senses."

Juliana laughed again, saying, "Persecutor, you think you are harming me, but Christ prevents me from feeling pain."

"Now you pretend to feel no pain, but lengthy tortures will wear you down. I shall easily conquer you," Aurelian boasted.

"The Lord Jesus Christ, Who always helps me, will never allow you to conquer me," replied the saint. "He lends help and will lend until my struggle is over. My God will force you to acknowledge His might and the power of Christian patience; moreover, He will require you to answer for the souls you have led to perdition and condemn you to roaring flames which shall never be quenched."

So saying, Juliana further enraged the Emperor, who ordered that a cauldron full of pitch be brought and a roaring fire lit beneath it. When the pitch was boiling furiously, Aurelian had both martyrs thrown into it. With one voice the saints prayed, "O Lord God of our fathers Abraham, Isaac, and Jacob, Thou didst descend into the Babylonian furnace with Shadrach, Meshach, and Abednego and prevent the fire from harming them. O Master Jesus Christ, unattainable Light, mystery and glory of the Father, right hand of God the Most High, Thou didst assume flesh and take up Thine abode among men to save the souls which our loathsome enemy the devil had corrupted

---

[3]Ps. 44

and hurled into the infernal abyss of Tartarus. Now Satan's disciple Aurelian hopes to lead us to perdition, but do Thou thwart him and deliver us from harm."

While the martyrs prayed, the seething pitch turned into cool water. Everyone was astonished by the Lord's power and glorified God, except for Aurelian. Thinking the saints had worked a miracle by sorcerous arts, he commanded that they be removed from the cauldron, in which no trace of pitch remained, but only cold water. The Emperor snarled, "The onlookers have been deceived by magic and believe that your God has cooled the kettle and delivered you, but I swear by my gods that I will confound your devilry. Fire and drawn-out tortures will exhaust you and compel you to sacrifice."

Saint Paul retorted, "We will never renounce the living God, Maker of heaven and earth, Who delivered us from darkness and protects us from your clutches! Never, persecutor, will you persuade us to worship dumb, lifeless idols. Employ every torment you know, and learn the power of God."

Aurelian had two gridirons heated over piles of charcoal brought from the public bath. When the beds reached glowing red, the saints were forced to lie naked on them. Next rendered swine fat was poured on the martyrs' bodies, and the Emperor bragged, "I have prevailed over your witchery and silenced you. Now you know not to trifle with me. If He can, let Christ come to your aid."

"Christ is already with us, preventing the fire from doing us harm, but you are unworthy to see Him," said Saint Juliana. "You should admit your folly and turn to Christ. If you repent, He will receive you, for He is compassionate, loves mankind, and is eager to pardon our iniquities. But if you remain an unbeliever, you shall be delivered to everlasting flames."

Seeing that the blazing couches were not burning the saints, two of the executioners exclaimed, "There is no God except the God of heaven, the Helper of Paul and Juliana!" The infuriated Emperor accused the men of accepting bribes from the Christians and showing mercy to the saints. For this he ordered both executioners decapitated.

As the soldiers were being led to death, the blessed Paul cried to them, "Have no fear! You shall not perish, but join the company of the saints and inherit the Kingdom of heaven."

When they heard this, the soldiers halted and prayed, "O Master, Lord Jesus Christ, the true God Whom Paul and Juliana preach, be Thou with us, for we die innocently." Upon completing their supplication, they were beheaded. Their names were Quadratus and Acacius.

After these soldiers were executed, the persecutor commanded others to resume the torture of Paul and Juliana. Upon the fire they poured a salt that made it spark violently, but without harming the blessed ones, who continued to reproach their tormentor. Put to shame before the crowd because he could not best the martyrs, Aurelian sent Paul and Juliana back to prison, where they were collared in heavy slabs of wood and shackled hand and foot. He also had sharp nails scattered on the floor beneath them, so that they would have no respite from afflictions, but be lacerated constantly as though by thistles or brambles. Furthermore, he forbade the guards to allow any Christian to visit the martyrs or provide them food and drink. At midnight, while the saints were lying on the nails and praying, light shone in the dungeon and an angel appeared. He said, "Paul and Juliana, servants of the Most High God, rise and glorify the Lord." Then he touched the saints, healing their wounds; and the collars and shackles fell from their bodies. Afterwards, the passion-bearers beheld two couches covered with fine sheets and a table set with delicious foods of every sort. The angel beckoned them, "Rest on the couches and eat what Jesus Christ has provided." The holy martyrs reclined, took bread and, raising their eyes to heaven, thanked God. Having eaten and drunk, they rejoiced and were strengthened. Seeing this, the other prisoners were amazed. They drew near, also partook of the food supplied by the Lord's invisible hand, and glorified God, Who had deemed His servants worthy of rich mercy. To a man they believed in the Lord and became Christians.

Three days later Aurelian sat upon his judgment seat, and the holy martyrs Paul and Juliana were brought to him. "Have torments convinced you to cease playing the fool, and to sacrifice to the gods?" he asked.

Saint Paul cried, "May all who love God ever play the fool, if this means remaining faithful to Christ! *The foolishness of God is wiser than men,*[4] and *the wisdom of this world is foolishness with God.*[5] If I were to forsake the true God and worship demons, it would mean that I had indeed lost my mind."

Again the Emperor was roused to anger. He ordered both martyrs suspended naked from a tree and their sides raked with iron claws. As they endured this, the saints prayed, "O Lord Jesus Christ, Son of the living God, Light of Christians and Rock of faith, reveal Thy countenance and help us! For Thy holy name's sake, we beg Thee never to forsake us." The Saviour responded by invisibly drawing near and easing their pain.

Stratonicus, the executioner assigned to rake Juliana's left side, was wounded by the martyr's beauty and refrained from gravely harming her. Saint Juliana perceived his thoughts and nudged his left leg, saying, "Do as the persecutor commanded. There is no need for you to show pity. Jesus Christ, the eternal God, Lord, and King, protects my soul and prevents my body from feeling pain."

Throwing aside his iron claw, Stratonicus approached the imperial tribunal and shouted, "Aurelian, godless persecutor, why are you so merciless to the Christians? What harm have the servants of God done to deserve such barbarity? Must they be punished merely for honoring Christ as Master of all?"

The Emperor was stunned and silenced. Finally, he sneered, "Have you also lost your mind, Stratonicus? Were you bewitched by Juliana's loveliness, or did you find the arguments of a woman so powerful you had no choice but to convert to Christian superstition?"

Stratonicus looked up to the tree and saw the faces of the holy martyrs shining like those of angels. He made the sign of the Cross and rushed to the vile heathen altar which had been erected there. Overturning and stamping it, he cried, "I am a Christian! Do with me as you like, persecutor." Infuriated, Aurelian ordered him beheaded.

Upon arriving at the place of execution, Stratonicus prayed, "O Lord Jesus Christ, made known in this city by Paul and Juliana, who are guarded by the might of Thy divinity and ever humiliate the oppressor, I beseech Thee: receive me into the

---

[4] I Cor., Ch.1   [5] I Cor., Ch.3

Kingdom of heaven. Although I have confessed Thy holy name only for a few brief moments, do not allow the tyrant Aurelian to prevail over me." With this, the sword fell. The Christians took Stratonicus' body and hid it.

For the rest of the day the holy martyrs Paul and Juliana were tormented, but no cruelty could exhaust their patience. Aurelian shouted at Saint Juliana, "Shameless, unbelieving woman, while yourself under torture, you corrupted the executioner. You alone brought about his death!"

The saint replied, "I neither corrupted him nor caused his death. Christ, Who chose me as His bride, deigned to call the soldier to Himself. Had the man been unworthy, he would never have attained a martyr's diadem. While burning in Gehenna, you will behold him rejoicing in heaven. You regarded this common soldier as utterly insignificant and far inferior to yourself, but when you see him crowned with glory by Christ in the celestial Kingdom, you will beat your despicable breast. How sorry you will be then! But your cries for mercy will remain unanswered."

At this Aurelian sent the saints back to prison. That evening Paul and Juliana were taken to the public bath and locked in. Meanwhile, the Emperor invited all the magicians and snake-charmers in the town to bring their most poisonous vipers, asps, and other serpents and release them in the building. The sorcerers filled the bath with venomous reptiles, but the creatures slid about harmlessly. For three nights and days the saints remained in the bath, completely unafraid and glorifying God. On the fourth night Aurelian sent servants to learn the martyrs' fate. Through the door the Emperor's men heard Paul and Juliana chanting psalms and singing the Lord's praises. They then climbed to the roof and, peering through a little window, saw light inside. Paul and Juliana were sitting, and an angel was warding off the snakes. The servants ran back and told Aurelian what they had seen and heard. The next morning the Emperor mounted his tribunal, ordered the wizards and snake-charmers to collect their serpents, and commanded that the martyrs be brought to him. Standing outside the doors of the bath, the magicians muttered enchantments, but the serpents ignored them. When the doors were opened, the snakes attacked their handlers and the crowd. Having mortally wounded many people, the serpents slithered away to freedom.

Before long soldiers arrived at the bath and informed Paul and Juliana that they must come to the Emperor. Aurelian greeted the martyrs cheerfully, saying, "I am glad that you are still alive and I can speak with you today. I swear by the gods that if you answer me honestly, I will reward you with high rank and many expensive gifts. My servants tell me that when they looked through the window into the bath, our master, the divine Apollo, was at your side, protecting you from the serpents. Is this true? Did you really see Apollo with your own eyes?"

"Apollo is a stranger to us. We have never seen him," answered Saint Paul. "We are servants of the true God, Who rewards with salvation those who labor for Him. Your soul, however, is lost, because you refuse to acknowledge the truth and repent. Obsessed with devising tortures, you have lost your mind. It was not Apollo that prevented the serpents from striking, but an angel sent by our Lord Jesus Christ."

Roused to fury, the tyrant commanded that Paul be beaten on the face with iron rods. "Haughty, senseless man," he exclaimed, "how dare you speak thus to me!"

After he was bludgeoned, Paul was dragged away from the judgment seat and Juliana called forward. "Juliana, mistress of my heart, do not imitate your foolish brother," the Emperor pleaded. "You are an intelligent and learned maiden. Heed my counsel and become my empress. I wish to marry you and erect golden statues of you throughout the realm."

The saint replied, "You will never deceive me, Aurelian, impious persecutor. You cannot lead astray the handmaiden of the Most High God; you cannot drag me to perdition. You hope to deprive me of the Kingdom of heaven and the glory of Christ, but this is impossible."

Aurelian then had Juliana taken away and Saint Paul brought back. He said, "Paul, your sister has just promised to sacrifice to our gods. I wish to marry her and make her empress. It is time for you to offer oblations as well. So doing, you will win my friendship and lofty rank and title."

"It is impossible that my sister has chosen you, a depraved mortal, and the demons you worship over Christ, the blameless, immortal Bridegroom. You lie brazenly because your parent is the devil, the father of lies[6] and your teacher. You imitate him and are incapable of winning over anyone, except by deceit. But your efforts are to no avail, for you will never lead us astray, even if you promise us the whole world," Paul said.

"Still you persist in berating me!" marveled Aurelian. "I swear by the gods that I will test every torture on you, and that no one will free you from my grasp." With this, he ordered a fire built and fourteen iron rods heated in it. Saint Paul was chained by the wrists and ankles to one of the blazing rods, which was driven into the ground. The rest were used to batter him by soldiers working in turns. One of the soldiers laid on blows, the other re-heated the rods as they grew cold. In addition, Aurelian commanded that Saint Juliana be taken to a house of ill-fame and raped. Learning this, many in the crowd, excited by Juliana's beauty, raced off like stallions in pursuit of the martyr.

When Saint Juliana reached the brothel, an angel appeared and told her, "Do not be afraid: He for Whom you labor, the Lord Jesus Christ, sent me to defend you. Seeing you preserved unharmed, all who fear Him will glorify His holy name." The degenerates rushed towards Juliana, intent upon forcing themselves on her, but the angel blinded them and swept them away like dust from the feet of Christ's bride. The evildoers vainly groped about the walls; however, they could not find Juliana. Witnessing this, the onlookers shouted with one voice, "Great is the God of Paul and Juliana, Who shelters and saves those who fear Him!" As for the blinded, they sank to their knees and begged, "Juliana, handmaiden of the Most High God, forgive us for attempting to defile you! We acted foolishly and sinned grievously; nevertheless, we beg you, as a servant of the good Lord, to entreat Christ to return our sight."

Feeling pity for the wretches, Juliana lifted up a bowl of water, looked up to heaven, and prayed, "O Jesus Christ, the true God and Saviour of all men, hearken unto Thy handmaiden and reveal Thy signs and wonders unto the people. Grant these men sight, that Thy holy name may be extolled." With these words, she sprinkled the eyes of the blind and restored their vision. The men thanked God on bended knees, then rushed to

---

[6]John, Ch. 8

the Christian church, where they again contritely acknowledged their sin. All became Christians and were deemed worthy of Holy Baptism.

In the meantime, additional torturers came to the aid of the two already beating Saint Paul with heated rods. The martyr cried to Aurelian, "Godless persecutor, what evil have I done to merit such inhuman punishment? Know that the Master, Jesus Christ, is easing my pain, but eternal fire awaits you and the devil, your inciter."

"Paul, where is your sister? You imagine she is still a virgin, but earlier today I sent her to a brothel to be raped," Aurelian mocked.

The holy martyr Paul answered, "I am certain that God, Who lightens my afflictions and delivers me from your wicked devices, will protect my sister and send an angel from heaven to guard her purity." Shortly afterwards he added, "Lo, my sister is returning, her virginity intact. She is coming to see my sufferings and wounds." This, because Saint Paul beheld with clairvoyant inner eyes everything that was occurring to Juliana. In fact, the persecutor had already sent orders for Juliana to be brought back from the house of ill-repute.

Saint Paul laughed for joy when his sister arrived, but Aurelian taunted her, "Juliana, did your lovers tire of your beauty?"

"Christ is my joy, beauty, and adornment," Juliana replied. "Because I am His lowly handmaiden and unfailingly trust in Him, He sent an angel to protect me. I glorify His holy name, for He alone is the God Who works wonders."

The Emperor had Paul loosed and told his servants to dig a hole twenty feet deep. The pit was filled with wood, which was set afire and burned to coals, upon which Aurelian commanded that Paul and Juliana be thrown. The holy martyrs approached the pit uncompelled, blessing God and entreating the help of Christ the Saviour. After making the sign of the Cross, the saints cast themselves onto the fire. While they hymned and praised the Lord, an angel descended from heaven, put out the coals, and swept them away. Everyone heard the saints chanting, "Blessed art Thou, O God, King of the ages, for Thou hast remembered our lowliness, overlooked our transgressions, and extinguished the fire. Thou hast preserved us, the humble, unharmed by the persecutor Aurelian."

Seeing the marvel, many of the heathen were stirred to compunction, renounced the idols, and believed in Christ. The Emperor ordered his men to stone the martyrs, but before they could obey, thunder roared and lightning flashed, a crimson cloud appeared in the sky, and fire fell from heaven. A voice sounded from on high, "Aurelian, you are bound for the flames of Gehenna, prepared for you and your father the devil." Aurelian and all the pagans were horror-struck. The tyrant had the saints removed from the pit and taken to prison, where they glorified God for all the wonders He had worked on their behalf.

Seven days later Aurelian sat upon the tribunal and instructed all the heathen priests to bring their gold and silver gods, adorned with precious stones, and to place his imperial robes at the idols' feet. The holy martyrs Paul and Juliana were then brought to him, and he told them, "You must worship the gods now. You have no hope of escape."

Saint Paul laughed defiantly and said, "Never, O persecutor, will we forsake the God Who made heaven and the earth. Abandon your hopes of winning us over to idolatry."

"So you think our mighty gods are idols? You are worthy of a bitter death!" cried Aurelian.

Saint Paul said, "Zeus, whom you call a god, was a mortal, an adept of the black art, the most lecherous and debauched of men. Whenever he saw a comely woman or girl and wanted to enjoy her favors, he would transform himself by sorcery, either into a bull, an eagle, or gold. Having deceived and defiled many, he came to be regarded as a god and was worshipped by the ignorant. I will not recount all his shameful, iniquitous, filthy deeds, lest the hearers be defiled and your anger roused, although truly, I do not fear your wrath. Another of your deities, next in rank after Zeus, is Apollo. Was he not a bastard, the son of Leto, who gave birth to him between two trees? Imitating his father Zeus, Apollo likewise committed many reprehensible deeds. And your highly revered god Dionysus, child of Semele, Cadmus' daughter, was he not of illegitimate birth as well?"

"You lie, impudent man!" shouted Aurelian. "Dionysus was the son of Juno, mother of the gods."

Again Saint Paul laughed. "Can a god be born of a mortal, become a god when he was not one before, and sire children with a woman?" he asked.

"How long will you continue to revile and blaspheme our gods, impious knave? Was not Christ, Whom you say is the God of heaven, the offspring of a woman?" the ruler replied.

"You are unworthy to learn divine mysteries, but I do not want the onlookers to become confused, so I must respond," said Paul. "In the beginning, God created heaven, the earth, the sea, and all things therein. He fashioned Adam, the first man, according to His own image and likeness: pure, guileless, and righteous. Placing man in a paradise of delights, God fashioned a helpmate for him from his rib. Unable to endure the sight of man enjoying such blessedness, your father the devil led astray Eve, the first woman, and through her persuaded Adam to transgress the Lord's commandment. Adam and Eve were expelled from paradise and had sons and daughters, so that their descendants filled the earth. Because of sin's entry into the world, the human race became subject to death, and all our forefathers, righteous and unrighteous, descended to Hades. As Christ's Apostle wrote: *Death reigned from Adam even over them that had not sinned after the similitude of Adam's transgression.*[7] Therefore, our Heavenly Father, God Almighty, took pity on the race of man, and rescued us. He sent His Son to assume human flesh and save Adam and those chained in Hades with Adam. A prince of the angels named Gabriel proclaimed to the holy, immaculate, most honorable Virgin the Incarnation of the Son of God, Who is the Word begotten of the Father before all ages: His wisdom, power, and right hand. The archangel announced to the Virgin, that scion of prophets and kings, *Hail, thou who art full of grace, the Lord is with thee,*[8] and, *The Holy Spirit shall come upon thee, and the power of the Highest shall overshadow thee: therefore also, that holy thing which shall be born of thee, shall be called the Son of God.* At this the Word of the Father, being God Himself, invisibly took up His dwelling in the most pure and sanctified womb and became flesh. The Son of God and Word of the Father was born of the blameless Virgin; He was clothed in a

---

[7]Rom., Ch. 5   [8]Luke, Ch. 1

body for the salvation of man. No one can see the true God as He is according to the divine essence, for *God is a consuming fire.*[9] No man on earth can behold the face of God and live; therefore, coming among us, our God assumed flesh. He was born and as a babe was nurtured with milk, while remaining perfect God. As a child he grew in stature, until He reached full manhood. He lived among men for thirty-three years. He passed through towns, villages, and countryside, preaching the Gospel to all and freeing those under the power of the devil. Then He willingly submitted to crucifixion in order to save the world, which was perishing in demonic deception. Having died in the flesh, He descended with His holy soul into Hades, crushed the brazen gates, and shattered the iron bolts. He broke the fetters with which the devil had bound his captives, and He led the souls of the saints out of darkness and up to heaven. On the third day after His crucifixion, He rose from the dead in the flesh, appearing to His disciples (called the apostles) and to many others who truly believed in Him. During the course of forty days, He ate and drank often with the apostles, then ascended into heaven, where He sits in the flesh on the right hand of God the Father. Now He reigns on high, and the Christians trample the devil as they enter the Kingdom of heaven, a realm to which you are an utter stranger. Your *part* and *lot*[10] are the fire of Gehenna, which is also the inheritance of your father Satan."

Aurelian gnashed his teeth and his face contorted with anger. "Long-winded fool, when will you cease railing against me and blaspheming the gods?" he ranted. "I tell you one last time: if you fail to sacrifice, I will destroy you."

Saints Paul and Juliana cried, "We are Christians and put our hope in Christ! We will never worship your gods; we will never serve demons; we do not fear torments. Torture us however you wish. We believe in God and shall conquer you, as our Saviour conquered the devil. Christ will enable us to prevail over any cruelty you devise."

At this Aurelian ordered Saint Paul roped to a tree and his face burned, while a herald shouted, "Do not revile the Emperor, lord of the universe; do not blaspheme the gods!"

---

[9]Deut., Ch. 4; Heb., Ch. 12   [10]Acts, Ch. 8

Presently the tyrant commanded that Juliana also be tied to a tree and burned. As fire was being applied to the martyr's face, Aurelian said, "Shameless wench, you must learn humility, as befits a woman."

"Aurelian, you demand that I show humility because you desire my submission; but at this very moment I see Christ, the living God, standing before me. I fear the Lord and can neither forsake Him nor worship demons," replied Juliana.

Humiliated and trembling with rage, the Emperor had the servants apply fire to every part of the martyrs' bodies. Seeing this, the people cried, "Your Majesty! It is unjust to torture these prisoners. If they will not sacrifice to the gods, execute them." Fearing an uprising, Aurelian sentenced the martyrs to beheading. Their corpses were to be cast as food to birds, dogs, and wild beasts.

The saints rejoiced as they were taken to the block, and they chanted, *"Thou hast saved us, O Lord, from them that afflict us, and them that hate us hast Thou put to shame."*[11] Fearing that his sister would be frightened if she witnessed his death, Paul asked that she be decapitated first. Juliana made the sign of the Cross as she joyfully bared her neck. The sword fell and Juliana reached the finish; whereupon, Paul lifted his eyes to heaven and thanked God, then crossed himself and met his end.

The martyrs' corpses were left unburied outside the city. Guards were posted nearby with orders from the Emperor not to allow the Christians to remove them. Meanwhile, dogs and wolves gathered around, not to feed on the bodies, but to watch over the relics. Also, birds of prey circled overhead and dove only to drive away flies. As the soldiers reported to Aurelian, this continued for seven days and nights. The Emperor could only say, "How powerful is Christian magic! These sorcerers continue to thwart us, even after their death."

On the eighth day the guards were withdrawn, and the Christians took the much-afflicted bodies of the holy martyrs Paul and Juliana and buried them reverently. Unto our Lord Jesus Christ, Who reigns with the Father and the Holy Spirit, be glory, honor, and dominion, now and ever and unto the ages of ages. Amen.

---

[11]Ps. 43

ε♠ε♠ε♠

According to *The Prologue* and the register of saints published in Kiev, the martyrs Paul and Juliana are also commemorated on August 7.

On the Same Day

The Life of Our Holy Monastic Father James the Faster, Who Fell and Repented

𝒥n the man who loves God and lives in accordance with the Saviour's commandments, humility is the wellspring of luminous virtues. Because he neither relies on his own strength nor thinks highly of himself, the genuinely humble man does not sink into despondency if he sins. Pride, to the contrary, is the ruin of the heedless, burdening them with vain cares and doing them irreparable harm. These truths are taught by many holy books, and especially by the present account, which instructs those who lead a heavenly life on earth to be vigilant, and *him that thinketh he standeth to take heed lest he fall.*[1] This narrative provides excellent guidance, an illustration of humbleness, and an example of a quick, vigorous arising from a stumble into sin. From it, we learn the power of repentance, which stirs the benevolent Master to deliver the wrongdoer from the gates of hell and tortures of Gehenna. With the aid of divine grace, the penitent can attain a state of virtue superior to that which he enjoyed before lapsing. And so, let us begin our story.

In Phoenicia, near the town of Porphyrionus, there lived a monk named James. Having renounced the vanity of this temporal existence, he took up his dwelling in a cave, where he lived for fifteen years. So harsh was his asceticism and lofty his virtue, that God granted him authority over demons and power to heal in the name of our Saviour Jesus Christ. Everyone marveled at James' holiness, and crowds of both the faithful and of Samaritans thronged to him. Being clairvoyant, the Lord's favorite knew who were the unbelievers and instructed them from the divine Scriptures. He converted many to the Christian faith. At length the devil, mankind's ancient foe and the hater of all Christians, struck back at James. Put to shame by the saint's good deeds and perfect life, the evil one laid his traps, hoping

---

[1] I Cor. Ch. 10

to ensnare the man of God and remove him from the cave. He entered into an unbelieving Samaritan living in Porphyrionus, as he once entered into Judas, and incited him to drive out James. The Samaritan assembled all his relatives, friends, acquaintances, neighbors, and servants, and with them went to the house of the accursed priest of their religion. A meeting was held, and all agreed that since James had converted many Samaritans to Christ, he must be expelled from the region. After much discussion, they also decided to allot twenty pieces of gold for hiring a woman of ill repute to seduce the hermit. Her money was to be doubled if she succeeded, as this would leave the Christians no choice but to allow the Samaritans to drive out James in dishonor.

Late one night James heard a knock at his door. It was the harlot, begging him to let her in. When the blessed one refused, she redoubled her pleas. Finally the saint opened the door and looked out. Certain that she was an apparition, James crossed himself and slammed the door in her face. Then, turning to the east, he fervently besought God to drive away the demon tempting him. But hours passed and the woman was still knocking and crying, "Have mercy on me, true servant of the living God! Open, lest the beasts prowling outside your cell devour me."

After considering how the woman might indeed be attacked by predators at such a late hour, the venerable James again looked out. He asked, "Where are you from and why are you here?"

"I live in a convent of virgins and was sent by the abbess to the city," replied the woman. "Night fell as I was returning, and I lost my way. Somehow I found your cell. I beg you, man of God, have mercy on me and do not permit me to become the prey of wild animals, but let me in. I will be gone at sunrise."

Moved by compassion, the godly James allowed the woman to enter and offered her bread and water, then retired to his inner chamber, leaving her in the outer room. After eating, the harlot rested a little. Presently she began feigning illness, weeping piteously, moaning, and entreating the saint's help. James looked through the little window on the inside door and, thinking she was sick, wondered what to do. The harlot begged,

"Father, show mercy and come trace the sign of the Cross on me. I have terrible pain in my heart."

Hearing this, the saint brought a burning lamp and holy oil to the woman. While heating his left hand over the lamp, he traced a cross in oil on her heart with his right hand, then rubbed in the oil with his warm fingers. Burning with unclean desire and hoping to corrupt the blessed one, the whore said, "Please, Father, keep putting on oil and warming my breast so that it will stop hurting."

Being simple and guileless, James had no inkling of her plan and did as she requested. Nevertheless, he knew how the cunning demons stir up carnal warfare, and he feared lest, while showing kindness to the woman, he bring about the perdition of his own soul. Repeatedly returning his left hand to the lamp for a period of two or three hours, he held it so close to the flame that his fingers burned off. By extreme pain the blessed one averted every demonic suggestion, not accepting a single unclean thought. Seeing what James had done, the harlot was moved to compunction and threw herself at his feet, weeping, "Woe is me, the debauched, blind one! Woe is me, the abode of the devil!"

The saint was taken aback and said, "Rise, woman." He lifted her from the floor and, after fervent prayer, demanded, "Tell me why you came here." With difficulty, she composed herself and explained that, beholding him lead an angelic life, the impious Samaritans (or rather, the devil himself) had paid her to seduce him. The venerable one sighed deeply and, tears falling from his eyes, thanked God for delivering him. He instructed the woman and blessed her, then sent her to the holy Bishop Alexander. The woman confessed all her sins to the Bishop, who catechized her. Convinced that her repentance was true, the Bishop without delay illumined her in Holy Baptism and entrusted her to a convent of virgins, where she was betrothed to Christ. After this he assembled his clergy and all the Christians, and expelled the entire Samaritan population from the town and surrounding region. He summoned the blessed James and, offering paternal counsel, encouraged him to continue leading a godly life. With the help of the Lord's grace, the former harlot pleased God and was granted authority over demons.

It came to pass that an unclean spirit entered the daughter of a certain wealthy nobleman, and the girl began crying out the name of the Lord's favorite. Her parents brought her to James and begged him to show mercy and drive out the unclean spirit. The saint prayed to God and laid his hand on the maiden, and straightway the Lord's power expelled the demon. When they saw their child in her right mind, the parents thanked God. In token of their appreciation, they sent the man of God three hundred pieces of gold. The righteous one not only refused the money, but would not even look at it, saying, "It is forbidden to buy or sell God's gifts. The Scriptures say, *Freely ye have received, freely give.*[2] It is best to give the gold to the poor. I live in the wilderness and have no use for it." With this he dismissed the nobleman's servants.

People burdened with infirmities of every kind were brought to the wonderworker, whose prayers restored them to perfect health. For example, a young man was paralyzed in both legs by a demon. His family brought him to Saint James and begged for his holy prayers. For three days the venerable one fasted and prayed, and the paralytic was healed. After blessing the youth, James commanded him to walk home.

Realizing that he was held in the highest esteem by all, the man of God feared that he would fall into vainglory. Fleeing the praise of men, he abandoned his first cave and took up his dwelling in a second, by a stream, about twenty miles from the city. For thirty years he lived there, praying and weeping night and day. In the beginning he sustained himself on plants that grew wild on the banks. Later he planted a small garden, where he worked for several hours each day to obtain his food. Eventually his fame spread so widely that monks from twenty or thirty monasteries, as well as many clergymen, began visiting him, seeking edification. Layfolk came in throngs to the cave for a blessing, prayers, and instruction in virtue. All received the spiritual profit they sought.

Even though this holy man was a repository of abundant divine power, he was permitted to take a grievous fall. Certainly, this occurred because he began to think highly of himself, con-

---

[2]Matt., Ch. 10

sidering that he had attained holiness and a God-pleasing life. The ancient adversary of mankind, envious of James' virtue and always digging traps for him, entered the daughter of a certain rich man and tormented her cruelly. The maiden cried, "I will not depart unless you take me to James the anchorite!" Her parents made the rounds of monasteries and hermitages until they found Saint James. Falling at his feet, they begged, "Have mercy on our daughter, who is being tortured by an unclean spirit! For twenty days she has eaten and drunk nothing, but continuously screams, tears at her flesh, and calls out your name."

So fervently did the blessed one pray for the maiden that the ground on which he stood trembled. After completing his supplication, the venerable James blew on the girl and commanded the foul spirit, "In the name of our Lord Jesus Christ, depart!" As though scorched by fire, the devil fled. The girl collapsed and remained speechless until James prayed for her a second time. When she came to herself, the man of God lifted her up and delivered her into the arms of her mother and father. Seeing the miracle, the parents glorified God, but were afraid that the demon might enter their daughter again; therefore, they entreated James to let her to remain with him for three days and recover her strength. To this the elder agreed.

In relating the deeds of those who have attained perfection, we must tell not only about their virtues, but about the temptations they undergo at the instigation of the wicked devil, who sometimes succeeds in ensnaring them. Hearing how even holy men stumble, those leading a celestial life on earth are put on their guard, as we said at the beginning. We have spoken about the wondrous deeds of this elder; now we must make known the storm that buffeted him, and also his grievous fall. But so doing, we will not hide the astonishing miracles he worked after fervently repenting. Verily, James' transgressions were as appalling as his earlier asceticism was laudable; but the distance he plummeted cannot be compared to the height to which he later ascended.

Seeing that the man of God was alone in the wilderness with the maiden, the devil waited for a convenient time, then assaulted him with a hail of dissolute thoughts and unclean carnal desires. When the harlot was sent by the Samaritans,

James burned his hand and controlled the passions. This time the wonderworker and expeller of demons burned so fiercely with lust that he forgot the fear of God, his ascetical labors, and the gift of healing vouchsafed him by the Lord. Despite our father's advanced age, Satan vanquished him. Thus James forced himself on the maiden and ruined her virginity, defiling himself and her and rendering useless all his self-mortification. Worse still, like a person slipping down a precipitous slope, tumbling from rock to rock and battering his body, James did not halt with this first crime. He added iniquity to iniquity, committing a second outrage. The enemy unnerved him with the thought that the girl would tell her parents about the rape, that he would be disgraced, and that retribution would follow. Reduced to fear and trembling, James killed the innocent girl, believing he could hide his first sin and avoid scandal. Then followed a third outrage, for the murderer did not bury the body, but heartlessly cast it into the stream. All this was the fruit of pride. If James had not thought himself a great holy man, he would not have suffered such a grievous fall and become in his old age a laughingstock to the demons, which he had held in derision and trampled from his youth.

After James committed these atrocities, the devil began driving him, like a prisoner in fetters, to the ultimate pit of perdition, to the worst offense of all: despair, the sin of Cain and Judas. The elder sat dejectedly in his cell wondering what to do next. His conscience would give him no peace, he sighed continuously, he dared not pray, and he shrank from turning his thoughts to God. He pondered fleeing to a faraway land, returning to the world, renouncing monasticism, and laboring for the devil in his old age. At length he abandoned the cave and hurried on his way, lashed by a tempest of thoughts.

In his mercy, Christ blotted out the sins of the whole world; and despite the elder's crimes, He Who desires that no man perish, but that all be saved looked down with compassion upon James. Intervening before the demons could claim total victory, our Saviour arranged for the hermit's repentance and amendment. In accordance with the Lord's unfathomable judgments, James happened upon a monastery. Entering it, he greeted the abbot and brethren. They washed his feet and offered him bread, but he refused it. When they insisted he eat, James sighed repeatedly and groaned, "Woe is me, the wretch! How can I raise my eyes to heaven? How can I call upon the name of Christ, Whom I have so grieved? How can I, a rapist and murderer, accept His gifts?" And he confessed everything before the entire brotherhood.

The superior and brethren were much disturbed by what they heard, but were also moved to pity. They consoled the elder and implored him not to despair, insisting that he remain at their monastery and repent. Nevertheless, he continued on his way back to the world. Providence next arranged his encounter with a holy anchorite whose cell was not far from James' path. The monk persuaded James to visit with him, washed the elder's feet, and offered him food. Reproached by his conscience, the elder sighed from the bottom of his heart and beat his breast, but would not eat. Falling at James' feet, the brother lamented with the elder and swore that he would not rise until James agreed to share a meal with him. Finally James relented and the two men partook of such food as one might find in a desert cell, then rose to pray. Afterwards, the anchorite requested James, "Father, say an edifying word about the life in Christ. Confirm your son's wavering heart, for I am troubled by many sinful thoughts."

James moaned, then wept and again beat his breast. "Brother, leave me in peace to bewail my iniquities," he answered. "I have greatly angered God, for in my old age, I have been vanquished by the devil and sullied myself like a youth. I am disgraced, bound for perdition, utterly lost. The passions I subdued as a young man have conquered me at the end of my days. And not only have I defiled myself with carnal sin: I have committed other, unspeakable outrages." Hearing this, the brother was deeply troubled and begged the elder to relate how the evil one had defeated him. He did so for two reasons: so that the elder would be moved to repentance as he told the story; and to stir himself to increased vigilance as he listened to it.

"I led the ascetic life in the wilderness for more than fifty years, laboring for the Lord and struggling against the passions," began James. "To preserve my purity, I burned off my fingers, as you can see. In His compassion, God deemed me worthy of abundant gifts of grace and worked numerous miracles through me, the sinner. Then a certain maiden fell under Satan's control. Her father and mother, hearing about the miracles I worked through the grace of Christ, brought the girl to me and requested my prayers. With God's help I expelled the devil. The parents asked that I allow their daughter to remain with me for three days to recover her strength. I agreed, the parents left, and straightway I began to burn with carnal desire. My mind was blinded, and forgetting God, the fires of Gehenna, and my years of ascetic labor, I violated the maiden. Afterwards, devil spurred me to worse atrocities: I murdered the girl and disposed of her body in a stream. Now, despairing of salvation, I have abandoned my cave and am on my way back to the world. Oh, how can I lift my eyes to heaven! I am certain that if I call upon Christ's name, fire will fall out of the sky and consume me."

As he spoke, James shed rivers of tears and uttered piteous cries. The brother was moved to contrition, embraced the elder, and kissed him, saying, "I plead with you, Father: do not give up your struggles; do not lose hope of salvation. Believe in the power of repentance and confess your sins to God. The Lord is rich in mercy, and His compassion ineffable. If God disdained repentance, how would David, who fell into the pit of adultery and murder after receiving the gift of prophecy, have obtained forgiveness? If repentance and bitter tears were futile, how could Saint Peter, to whom the Lord entrusted the keys to the Kingdom of heaven, have secured pardon after thrice denying the Master during His voluntary Passion? Indeed, after his repentance, the Apostle was counted worthy of higher honor than before his fall and was made chief shepherd of Christ's sheep. Therefore, let us repent, while there is still time." Besides offering encouragement, the hermit urged James to remain with him; however, the elder refused. Fearing lest the elder perish in the slough of despondency, the anchorite fell at James' feet and pleaded that he reconsider, but to no avail. Lamenting bitterly and weeping, the brother finally let James go, giving him some food for the journey. He accompanied the elder for two miles, all the while exhorting him to repentance. Then, having embraced James and tearfully kissed him farewell, he returned to his cell.

James continued on his way back to the world, but soon the voice of conscience prevailed. Leaving the path, he found a burial cave, in which were old bones crumbling to dust. He pushed the bones to a corner and took up his dwelling there. Falling to his knees, he beat his breast, wailed, and prayed thus: "How can I lift up mine eyes to Thee, O my God? How shall I begin confessing my sins? How can I make entreaty with an unclean tongue and defiled lips? For which sin should I first ask pardon: for rape, or murder? Forgive my crimes, O most kind Master; be merciful to me the unworthy, O most compassionate Lord. Destroy me not on account of my foul deeds. I have defiled myself and shed innocent blood; I have cast away my victim's corpse in a stream, feeding it to beasts and birds. But now, O Lord, Who knowest all things, I confess my transgressions and beg forgiveness. Disdain me not, O Master, but in Thine ineffable love for man, have mercy on me, the impious, vile one. Reveal Thine infinite goodness and cleanse all my sins. Do not allow the enemy to drown me in the abyss of iniquity; do not permit the serpent to devour me in the bottomless pit."

For ten years the blessed James repented, buried like a corpse in the sepulcher with dead men's bones and cut off from the living. Whenever anyone came there, the elder would say nothing to him, even if asked a direct question. Instead, he remained in the grave and spoke only to God, confessing his sins. He subsisted on the wild herbs growing in the wilderness, and of these he partook barely enough to prevent starvation. The whole ten years he spent weeping, sighing, and praying, shouting to God his transgressions and beating his breast.

The all-compassionate and most merciful Lord, Who desires not the death of the sinner, but that he should turn to life, accepted the elder's lengthy repentance. He heard James' lamentation and confession, forgave his offenses, and restored to him the gift of wonderworking. The first miracle James wrought after his repentance was the following. A hot, dry wind was scorching the land, which was already suffering from drought. The entire population was fasting and praying to God for rain. While matters were in this state, a voice from heaven spoke to the Bishop of the town, a man of virtue. It said, "In such-and-such a burial cave there lives a holy elder. If he prays for you, the wind will cease, the rain will fall, and the earth will bring forth her fruits."

The next day the Bishop assembled the clergy and laity and announced the revelation, then led a procession to the sepulcher. The hierarch and his flock beat on the doors, imploring God's favorite to show compassion and pray for them, so that the Lord would turn away His righteous anger and end the drought. But there was no reply from the grave, because James dared not lift his eyes to heaven and intercede for others. Instead, he continued beating his breast and repeating, "Have mercy, O Christ, and forgive my grievous transgressions."

For hours the Bishop knocked, while entreating the elder's prayers, but James did not respond. Finally, he and his flock returned to the city, downcast and weeping. They went directly to the cathedral, where they performed a Service of Supplication. Outside, the dry wind was howling and hunger was stalking the land; inside, the weeping crowd, although exhausted from fasting, cried out to God. And it came to pass that the celestial voice again spoke to the Bishop, saying clearly, "Go back to My servant James, whose presence I disclosed earlier. If he prays for you, the land will be saved from disaster."

The Bishop, his clergy, and the people returned to the tomb and once more implored God's servant to pray for them. Finally, they forced the doors and carried out the saint. Unwillingly, the blessed James raised his eyes and hands and said a lengthy prayer. He had not yet completed his petition when the wind stopped and rain began pouring out of the sky. This came to pass because the Lord does the will of them that fear Him, *and His ears are opened to their supplication.*[3] On that day the words of the prophet were fulfilled: *Then shalt thou call, and God shall hear thee, and shall say to thee, Behold, I have come.*[4] Astonished and overjoyed at the miracle, the Bishop and his flock sang a triumphal hymn of thanksgiving and gladness to God and extolled the Lord's favorite, Saint James. Every year thereafter they celebrated the anniversary of their deliverance from tribulation by God's mercy and the prayers of the blessed elder.

Some time later Heaven directly revealed to the venerable

[3]Ps. 33   [4]Is. Ch. 58

James that his repentance had been accepted and his sins for-given. He began to perform numerous miracles by the grace of Christ, curing diseases of every sort and casting out demons by a mere word. Within a short time he had worked more wonders than in all the years prior to his fall and repentance.

Before the year was out, it was made known to James that his end was at hand. He summoned the Bishop and requested that he be buried in the sepulcher in which he lived. A few days later, James, the God-pleasing penitent, fell asleep in the Lord, and his holy soul took up its abode with the saints in the celes-tial land of divine blessings. The venerable James was seventy-five years old when he died. Word of his passing spread throughout the region and drew to his funeral enormous crowds bearing candles and censers. The Bishop presided over the rites and was assisted by all his clergy. Having chanted fit-ting dirges and anointed the holy remains with costly perfumes, they reverently buried the corpse in the sepulcher, as the saint had directed. Later, the Bishop erected a church outside the town and dedicated it to Saint James. The honored relics were enshrined there, and a feast was celebrated annually in honor of God's favorite, our venerable father James, and unto the glory of Christ God, Who is praised forever with the Father and the Holy Spirit. Amen.

On this same day we commemorate Saint Gregory, Bishop of Constantia in Cyprus, who reposed in peace.

On this same day we commemorate the translation of the honored relics of the holy Prince Wenceslaus of the Czechs, who was murdered by his brother Boleslav. Saint Wenceslaus' remains were transferred from Boleslavgrad to Prague and laid to rest in the Church of Saint Vitus.

On this same day the blessed Prince Basil of Rostov was slain by Batu, Khan of the Tartars. His life may be found in *The Prologue.*

The Fifth Day
of the Month of March

The Passion of the
Holy Martyr Conon of Isauria[1]

Saint Paul, apostle of the Gentiles, was the first to preach the faith of our Lord Jesus Christ in Isaura, the chief town of the land of Isauria, and to make converts of its citizens. In those days there was a man called Nestor living in the village of Bidane, two miles from Isaura. His wife Nada bore him a son, Conon, about whom our story will tell.

When Conon reached manhood, his parents betrothed him to a beautiful maiden named Anna. Prior to the nuptials, however, the Holy Archangel Michael, resplendent with light, appeared in human form to Conon. He instructed the youth in the faith, then led him to a river, where he baptized him in the name of the Most Holy Trinity. Before disappearing, the Archangel Michael imparted to Conon the divine Mysteries and traced the Sign of the Cross over him, so that the young man was filled with the Holy Spirit.

Conon's wedding day arrived and while the guests celebrated, the youth and his bride were led into their room. As he put out the candle burning in the bridal chamber, Conon asked the maiden, "Which is superior, light or darkness?"

"Light, of course," replied the maiden.

Then Conon, inspired by the Holy Spirit, explained that the Lord Jesus is the true light, and that the works of the flesh and the impious religion of the heathen are darkness. He exhorted

---

[1]From *The Great Collection of Readings*

his bride to preserve her purity and believe in Christ God, and the seed of his word fell on rich loam in her heart. The maiden agreed to everything he proposed, and the couple resolved to keep their virginity. Living as brother and sister, or rather, as two angels, Conon and the maiden burned with seraphic love for God and toiled ardently for the Lord. Before long the blessed Conon led his parents to Christ. Having persuaded them to renounce the idols, he baptized them with his bride. Instructed and guided by Saint Conon, the family led a God-pleasing life. Eventually Conon's father, the blessed Nestor, was deemed worthy of a martyr's crown, being put to death by idolaters whom he had upbraided for their errors. Then Conon's mother, the blessed Nada, reposed peacefully in the Lord, having held fast to a sound confession until her last breath. Finally, the holy virgin Anna, Conon's bride, departed to the immaculate bridal chamber of Christ, the Heavenly Bridegroom. After this, Conon lived alone with God, exercising himself in contemplation, fasting, and every ascetical labor. By night-long vigils he mortified his flesh and subjected it to the spirit. The Holy Spirit shed His grace upon Conon, who guarded it as a hidden treasure until he reached old age and his sanctity was manifested to the world. This happened in the following manner:

In the wild mountains of Isauria there was a dark, haunted cavern that served as a temple for the pagans. In it stood a large stone idol of the vile god Apollo, which was the object of fanatical devotion on the part of the local population. Every year on the loathsome feast of the god, the Isaurans would celebrate there, offering sacrifices. As the time of the festival approached and the townsfolk were preparing to visit the sanctuary, Conon, moved by the Holy Spirit, betook himself to the city. A crowd had assembled there, armed as if for battle. Some of the men were on horseback, some on foot. Conon cried to them, "Isaurans! I must have a word with you. Why are you arrayed for combat? Have you been called up to repel invaders?"

"Nothing of the sort," they replied. "We are on our way to sacrifice to Apollo and celebrate his feast."

"Who is Apollo?" asked the saint. "What sort of power does he possess?"

"He is our protector and provides us with every blessing,"

they asserted. "He strengthens us in battle, as he did our fathers, who taught us to worship him."

"Your fathers were oafs, duller than oxen," said Conon. "Had they known the true God, they would not have held a deaf, dumb, useless idol in such esteem. Allow me to do as I please to your god, and I will show you his feebleness. If I smear him with paint, can he wash himself clean? If I take a hammer to him, can he restore his own likeness? If I offer him food, can he take it and eat? How long before you understand? Hear me, for I am your fellow-countryman, but a stranger to your deeds. Renounce idolatry and I will teach you to worship the God Whose throne is on high. He is invisible, but sees everything. It was He Who created heaven, earth, the sea, and all that therein is. He is a mighty God, Who delivers His servants and smites His adversaries: those who worship idols and offer oblations to demons. He has no need of bloody sacrifices, but desires that His worshippers renounce evildoing and acknowledge Him as the true God. He is the Father of our Lord Jesus Christ, through Whom He created the ages and from Whom He is inseparable. The Father and the Only-begotten Son live and reign with the Holy Spirit, Who proceeds from the Father. These three hypostases are one God. His enemies, idolaters, He destroys with fire; but He loves them that love Him and glorifies them that glorify Him. Supremely compassionate, He has mercy on all who believe in Him and call on Him in truth."

As the Lord's favorite said this and much else in a similar vein, the crowd became agitated. Some of the people wanted to murder him, but they were restrained by others, who wished to hear what else Conon had to say. When the uproar had subsided a little, the heathen asked Conon, "Can you prove that your God is greater than Apollo, whom we revere more than any other deity? Have your God show His power, and we will believe in Him."

Putting his trust in the Lord, Conon responded with this challenge: "Many of you are mounted, and those who are not are strong, young fellows. Race me to your temple at the cave of Apollo. You leave first, and I, a feeble old man, shall follow on foot. All of us will swear to acknowledge the winner's God as true. If you horsemen or you strong young runners reach

Apollo's cave before me, it will prove your god's mightiness; but if I arrive first, it will show that my God is greater than yours, and you must accept Him."

The heathen agreed and gave their word to observe Conon's terms. "It will take the old man four days to reach the temple," they laughed. "The cave is far away and the path winds through mountains and ravines."

The pagans set out, trusting in their steeds and their well-muscled legs. Behind them shuffled Saint Conon, praying fervently. He had not walked far when the holy chief commander Michael appeared and instantaneously transported him to the cave. Then the archangel bewildered the heathen, so that they lost their way. Horses and men tripped, tumbled down the slopes, and were injured. Some of the pagans wandered aimlessly; others were trapped in the gorges. Not one reached Apollo's cave that day or night. The next morning Saint Conon headed back to ridicule the Isaurans. They were astonished to see him, but he mocked them, saying, "What is taking you so long? I tired of waiting, so I came to fetch you."

Wounded and exhausted, the pagans begged Conon to help them regain the trail. Conon led them all the way to the temple, saying, "Because I arrived first, you must admit the superiority of my God and believe in Him, as you agreed. You must also turn over your god to me, so that I may punish him for deceiving you for so long."

"No, no, do not blame our god or harm him!" the heathen cried. "It was our fault we lost the way."

Clearly, the pagans had no intention of keeping their promise. The saint demanded angrily, "If you will not believe in my God, will you believe in yours? If he speaks, will you heed him?"

"Certainly," they replied. "Our faith in Apollo is as strong as ever."

When the heathen had confirmed with the most solemn oaths their willingness to believe whatever Apollo said, Conon shouted into the cave, "My Lord Jesus Christ orders you to emerge!" Straightway the lifeless statue trembled; then it toppled from its pedestal and crawled to the blessed one, rising only after groveling at Conan's feet. Frightened out of their wits, the pagans screamed wildly and fled. Conon hardly succeeded in halting and quieting them. Then he returned to Apollo. The pagans watched apprehensively, and Conon ordered the statue, "Tell us, lifeless image: Who is the true God? You, or the Lord Jesus Christ, Whom I preach?"

At these words, the idol crashed to the ground and broke into pieces. Beholding the miracle, everyone shouted, "There is one true God, the God of Conon. He has conquered!" Many of the citizens believed in Christ God, smashed their idols, and accepted Holy Baptism. Some, however, were hardened in unbelief and would not convert. They mourned the destruction of Apollo. Nevertheless, even these were eventually drawn to the faith by other miracles worked by Saint Conon.

There was another cave in the wilds of Isauria which was home to a ferocious demon. Like a bandit or a barbarian raider it would kill men and domestic animals that passed by. Sacrifices and tears of pleading did nothing to appease the evil spirit, which became, if anything, even more vicious. Matters being in this state, the townspeople assembled and appealed to Conon to drive the demon out of their land. The believers asked with faith, trusting in the power of Christ which dwelt in Saint Conon. The unbelievers asked in order to test the saint, doubting that he could expel such a fierce demon; moreover, they secretly hoped that the devil would murder the Lord's favorite. Having agreed to help, the saint proceeded to the cave, with all the people following. The crowd stood afar off, shaking with fear, but the saint went directly to the entrance and in the name of Christ enjoined the unclean spirit to show itself. The demon was ashamed of fleeing before so many people. It begged Conon to let it simply vanish, pleading that it was too horrifying for human eyes to behold, but the blessed one threatened dire punishments if it would not come out for all to see. Slowly, the imp assumed the form of an ugly old woman, trembling and covered with gashes, and hobbled out of the cave. Saint Conon forbade the hag to do further harm and condemned her to the fires of Gehenna. Straightway the fiend vanished and everyone shouted, "Great is the God of Conon!" Many heathen converted to Christ, and Saint Conon taught the people for a long time. When he was done, the man of God went back with them to the city, chanting hymns of praise to Christ the true God. Saint Conon intoned each verse, and the newly-won faithful repeated his words.

After this Saint Conon returned to his father's house in Bidane. He healed the sick among the believers, expelled demons from the possessed, and worked miracles of every kind. One time, thieves stole a hoard of gold from a leading citizen of Isaura. Many were accused and questioned under torture, and the jails were full of innocent people, but no treasure could be found. Finally, both the nobleman and the kinsfolk of the prisoners went to the saint for help. Falling to their knees, they begged him to reveal where the gold was hidden. Conon was moved to compassion for the falsely charged, and he straightway betook himself to the forum of the city. There he raised his hands to heaven and prayed fervently until God granted him knowledge of the treasure. Without delay, Conon set out, with an enormous crowd following him. Deep in the wilderness, the holy chief commander Michael pointed out to him a rock, beneath which the gold-hoard was hidden. Saint Conon commanded the people to uncover the gold and take it back to the city. The whole town was astonished and glorified the Lord. But when the nobleman asked the saint who had stolen it, Conon replied, "Be satisfied you recovered everything, and make certain all the prisoners are released." The nobleman obeyed the saint, and word of the miracle spread throughout the land, so that many turned to God and Christ's Church grew day by day.

Once, Saint Conon was sitting quietly in his house when a horde of demons drew up ranks and advanced to attack him. These were wicked spirits that Conon had expelled from people and pagan temples and were living on the island.[2] Seeing hell's warriors approach, the saint halted and bound them by the name of Jesus. The devils begged Conon to punish them any way, but not to imprison them in the abyss. Having forbade them to harm people ever again, he condemned them to various tasks: digging in gardens; removing weeds, thorn bushes, and nettles; plowing and sowing; guarding fruits and vegetables

---

[2]There is no indication in the text as to what island this might have been. (Tr.)

as they ripened; herding flocks and protecting them from wild animals; hewing wood and hauling water. In a word, he enslaved them, and they were forced to do every servile chore. They toiled for him submissively, carrying out their tasks just as he required; for they were bound with the invisible chains of God's power and helpless to defy the Lord's favorite.

It happened that thieves descended upon the saint's house by night, since it was widely rumored that he was rich. They tied up Conon and tortured him, demanding that he reveal where his gold was hidden. While they were pummeling the saint, God ordered Conon's demonic servants to the scene. The devils laid hold of the robbers and beat them senseless, lit the oven and roasted the thieves' flesh, and also untied the Lord's favorite. None of the thieves would have survived had not the blessed one intervened. The saint prayed for the robbers until they came to. He reproved them and forbade them to continue their life of crime, then allowed them to depart.

Not only did the demons, at God's command, rescue Saint Conon from the hands of robbers: they defended his good name. Anyone who reviled the saint was invisibly pummeled by the wicked spirits with such ferocity that the name of Conon came to be regarded with fear and awe. Thus, two idolaters were fulminating against Conon when the demons assaulted them and dragged them by the hair to the saint's feet. After this, the unbelievers were afraid even to think ill of Saint Conon. When a thief sneaked into Conon's orchard, the invisible guards seized and beat him, then took him, his donkey, and his bag of pilfered fruit to the blessed one. Conon urged the man not to steal and let him go his way. Again, at harvest a poor widow, carrying her only child, went into the fields to glean. She put down the boy and was working some distance away when a wolf dashed out of the forest and snatched him. The laborers chased the beast into the woods but could not catch it or retrieve the child. No choice remained but for the woman to appeal to Saint Conon, who lived nearby. She fell at the blessed one's feet and washed them with tears, and he called for the assistance of his invisible slaves. A moment later they delivered the wolf, with the boy in its jaws. Conon handed over the child to his mother safe and sound and sent the wolf on its way. Some time later evil spirits that had not been bound by the wonderworker began afflicting the Isaurians with various diseases, especially the pox. Perceiving that demonic malice was at work, Saint Conon prayed and was given authority over the guilty fiends. He ordered the devils to present themselves, forbade them from doing further harm, and exiled some to the wilderness and some to the infernal abyss. The rest he bound and confined in thirty clay jugs which he sealed with lead. Having traced the sign of the Cross over the vessels, he buried them beneath the foundation of his house.

By and by persecution of the Christians began and an officer named Magdonius was sent to Isauria with an imperial decree commanding that everyone sacrifice to the gods. First Magdonius tortured to death Saint Onesimus, in the village of Usorobus. Then he seized Conon and tortured him viciously. When they heard this, the Isaurians took up arms and marched toward Usorobus with the intention of killing the commander. Magdonius and his cavalry rode away, escaping the Isaurians, who found the holy martyr tied up and covered with bloody wounds. They unbound him and wept for him, and were sanctified by daubing themselves with his blood and kissing the wounds he endured for Christ's sake. But Saint Conon was very sad that the Isaurians did not abandon him to a gruesome death for Christ.

The holy martyr was taken back to his home in Bidane, where the faithful treated his wounds. Two years after being tortured, he reposed in the Lord. All of Isauria lamented his passing. Saint Conon was buried with his righteous parents and his holy bride, who had kept her virginity intact until the end of her days. After his funeral, the Isaurians decided to convert his parents' home into a shrine dedicated to the martyrs. While enlarging the building, they dug into the foundation and found the thirty clay vessels in which Conon had imprisoned the demons. Hoping the jugs held gold or silver, the workers broke open one of them. Foul, black smoke belched out, darkening the sky, and a fierce wind arose. Some of the workers fainted in terror; the others took to their heels. The demons flew about and screeched one another's names, frightening the rustics so badly that no one dared venture out of his house until the next morning. Even so, the peasants had no peace that night, because the wicked spirits appeared in various forms to man and beast. In this way God chastised the Isaurians for their greed. Only when the villagers appealed to Saint Conon did the demonic apparitions cease. The remaining twenty-nine vessels were left undisturbed beneath the foundations of the church of Saint Conon, through whose holy prayers may we ever be preserved unharmed by demonic attack and glorify the Father, Son, and Holy Spirit, one God in Trinity. Amen.

On the Same Day
The Commemoration of the Holy Martyr Conon the Gardener[1]

This Saint Conon lived during the reign of the Emperor Decius and was born in Nazareth of Galilee. From thence he moved to the village known as Carmelas, near the town of Magydos in Pamphylia, and planted a garden, which provided his food. A simple, guileless Christian, Conon knew no letters but only to write his name in the Book of Life.

As soon as he learned about Conon, the Governor, Publius, sent troops to arrest him. The soldiers mocked Conon, pretending to come as friends; the saint, however, greeted them warmly and sincerely. When they told him that Governor Publius required him to present himself, Conon said, "Why does he want me? I am a Christian. Let him summon those who believe as he does."

The soldiers bound Saint Conon and took him to the Governor, who demanded that he worship idols. Sighing from the bottom of his heart at the blindness and delusion of the unbelievers, the martyr rebuked Publius and steadfastly confessed Christ. The Governor answered by driving nails through Conon's feet and forcing the saint to run before a chariot until he collapsed. After praying, the blessed one surrendered his soul into God's hands.

---

[1]From *The Prologue*

On the Same Day

The Commemoration of Our Holy Monastic Father Hesychius the Faster [1]

Hesychius, God's great favorite, learned from earliest childhood to love virtue and despise every attachment to worldly things. He became an abode of the Holy Spirit and unceasingly longed for the blessings of the heavenly Zion. Yearning for the celestial homeland, he forsook his earthly birthplace, Andrapa (which is inland from Adraneia), and ascended Mount Maion. The demons living on the mountain were afraid the saint would remain there and expel them, so they entered two men, John and Hilarion, who stopped God's chosen and warned him, "Are you aware, sir, how dangerous this peak is? It is the haunt of carnivorous beasts and murderous bandits. If you go further, your death is certain. Turn back or you will not survive the day."

Perceiving by the Spirit that the demons were trying to rid themselves of him, Hesychius answered, "Because of the multitude of my sins, I am worthy of death. I have come to this mountain because I want to be killed by wild animals or highway robbers." He then uttered a prayer and by the power of the Cross expelled the unclean spirits from the men. Afterwards, Hesychius continued on his way until he reached a spot that suited him. There he built a cell, planted a garden, and took up the hermit's life.

Once, a flock of birds flew into the garden and destroyed Hesychius' vegetables. Then other birds descended and began devouring the seeds he had planted. The saint prayed, and suddenly the birds that had eaten the vegetables fell from the sky. Their wings remained outspread, but they could no longer fly. Those that were greedily pecking at the seed also found they could not move their wings and dragged themselves along the ground as though they had been poisoned. The whole garden

---

[1]From Greek manuscripts

was crawling with flightless birds. A little while later the venerable one, moved by compassion, emerged from his cell and commanded the birds, "Depart, and find other food. I forbid you to eat the labor of monastics." No sooner had he said this than the birds flew away, never to return to the garden.

The saint found a spring in a nearby ravine and built a chapel there, which he dedicated to the holy Apostle Andrew. Once, while he was at the chapel practicing mental prayer with his disciples, a possessed maiden was brought to him by her parents. Falling at the feet of the saint, the father and mother begged him to drive the unclean spirit out of their child, which the venerable one promptly did. Afterwards, Saint Hesychius announced to the parents, "Thus says the Holy Spirit: 'After Hesychius' death, a community of holy nuns shall live here. By their prayers the regiments of demons shall be expelled from this place.'" In time the prophecy was fulfilled.

Once the venerable Hesychius was leaving his cell and a heavily loaded wagon was passing by. One of the oxen tripped and fell to the ground. The driver tried to help it to its feet but, like a huge stone, the beast could neither move nor be moved. The driver pushed and shoved until he was reduced to tears. This pitiful sight moved the saint to come over and pet the ox's shoulders. He urged the beast, as though it could understand: "Rise, lazy creature, and pull, lest the enemy see your fall and take advantage of it." Then he traced a cross over the animal, which regained its feet and began pulling with great strength. The astonished driver made a prostration to the saint, thanked him, and happily continued on his way.

Striving daily to attain new heights of virtue, the man of God was deemed worthy to converse with the celestial powers. Thirty days beforehand, an angel brought him the glad tidings of his departure to the Lord. After this, Hesychius devoted himself to instructing his disciples. At midnight just prior to his repose, a light shone from heaven, illumining both his cell and the surrounding area. The venerable one uttered his last words—"O Lord, into Thy hands do I commit my spirit"—and his soul flew off for the mansions of heaven.

The godly Hesychius' sacred and honored body was laid to rest in a sepulcher by the holy gates of the previously mentioned chapel of the Apostle Andrew the First-called. Later, the incorrupt relics were transferred to Amaseia by Theophylact, bishop of that town, during the reign of Constantine and Irene, in the year 6300 from the creation of the world.[2] As the saint had foretold, a convent for virgins was built in the wilderness at the place where he had struggled.

≷♠≷♠≷♠

On this same day we commemorate the holy martyr Eulogius of Palestine. The son of wealthy heathen parents, he distributed his inheritance to the poor and became a pauper for Christ's sake. While travelling through Palestine, teaching the pagans and converting many to Christ God, Eulogius was denounced to the Governor, who subjected him to many tortures and beheaded him.

On this same day we commemorate the holy martyr Eulampius, who was decapitated for Christ's sake. We also commemorate the repose of the venerable Mark the Ascetic, mentioned in the Life of our holy monastic father Macarius of Alexandria, whose feast is January 19.

On this same day we commemorate the translation of the relics of the holy, right-believing Prince Theodore, wonderworker of Smolensk and Yaroslav, and of his sons David and Constantine.

---

[2]In the year 792 from the Incarnation of Christ (Tr.)

The Sixth Day of the Month of March

The Passion of the Holy Forty-two Martyrs Captured at Amorium and Put to Death in Syria[1]

$\mathcal{T}$he Greek Emperor Theophilus was the son of Michael the Stammerer, a native of Amorium. He often waged war upon the Ishmaelites,[2] with varying success. Once, he attacked the Hagarene Caliphate and besieged a town called Zapetra, whence hailed the family of al-Mu'tasim, ruler of the Saracens. Al-Mu'tasim (also known as Abu-Ishaq) was elsewhere at the time and sent envoys to the Emperor Theophilus, entreating him to lift the siege and spare Zapetra; but Theophilus paid no heed. He took the town, razed it, and returned to Constantinople with much booty.

Al-Mu'tasim was infuriated by the destruction of Zapetra and, hiring troops from Babylon, Phoenicia, Palestine, Coele-Syria, and faraway Africa, soon assembled an enormous army at Tarsus. His plan was to capture the splendid Phrygian city of Amorium, birthplace of Michael the Stammerer, Theophilus' father, thereby avenging the Greek victory. Learning this, the Emperor hired troops from the East and West, as well as from Persia, and set out to engage the foe. When he reached the Phrygian town of Dorylaeum (three days away from Amorium), he met with his counselors. Because they possessed intelligence

---

[1]From George Kedrinus, Leo the Grammarian, Evodius Synchorus, and other sources
[2]The Arabs (Tr.)

about the size of the Hagarene army, which was much larger than the Greek, their advice was to avoid battle, evacuate the inhabitants of Amorium, and settle them in other fortified towns. To this the Emperor replied that it was cowardly to shirk combat and to permit such a beautiful city to be devastated without even attempting to defend it. Spurning the opinion of the nobles, Theophilus marshaled his troops and sent reinforcements to Amorium. The commanders of this detachment included the patricians Constantine the *Drungarios*,[3] Aetius, and Theophilus; Theodore Krateros the *Protospatharios*;[4] the *turmarchai* Melessenus and Callistus;[5] Basoes; and many other renowned officers.

Before long the armies of Theophilus and al-Mu'tasim clashed. Many fell on both sides, and at first the Greeks had the upper hand, but later God allowed the tide to turn, because He was wroth with Theophilus, who was an iconoclast. Christ our Master sapped the Greeks of courage, and when the Saracens began to prevail, the imperial army turned tail, abandoning Theophilus. Had it not been for the magnificent stand of his Persian mercenaries and the setting of the sun, the Emperor doubtless would have perished. Moreover, the King of heaven, *Who will not be angered unto the end,* nor *be wroth unto eternity,*[6] had mercy upon the Christians. There was an unexpected rainstorm which rendered the Hagarene archery ineffective and halted the foe's pursuit of Theophilus and the routed Greek troops.

After the bloody triumph, the Caliph advanced directly to Amorium. His men surrounded the city with trenches and a lengthy blockade ensued. Meanwhile Theophilus, having fled in shame to Dorylaeum, sent emissaries with many rich gifts to al-Mu'tasim, begging the barbarians to retire. Still furious

---

[3]*Drungarios*: originally a commander of 1,000 men. Over the centuries, the authority of the drungarioi decreased, until they were little higher than common soldiers. (Tr.)

[4]*Protospatharios*: a dignity in the imperial hierarchy usually conferring membership in the Senate. Protospatharioi were generally the commanders of themes, the military divisions of the Empire. (Tr.)

[5]*Turmarch*: an officer subordinate to the commander of a theme. Turmarchai had charge of subdivisions of themes and were sometimes commanders of naval units and littoral districts. (Tr.)

[6]Ps. 102

because of the destruction of Zapetra, the Caliph laughed at the Emperor's entreaty and presents, calling Theophilus a coward. He had the envoys clapped in irons until the campaign was over and ordered fierce assaults on the city. Due to the spirited resistance of the defenders, the only result of these was numerous Saracen casualties, including prominent commanders. Realizing he could not take the city by storm, al-Mu'tasim was greatly disheartened and decided to lift the siege and retreat. Then Vaditzes, an officer of the garrison, having quarreled with his immediate superior, decided to betray Amorium to the enemy. After the Saracens had already begun to withdraw, Vaditzes shot into their lines an arrow to which was tied this message: "Why are you accepting defeat after the town has been cut off for so long and while such enormous forces remain to you? Take courage and attack the wall near the pillar with a carving of a lion in marble, above which is a sculpted date palm. I will be posted in that area. The defenses there are weak, and with my help you will easily conquer the city. I am certain you will generously reward my assistance."

The note was taken with the arrow to al-Mu'tasim, who read it and rejoiced greatly. Without delay he ordered a major assault upon the indicated stretch of fortifications and, with the help of the wicked traitor, the Hagarene army broke into the city. A terrible slaughter ensued, rivers of Christian blood flowing through the streets. The population was put to the sword and the buildings were torched. This is how the Lord punished His people for the heresy spreading at that time among the Greeks. In a single day the fair city of Amorium was destroyed by fire and the sword because of the sins of the impious Emperor Theophilus, who had stripped the churches of their beautiful icons and cruelly tortured many holy confessors for venerating the sacred images. Seventy thousand men survived the carnage and flames, only to be decapitated by order of the Caliph; however, al-Mu'tasim spared forty-two commanders assigned by the Emperor to defend the city. These included the officers already mentioned by name. Countless women and children were taken captive and divided among the Saracen troops.

Al-Mu'tasim showed Theophilus' emissaries the wreckage of the city and sent them back to the Emperor. When they told

Theophilus what they had seen, he was overcome by grief and dispatched messengers to al-Mu'tasim offering to ransom his officers for two hundred *centenaria*.[7] The Caliph refused to release the captives for that amount, saying that he had spent a thousand centenaria to raise his army. Having mocked the Emperor's letter, he contemptuously expelled the messengers. Theophilus fell ill from grief and never fully recovered, although he lived several years longer. The captives were taken to Syria. As for Vaditzes, the betrayer of the city, he renounced Christ and embraced the impious religion of the Saracens.[8] The apostate was rewarded with rank and wealth by the Caliph.

Upon arrival in his own country, al-Mu'tasim shackled the Greek officers, cast them into a gloomy dungeon, and put them in stocks. But the saints in prison suffered less at the hands of the Hagarenes than of the vicious apostate Vaditzes.

One day, several men came to the dungeon and, feigning compassion, gave the saints a few coins as alms. So doing, they advised the captives to show pity on themselves and gain their freedom by accepting the Mohammedan religion. The saints refused the deceptive offer, preferring to endure privation, life-imprisonment, and even the cruelest death, rather than to become followers of the loathsome Mohammed. Many times the deceivers returned and repeated their blandishments, but to no avail, even though in the name of the Caliph they promised freedom, honors, and many gifts.

On another occasion several of the highest-ranking Hagarene nobles brought alms to the prisoners, sat with them, and lamented their fate. After this false show of sympathy, the noblemen commented to one another, "Oh, what misfortunes result from unbelief in the great prophet Mohammed! Were not these men, who are now loaded with chains, favorites of their sovereign and renowned for valor among their fellow-countrymen? Were they not commanders of the great castle-city of Amorium and an army of more than seventy thousand? Yet

---

[7]*Centenarion:* money of account, equivalent to a hundred Roman pounds of gold coins. The Roman pound approximately equals three-quarters of an English pound. (Tr.)

[8]Islam (Tr.)

they have fallen into the hands of our *protosymboulos*[9] (as their ruler was called). Who brought low their might? Why would they have come to such a pass, unless it were for rejecting the illustrious prophet Mohammed, whose servants have won a splendid victory. Still, it is understandable why they do not believe in him. They are untaught and do not know him. But those who sin in ignorance are easily forgiven." Then the nobles said to the holy captives, "Sirs, you know our sympathy for you; now heed our advice. Turn aside from the narrow way which the Son of Mary commands you to tread, and travel the path indicated by our famed prophet, which is wide both in the present and the future age. Why do you disbelieve the prophet when he assures us that in this life God rewards with every enjoyment those who submit to Him and in the next makes them heirs to paradise? Does God lack for gold or any other bright thing? Repudiate the doubt of the ignorant, for it is senseless to decline the rich gifts God bestows both here and yonder. Or do you think to control the divine bounty, now rebuffing God's benefits, now securing His blessings at whim? Overweening pride impels you to spurn God's generosity and to rouse His wrath. If you wish to give something to your slaves and they disdain your liberality, do you not become angry with them? Do you not punish them for insolence? If you, being mortal men, will not suffer such an insult, how shall the immortal God endure? Therefore, accept the doctrine of our prophet, and you will escape present tribulations and enjoy the divine boon granted us in this life and after death. Seeing how difficult it was for men to fulfill the law of Jesus, our compassionate God sent His prophet Mohammed to ease our plight. Freed from all burdens and afflictions, we may now revel in every temporal pleasure and still inherit celestial delights, being saved by faith alone, without deeds of virtue."

As the Hagarenes prated, the wise prisoners exchanged knowing glances and laughed softly. They quoted the psalm verses, *"Transgressors have told us fables, but they are not like Thy law, O Lord. All Thy commandments are truth."*[10] Then they asked

---

[9]*Protosymboulos:* a Greek title meaning "first councillor" or "the chief minister of state," but here used for the Caliph himself (Tr.)
[10]Ps. 118

the Saracens, "Is this really the teaching of your prophet? Do you truly believe that we can please God if we are in bondage to every impure desire and passionate yearning? Do you think that we can be counted righteous if our mind is so enslaved by pleasures that we cannot even conceive of restraining ourselves with the bridle of abstinence? Friends, a dissolute man is worse than an irrational animal. We have no intention of degrading ourselves. Do not expect us to renounce the noble, upright principles of the Christian faith. We are disciples of the martyrs, who cried to the Lord, 'Never shall we repudiate Thee! *For Thy sake we are slain all the day long, we are counted as sheep for the slaughter.[11] Neither things present, nor things to come, nor any other creature shall be able to separate us from the love of God, which is in Christ Jesus.'"*[12] Hearing this, the Hagarenes realized that they had failed in their design, and so departed.

At another time the Caliph sent gymnosophists[13] to the saints. After giving the captives alms, these deceivers asked, "What is impossible for God?"

"Nothing," replied the saints. "Omnipotence is an innate characteristic of the Divinity."

The gymnosophists proposed, "If nothing is impossible for God, let us consider on whom, in His omnipotence, He has chosen to shower blessings at the present time: the Greeks or the Ishmaelites? To whom has God given the most fertile and desirable parts of the earth, to you or to us? Who has the larger army? Whose regiments are cut down like straw? Is God unjust? If He had not adjudged us faithful keepers of His commandments, would He have blessed us so richly? And is it not because you reject His prophet Mohammed that He has subjected you to us and made you our captives?"

The saints retorted, "If you believed the testimony of the prophets, you would understand that your reasoning is false. Your contention is not supported by divine Scripture. Answer this: Two men quarrel over ownership of a field. The first argues and shouts that the property belongs to him, but can produce

---

[11]Ps. 43   [12]Rom., Ch.8
[13]*Gymnosophystai:* the name by which the ancient Greeks designated the ascetic philosophers of India (*gymnos* "naked" and *sophistes* "teacher of wisdom") (Tr.)

no witnesses at all. The second does not strive or contend, but has many honorable, trustworthy witnesses, ready to testify that the field is his. Which of the two would you, Saracens, declare the owner?"

The philosophers answered, "The field of course belongs to the man with the witnesses."

"That is correct," agreed the saints. "We apply the same logic to your teacher Mohammed and to the Only-begotten Son of God, our Lord Jesus Christ. All the ancient, holy prophets foretold the coming of our Lord into the world, and Jesus Christ fulfilled their prophecies when He assumed flesh from the pure Virgin. Many times have we heard you Saracens testify that you accept this. But what can we say about your great prophet and lawgiver Mohammed? Why did not at least one or two of the prophets testify concerning him, making it clear that he was truly sent by God?" This argument put to shame the gymnosophists, who could make no rebuttal.

Then Saint Basoes smiled, "But the Hagarene lawgiver does have a true and glorious witness who prophesied about him: the holy Isaiah. I would cite his words, but they might grieve our wise visitors."

"We shall not take offence," the gymnosophists assured him. "We have been taught to forgive those who sin out of ignorance, even if they malign our prophet."

"Is it not your belief that Mohammed is the last, the seal of the prophets?" asked the saint.

"It is," they replied.

Then Saint Basoes said, "Isaiah, whom you also confess to be a prophet of God, testified, *The Lord will cut off from Israel the head and tail.*[14] Further on, Isaiah himself interprets his own words, explaining that *the head* means those who respect persons and render unjust judgment, and *the tail* means *the prophet that teacheth lies.* Do not be offended, my friends, but is not your prophet *the tail*, the very last of the prophets, according to your belief? And does not your lawgiver teach iniquity? For example, he says that if a man hates his wife and divorces her, he cannot take her back until she lies with another man. We could point out

---

[14]Is., Ch. 9

many other infamous ordinances in Mohammed's law, but modesty constrains us to silence. Sufficient are Isaiah's words: *The prophet that teacheth lies, he is the tail.* They can refer only to Mohammed."

The gymnophists protested, "We can philosophize to our heart's content, but who can challenge God's will? Mohammed was ordained by God, Whose laws he delivered. He has no need of human witness."

"Can God have given a law permitting you to have many women, with whom you enjoy yourselves all night during your period of fasting, indulging in gluttony and carnal relations?" asked Saint Basoes.

"He did give such a law," affirmed the gymnosophists.

"We wish to return to your original contention," the other saints said. "You maintain that whoever has the mightiest army and wins victories necessarily has the best religion. If you judge matters of faith on the basis of military strength, remember the ancient Persians, who conquered many lands and subjugated almost the whole world. Afterwards arose the empire of the Greeks, ruled by Alexander the Great, vanquisher of the Persian Empire. Next Rome established its dominion over all the earth. So, did they have the true faith? They were all successful in war, but utterly idolatrous and ignorant of the true God, the Creator of the universe. How then can you insist that your recent victory over us proves the truth of your religion? God permitted you to defeat us because of our sins. Often we Christians, who worship God correctly, overcome our foes, with the Lord's help. Again, when we have angered Christ the Lord and fail to repent, He allows the ungodly to punish us for our transgressions. Nevertheless, while being chastised, we do not deny our Master, but beg His mercy, trusting that He will have pity on us. As for Mohammed, whom no prophet accredits and who teaches contrary to the saints of old, we utterly reject him." The gymnosophists, seething with anger, returned in shame to the Caliph.

For seven years the saints languished in the narrow, gloomy dungeon, loaded with shackles.[15] Day and night they exercised

[15]During the saints' imprisonment, al-Wathiq succeeded his father al-Mu'tasim as Caliph. (Tr.)

themselves in prayer, unceasingly chanting the psalms of David and thanking God for His spiritual blessings. By means of lengthy imprisonment, the Lord cleansed the sins they had committed during the years they had enjoyed comforts. Furthermore, He strengthened them in patience to a degree they could not have imagined before.

While the holy martyrs were steadfastly enduring their lot, the apostate Vaditzes, who had betrayed Amorium to the barbarians and denied Christ, came to the prison. It was the evening of the fifth of March. Through a window, he called to one of the prisoners, Constantine, former notary of the patrician Constantine. "For many years I was a dear friend of your master Constantine the patrician," whispered the deceiver. "I was told by a reliable informer that the Caliph intends to slay all of you tomorrow, unless you convert. You are a prudent man: advise your master to stay alive by pretending to accept the Saracens' religion. You also should feign conversion. In your minds remain steadfast in the Christian faith. Christ will understand that you acted thus only to escape the Caliph's wrath."

The devout notary traced the sign of the Cross upon himself with his right hand and said to the apostate, "Depart, worker of iniquity!"

Vaditzes slunk away, but Constantine the patrician asked his notary, "With whom were you speaking through the window? What was he saying?"

Fearing that some of the prisoners might waver or panic if they heard their death was immanent, the notary took aside his master. When he learned what Vaditzes had related, the patrician thanked God, saying, "May the Lord's will be done." Then he suggested to his companions, "Brethren, let us spend the whole night in prayer." Everyone rose and prayed, chanting psalms until morning.

At dawn the Caliph sent to the prison one of his most brutal officers and a company of soldiers. The officer took the forty-two martyrs from their cell to the courtyard of the dungeon, barred the gates, and asked the captives, "How many years have you been here?"

"Why do you ask the question, when you know the answer?" responded the saints. "We have been here seven years."

"Such a long time has passed, and you still do not appreciate the compassion of our just ruler!" marveled the officer. "He has spared you for years, though he could have put you to death at any time. You should be grateful for his mercy, pray for him, and love him with all your heart."

The saints said, "Our law commands us to pray for those who persecute, oppress, and offend us; therefore, we do pray for your ruler. We cannot, however, love him with all our heart, because the holy Prophet David forbids this when he cries to God, *As for them that hate Thee, O Lord, have I not hated them?*"[16]

"How can you pray for someone you hate?" the officer hissed. "Clearly, you lie when you profess to pray for the Caliph."

"We indeed speak the truth," said the martyrs. "We pray that God enlighten his soul, which is blinded by unbelief. May he find the path of righteousness and piously worship God, accepting the true Christian faith and renouncing the false religion he now confesses. If your ruler were to convert to the true faith, we would not only love him with our whole heart, but revere him greatly, following the example of David, who said, *To me, exceedingly honourable are Thy friends, O Lord.*"

"The princes of the Greeks and Romans are fools if they think our nation could have attained such power without God's aid," scoffed the Hagarene. "If God hated us, He would not favor us so. He would not have multiplied us and extended our rule over so many lands."

"We never claimed that you are not overshadowed by providence," the martyrs said. "Providence has charge over every man on earth. A man may be ignorant of God or offend Him by iniquitous deeds; nevertheless, he cannot live or act apart from providence. We say only that you do not believe correctly in the true God. While confessing Him to be the Fashioner of all creation, visible and invisible, you mock Him by maintaining that He is the Cause of both good and evil, truth and falsehood, righteousness and unrighteousness, humility and pride, meekness and wrath, chastity and fornication, the virtues and the opposing vices. If what you say about God were true, we would freely admit that you have a correct understanding of Him. But

---

[16]Ps. 138

your confession differs from the truth as darkness does from the light of the sun. We cannot pretend that you have a true understanding of God, or refrain from setting you right. You most certainly have aroused the Lord's anger, even if you are preserved by providence."

"So do you imagine that there is a second god, the author of every evil and sin?" the officer demanded. "How can there be two gods, one good and one bad? How could the world escape destruction, with two gods battling over it?"

The saints explained, "We do not say that there is a second god, who created evil and is at enmity with God the Creator of everything good, but that one of the angels, having free will, chose what is harmful and contrary to the good. Loving evil, he first hated God his Maker, then hated man. He was permitted to test the disposition of our will, to see whether it was inclined toward God or wickedness. This fallen angel has led you astray, and you perversely ascribe his maleficence to God, Who is passionless and immutable."

"Our prophet Mohammed insists that Almighty God is responsible for every evil deed of man, no less than every good deed," said the Hagarene.

To this the saints replied, "Then it is clear that Mohammed has invented and commanded you to worship a new god who never has existed nor ever will exist, a god like unto the *agathos daimon*[17] of the ancient Greeks. But we know and confess the true God proclaimed as the Creator of everything good by the holy prophets in the Old Testament and by the holy apostles of Christ in the New."

"I have been sent to persuade you to join in worship today with our devout *protosymboulos* and caliph, according to the custom of our religion. Will you agree? I know that certain of you are of a mind to do this. As for the others, they will see how those who comply are rewarded, and will have reason to lament their obstinacy and poor judgment," threatened the officer.

---

[17]*Agathos daimon:* originally, the "protective spirit" of individuals and families. In time the *agathos daimon* was associated with Tyche, goddess of fortune, as an impersonal providence. The ambiguity of his character was emphasized by his depiction either as a serpent, or a youth holding a horn of plenty and ears of grain. (Tr.)

With one voice the saints replied, "We pray that not only your ruler, the *Protosymboulos*, but the whole race of Saracens will renounce the error of the ungodly Mohammed and offer fitting honor and worship to the one true God preached by Christ's apostles and prophets. We cannot forsake light and willingly enshroud ourselves in darkness."

"Be careful what you say, lest you regret it later," warned the officer. "If you remain unsubmissive, you will not escape severe punishment."

"We entrust our souls to God, Who is immortal and just. We will hope in Him until our last breath and never renounce our faith in Him," said the martyrs.

"On the dread day of judgment your orphans and widows will bear witness against you," said the Ishmaelite. "The only reason they are not at your side today is because you refuse to obey the Caliph and renounce your faith. If you yield, our mighty caliph will order your child-emperor to send your wives and children. I assure you that if you acknowledge the prophet Mohammed, you will soon have the joy of seeing your families. The country of the Greeks is now ruled by the Empress Theodora, on behalf of her little son Michael, and she is in no position to disobey the command of our illustrious *protosymboulos*. Do not be troubled over how you will support your families: our generous caliph has decided to turn over to you the entire tax revenue of Egypt for a whole year, if only you become his friends. You will be rich men, as will your descendants unto the tenth generation."

Burning with divine zeal, the saints shouted fearlessly, "Anathema to Mohammed and to all who regard him as a prophet!"

The infuriated officer ordered his soldiers to tie the saints' hands behind their backs and lead them to the place of execution. An enormous crowd of Saracens and of Christians living among the Saracens gathered to see the martyrs put to death. When the passion-bearers were not far from the bank of the Euphrates River (on which the great Saracen city of Samarra[18] is located), the officer called for one of them, the holy Theodore

---

[18]Then capital of the Caliphate (Tr.)

Krateros, whose name means "the strong" or "the brave." He said, "I have it on reliable report that you were once a clergyman, but renounced the priestly rank, took up arms, and shed blood in battle. Why do you hypocritically pretend to be a Christian when in your heart you long ago rejected the Christian faith? It would be best if you embraced the teaching of the prophet and apostle Mohammed, receiving from him help and deliverance from death. Having freely renounced Christ, it is certain you can have no boldness before Him nor expect His aid."

Christ's valiant martyr Theodore replied, "You lie, saying that I renounced Christ God. I only left the ranks of the clergy because of my unworthiness, which is good reason my blood should be shed for the faith of Christ. If I die for love of the compassionate Master, He will forgive the sins I once committed. If you had a slave who fled, but then returned to you and proved his loyalty by dying for your sake, would you not forgive his flight?"

"Have it your way," said the officer. "I was merely suggesting that you save your own life."

Presently Ethiopian executioners bared their swords and ordered the martyrs to stand a distance from one another. Theodore Krateros found himself nearest to Constantine the patrician. Fearing lest Constantine waiver if he saw him beheaded, Theodore said, "Hear me, my lord! You were our leader and surpass us all in virtue; therefore, you should have the honor of being the first martyred. The earthly Emperor recognized your superiority by entrusting you with command and lavishing gifts on you, so you should be first to receive a crown from Jesus Christ, the King of heaven."

Saint Constantine replied, "You are first in valor; therefore, you should be first to lay down your life for Christ. We shall imitate your brave example."

After praying, Saint Theodore commended his soul to God, approached the executioners, and met his glorious death. Then the other saints, according to rank, offered their necks to the sword. They hurried to die as though they were being summoned to an imperial banquet, not showing the least fear or agitation. The Saracen officer was amazed at how joyfully the martyrs confronted their end.

The holy forty-two martyrs were beheaded for the Lord on the sixth day of March.[19] After they were put to death, the Caliph commanded that the apostate Vaditzes be slain, saying, "If he had been a true Christian, he would never have denied his religion. If he did not keep faith with Christ, he will not do so with Mohammed. If he betrayed his fellow-Christians into our hands, he will turn on us in our hour of need. If he was disloyal to his own people, he will not remain true to us." Thus the wretch was decapitated, receiving from the Saracens a just reward for delivering into their possession the splendid and glorious Christian city of Amorium.

The next morning, on orders from the Caliph, the remains of the holy forty-two martyrs were cast into the river Euphrates, as were those of the apostate. Not many days later, the bodies of the martyrs were found on the opposite bank with heads reattached. The corpses lay side by side, neatly arranged according to rank. The renegade's carcass washed up a good distance away, and the head was not joined to it. Local Christians gave fitting burial to the saints' bodies, but the iniquitous traitor was devoured by crocodiles. For all this, glory be to Christ our God, Who is worshipped forever with the Father and the Holy Spirit. Amen.

---

[19]From Symeon Logothetes

On the Same Day

The Passion of the Holy Monastic Martyr Conon and His Son, Also Named Conon, Who Suffered in Iconium[1]

During the reign of the persecutor Aurelian, a nobleman named Conon lived in the city of Iconium. He and his wife were deeply pious, burning with love for the celestial homeland and preferring heavenly to earthly honors and glory. For a long time they entreated God to grant them a son. The Lord heard their prayer, and Conon's wife bore a child. On the very day she gave birth, the devout mother departed to the Lord, having firm hope for salvation, in accordance with the Apostle's words: *The woman shall be saved in childbearing.*[2] The boy was named Conon, after his father.

The blessed widower Conon spent all his days and nights in prayer. When his son reached the age of seven, he distributed among the poor everything he owned, took the child to a monastery, and himself received the tonsure there. God granted him the grace to give sight to the blind, cleanse lepers, cast out demons, and work many other glorious miracles.

Every spring the river flowing through Iconium overflowed its banks, flooding fields, gardens, farmhouses, and villages. One year, the floodwaters raged out of control and all the peasants implored the man of God for aid. Falling at Conon's feet, they begged, "Help us, servant of the Lord! The river has submerged our homes and land, and no one can cross it."

"Brethren, I am sinful and unworthy," protested the saint. "I can do nothing for you."

Not willing to accept this answer, the people shouted again and again, "Saint Conon, servant of God, help us!"

Conon went to the river, lifted his eyes to heaven, and prayed, "O Lord Jesus Christ! Once Thou didst hearken unto

---

[1]From Greek manuscripts and *The Great Collection of Readings*
[2]II Tim., Ch. 2

Thy servant Moses and lead the sons of Israel dry-shod through the Red Sea. Now hear me, O Master, for the sake of this people, that they may witness Thy miracles and glorify Thy blessed name forever."

The crowd added the Amen, and suddenly the waters parted, half reversing their course, half continuing downstream. With one voice men and women shouted praise to God, the Deliverer of all who hope in Him. Peasants living downriver began returning with their animals to the homes they had abandoned. Upriver, however, the waters that turned back flooded not just low-lying villages and woods, but high ground as well. Again all hastened to the man of God and poured out their woes; again Conon went to pray at the river. Tracing the sign of the Cross over its surface, he cried, "Heed the command of God Almighty, gather the waters within your banks, stay in your course, and never again touch the dwelling-places of men!" Like a slave obeying his master, the river hearkened unto God's favorite. The waters, which had risen up like a mountain, straightway fell back to their usual bounds and thenceforth always remained within them. Thus the word of the Lord was fulfilled: *If ye have faith as a grain of mustard-seed, ye shall say unto this mountain, Remove hence to yonder place, and it shall remove.*[3]

In his zeal for men's salvation, the blessed one destroyed many heathen temples and converted numerous unbelievers to the faith, not only in the town of Iconium, but in the surrounding countryside as well. By and by rumor of his doings reached the ears of the impious Count Domitian. The evildoer hurried to Iconium, striking terror into the hearts of the citizens. No one dared acknowledge openly that he was a Christian, and many fled to the mountains, preferring to live among wild beasts rather than renounce the faith. Prompted by Satan, Domitian ordered his troops to capture the man of God. When the soldiers brought Conon to him, Domitian smiled, "Greetings, noble elder!"

"Greetings to you," answered Conon.

"Your appearance is exactly as was described to me," said Domitian. "You are a handsome, respectable-looking man; your

[3]Matt., Ch. 17

eyes are penetrating and shine like the stars; and you have reached a venerable age. Nevertheless, I am told that you are poisoned with the lethal venom of Christianity and are both deceived and a deceiver of others. This I find hard to believe. You are clearly a person of noble birth and must be a devout adherent of our religion."

The blessed Conon replied, "It is written that we should follow wise counsel, not foolish. Why have you rejected our Lord, Who was seized and condemned to death, crucified and laid in a sepulcher? Why do you not marvel at His Nativity from the immaculate Virgin, who gave birth as a virgin and remained a virgin afterwards? Why are you not amazed by the Nativity proclaimed by angels, who rejoiced, chanting, *Glory to God in the highest, and on earth peace, good will toward men?*[4] Why are you not astonished by the power of Him Who fed five thousand men with five loaves of bread and two fishes? Save Christ, who has ever opened the eyes of a man born blind; restored life to someone dead for four days (the famed Lazarus); suffered willingly for the salvation of the world; or rent rocks, opened graves, and caused many bodies of the saints to rise by His own death and Resurrection?"

"If your claims were true, then the entire world would accept Christ, and Zeus' power would be broken," scoffed Domitian.

"The power of Zeus and all your gods shall be broken by the infinite might of the Lord Jesus Christ, Who commanded me to proclaim the truth," declared Saint Conon. "I shall ever abide in that truth: the eternal law of Christ. Our Lord said, *I am the way, the truth, and the life.*[5]*He that believeth in Me, though he were dead, yet shall he live. And whoever liveth and believeth in Me shall never die.*[6] We the faithful *must through much tribulation enter into the Kingdom of God.*[7] As for the sons of this world, who live spaciously, enjoying temporal pleasures, they *shall be cast into outer darkness: there shall be weeping and gnashing of teeth.*"[8]

Roused to anger, Domitian commanded that Saint Conon be pummeled and subjected to various torments. "I am glad you

---

[4]Luke, Ch. 2   [5]John, Ch. 14   [6]John, Ch. 11
[7]Acts, Ch. 14   [8]Matt., Ch. 8

are so quick to employ torture," Conon said. "Use the utmost brutality, so that I may receive a better reward from my compassionate Christ."

Domitian said, "Accept my good advice: submit, and you will enjoy earthly delights with us."

"My purpose is to save my soul, not my body," replied the martyr. "I wish to enjoy spiritual, not physical delights. You, impious one, and your father the devil are destined for unending torments in hell."

"What rank do you hold in your religion, wicked elder?" inquired the Count. "Are you a priest?"

"I am a simple man and unworthy of such an exalted rank. Those who hold the priesthood spiritually rejoice with Christ and His holy angels," the martyr explained. "Nonetheless, I also rejoice in Christ and worship Him."

"Are you married?" asked Domitian.

"I had a wife, briefly; but she departed to Christ our God," the saint answered.

Domitian continued, "Do you have children?"

"I have a son, who remained in my cell. I hope he will also have the opportunity to stand before your judgment seat," said Conon.

"Will he worship the gods?" demanded the Count.

"The branch is like the tree. I urge you to bring him here, so that we may receive the crown of martyrdom together," Conon said.

Without delay the Count sent troops to bring the younger Conon. When the son arrived, Domitian asked the father, "How old is the boy?"

The elder explained, "He was seven when I took him to the monastery, where he learned to read. At twelve he was made a lector. He is now seventeen and, by the grace of Christ, has been ordained a deacon. From his earliest years I have taught him to lead a chaste, sober life. He is worthy to be martyred; therefore, continue my torture and let him share in it, that we may be crowned together by Christ our God. We are Christians and eager to die for Christ."

"What is your son's name?" asked Domitian.

"Conon, the same as mine," replied the elder.

Then Domitian addressed the younger Conon, saying, "Your father has reached old age, was married, sired a child, and has enjoyed this life for many years. It is understandable that he is ready to die. You are young and have had no experience of pleasures. Do you truly wish to perish with your father?"

"It was my father (with the Lord) who brought me into this world, and it was he who taught me to know the one true God, Creator of all things visible and invisible," said the deacon. "He showed me the path of salvation and led me to understand that this life is but death and that all who love temporal life die unto eternity. However, the life offered by our Master Christ to those who love Him is endless. My father also taught me that the unquenchable fire of Gehenna awaits impious idolaters whereas Christ our God (for Whose sake *the world is crucified unto* us, *and we unto the world)*[9] has reserved unfading garlands of celestial glory in the everlasting Kingdom for His faithful servants. I say with my Master Christ, 'As *My Father worketh, I work;*[10] and, *The Son can do nothing of Himself, but what He seeth the Father do.'*"

"Your father is about to perish in agony," said Domitian. "Are you prepared for the same destruction?"

"I intend to die with my father, that I may live with him in the Kingdom of our Master," affirmed the deacon. "Martyrdom for Christ is not death, but the portal to everlasting life."

"This youth is even more sharp-witted than you," Domitian said to the elder Conon. "His only faults are ignorance of the truth and failure to pay homage to our gods."

The elder answered, "The young man knows the truth well and with me reveres Him Who said, *I am the truth.*[11] Never will he or I worship statues of your false gods, the demons."

"This is your last warning: Bow down before the gods, save yourselves from gruesome tortures and death, and be enriched by our gifts," urged the Count.

"O wicked renegade from God, thirsty blood-drinker, persecutor, and most impious of men, I have already told you that I am a Christian and want to die for Christ with my son!" repeated the elder. "You are drunk with malice, utterly insane, and cannot remember a word I say."

---

[9]Gal., Ch. 6   [10]John, Ch. 5   [11]John, Ch. 14

At this Domitian ordered a gridiron couch heated to glowing-red and the saints stripped naked and laid on it. Servants stuffed blazing coals beneath the bed and poured boiling oil over the martyrs' bodies, but without doing them any harm. The elder Conon taunted Domitian, "Have you forgotten my request that you torment us cruelly? Where are the real tortures?"

Next the persecutor had a copper kettle filled with molten lead, sulphur, and pitch. The cauldron was brought to a boil, and the holy martyrs were thrown into it. "If the bed was not hot enough for them, let them stew in the pot," muttered the Count. "We shall see whether their God delivers them."

As the saints stood in the cauldron, they raised their eyes to heaven and prayed, "O Lord our Creator, hearken unto our supplication, and send Thy holy angel to cool us like the Three Youths in the fiery furnace of Babylon! Hear us, O Master, and come quickly to our aid, that all may know that Thou art the Son of the living God and Deliverer of the world."

Straightway, the Lord sent His angel to bedew the fire and cool the kettle. The angel greeted the Lord's favorites, "Peace be unto you, valiant warriors and steadfast strugglers! Do not be afraid, for Christ is with you. He will see to it that you gain the victory and inherit everlasting joy."

After this Count Domitian commanded that the holy martyrs be suspended upside-down over a burning heap of foul-smelling rubbish. The elder Conon laughed, "Fool, the flames are not reaching us and smoke can do us no harm"; but the Count left them to hang. The younger Conon joined his father in ridiculing Domitian, saying with him, "Wretch, your wicked devices have come to nought. Just two soldiers of Christ are enough to break your power and put to shame your father the devil."

Thoroughly humiliated and seething with anger, Domitian was uncertain what to do next. At length he ordered that the saints be brought down and sawn in half. Before the servants began to saw, the martyrs requested time for prayer. The servants consented, and the saints prayed thus: "O Master, God Almighty, Creator of heaven and earth, King of kings and Lord of lords! We thank Thee for deeming us worthy to suffer for Thy holy name, for strengthening us amid torments, for preventing Thine adversaries from exulting over us, and for making us victors over the devil. We glorify Thee, Christ God, almighty, all-benevolent Lover of mankind; and we beseech Thee: grant peace unto Thy Holy Church throughout the world, subdue her oppressors, and quickly destroy the vile heathen temples. Manifest Thy power and spread the praise of Thy holy name; preserve and increase the race of Orthodox Christians unto the end of the world. Furthermore, we entreat Thee, O Master, to permit us to depart this life in peace. Let not the persecutor's orders be fulfilled, but spare us from being sawed in half, lest our enemy have the satisfaction of destroying us. Let Thy mercy go before us and lead us to Thee. Let Domitian know that we are Thy servants, that Thou art with us, and that Thou art almighty. May all who hear of our passion forever glorify Thy holy name, O Lord."

When the saints said the Amen, a voice sounded from heaven, calling them to the celestial abodes. The holy martyrs made the sign of the Cross and committed their souls into God's hands. A mighty earthquake brought down the pagan temples and all the idols in the city were shattered. Domitian fled and cowered in his headquarters. Upon learning what had happened, the brethren of the monastery came and removed the sacred corpses. After anointing them with sweet spices, they held a magnificent funeral and committed to the earth the honored remains, glorifying the Father, Son, and Holy Spirit, the one God in Trinity, extolled by all creation forever. Amen.

☙✾❧✾❧

On this same day we commemorate our venerable father Arcadius of Cyprus. He became a monk at an early age, during the reign of Constantine the Great. Arcadius was the elder of the holy martyrs Julian the Physician and Eubulus, who suffered under Julian the Apostate. Saint Arcadius buried his disciples and then, sending up thanks to God, departed this life.

The Seventh Day of the Month of March

The Passion of the Holy Hieromartyrs Ephraim, Basileus, Eugene, Elpidius, Agathadorus, Aetherius, and Capito, Who were Bishops of Cherson at Various Times[1]

$\mathcal{I}$n the sixteenth year of the reign of Diocletian, the Most Holy Patriarch of Jerusalem Hermon sent bishops to various countries and tribes to proclaim the word of God and preach Christ as once did the apostles. Two of the hierarchs, Ephraim and Basileus, went to the land of the Tauroscythians[2] and labored in the town of Cherson, declaring the true God to the unbelieving people and enlightening those benighted by idolatry. Eventually Saint Ephraim left Cherson to the care of Saint Basileus and went to preach to the Scythians living near the Danube River. He converted many and, after toiling and suffering much on behalf of the gospel of Christ, was beheaded by the sword on the seventh day of March.

Saint Basileus continued to denounce the errors of the heathen Chersonites and demonstrate the way to salvation, thereby

---

[1]From Greek manuscripts
[2]The Tauric Chersonese, now known as the Crimea (Tr.)

rousing the anger of the citizens. The pagans seized him, beat him mercilessly, and drove him from the town; whereupon, he took refuge in a cave on a mountain twelve miles away. The mount was known as *Parthenon*, meaning "of the virgins," because on it there was a temple full of statues of Greek virgin-goddesses. Living on the mountain, Saint Basileus rejoiced in spirit because he had been deemed worthy to endure wounds and banishment for Christ; but he also mourned the perdition of the Chersonites. He never ceased shedding tears for those lost souls, deceived by the devil, or beseeching God to bring about their conversion.

It happened that the only son of a prince of Cherson died and was buried outside the city. Overcome by grief, his parents would not leave after he was committed to the earth, but remained at the grave, weeping into the night. When they finally fell asleep, the boy appeared to both of them in dreams, saying, "Why do you vainly hope that our gods will restore me to you? They cannot raise me, for they are idols without souls, devised by wicked spirits to delude and ruin men. If you wish to have your sorrow assuaged and to see me alive again, request the stranger who was beaten and driven out of the city to pray for me to his God. Believe in the one true God Whom the stranger preaches and Who alone has power over the quick and the dead. He can restore me to life, by the prayers of that man whom you mistreated."

The parents awoke and told each other what they had dreamed. They were amazed and overjoyed that their dreams were the same and hastened to the city to tell their kinfolk and friends. At first light they began searching for the man of God, and they found Saint Basileus in his cave. The Prince and his household fell at the hierarch's feet, begging him to raise the dead boy. "I am a sinner," protested the holy Bishop. "I cannot do this unless you believe in the God Whom I preach. He alone has power to restore the dead to life."

"If you return the child to life, we shall do whatever you require," they promised.

God's hierarch went to the tomb and the Prince's servants rolled away the stone blocking the entrance. After tracing the Cross over the corpse, Basileus prayed for a long time. Then he blessed water and poured it on the body, invoking the Holy Trinity as in the rite of Baptism. Straightway the boy returned to life and glorified God. Fear and trembling came upon everyone present, and the parents' joy knew no bounds. All the people fell at the feet of the holy Bishop, glorifying him and confessing as true and almighty the God he proclaimed. They escorted Saint Basileus to the city in triumph, and the Prince and his entire household were baptized into Christ. Many other citizens learned of the miracle and joined themselves to the believers. Christ's Church flourished in Cherson, and one by one the heathen sanctuaries were pulled down.

Chafing at the sight of his ruined temples, the devil entered the hearts of the Jews of Cherson, who incited the heathen to assault the Christians and especially their leader, Saint Basileus. "If we murder their teacher," reasoned the Lord's enemies, "we can easily suppress the Christians." A mob of unbelievers assembled and without warning attacked God's hierarch. The evildoers dragged Basileus out of his room, bound his feet, and hauled him through the streets, beating him with staves and stones and trampling him. When they reached a pillar surmounted by a cross which the Christians had erected, the Lord's hierarch surrendered his holy soul into the Master's hands. The martyrdom took place on March 7, the very day Saint Ephraim was beheaded in Scythia.

Saint Basileus' corpse was dragged through the city gates and thrown to dogs and to birds of prey, but remained unconsumed, although it lay without burial for many days. At night a brilliant star shone upon the martyric remains, which a wolf guarded from dogs; and by day an eagle soared over the relics, keeping other fowl at bay. Finally one night the Christians retrieved the body, which they buried with reverence.

After the death of the holy Bishop Basileus, one of his disciples sailed to the Hellespont, where three bishops were proclaiming the gospel of Christ. Their names were Eugene, Elpidius, and Agathadorus. Like Saints Ephraim and Basileus, they had been commissioned to preach by the Most Holy Hermon, Patriarch of Jerusalem. Basileus' disciple related the saint's martyrdom to the three bishops, who glorified God for vouchsafing the crown of suffering to His favorite. After some deliberation, the bishops took ship to Cherson, intending to follow Saint Basileus' example. Preaching Christ God there, they daily increased the number of the faithful. At length the devil incited the Jews and pagans against them, as he had against Saint Basileus. The mob seized the bishops, bound them, and dragged them through the streets, pounding them with clubs and rocks until the victims delivered up their holy souls into the hands of the Lord. Although the martyrs' bodies were taken to a cemetery outside the city, they were not interred, but left as food for dogs and birds; however, the Christians secretly removed them and gave them an honorable burial. The three bishops Eugene, Elpidius, and Agathadorus suffered on the seventh day of March, one year after the martyrdom of Saint Basileus.

Several years later, when Constantine the Great reigned and had espoused the holy faith, the Patriarch of Jerusalem sent another bishop, Aetherius, to Cherson. Aetherius found that the heathen were bitterly resisting the spread of the Christian faith and were oppressing the believers; therefore, he sailed to Byzantium and protested to the Emperor. Constantine issued a decree ordering that the Christians be permitted to live unharried in Cherson, that they enjoy absolute freedom to assemble and glorify God, and that anyone who dared harass them be expelled from the town. Aetherius returned with the edict, which brought joy to Christ's flock and consternation to the godless. After building a church in the city for the Christians and setting in order the affairs of the diocese, Aetherius again sailed to Byzantium, in order to thank the Emperor for his patronage. On the voyage back to his see he took ill, and when the ship reached the island called Aasus, Aetherius was translated from this earthly life to life eternal. Over his tomb the faithful erected a column, and a grove of tall trees grew up there, such that the saint's burial place could be spotted from afar. Like the earlier martyred bishops, Saint Aetherius died on the seventh of March.

The Christians bitterly lamented the loss of their pastor and sent the Emperor word of his repose, with a request for a successor. Constantine appointed the blessed Capito bishop of the Church of Cherson. When Capito arrived in the city, he was greeted joyfully by the faithful. Numerous unbelievers also turned out to meet him, clamoring for a miracle as testimony to the truth of the Christian faith and promising to convert if the hierarch satisfied their demand. They shouted, "Let the Bishop enter a fiery furnace! If he is not harmed, we shall accept Baptism."

Putting his trust in God, Saint Capito ordered a fire built in a furnace. He put on liturgical vestments and contritely begged the Lord to reveal His divine power as He once had for the youths in Babylon, so that the unbelievers would convert. A deacon exclaimed, "Let us attend!" and the Bishop entered the blazing furnace, in which he stood for a full hour, with hands uplifted to heaven. Afterwards, holding hot coals in his phelonion, Capito emerged from the oven unharmed. Seeing that not even his robes were singed, the people cried as with a single voice, "There is only one God, the God of the Christians! He is great and mighty, and has preserved His servant in the fiery furnace." On account of this miracle, all the unbelievers of Cherson and the surrounding region accepted the Christian faith. Word of the marvel was sent to the great Constantine and to the holy fathers assembled at the First Ecumenical Council in Nicaea. They glorified God and were astonished by Saint Capito's firm faith and boldness before the Lord.

Several years later, the holy Bishop was sailing from Cherson to Constantinople. A storm arose and the winds blew his ship onto shore at the mouth of the river Danube. The godless people living there stole everything in the boat, enslaved the crew and passengers, and drowned God's hierarch Capito. It was on the twenty-first day of December that Saint Capito was murdered; nevertheless, he is commemorated with the other bishops of Cherson, who died on March 7, because his soul joined their company in heaven. Like the seven chief angels,[3] the seven holy bishops of Cherson now stand before the Holy Trinity—Father, Son, and divine Spirit—glorifying the one God with all the saints unto the ages. Amen.

---

[3]The seven chief angels are Michael, Gabriel, Raphael, Uriel, Salathiel, Jegudiel, and Barachiel. (Tr.)

On the Same Day

The Commemoration of Our Holy Monastic Father Emilian

In the city of Rome there once lived a man named Victorinus who, beginning in his youth, committed numerous sins. In old age, however, fear of divine judgment impelled him to repentance, so he went to a monastery and begged the abbot to admit him to the brotherhood. The hegumen accepted Victorinus and named him Emilian in the tonsure. Emilian utterly renounced all worldly attachments, submissively carried out every task given him, and unsparingly mortified his flesh. Death was his continuous meditation. He was ever preparing to answer for his sins before the dread tribunal on the Day of Judgment and so feared the eternal tortures of Gehenna that he utterly wasted his body. The devout brethren of the monastery were amazed by his asceticism, humility, and zeal for toil. To the best of their ability they imitated his way of life and especially his obedience, striving by labors of repentance to cleanse their souls. Daily they were aroused to virtue by seeing Emilian hungry, thirsty, making prostrations, depriving himself of sleep, and availing himself of every opportunity to torment the flesh.

The monastery where Emilian lived was on a high mountain, and on one of the slopes there was a cave. Late every evening the blessed Emilian, unbeknown to all, would slip away to the cave and remain there until shortly before Matins, weeping for his sins and praying. This went on for a long time, until one night the abbot noticed him leaving. Wondering where Emilian was going, the hegumen secretly followed him and saw him enter the cave and pray with uplifted hands. The abbot decided to remain nearby and question the saint when he emerged; but while he was waiting, a light more brilliant than the rays of the sun burst out of heaven, illumining the mountain and bathing Emilian's head. Awe-struck, the superior fled for the monastery, trembling violently and stumbling all the way. As he neared the gates, a voice from on high thundered, "Emilian, your sins are remitted!" Terrified, the abbot hid in his cell and did not leave until it was day.

The hegumen wanted to edify all the brethren, so he put off questioning Emilian until the end of Matins, when the whole community was present. Plucking up his courage, he asked, "Brother, where were you last night?"

The godly one made a prostration to the abbot and replied, "I was sleeping in the monastery, as were the others."

The superior refused to accept this answer and demanded that Emilian reveal how God shows mercy to truly repentant sinners. Unwillingly, the saint told the brethren about the light and the voice that spoke from the throne of divine compassion. To his words the hegumen added these: "Consider, beloved: Almighty God our Creator, Who is near to those that repent, could have pardoned Emilian silently. Instead, He confirmed the sinner's forgiveness by means of the voice as well as the light. He did this to stir our hearts to repentance, and to assure us of His compassion and love for man."

Having received a pledge of forgiveness, the venerable Emilian lived in a state of spiritual joy until he was called to the ineffable Light. Now he dwells in the celestial mansions of the righteous, where the voice of gladness is heard unto the ages.

A Narrative About the Recluse to Whom God Granted a Revelation Concerning Those Who Accept Alms

$\mathcal{I}$n a certain monastery there was a recluse who from his youth led a holy life. Having renounced every temporal pleasure, he withdrew to a little cell, where he labored for God, mortifying his flesh by fasting and all-night vigils. Whenever he prayed, the elder shed abundant tears for himself and the world. His mind was fixed on the Lord, and he ate but once a day, when the cellarer brought him meager rations. The God-fearing local Christians provided gold, silver, pleasing foods, and wine to the brethren; but the recluse never accepted any of these.

One day the mayor of a nearby town came to the monastery and gave each brother a silver coin. He begged the recluse to take a gold piece; and the elder, not wishing to grieve the noble donor, broke his rule and put the money in his satchel. After saying his rule of prayer that night, the elder lay down upon his rush mat. As soon as he fell asleep, he saw himself in a dream with the brethren in a vast field of thorns. An awe-inspiring young man (this was an angel of the Lord) appeared and ordered the monks, "Mow the thorns!" Then he approached the elder and commanded him, "Gird yourself and mow the thorns!" When the recluse hesitated, the angel demanded, "Why such sloth? Yesterday the pious mayor hired the other monks for a silver coin apiece, whereas he paid you in gold. You were given more and should work harder than they. The thorns are the sins of the almsgiver. Help the brethren cut them down."[1]

The recluse awoke very troubled. After pondering the dream, he sent for the mayor and begged him to take back the gold piece. The devout nobleman refused, saying, "Keep what is yours, Father, or give it to someone else, if you choose."

"I do not have strength to mow the thorns of my own sins, much less those of another," protested the elder. So saying, he threw the gold piece out of the window and closed the shutters.

---

[1]He who accepts alms is obligated to labor spiritually on behalf of his benefactor, especially by praying for him. (Tr.)

Moved to compunction, the mayor corrected his faults. Moreover, heeding the scriptures which teach that sins are cleansed by faith and almsgiving, he became a generous benefactor of the poor.

❧❧❧

On this same day we commemorate our venerable father Paul the Confessor, Bishop of Prousa in Bithynia. He endured much suffering at the hands of the iconoclast heretics and was exiled by them because of his devotion to the holy images.

The Eighth Day
of the Month of March

The Commemoration of
Our Venerable Father Theophylact,
Bishop of Nicomedia

The devout Theophylact came to the Imperial City from the lands of the East while the heresy of iconoclasm was troubling the Church. He became a close friend of the great luminary Tarasius[1] while that saint was still a senator and the chief imperial secretary.

When the brutal iconoclast Emperor Leo Copronymus[2] died, the tyrant's wife Irene and son Constantine inherited the throne, and Patriarch Paul, known as "the Merciful,"[3] elected to retire. Saint Tarasius then became patriarch, convened the Seventh Ecumenical Council, and anathematized iconoclasm. At that time the blessed Theophylact and Saint Michael of Synnada[4] forsook the world and were sent by the Most Holy Tarasius to a monastery on the shore of the Black Sea. Devoting themselves to the strictest asceticism, both advanced in virtue and attained boldness in prayer before the Lord.

Once, at harvest, there was a drought and extreme heat, so that everything was suffering from thirst. The saints prayed to God and made an empty bronze kettle bubble over with water.

---

[1]Commemorated on February 25
[2]The son of Constantine Copronymus or "the dung-named," so-called because he defecated while being baptized. Leo Copronymus is usually called Leo the Khazar, since his mother was a Khazar princess. (Tr.)
[3]Commemorated on August 1 (or August 30 – Tr.)
[4]Commemorated on May 23

This was like two ancient miracles worked by the Lord: the first, when He brought forth a stream from a rock in the desert for Israel;[5] the second, when He slaked Sampson's thirst with water flowing out of an ass' jawbone.[6]

Because our venerable fathers Michael and Theophylact shone like stars with virtue, Patriarch Tarasius deemed them worthy of exalted rank, consecrating Michael bishop for Synnada and Theophylact for Nicomedia. The holy churches erected in Nicomedia by Saint Theophylact testified to his care for the spiritual needs of Christ's rational flock; while the hospitals and hostels showed his concern for orphans, widows, and other poor folk. Every day Theophylact gave abundant alms to the needy. With his own hands he ministered to the sick, blind, and lame, and he frequented almshouses and city squares looking for victims of leprosy. Not the least repulsed by the hideous disease, he would cleanse the lepers' ulcers with warm water he carried in a jar for this purpose.

After the Most Holy Tarasius departed this life, the wise Nicephorus became Patriarch of Constantinople. In those days the godless iconoclast Leo the Armenian ascended the throne, and the tempest of heresy again buffeted the Church. Rising to the defense of the faith, Patriarch Nicephorus summoned the bishops Emilian of Cyprus, Euthymius of Sardis, Joseph of Thessalonica, Eudoxius of Armenia, Michael of Synnada, and the blessed Theophylact, and with them appeared at court. Quoting the Holy Fathers at length, the hierarchs attempted to persuade the impious ruler not to disturb the Church of Christ by re-introducing the heresy condemned by the Seventh Ecumenical Synod. Their efforts were unsuccessful and only aroused the fury of the Emperor, who was full of the serpent's venom. When the other prelates had spoken their piece, the blessed Theophylact warned Leo, "By opposing the ancient tra-dition of the Holy Fathers, you are trying God's forbearance, endangering your salvation, and troubling the Church. Unexpected misfortune and cruel destruction await you, and no one can deliver you from them." The Emperor flew into a fury, drove the hierarchs out of the palace, and banished them to remote places. The Most Holy Patriarch Nicephorus was sent to the island of Proconnesus; Saint Michael, Bishop of Synnada, to Eudocias; Saint Theophylact to Strobulus, a maritime town in the theme of Cibyraeots; and the others to different destinations. Theophylact, Christ's confessor and mighty champion of piety, remained in exile until his death thirty years later and endured every deprivation and hardship.

As foretold by our saint, Leo the Armenian's end was unexpected and violent. On the very day of Christ's Nativity, he was cut down by his own soldiers in church during Matins. His successor on the throne, Michael the Stammerer, and his son Theophilus were both iconoclasts. After they died, the scepter was inherited by the Empress Theodora and her son Michael III. Saint Methodius was elevated to the patriarchal throne, the iniquitous heresy was eradicated, and the light of Orthodoxy again shone brilliantly. It was then that the honored remains of our holy father Theophylact were translated to Nicomedia from their burial-place and enshrined in one of the churches built by the saint, to serve for the defense of the city and the glory of Christ our God.

On the Same Day

The Passion of the Holy Hieromartyr Theodoritus, Presbyter of Antioch[1]

$\mathcal{T}$ he great Emperor Constantine and his son Constantius built a beautiful cathedral in Antioch called "the golden church" by the people. It was adorned with gold mosaics, its roof was gilded, and in it were kept innumerable ecclesiastical vessels, all fashioned of gold or pure silver. In order to provide for the many clergymen attached to the cathedral, the emperors richly endowed it. Among the clergy of this great church was the presbyter Theodoritus, who was charged with care of its sacred vessels and other treasures. From his youth, Theodoritus led a virtuous life and was staunchly devoted to Orthodoxy. In him were fulfilled the words of Scripture: *With the heart man believeth unto righteousness; and with the mouth confession is made unto salvation.*[2] By fasting, prayer, almsgiving, and diligence in fulfilling his pastoral and liturgical duties, Saint Theodoritus greatly pleased God.

When Constantius died, Julian the Apostate became emperor. At first Julian pretended to be a devout Christian and returned from banishment all the hierarchs exiled for piety by Constantius,[3] but when he felt secure on the throne, he openly denied Christ. In his heart, he had apostatized many years before, becoming a servant of the demons and an adept of the black art. He began to persecute the Church of Christ, although he did not slaughter the Christians wholesale. Instead, he arrested, tortured, and slew the most eminent clergy, as well as devout laymen of noble birth. God's churches were removed from Christian possession and converted to heathen temples, and ecclesiastical treasures were confiscated. In justification of this shameless plundering, the knave argued, "The Christians should be happy to lose their wealth, since Christ enjoined

---

[1]From *The Great Collection of Readings* and other sources
[2]Rom., Ch. 10
[3]Constantius favored the Arian heresy. (Tr.)

them to poverty and forbade them to acquire gold or silver."
During this time of trial, the golden church of Antioch was
despoiled. All of its sacred vessels were looted and taken to the
imperial treasury, the clergy were scattered, and Saint
Theodoritus was tortured and put to death. This took place in
the following manner.

The Emperor Julian had an uncle, also named Julian, whom
he appointed governor of the eastern provinces and charged
with persecuting the Christians. The elder Julian had been a
Christian, but to please his nephew he renounced Christ and
worshipped idols. Before the Emperor's arrival in Antioch,[4] his
uncle and another courtier, the imperial treasurer Felix, came to
the city. Knowing the cathedral's wealth, the nobles seized the
blessed presbyter and *skevophylax*[5] Theodoritus. After taking
from him the keys to the sacristy, they bound and imprisoned
him. Meanwhile, the other clergymen fled in terror and hid,
each wherever he could.

Escorted by a large troop of soldiers, Julian and Felix entered
the cathedral, their eyes greedy to take for the treasury everything of value, especially gold and silver. Julian shamelessly
ventured into the sanctuary, which he looted and defiled, daring
even to urinate on the altar table. When the sacred vessels had
been heaped on the floor, he sat on them and mocked and cursed
our Lord Jesus Christ. A man named Evzoes was watching this
and warned him of God's punishment, to which Julian responded
by buffeting him on the head. "Providence does not protect the
Christians!" shouted the thief. "They are bereft of divine care."

Having plundered and desecrated the church of God, the
impious Prince turned his attention to the torture of Saint
Theodoritus. The Lord's servant was presented at the tribunal
of the unjust judge, who asked him, "Why, Theodoritus, did
Constantine destroy the temples of the ancient gods, adorn the
sepulchers of the dead, and build churches to house corpses?"

The saint replied, "From the days of our forefathers we
Christians have built holy churches and adorned the sepulchers

---

[4]Julian the Apostate stopped in Antioch on his way to fight the Persians.
(Tr.)
[5]*Skevophylax*: the clergyman, usually a priest, charged with care of the
liturgical vessels and other valuables of a church. (Tr.)

of the saints glorified by God. You, O Prince, once knew the God of the Christians. How is it that you turned to idolatry?" At this the Governor commanded his servants to strike Theodoritus upon the face. In response to the blow, Theodoritus reproached the apostate, saying, "It is a sin, Julian, to adore as gods idols made from wood or stone."

Then the persecutor accused Theodoritus of using his position as skevophylax to enrich himself and ordered that the martyr be stripped naked, suspended from a tree, and raked with iron claws. For three hours the servants tore away Theodoritus' flesh. Rivers of blood flowed, but the blessed one felt no pain and his face shone with joy. "Wretch, sacrifice to the gods, and no charges will be brought against you for pilfering the treasures of the Church. Unless you offer oblations, you will perish in agony," Julian threatened.

"Wretch," said the saint, "you and your wicked emperor shall burn in everlasting fire for renouncing Christ and joining yourselves to Antichrist. I am guilty of no theft and in debt to no one, except my Lord Jesus Christ. My obligation to Him is to remain steadfast in the true faith until my last breath."

"Theodoritus, if you renounce the warlock whom you call the Son of God, I will reward you with rank and gold," Julian promised.

"*Thy money perish with thee*,"[6] answered the holy martyr. "I put my hope in the Lord, Who rewards His servants not with earthly, corruptible gifts, but with celestial and incorruptible."

Next the persecutor had Theodoritus' sides scorched with candles. While the flame was being applied, the martyr raised his eyes to heaven and prayed. Straightway, a divine power threw the torturers to the ground, knocking them senseless. When they came to themselves, they could only regain their feet with help from Julian and the other nobles. The Governor asked the servants, "What made you fall asleep? My orders were to sear the flesh off the godless Christian."

"Because impiety has blinded the eyes of your soul, you could not see the angels defending God's slave," replied the torturers. "Even now, four angels are conversing with Theo-

---

[6]Acts, Ch. 8

doritus and threatening us with dire punishment if we make another attempt to harm his sacred flesh. Look to your soul, blasphemer, and prate no more, but accept the God of the Christians, in Whom we now believe." Bewildered but unmoved, the Governor commanded that the servants be drowned.

As the servants were being led away, Christ's holy martyr exclaimed, "Walk the path of blessedness in peace, children! I shall follow you. We shall rejoice together eternally in the Kingdom of heaven." The servants were thrown overboard into the sea and their bodies descended to a watery grave, but their souls were crowned with diadems of martyrdom by Christ God, in Whom they believed.

Again turning his attention to Saint Theodoritus, the loathsome Prince demanded, "Sacrifice to the gods!"

Being filled with the Spirit of prophecy, the saint forewarned, "Your crimes will secure for you damnation, O most impious, most wicked of men. Soon you will be eating your own excrement and vomiting your vile soul into unquenchable fire. Your iniquitous emperor will follow you into the abyss after he is slain in battle with the Persians, for an invisible hand will strike him down and hurl him into nethermost flames." Infuriated by the saint's words, Julian immediately pronounced the sentence of death. The blessed Theodoritus hurried to his execution, praying for himself and the whole world. He was beheaded with an ax and his holy remains were buried by the faithful, who remembered his prophecies and awaited their fulfillment.

It was not long before both Julians, uncle and nephew, perished miserably. The uncle, prince of the eastern lands and murderer of Saint Theodoritus, fell gravely ill, receiving his just deserts for daring to urinate on God's altar and sit upon the sacred vessels while blaspheming Christ and everything holy. His bowels filled with worms, which crawled out of his rectum.[7] The disease was beyond the skill of physicians and hourly grew worse, the worms quickly eating through his flesh, on which God's avenging hand lay heavy. Then came to pass the saint's prediction that Julian would chew his own filth, for the wretch's

[7]From Sozomen and Chrysostom's Homily on the Heathen

intestine and bladder became obstructed, and his profane mouth filled with waste. By the time he spewed up his soul, every inch of his body was alive with worms. Before long, divine judgment also overtook his friend Felix, the imperial treasurer. His inwards split apart, and blood dribbled continuously from his irreverent mouth. Within a few days Felix surrendered his miserable soul to the fires of Gehenna.

All this was reported to the impious Emperor Julian, who upon arriving in Antioch dared not dishonor the relics of the holy hieromartyr Babylas, as he had intended, but merely ordered the Christians to remove them from the church near the shrine of Apollo at Daphne.[8] After leaving the city, Julian invaded Persia and was killed during battle. When they learned that the prophecy of the holy hieromartyr Theodoritus had been fulfilled in every detail, the faithful praised Christ our God Who, with the Father and the Holy Spirit, is glorified forever. Amen.

❧❧❧

According to *The Prologue*, the holy Apostle Hermas is commemorated on this day. He is also commemorated in November[9] with other apostles of the Seventy.

According to *The Prologue*, our holy monastic father Dometius reposed in peace on this day. We could not find a Life of this saint. Besides this Saint Dometius, there is another, a monastic martyr commemorated on August 7.

---

[8]An account of this may be found in the Life of Saint Babylas, under September 4.
[9]On November 5 (Tr.)

The Ninth Day
of the Month of March

The Passion of the
Holy Forty Martyrs
of Sebastea in Armenia[1]

During the reign of the impious Emperor Licinius, there was a cruel persecution of the Christians, and the faithful were required to sacrifice to the idols. In those days the commander of the garrison of Sebastea in Armenia was Agricola, a man of violent temper and a zealous champion of idolatry. There were many Christians in the imperial army at that time, and they also were required to offer oblations to demons.

In Agricola's regiment forty men from Cappadocia, devout believers in Christ God, formed a single unit. All were mighty warriors, and three were especially well versed in sacred Scripture: Cyrion, Candidus, and Domnus. When it was reported to Agricola that there were Christians among his troops, he had the offenders arrested and brought to him. His intent was to force them to worship idols. "In combat you proved yourselves of one soul and one mind and demonstrated

---

[1]From Metaphrastes; Evodius, Bishop of Caesarea; and other sources

exemplary bravery," said Agricola to the martyrs. "Now you would do well to show the same unity, obeying the imperial decree and sacrificing to the gods. Submit willingly and escape torments."

To this the blessed soldiers fearlessly replied, "If we were invincible when fighting for the earthly Emperor (as you admit), we will certainly prevail over your cunning and wickedness as we contend for the immortal King."

"Your choice is either to sacrifice to the gods, or to disobey and be disgraced and stripped of rank. Consider well what is to your advantage," counseled Agricola.

"The Lord will provide what is to our advantage," said the soldiers.

"You must quickly renounce falsehood and offer oblations to the gods tomorrow," Agricola insisted.

With this, he had the martyrs cast into a dungeon, where they fell prostrate in prayer, crying to God, "Deliver us from temptation, O Lord, and from the snares of the lawless." Later that evening the saints chanted psalms, beginning with, *He that dwelleth in the help of the Most High shall abide in the shelter of the God of heaven.*[2] Saint Cyrion intoned each verse, and Candidus, Domnus, and the others sang it. At midnight, when they had completed their supplication, the Lord spoke to the martyrs, saying, "You have made a good beginning; *but he that endureth to the end shall be saved.*"[3] Hearing this, all were astonished and filled with joy. Not one of the saints slept that night.

The next morning Agricola assembled his officers and commanded that the holy forty soldiers be brought to him. When they were presented, he said, "I do not wish to flatter you, but tell you truly: our emperor has many legionnaires, but none are as handsome, stalwart, resourceful, or deserving of respect as you. Do not turn my admiration into hatred. It is in your power to retain my esteem or arouse my animosity."

"Your name matches your character, Agricola," retorted Saint Candidus. "You are savage and a deceiver."[4]

---

[2]Ps. 90   [3]Matt., Ch. 10
[4]*Agrios* means wild or savage in Greek; *kolax* means a flatterer or deceiver. (Tr.)

"I repeat: it is in your power to retain my esteem or arouse my animosity," said the commander.

"Since the choice is ours, we will have your animosity," Candidus said. "We loathe you and desire the favor and love of our God. You lie, saying that we enjoy your affection and admiration, for you are a merciless brute, an enemy of the Lord. You are lawless and consumed by envy, benighted by delusion, and by extreme cruelty have shown that you deserve your name."

His anger provoked, the commander gnashed his teeth like a lion and ordered the saints clapped in irons and returned to the prison. At this Saint Cyrion reminded him, "The Emperor has not authorized you to torture us."

Taken aback, Agricola told the guards not to fetter the saints or do violence to them, but merely to escort them to the dungeon. Although he changed the order, the commander instructed the jailer to observe the prisoners closely and send word to Prince Lysias, requesting him to come to Sebastea.

While in the dungeon, the saints hearkened day and night to Saint Cyrion's teaching. The blessed Cyrion exhorted them, "Brethren, Providence arranged for us to be comrades while we served in the vain, temporal army, and I trust that we shall remain together for all eternity. As we lived in unity of soul and mind, so let us die united; as we pleased the mortal Emperor, let us please Christ God, the immortal King."

A week passed, and the saints were still in the dungeon. Then Lysias arrived in Sebastea, and on the eighth day of the saints' imprisonment, he and Agricola commanded that the holy soldiers be presented to them for questioning. As the martyrs were being led to the unjust judges, the blessed Cyrion exhorted his companions, "Have no fear, brethren. Remember how God hearkened unto us whenever we sought His help before combat. He always granted us victory. You recall the great battle in which the rest of the army was put to flight and we were surrounded by the foe. We wept and prayed to the Lord, and with His assistance prevailed. Despite the horde of adversaries and the fury of the contest, not one of us was harmed, but we wounded many of our enemies and routed their entire force. This time we face only three opponents: Satan, Lysias, and Agricola or, better to say, the devil alone. He will never defeat us! Now, let us have recourse to fervent prayer, as always in the past. With God on our side, we fear neither fetters nor torture. It was ever our rule to sing before battle, *O God, in Thy name save me, and in Thy strength do Thou judge me. O God, hearken unto my prayer, give ear unto the words of my mouth.*[5] Let us sing this psalm, and the Lord will hear and aid us."

The martyrs were chanting the psalm when they reached the tribunal. The whole town had turned out to watch the proceedings. Lysias studied the prisoners and announced, "I think these men desire promotion." Then he addressed the martyrs, saying, "You will earn high rank and other rewards if only you obey the imperial ordinances and sacrifice to the gods. If you refuse, you will be dismissed from the army and put to torture."

"Punish us as you say!" exclaimed Saint Candidus. "For us, nothing is dearer, nothing higher than Christ our God."

Straightway Lysias ordered the saints beaten upon the mouth with rocks. "Prince of darkness and master of iniquity, be diligent at your work, so that you may see God's retribution!" Candidus taunted him.

Agricola was infuriated by the servants' failure to silence the martyrs. Gritting his teeth, he shouted at the slaves, "Indolent, worthless knaves, I will have your heads!"

The slaves began pelting the martyrs with stones, but hit one another instead. Seeing this, the holy passion-bearers grew bolder in the Lord and relentlessly taunted the persecutors. Prince Lysias hurled a rock at one of the saints, but it smashed Agricola's face. "Our enemies have lost their strength and are collapsing," said Cyrion. *Let their sword enter into their own hearts and let their bows be broken.*[6]

Blood gushing from his mouth, Agricola muttered, "By the gods, I swear that a sorcerous power helps these villains."

"In the name of Christ, I assure you that God helps us," said Domnus: "the same God Who puts you to shame for slandering His Son. Do you enjoy humiliation, O fool, stranger to truth, abyss of diabolical gloom, sower of the seed of deception? You, Agricola, are the devil's head of wickedness, and Prince Lysias is his tail of wrath. Both of you are Satan's servants. If your first

---

[5]Ps. 53   [6]Ps. 36

attempt to harm us has failed to convince you that we are assisted by God's power, then punish us by other means."

"Why, deluded foes of our gods and strangers to their mercy, do you refuse to offer oblations?" the servants asked.

Cyrion answered, "We worship the one God, His Son Jesus Christ, and the Holy Spirit. We shall complete the course without flinching, triumph over you deceivers, and win garlands of eternal life."

Because he wanted time to decide their fate, Prince Lysias commanded that the saints be returned to prison. In the dungeon, the martyrs chanted, *"Unto Thee have we lifted up our eyes, unto Thee that dwellest in heaven. Behold, as the eyes of servants look unto the hands of their masters, so do our eyes look unto the Lord our God, until He take pity on us."*[7]

At the sixth hour of the night, after the martyrs had completed their prayer, the Lord spoke to them again, saying, *"He that believeth in Me, though he were dead, yet shall he live.*[8] Take courage and do not fear fleeting torments. Endure a little while, remain vigilant, and you shall be crowned," Strengthened and consoled by Christ the Lord, the martyrs rejoiced in spirit the whole night long.

At dawn the persecutors had the saints brought to them. The holy martyrs said to the impious judges, "Do with us as you wish. We are Christians and will not bow to idols."

As the passion-bearers spoke, the devil could be seen standing beside Agricola, holding a sword in his right hand and a serpent in his left. He whispered into Agricola's ear, "You are mine; be about your work!" Immediately the commander and the Prince ordered the forty martyrs bound and taken to a large lake near Sebastea. It was wintertime, the frost was heavy, and a fierce wind blew. The sun was sinking when the martyrs reached the lake. The saints were forced into the water and guards were set under command of the prison warden, but a warm bath was prepared on the shore for any of the martyrs who might reconsider and agree to worship idols. As darkness drew on, it became extremely cold. Ice covered the Christians' bodies, and one of them could endure no longer. Abandoning

---

[7]Ps. 122   [8]John, Ch. 11

the choir of the saints, he sought refuge in the bath, but as soon as he entered, he gave up the ghost. The others saw this and with one soul and voice cried, *"Was the Lord displeased against the rivers? Was Thine anger against the rivers? Was Thy wrath against the sea?*[9] He who fell from among us *was poured out like water, and scattered are all his bones,*[10] but *we will not depart from Thee. Thou shalt quicken us, and we will call upon Thy name,*[11] which the whole of creation praiseth: *dragons and all abysses, fire, hail, snow, ice, and blast of tempest.*[12] Thou didst walk upon the sea as though on dry ground; Thou didst calm the waves with the gesture of Thy hand. Thou art the same Lord that heard Jacob's prayer and delivered the patriarch from his brother Esau, that rescued Joseph from calamity, that gave ear unto Moses and granted him power to work signs before Pharoah and the Egyptians, that divided the sea and led the people through the wilderness, and that hearkened unto the holy apostles. Be Thou attentive to us now, O Lord, for we are brought very low, and do not let the turbulent water swallow us. Help us, O God our Saviour: our feet stand in the freezing water and are bleeding. Ease our pain and warm our bodies, for in Thee, O Lord our God, do we hope. Let us not be put to shame, but make it known to all men that we who call upon Thee have been saved."

Three hours after nightfall a shaft of light shone from heaven upon the martyrs. It was bright as the sun at harvest time, and it heated the air, melting the ice and warming the lake. Sleep had overcome the guards, except for the prison warden. Hearing the martyrs praying, the warden (whose name was Aglaius) marveled at how the soldier who fled to the bath had straight-way melted, as it were, from the heat, whereas the others had survived the cold. He beheld the light shining upon God's favorites and, looking into heaven, saw thirty-nine brilliant diadems descending upon the heads of the saints. "Were there not forty prisoners?" he asked himself. "Why are there only thirty-nine crowns?" Then he understood that the soldier who had sought refuge in the bath had excluded himself from the choir of the saints and lost his crown. The warden woke the guards,

---

[9]Hab., Ch. 3   [10]Ps. 21
[11]Ps. 79   [12]Ps. 148

threw off his robes, and ran into the lake, shouting, "I too am a Christian!" Joining himself to the company of the martyrs, he confessed, "O Lord God, I also believe. Number me with Thy servants and vouchsafe me to suffer with them, that I may be tested and found worthy of Thee." Thus the fellowship of saints regained its perfect number.

Seeing himself vanquished and humiliated, the devil assumed human form and wept bitterly, lamenting, "Woe is me! I have been defeated and reduced to a laughing-stock. No faithful ally or devoted servant remained at my side to assist me in battle. What am I to do? I can stave off utter ruin only by persuading my prince and my commander to burn the Christians' bodies and scatter the ashes on a river, so that no relics remain."

Meanwhile, Saint Cyrion cried, *"What God is as great as our God? Thou art God Who workest wonders.*[13] Thou, O Master, didst join to us him who was against us, restoring our number to forty and putting Satan to shame." Then all the martyrs chanted the psalm, *Save me, O Lord, for a righteous man there is no more.*[14]

At dawn the godless persecutors came to the lake and saw that the holy martyrs were alive and unharmed by the cold. They tested the water, and finding it to be warm, declared that only by sorcery had the prisoners survived. They were especially amazed that the prison warden had joined the martyrs in the lake, and they asked the guards, "How did this happen?"

"We fell asleep," admitted the guards, "but the warden remained on watch. When he woke us, a brilliant light was shining on the prisoners in the water. The next thing we knew, the warden had thrown off his clothes, was running to join them, and was shouting, 'I too am a Christian!'"

The enraged persecutors ordered that the saints be dragged to shore and thence to the tribunal in the city, where their legs were shattered with sledgehammers. The devout mother of Meliton, one of the youngest martyrs, watched this inhuman punishment and encouraged her son to remain steadfast. Fearing lest, because of his youth, he shrink from death, she stretched out her arms to him and gazed at him lovingly. "Sweetest son," she implored, "be patient; you will finish the

---

[13]Ps. 78   [14]Ps. 11

course quickly. Do not be afraid. Christ is beside you and aids you."

Under the blows of the hammer, the saints uttered their last words: *Our soul like a sparrow was delivered out of the snare of the hunters. The snare is broken, and we are delivered. Our help is in the name of the Lord, Who hath made heaven and the earth.*[15] Having said the Amen, all the martyrs except Meliton surrendered their souls into the hands of the Lord. The persecutors ordered their lackeys to transport the bodies to the river for burning. As the wagon pulled away, Meliton's mother saw that her son was being left behind. Exchanging womanly weakness and fear for the strength and courage of a man, she hoisted Meliton over her shoulder and chased the wagon. Meliton joyfully breathed his last just before his mother caught up to it and threw him onto the pile of bodies.

Coming to the riverside, the servants heaped up a large quantity of kindling and wood and set the corpses ablaze. The martyrs' flesh was consumed by the fire, but their bones did not burn. "If we leave the bones here, the Christians will collect them, break them into little pieces, and fill the world with them, perpetuating the memory of these criminals," reasoned the persecutors. "We should throw the bones into the river, so that no trace of them remains."

Hoping to assign the martyrs to oblivion, Lysias and Agricola had the servants cast the relics into the water, but *the Lord,* Who *keepeth all* the *bones*[16] of His favorites, did not allow even the smallest of them to be lost. After three days had passed, the holy martyrs appeared to the blessed Peter, Bishop of Sebastea, saying, "Go to the river by night and recover us." The Bishop took pious members of his clergy to the river in the deep of night and saw the relics in the water, glowing like stars. Even the least fragments were clearly visible. Having collected all the remains, the Bishop enshrined them in a place of honor.

These holy martyrs suffered for Christ, were crowned by Him, and shine as luminaries throughout the world. They believed in the one God, confessed His Son Christ, refused to deny the Holy Spirit, and were glorified by the life-creating

[15]Ps. 123   [16]Ps. 33

Trinity. Their Passion is a memorial and guide to salvation for all who have faith in the Father, Son, and Holy Spirit. The names of the holy Forty Martyrs are Cyrion, Candidus, Domnus, Hesychius, Heraclius, Smaragdus, Eunoicus, Valens, Vivianus, Claudius, Priscus, Theodulus, Eutychius, John, Xanthias, Helianus, Sisinius, Angus, Aetius, Flavius, Acacius, Ecditius, Lysimachus, Alexander, Elias, Gorgonius, Theophilus, Dometian, Gaius, Leontius, Athanasius, Cyril, Sacerdon, Nicholas, Valerius, Philoctimon, Severian, Chudion, Meliton, and Aglaius.

The Forty Martyrs were arrested four days before the calends of March, that is, on the twenty-sixth of February. They surrendered their souls to God seven days before the ides of March, on the ninth day of that month, while Licinius reigned on earth, but our Lord Jesus Christ ruled all creation. Unto Him, with the Father and the Holy Spirit, are due all glory, honor, and worship unto the ages. Amen.

ぎ♠ぎ♠ぎ♠

On this same day we commemorate the holy martyr Urpasianus, who was put to death for Christ in Nicomedia by the Emperor Maximian.

On this same day we commemorate Saint Caesarius, brother of Saint Gregory the Theologian.

According to *The Prologue*, the holy martyr Dionysius of Corinth is commemorated on this day, rather than on March 10 with the holy martyr Quadratus.

According to *The Prologue,* a Saint Tarasius also is commemorated on this day, but no information about him is provided. The only Saint Tarasius in the calendar is the Patriarch of Constantinople whose feast is February 25.[17]

---

[17]There is also a Saint Tarasius of Glushitsa, but he is commemorated on October 12. (Tr.)

The Tenth Day of the Month of March

The Commemoration of the Holy Martyrs Quadratus, Cyprian, Dionysius, Anectus, Paul, Crescens, and Others with Them[1]

The holy martyr Quadratus was born and raised while impious emperors and princes were persecuting the faithful. Christ's confessors were undergoing brutal tortures and being put to death, and fear drove many believers to abandon their homes and possessions, flee the towns, and hide in the mountains. Their gaze intent on the pure and holy faith of Christ the Lord, they preferred to live in the dens of the earth with wild beasts rather than with godless idolaters. During those difficult times the devout woman Rufina, although with child, left Corinth to escape the persecution and wandered through trackless wastelands. There she bore a son, whom she named Quadratus. Rufina survived childbirth only a few days; but God, Who *giveth food to all flesh*,[2] and opens His *hand* and fills *all things with goodness*,[3] took the infant under His protection, becoming its father and mother, guardian and nourisher. The Lord commanded a cloud to descend and drop sweet dew into the babe's mouth, feeding him as it were on milk and honey until he was old enough to eat the plants that grew in the mountains. Like Saint John the Baptist, Quadratus spent his childhood in the wilderness: he was preserved by the Lord and instructed by the Holy Spirit, Who guided him to divine vision.

---

[1]From Metaphrastes and Nicephorus Gregoras
[2]Ps. 135   [3]Ps. 102

Quadratus was already a youth when he was found by believers, brought to the city, and taught to read. Later the saint trained as a physician, but he cured diseases not so much by medical science as by the healing grace bestowed on him from above. Accustomed as he was to stillness, he avoided human companionship, eventually returning to the mountains, where he could be alone and exercise himself in meditation on God. Although he visited the city on occasion for the benefit of others, treating illnesses of the body and ministering to spiritual infirmities by proclaiming the word of God, he did not tarry there. Instead, he hastened back to his beloved wilderness, where he lived as a hermit until old age.

Quadratus' most frequent visitors were several admirers who delighted in his venerable countenance and divinely inspired discourses. Among these were Cyprian, Dionysius, Anectus, Paul, and Crescens, who underwent torments for Christ the Lord with the blessed anchorite. Their sufferings began when the impious Roman Emperor Decius sent Governor Jason to Corinth with orders to torture and execute Christians. Jason arrested many of the faithful, including Quadratus and his five disciples. After our saints had been chained in a dungeon for several days, Jason mounted his tribunal and commanded that they and the other Christians imprisoned with them be presented to him. The senior Christian was Saint Quadratus who, like a commander marching before his troops, led Christ's chosen phalanx into battle. He would answer the tyrant fearlessly on behalf of all the Christians.

The persecutor began by asking, "Quadratus, what made you lose your mind? Why have you chosen bonds and imprisonment over the pleasures of home and friends? On what do you set your hope? Submit to the imperial ordinances and worship the gods, so that you may share our happiness and enjoy this life."

"Those with a carnal mind cling to fleeting pleasures, but we should love the Giver of life more than life itself," said Quadratus in reply. "The Giver of life is God, to Whom we owe thanks and praise. We proclaim His glory by striving for virtue and by suffering for Him, and must not love this life so much that we adore idols in order to prolong it. We acknowledge as good and true no deity except Christ Jesus the Saviour, Who suffered and died for us and has ever enriched us with the gifts of His grace. The mark of a righteous man is willingness to endure torments for piety and the true faith. If anyone attempts to seduce and pervert the zealots of divine mysteries, *let him go forth condemned and let his prayer become sin.*[4] We must choose what is better and avoid blindly following pretenders to virtue; we must carefully discriminate between good and evil, and understand the danger posed by men who would lead us astray. Our forefathers directed us to the best path; therefore, do not waste your time attempting to persuade us to forsake Christ and adopt your beliefs. Divine truth is an excellent counselor and the tenets of piety are most persuasive. The one is consistent with the other, and both unite us to God. Consider this also: the law of nature requires that every mortal die. No one can escape this. At the hour of death, our wicked schemes come to nought and temporal glory is swept away like dust. Good and noble deeds, however, redound to the everlasting glory of the virtuous; therefore, we are determined to suffer valiantly for Christ and serve as worthy models for all who would emulate us. Those who reason and believe correctly are deeply inspired and guided to perfection by devout exemplars."

"Quadratus, you preach Christ, Who was a mere man," said Jason. "Be careful because, so doing, you demean the nature of the gods. If you wish to be a model of virtue, then show gratitude to whichever deity has watched over you since childhood."

"If you can control your temper, O Governor, I will explain myself further," proposed Quadratus, "although I am little accustomed to discourse about lofty matters."

The Governor said, "Speak, Quadratus. Tell us your beliefs concerning Christ."

"In the beginning," explained the saint, "God brought everything visible into existence by His Word and established it by the power of His Holy Spirit. He Who willed is called the Father; He Who created, the Son; He Who upholds creation, the Holy Spirit. Having fashioned everything beautifully, excellently, and

---

[4]Ps. 108

for a specific purpose, God wanted someone to enjoy what He had made and glorify the Creator out of gratitude for it. This is why He also created the human race, giving it dominion over the earth. The Lord breathed the spirit of life into the first man and put him in a paradise of ineffable delights. Dwelling in the wondrous garden with the helpmate God provided him, man rejoiced in its many splendid sights. Our first parents reflected on the high honor God had bestowed upon them, and they realized that they must worthily thank their Creator and Benefactor. They led a virtuous life and at first observed God's commandment not to taste the fruit of a certain tree. But then the devil, that wicked seducer consumed by envy, who has deceit on his lips and hatred in his heart, spewed upon them his venom. Determined to deprive them of paradise, he urged them to transgress the Lord's commandment. They disgraced themselves by agreeing to his evil counsel and thus fell away from the grace of God, being driven out of the garden where they had lived with the Creator. From that moment the sharers in God's glory were condemned to a pitiful existence: they were bound with fetters of sin and became prisoners of vain desires. Nevertheless, the Lord took pity on His creatures and showed Himself merciful to their weakness. Concealing His divinity beneath human flesh, He came to dwell with us, the wretched and lost. He liberated us from bondage to the enemy, led us to freedom who were enslaved to the kingdom of death, and delivered us from perdition. *When the fullness of time came, God sent forth His*[5] Word, Who took up His dwelling in the all-pure womb of the Virgin Theotokos and clothed Himself fully in humanity. The immaculate Lady conceived by the Holy Spirit and bore God in the flesh, and we beheld God the Son and Word, Whom we call Christ, vested in a body. Having revealed Himself to us in the humanity taken from the Virgin, Christ entered into combat with the armies of our foe and expanded the boundaries of the heavenly kingdom. He abolished the laws of mortality and by His divine power shattered death's chains. He demolished Hades and led out of it our first parents and a multitude of their descendants. Because He delivered from per-

---

[5]Gal., Ch. 4

dition every nation and land, He won the title 'Saviour.' Christ opened the treasures of His compassion to enrich all; He freed mankind from the tyrant's tortures; He ever preserves His inheritance intact and safe from destruction. Nothing is hidden from Him: neither the hour of our birth, nor the length of our life, nor the time of our death. He knows all things, for whatsoever the Father ordains, the Son brings to pass. This then is Christ, Whom we preach. He it is Who saves the human race; He it is Who bestows upon us the inexhaustible riches of divine goodness. He is always and everywhere present, abiding with His servants and assisting them."

The Governor marveled at Saint Quadratus' teaching; nonetheless, he refused to believe the truth and said, "However high-flown your words, I am not deceived. You attribute human characteristics to your God, alleging that He was contained in a virgin's womb. If, as you assert, Christ was born of a virgin, then you have a God here on earth in human flesh, and another, the true God, elsewhere."

Saint Quadratus replied, "Impious men ought not investigate matters of faith. Not everyone is permitted to understand lofty truths, and we are forbidden to reveal holy things to incorrigible unbelievers. The Son of God deigned to abase Himself, assuming the guise of a servant. Being God, He consented to become man, to wrest us from enslavement to demons. You are a godless infidel, and these matters are beyond your comprehension. Know, however, that you shall never sunder us from Christ, either by violence or by guile."

The Governor commanded his merciless lackeys to strip naked Christ's illustrious servant and batter him with a rod. As he bravely endured the cruel beating, Quadratus asked the persecutor, "When will you realize, Governor, that by violence you will never persuade anyone that your religion is true? You only make it clear that you are a brute, whereas by limiting yourself to exhortation, you would at least show that you are mild and kind. You are wasting your time, attempting to force us to worship idols. Fear will never compel us to abandon piety. We are burning with love for Christ and pay no heed either to your cajolery or to your tortures. Christ lightens our tribulations and pain with the hope of celestial reward, making us steadfast and invincible in the contest of suffering." The maddened persecutor responded by ordering the saint suspended upside-down, his body raked with iron claws, and a fire lit beneath him; however, the passionbearer endured manfully and remained unconquered.

Next the Governor tried to beguile Saint Cyprian, but the young martyr rejected every blandishment and prepared himself for torture. As Cyprian and the others were removing their cloaks in anticipation of torments, Saint Quadratus instructed them, "Friends and co-strugglers! Remember that in His kingdom the Lord rewards piety with honor, and martyrdom with glory. Remember that you have been deemed worthy of the mercy of Jesus Christ, Who will soon manifest His aid to you from heaven. Now is the time to contest, now the time to prove your unwavering faith in Christ God. Do not hesitate, but fulfill the law of love and surrender your souls to the Beloved. Be examples for all who wish to suffer for Christ. Remain steadfast, and astonish the onlookers by your patience. Let your bravery prove that good is superior to evil. Remain true to piety and united in your confession of our common faith, for you will soon be standing before God's dread tribunal. Remain on the path of virtue, and you will quickly finish the course and reach Christ. Profess the merciful God with a pure heart and do not fear to sacrifice the flower of your youth. Life unfading and unaging awaits you. You stand near the portal to eternity, so keep in mind that you are young and strong and can bear torments for Christ more easily than the old. Boldly offer your flesh to the torturers, manfully endure their brutality, vanquish the foe, be glorified by the Lord, and join the ranks of holy martyrs in heaven."

Hearing this exhortation, the persecutor flew into a rage and had Cyprian stripped naked, suspended like Quadratus, mangled, and burned. Afterwards, Dionysius, Anectus, Paul, and Crescens were subjected to the same torments. Since the tortures failed in their purpose, Jason commanded that the martyrs be fed to wild beasts. When the animals refused to harm them, the Governor condemned the saints to decapitation. First, however, he had them dragged by the feet through the city. A huge mob, including many children, beat the passion-bearers with staves and rocks, and followed the sufferers out of the walls to the place of execution. There the saints requested a little time for prayer and, after offering fervent supplication to God, bared their necks to the sword. The holy martyrs were beheaded on the tenth day of March. A spring burst out of the ground darkened by their blood, its pure water serving as a constant reminder to the Corinthians of the saints' passion. After Quadratus, Cyprian, Dionysius, Anectus, Paul, and Crescens were executed, the other Christian prisoners were tortured and put to death by various means. The throat of a second martyr named Dionysius was slit with a knife; and Victorinus, Victor, and Nicephorus were crushed in a large stone mortar by Tertius, who succeeded Jason as governor. Claudius' arms and legs were cut off; Diodorus peacefully surrendered his spirit to God amid the flames into which he had rushed eagerly, regarding them as his magnificent bridal chamber. Serapion was beheaded; Papias was drowned; Leonidas was brutally tortured by Venustus, Tertius' successor, then cast into the sea.

Many holy women who had laid up in their hearts Quadratus' teaching and wished to emulate the saint were also tortured for Christ's sake. These included Chariessa, Nunechia, Basilissa, Nika, Gala, Galina, and Theodora. After being sent to the Lord by beheading, drowning, or other means, they were numbered among the martyrs with their guide Quadratus, and received the garland of victory from the right hand of Christ God. Unto Him be glory, with the Father and the Holy Spirit, unto the ages. Amen.

On the Same Day

The Passion of the Holy Martyrs Quadratus of Nicomedia, Satorinus, Rufinus, and Others[1]

During the reign of the impious Roman Emperor Decius and his successor Valerian, the faithful were arrested in various towns and villages and imprisoned at Nicomedia, a city of Bithynia. Soon the Christians of Nicomedia feared for their own safety, the more so after they learned that Decius was in Caesarea and traveling in their direction. Anticipating persecution, many believers fled to the mountains and hid, but others courageously remained in their homes and awaited the hour when they would be called to glorify the Lord by enduring torments. One of the Christians who stayed in the city was the blessed Quadratus, a tall, handsome, devout, well-spoken nobleman. Quadratus bribed the warden and guards and obtained unhindered access to the Christians languishing in prison. He supplied all the needs of the brethren, encouraged them to endure every torture out of love for Christ God, and reminded them of their eternal reward in the Kingdom of heaven.

The day of judgment for the Christians dawned and the Proconsul Perenius, who had been sent by the Emperor, entered Nicomedia. Perenius sat upon his tribunal before all the citizens and called for the martyrs. Arriving with his charges, the *commentarisius* or warden of the dungeon announced, "Behold, Your Excellency, the whole lot of iniquitous Christian prisoners stands before you!"

The Proconsul commanded God's servants, "Tell me your name, rank, origin, and place of birth."

Behind the crowd stood the blessed Quadratus, who saw that the weaker brethren were pale with fear. Anticipating that they might renounce Christ under torture, he shouted, "We are Christians and all of us noble slaves of Jesus Christ our Lord, the

---

[1]Abbreviated from *The Great Collection of Readings*

invisible God! Our homeland is heaven, where God settles those who trust in Him."

The Proconsul was amazed by Quadratus' boldness and told his servants, "Bring that madman here."

The blessed Quadratus heard what the Proconsul said and quickly pushed his way through the crowd. Reaching the tribunal before he could be seized, Quadratus made the sign of the Cross and announced to the persecutor, "As you and everyone here can see, I have come willingly to speak on behalf of my brethren and contend with the devil. Do not delay, but test our courage and learn that we are Christ's invincible soldiers."

"Tell me your name and origin, fool," demanded Perenius.

"I already told you that my brethren and I are Christians, that is, Christ's slaves. We derive both nobility and our name from serving Christ," said Quadratus.

"Listen to me, friend," said the Proconsul. "If you sacrifice with us to the gods, I am willing to recommend you to the Emperor for commander in the army."

"Proconsul, you allege that there are many gods, but in truth *there is* only *one God* and *Father, of Whom are all things,*"[2] Quadratus replied.

"There are many gods," insisted Perenius, "but the Emperor requires only that you sacrifice to the twelve chief deities."[3]

"Anarchy results when numerous petty rulers vie for power. There is but one Master of heaven and earth, one King and God: our Lord Jesus Christ," proclaimed the saint.

"How dare you call our gods petty rulers!" the Proconsul cried. "Hear what Homer writes about mighty Poseidon:[4] 'The father of the gods gathered the clouds, stirred up the winds, blackened the heavens, and caused thunder to roar, spreading his dominion over dry land and all creation.'"

"So you believe what Homer and the other poets teach about your gods?" asked Quadratus.

"Of course," said the Proconsul.

---

[2] I Cor., Ch. 8
[3] The twelve chief deities were Zeus, Hera, Poseidon, Demeter, Apollo, Artemis, Hephaestus, Athena, Ares, Aphrodite, Hermes, and Hestia. (Tr.)
[4] Neptune

"Then you believe that your deities are adulterers; shameless, insatiable fornicators; and perverts. I am perplexed by you, Proconsul: you adore divinities who commit crimes far worse than those for which you torture and execute men. Better to punish the gods for their innumerable abominations. You show no clemency to mortals who break the law, but praise and worship lawless deities. How can you fail to understand that there is nothing divine in such ignoble, spiritually lifeless gods?" wondered Quadratus.

The Proconsul said, "The Emperor will punish me if I tolerate your insolence any longer. Sacrifice now; otherwise, I will deliver you at once into the hands of the torturers."

"Neither you, nor your emperor, nor your father Satan can silence me," answered Quadratus.

At this the Proconsul ordered that Quadratus be stretched out naked on the ground and whipped with leather straps. As the saint was being lashed, Perenius demanded, "Tell me your name!" When the saint did not reply, the Proconsul asked the onlookers, "Who is this rogue and what is his name?" Persons who knew the martyr told the Proconsul that he was Quadratus, a man of very high birth. Hearing this, Perenius commanded the servants, "Loose the prisoner." Quadratus put on his robes, and the Proconsul bade him approach and said to him, "You have embarrassed the both of us. Why did you not say that you are a nobleman? Why do you demean your rank by professing the contemptible errors of the Christians? You have shamed yourself and your whole family!"

I have chosen rather to be an outcast in the house of my God than to dwell in the tents of sinners,[5] rejoined the saint.

"Submit to me and sacrifice to the gods, unless you wish to die as a criminal," said the persecutor. "The Emperor and his counselors have decided that not one Christian is to be spared. Their wise decision has already brought many admirable persons to renounce Christian error."

"Blessed is the man that hath not walked in the counsel of the ungodly, nor stood in the way of sinners, nor[6] been led astray by the

---

[5]Ps. 83   [6]Ps.1

errors of this vain world," replied the martyr. "Those who have obeyed you and apostatized have perished and *are like the chaff which the wind doth hurl away from the face of the earth."*

Then the knave began to weep into his handkerchief and pleaded, "Quadratus, do not reject this life and its pleasures! Do not choose death."

"Treacherous dog! Cunning serpent!" cried the martyr. "Your false tears cannot deceive me. You are wasting your time, attempting to lead astray God's servant."

Maximian, one of the officers standing nearby, reproached the martyr, saying, "Thankless wretch, my lord the illustrious Proconsul feels pity for you, and you repay him with insults!"

"Your Proconsul was born to inherit perdition," said the saint. "If he wants to weep, let him lament the hour his mother bore him. In any case, Perenius does not require your help to ascertain that I am a Christian and to put me to death. But may you inherit the damnation our Lord Jesus Christ has prepared for him, if you join in my condemnation."

The prison warden told the Proconsul, "Master, if you allow this fellow to revile you, he will soon be fulminating against the emperors. If we do not destroy him now, he will put us in grave danger."

The martyr sighed, *"Why have the heathen raged, and the peoples meditated empty things? The kings of the earth were aroused, and the rulers were assembled together, against the Lord, and against His Christ.*[7] Again foolish men and arrogant are judging Christ, Who suffers in the person of His faithful servants, who are His members."

"Strip the ingrate and flog him more cruelly than before!" Perenius commanded the servants. "He must learn to obey the imperial ordinances and worship the gods."

While being scourged, Quadratus prayed, "Glory be to Thee, my Lord and God, Jesus Christ! Thou hast permitted me, the iniquitous and unworthy, to suffer on behalf of Thy holy name; may I also be numbered among Thy beloved servants. I thank Thee for Thy kindness, and beg Thee to fill me with Thy Holy Spirit. Guide me, enable me to remain steadfast in the faith, and

[7] Ps. 2

enlighten me with Thy wisdom. Be my helper, O Master: send Thine aid now and come now to my defense. Strengthen me, so that I may prevail over the ungodly and Thy holy name may be glorified in me. Lead me to Thy heavenly Father and confess me before Him, saying, 'Behold, this man is Thy loyal servant.' Yea, Lord Jesus Christ, assist me in completing the course well."

Five floggers wore themselves out lashing Saint Quadratus. Torrents of blood flowed from the blessed one's back, and pieces of the martyr's flesh were strewn on the ground. "Have you finally learned to believe in our gods, Quadratus?" asked the Proconsul.

The idols of the nations are of silver and gold, the works of the hands of men,[8] answered the saint. *They have a mouth, but shall not speak. Let those that make them become like unto them, and all that put their trust in them.*

"With these dark sayings you blaspheme our gods!" the Proconsul exclaimed.

"Blind fool, you take for light the darkness of this deceptive age and cannot see the effulgence of truth. You should heed me when I attempt to illumine your soul with the teachings of our fathers," advised Quadratus. "Know that I will neither sacrifice to your gods nor submit to the commands of the Emperor and his counselors. Continue your grisly work and send me quickly to the King of heaven!"

The persecutor swore, "The gods are my witnesses that I will prolong your worthless life and you shall suffer horribly."

At sunset the flogging ceased and the saint was taken to the dungeon with the other Christians. He was laid on small, sharp nails and a huge rock was placed on his chest, while his feet were put in stocks and his body was wrapped in a heavy chain. Quadratus was left thus for many days, but with His glorious, almighty right hand Christ God strengthened the martyr and enabled him to endure sufferings humanly impossible to bear. At length Perenius left Nicomedia for Nicaea, taking along Quadratus and the other Christian prisoners. Upon arriving in Nicaea, the Proconsul went to a heathen temple and worshipped devils; at the same time, he commanded that the

---

[8]Ps. 113

Christians also offer oblations to the wicked spirits. When Christ's servants were taken to the demons' sanctuary, Quadratus persuaded the guards to allow him to speak with the Proconsul. Perenius was astonished to see that the commander of the Christian phalanx had been entirely healed by the Lord, that his face was radiant and wore a joyous expression, and that he was again the very picture of courage and physical strength. Nevertheless, he greeted the martyr with the words, "Sacrifice to the gods, Quadratus!"

"I am the servant of Jesus Christ, and to Him do I offer myself as a sacrifice," replied the saint. "As for your *gods, that have not made the heavens and the earth, even they shall perish.*"[9]

"You must obey the Emperor, for your Scriptures teach, *Render to Caesar the things that are Caesar's, and to God the things that are God's,*"[10] argued the Proconsul.

"We should indeed *render to Caesar the things that are Caesar's, and to God the things that are God's,*" agreed the saint. "I paid Caesar the usual tax when I purchased my estate; now I must give God His due, remaining steadfast in my confession. The earthly Emperor offers Christians the choice of either sacrificing to idols or being put to death. We are ready to die for Christ our God not once, but repeatedly."

"Many Christians have offered oblations to our gods. Do you think you are better than they?" scoffed the Proconsul.

"As long as I refuse to bend the knee before idols, I certainly am better than those who renounce God their Creator," said Quadratus. "But where are the Christians who worshipped your gods? I do not see them." Upon this the Proconsul ordered the apostates brought to him.

Meanwhile, Saint Quadratus, who until this time was bound, asked to be loosed. Thinking that the prisoner wished to worship the gods, the Proconsul agreed. Quadratus ran to a large idol, threw his arms around its feet, and hurled it to the floor. After destroying the first statue, Quadratus rushed to do the same to the others, but soldiers and heathen priests laid hold of him. The infuriated Proconsul ordered that Quadratus be removed from the temple, suspended, and raked with iron

---

[9]Jer., Ch. 11   [10]Mark, Ch. 12

claws from head to toe. As the saint was being tortured, the apostates arrived. Quadratus reproached them, saying, "Wretches! What torments convinced you to repudiate Christ the Master and align with the devil? Do you not believe in the general resurrection, divine judgment, the abyss of hell, unquenchable fire, or the worm that never sleeps? What answer will you give on the great and glorious day of our Saviour's coming? What will be your defense when Jesus Christ judges the quick and the dead? Open your inner eyes and see how low you have fallen. You have bartered the eternal Kingdom of heaven for this worthless temporal life; you have scorned the kind, loving Master and become pitiful slaves of Satan, who misuses and ultimately destroys all who are in bondage to him. When our Lord returns, He will bind the devil with unbreakable bonds and hurl him into the fiery abyss, together with his servants. Realize what you have done! A few fleeting tortures have terrified you, and you have condemned yourselves to perpetual suffering. Ponder the day when you will stand before the tribunal of Jesus Christ, *Who will render to every man according to his deeds.*[11] Remember the Lord's words in the Holy Gospel: '*Fear not them which kill the body, but are not able to kill the soul: but rather fear Him Which is able to destroy both soul and body in* the flames of *Gehenna.*'"[12]

Weeping bitterly, the fallen Christians told him, "Servant of God, we were afraid of torments and were led astray. Like lost sheep we fell prey to wolves. This happened because of our sins. We forfeited everlasting life, wishing to prolong this fleeting one. How can we escape our miserable plight?"

To their tears the blessed Quadratus responded with joy. "Take courage, brethren; do not despair. Christ the Lord is merciful," he reassured the lapsed. "Fall prostrate before Him, lament, and beg forgiveness. Step forth and confess Christ, and you will be cleansed in your own blood."

The penitents cast themselves to the ground and lamented for a long time, throwing ashes on their heads and beating their breasts with rocks. So loud were their sobbing and mourning that all the citizens of Nicaea came to see what was happening.

---

[11]Rom., Ch. 2   [12]Matt., Ch. 10

Everyone was amazed by their fervent repentance. Because of the commotion, Perenius came out of the temple and ordered that Saint Quadratus be raked more cruelly than before and that his sides be burned with candles. Quadratus prayed long and earnestly for the penitents, begging the Lord to accept their remorseful cries. He ended his supplication with these words: "Yea, Master, Lord Jesus Christ, punish me in their stead, but have mercy on them"; whereupon, his torturers collapsed like dead men. A radiant cloud overshadowed the saint, the Christian prisoners, and the penitents; but gloomy darkness enshrouded the Proconsul, his advisers, and the other heathen. The pagans were terrified, certain that the town was about to collapse and that they would be buried in the rubble.

After lengthy silence the faithful heard holy angels praising and glorifying God. Another two hours passed and the dense murk enveloping the pagans dissipated. The unbelievers saw heavenly light shining on the Christians, but the Proconsul had no sooner recovered from his stupor than he commanded that the penitents be seized. All who had heeded the martyr's exhortation and returned to Christ were bound and sent to a dungeon with the other Christians. At the same time, Saint Quadratus was let down from the tree and was likewise fettered and imprisoned.

The next morning Governor Perenius sat upon the tribunal and had the Christians, except Saint Quadratus, brought to him. Employing both flattery and torture, he spent the whole day attempting to win over the martyrs to his vile gods. Finally he realized that the saints were resolute in their confession and that no matter how many stripes were laid upon them, they would never yield, so he sentenced them to be burned alive. The holy sufferers were overjoyed to hear this and glorified God. Each passion-bearer was sent to his native town and immolated, thereby attaining the celestial homeland.

Meanwhile, the Proconsul received instructions from Decius requiring him to traverse town and country and force any Christians he found to sacrifice. If they refused, he was to torture them to death. In consequence of this, he left Nicaea and went to Apameia, taking Saint Quadratus and intending to compel the local believers to offer oblations to idols. Upon arrival in Apameia, Perenius entered a heathen temple and worshipped the idols, then asked the holy martyr, "Are you ready to sacrifice, wicked sorcerer?"

"I am a Christian and ignorant of the black art. I am opposed to all wickedness and determined never to offer oblations either to your father Satan, overlord of sorcerers, or to his demons," answered the martyr.

"What am I to do with this despicable Christian? What torture should I employ against him?" the Proconsul asked his advisors.

Seeing the martyr's flesh already torn and shredded, his bones laid bare, and every member of his body wounded, Perenius' underlings were at a loss what to answer; but their perplexity did not hinder the Governor from quickly devising new cruelties. He straightway ordered that Quadratus be put into a sack with various reptiles and thrown into a deep pit of mud. At dawn he ordered that the sack be brought up, thinking that Quadratus would be dead; but lo, to the astonishment of all, the martyr was unharmed. Lifting his eyes to heaven, the saint said, "I thank Thee, O Lord Jesus Christ, that the blows of mine enemies are made *as an arrow of infants*[13] and that their strength hath waned. Thou hast given me courage and might, and I have humiliated Thine adversaries, unto the glory of Thy holy name." Then he turned to the Proconsul, saying, "Oaf! Are you completely inept? You must devise better tortures. These are useless."

The enraged Governor announced that he would take Quadratus to Caesarea, his next destination. He warned the martyr, "Wretch, if you contrive any more sorcerous illusions, I will torment you continuously on the way."

Upon arrival in Caesarea, the Proconsul went to a heathen sanctuary and sacrificed to idols, then had Quadratus brought to him. He told the saint, "You have suffered enough; now offer oblations to the gods."

Saint Quadratus replied, "I thought you were merely playing at torturing me. Are you already exhausted? I am not the least fatigued, but am eager to endure more pain for my God."

---

[13]Ps. 63

The incensed Proconsul commanded that the martyr be stripped naked, suspended from a tree, and flogged mercilessly. The servants carried out the order, but little remained of Quadratus' flesh, so they mostly whipped bare bone. While under the lash, the saint chanted, *Many a time have they warred against me from my youth, and yet they have not prevailed against me. The sinners wrought upon my back, they lengthened out their iniquity.*[14]

Roused to fury by the psalm, the Proconsul shouted to his slaves, "Lay it on harder! He still feels no pain."

The saint joined in, "Yes, thrash me harder! Destroy what is left of my flesh, so that my soul may prosper."

"Knave, you are certainly possessed by a devil!" exclaimed the Proconsul.

"I am not possessed by a devil, but possess authority over your father Satan and his thralls, the demons," replied the saint. "By the grace of my Christ, I order about Satan's whole infernal army, and it must do as I say. All the regiments of Hades fear me. Seeing on me the dread and invincible emblem of Jesus Christ[15] and sensing the power of the Lord's grace, the demons quiver like terrified rabbits." Then, after a few moments of silence, the martyr cried, "Glory to the Father, Son, and Holy Spirit, now and ever and unto the ages of ages!"

In the crowd there were many Christians, who responded, "Amen!" Enraged by this, the Governor ordered that two of the Christians nearest him, men of noble appearance, be stripped naked, suspended, flogged, and raked with iron claws. The servants interrupted Quadratus' torture in order to deal with these two Christians, whose names were Satorinus and Rufinus. As their flesh was being torn away and their entrails were spilling to the ground, Satorinus and Rufinus begged Quadratus and all the brethren to pray for them. The blessed Quadratus implored the Saviour, "O Lord Jesus Christ, Son of the invisible Father, look down upon the humble and have mercy on them. Grant patience and invincible might to Thy sufferers, that they may persevere to the end, gain victory, and humiliate the foe."

---

[14]Ps. 128   [15]The holy cross (Tr.)

When Satorinus and Rufinus were so weakened by torture that they could no longer speak, the persecutor had them untied and beheaded. Thus the souls of the two martyrs departed together to heaven, where the Ruler of the contest, Christ the Lord, Who is one hypostasis in two natures, awaited them. Then Perenius went to Apollonia, taking Saint Quadratus and other Christians whom he had seized in Caesarea. Entering the temple of Apollo, Perenius told Quadratus, "If you worship the gods, I will order physicians to attend to you. Render Asclepius his due, and he will heal you. Fear our mighty deities and adore the great Apollo; Heracles;[16] Zeus,[17] father of all gods; glorious Ares;[18] and dread Poseidon,[19] awesome ruler of the sea. Worship the sun likewise, for it is immortal and shines upon all things, from heaven to earth."

The saint answered, "I worship the true God: Father, Only-begotten Son, and Holy Spirit. Before the Lord's power, majesty, and ineffable glory do I tremble. I ever praise God's infinite might, but will never adore lifeless statues, the work of men's hands. I fear neither the demons nor you, for your authority will soon come to an end. A few days hence I shall depart to the Lord, but you shall weep bitterly for all eternity because you refuse to acknowledge God your Creator. Child of Satan, ally of wicked demons, you are more senseless than a hog! Rabid cur, blood-drinker, serpent, you are more eager than any beast to devour the loathsome carcasses of the sacrificial victims of your gods! Are you not ashamed to rave like a madman? Do you not realize your blindness? What good is it to offer animals and birds as oblations to inanimate divinities that cannot hunger? If you put food to an idol's mouth, does it eat? Tell me, what nourishment do your stone or wood deities prefer: goat, beef, or chicken? Doomed fool! You have fallen into the pit of perdition and hope to bring us down as well." At this the Proconsul flew into a rage and had vinegar and salt poured on the martyr's wounds, which were then scoured with sackcloth. Afterwards, Quadratus' sides were burned with red-hot iron. Towards nightfall the martyr was cast into prison.

---

[16]Hercules   [17]Jupiter
[18]Mars   [19]Neptune

The next morning Perenius left Apollonia and began traveling toward the Hellespont. He took with him the Christian prisoners in chains, including the holy martyr Quadratus, who was transported in a wagon because his wounds prevented him from walking. At the river Rontacus, Perenius was met by the military commander of the region. All the local Christians had assembled there under pretext of greeting the Proconsul, but actually out of desire to see and honor the great-martyr Quadratus, whose fame had spread throughout Asia Minor and beyond. The Proconsul and the commander spent the night in a hamlet further on the way, and the next morning Perenius decided to sacrifice to the demons, since the village was full of idols. He also wanted to force the Christian prisoners to sacrifice, and began by ordering that Quadratus be presented to him. Because the saint could not walk, he was wheeled in a cart to the altar. Although physically weak, Quadratus rejoiced in God his Saviour and was smiling. A large number of people had gathered to see Christ's martyr contest. "Have you come to your senses, Quadratus?" asked the Proconsul. "Are you ready to worship the gods, or are you still out of your mind?"

In a loud voice, so that all could hear, the martyr answered, "I have known Christ as the true God since I was a babe in swaddling. Do you expect me, a Christian from my mother's womb, to acknowledge another God?"

Perenius ordered that the saint be placed on a blazing gridiron. "There is no need to lay me on the grating. I will mount it willingly," declared the saint. Strengthened by Christ, Quadratus approached the flames, then crossed himself and happily lay on the blazing couch, as though it were a soft bed. The fire did not harm God's servant; rather, its natural qualities were diminished so that it became his slave, warming and providing comfort to his much-afflicted, longsuffering body. As the devil's lackeys tossed pitch, oil, and cotton into the flames, the saint chanted, *O God be attentive unto helping me; O Lord, make haste to help me. Let them be shamed and confounded that seek after my soul.*[20] He also mocked the persecutor, saying, "The fire has cooled and the couch become soft, but your heart is still hard as stone.

---

[20]Ps. 69

Thank you for providing me such a comfortable bed: I was worn out from travel." With this Quadratus rolled onto his side and enjoyed a little rest.

For several hours the saint remained on the blazing couch, alive and unharmed. Finally, the exasperated persecutor commanded that he be decapitated outside the village. Quadratus walked quickly to the place of execution, requiring neither transport nor assistance. On the way he chanted, *Blessed be the Lord Who hath not given us to be a prey to their teeth.*[21] A number of the brethren followed and joined him in song.

Christ's holy great-martyr was beheaded on March 10, the day on which his namesake and friend Quadratus of Corinth and those with him gained the crown of martyrdom. At that time Decius and Valerian[22] wielded authority over the Greeks and Romans, but the Lord Jesus Christ ruled over the Christians. Unto Him be glory and dominion with the Father and the Holy Spirit, now and ever and unto the ages of ages. Amen.

---

[21]Ps. 123

[22]It was two years after Decius' death that Valerian came to the throne. During Decius' reign, however, Valerian exercised almost unlimited civil authority as censor. (Tr.)

On the Same Day

The Commemoration of Our Holy Mother Anastasia the Nun, Who Assumed the Name Anastasius and the Identity of a Eunuch

During the reign of Justinian the Great, the ranking noblewoman at the court of Constantinople was the pious widow Anastasia. Her physical beauty was exceptional, and her spiritual beauty even more so, for she nurtured in her heart the fear of God and scrupulously observed the Lord's commandments. Having adorned her soul with virtue, Anastasia attained such modesty and humility that everyone was edified by her life and many strove to emulate her. The Emperor held her in the highest esteem. It was to be expected, then, that the devil, the sower of tares and adversary of good, who never ceases to war against the race of man and incite enmity, would attack the blessed Anastasia. He did this through the Empress Theodora, who loathed God's blameless handmaiden. Mulling over her plight, the divinely wise one reasoned, "Anastasia! Here is a chance to save your soul. Give place to the Empress' wrath and you will win the Kingdom of heaven."

Abandoning most of her vast wealth, the blessed one secretly left court and sailed to Alexandria. Three miles outside that city she built a small convent, took up her dwelling there, and began laboring for God alone. She kept her hands busy with spinning and needlework, and ever recited psalms and sang God's praises. The community came to be known as "The Convent of the Patrician Lady" because of the blessed one's rank. It grew and became famous, enjoying abundant prosperity until the Hagarene conquest of Egypt.

Several years after Saint Anastasia left the Imperial City, Theodora died. Justinian remembered the respected noblewoman and dispatched servants to search for her throughout the Empire. Hearing about this, God's lamb left her monastery one night, went to Abba Daniel in Scete, and related her story to him. The elder clothed Anastasia in men's monastic garb, renamed her Anastasius, and settled her in a cave some distance from the lavra. He provided Anastasia with a rule of life, forbade her to receive visitors or to leave, and instructed her to say she was a eunuch, if anyone chanced upon her. He also appointed one of his disciples to supply her with a small loaf of bread and a pot of water every week. The disciple was to leave the provisions near the cave and withdraw after the anchoress said a blessing. For twenty-eight years Anastasia remained in the grotto, never leaving it or seeing anyone. Possessing a firm, manly character, she unfailingly carried out the rule given her by the elder. No one came to visit her and, indeed, no one knew she was living there, besides Abba Daniel and the disciple, who was told Anastasia was a eunuch.

The tongue cannot tell, nor can the mind imagine all the labors performed by the saint for God during the many years she lived in seclusion. Who can relate her tears, sighs, lamentation, vigils, chanting, prayers, prolonged reading, standing, prostrations, fasting, and privations? Who can describe the demonic assaults she endured or her battles with the spirits of wickedness, which constantly reminded her of the pleasures of the world and the flesh? It is almost inconceivable how the saint, being of the gentlest birth and highest rank, accustomed to living in the imperial palace and dining with countless noblemen and noblewomen, could have endured so long in that den of the earth, continuously engaged in fierce combat with devils. It is astonishing how the Lord's favorite not only disdained the luxuries she had once enjoyed, but even eradicated the very remembrance of them from her mind. Having attained extreme humility by the narrow, sorrowful path of asceticism, she became a chosen vessel of the Holy Spirit.

At the end of her twenty-eighth year as a hermitess, the victorious, God-pleasing spiritual athlete neared the finish line. Foreseeing her departure to the Lord, she wrote this message to the elder on a shard: "Reverend Father! Come quickly with your disciple. Bring picks and shovels to bury your son, the eunuch Anastasius." She left the potsherd outside the cave.

That night God revealed to Abba Daniel what Anastasia had done. The elder commanded his disciple, "Run, child, to the cave where our brother Anastasius the eunuch lives. Near the entrance there is a piece of pottery he has inscribed. Bring it to me quickly."

The brother found the shard and delivered it to Abba Daniel, who read it and wept. Then, taking everything necessary for a burial, elder and disciple set out for the cave. They found the eunuch burning with fever. Abba Daniel fell on the saint's breast, weeping, "You are blessed, Brother Anastasius, for you disdained the pleasures of court and spent your whole life preparing for the hour of death!"

Anastasia said, "You are also blessed, O new Abraham!"

"Pray to the Lord for us," the elder begged.

"Reverend Father, it is I who need your prayers at this hour," the saint rejoined.

"If I were to die before you did, then I would certainly pray for you," said the elder.

At this Anastasia sat up on her rush mat, kissed the elder's head, prayed for him, and called down the Lord's blessing upon him. Then the elder had his disciple prostrate himself before the saint and ask for a blessing. "May the God of my fathers, Who is present before me and is about to separate my soul and body, Who knows all my labors and everything I have suffered for His sake, anoint this man with the spirit of his elder, as He once anointed Elisha with the spirit of Elijah," said the venerable one. After this the eunuch, tears flowing down his cheeks, whispered to Abba Daniel, "For the Lord's sake, Father, do not remove my robes when I die. Keep my secret."

Saint Anastasia partook of the immaculate Mysteries of Christ and then said to Abba Daniel, "Father, trace the sign of the Cross of Christ over me and pray for me." Afterwards, her face blazed like fire, and she looked into the eastern sky, crossed herself, and uttered these last words: "O Lord, into Thy hands do I commit my spirit." Thus she fell asleep in the Lord.

The two monks began digging in front of the cave. When the grave was completed, Abba Daniel removed his rason and told his disciple, "Child, put this on our brother." While carrying out the elder's command, the disciple noticed that Anastasia's breasts were those of a woman, although withered like dry leaves. For the moment he said nothing to the elder, but assisted him in committing the saint's corpse to the earth and chanting

the usual funeral hymns. Later, while the two men were returning to their cells, the disciple asked Abba Daniel, "Father, did
you know that the eunuch Anastasia was actually a woman?"

"I did, child," said the elder. "I gave her men's clothing and
the name Anastasius to prevent scandal and rumors. The
Emperor Justinian's servants searched for her everywhere, but
by the grace of God could not find her." Abba Daniel told his
disciple everything about the saint, and eventually all the
monks of Scete learned the story. The venerable Anastasia's Life
was recorded for the edification of posterity and unto the glory
of Christ God, Who is wondrous in His saints throughout the
ages. Amen.

The Eleventh Day
of the Month of March

The Commemoration of
Our Father Among the Saints
Sophronius the Wise,
Patriarch of Jerusalem

Saint Sophronius, namesake of chastity, was born in Damascus to devout, temperate, noble parents, Plinthus and Myra. From his youth he conducted himself in a manner worthy of his name. He loved both spiritual and secular wisdom and kept his virginity as unsullied as on the day he came forth from his mother's womb. Saint John of the Ladder teaches, "Chastity is the name common to all the virtues,"[1] and Sophronius strove to acquire each and every one, especially spiritual wisdom and virginal purity. Having thoroughly acquainted himself with secular philosophy, he won the title *sophist*,[2] which means "a man of wisdom." In those days this was a most illustrious appellation, given only to leading philosophers, such as Libanius the Sophist, friend of Saint Basil the Great.[3] Then the blessed Sophronius decided to seek spiritual wisdom and began visiting monasteries and hermitages. He was profoundly edified by the fathers of the desert. Afterwards, he went to Jerusalem and made the rounds of monasteries near the Holy City, including the coenobium of Theodosius the Great. There he met the

---

[1]*The Ladder*, Step 15
[2]In later Roman times, this term was the designation for teachers of one of the most valued parts of higher education: the use of rhetoric as a purely literary exercise. (Tr.)
[3]Libanius was one of Basil's teachers. (Tr.)

learned monk John Moschus or Eucrates, a virtuous presbyter and master of the spiritual life. Sophronius cleaved wholeheartedly to John, as a son to his father or a pupil to his teacher. Until the end of John's life he followed the elder everywhere, traveling from one monastery or desert cell to the next and making the acquaintance of many fathers, whose lives are recorded in the *Leimonarion* or *The Spiritual Meadow*. Sophronius helped John write this book, which was endorsed by the Seventh Ecumenical Council. In it, the blessed John calls the venerable Sophronius "The Sophist" and his lord and master. Foreseeing in the Spirit that Sophronius would become an eminent pastor and unshakable pillar of the Church, John regarded him less a disciple than a friend, companion, and fellow-laborer.

Prior to his tonsure, Sophronius lived for some time in Palestine with the venerable John, first at the coenobium of Theodosius the Great, later in the wilderness of the Jordan, last at the New Lavra founded by Saint Sabbas. After this, Persian raids compelled John and Saint Sophronius to seek refuge in Antioch the Great. At that time Chosroes the Younger, Shah of Persia, attacked the Greek Empire because the tyrant Phocas had murdered the Emperor Maurice and usurped the throne.[4] A few years earlier, Maurice had sheltered Chosroes when the latter was driven across the border by a rebellion. He became a second father to Chosroes and with funds and troops helped him regain power. As a result, peace was concluded between the two realms, which had warred for centuries. Chosroes was deeply grieved by the execution of his benefactor and broke the peace treaty. The Persian Army conquered many provinces of the Greek Empire, including Syria, Phoenicia, and Palestine. The fathers leading the ascetical life in those countries abandoned their monasteries and desert cells and fled to safer places, and Saints John and Sophronius left the Holy Land. After their departure, the invaders captured Jerusalem, seizing the Cross of Christ and the Most Holy Patriarch Zachariah and taking them to Persia. For fourteen years the honored and life-giving Wood remained in captivity, to the distress of all Christians.

[4]The Greek author Nicephorus explains this at length in chapter eighteen of his history.

Having taken up their dwelling in Antioch, John and Sophronius began visiting the virtuous ascetics of the region. Like bees flying from one blossom to another, they went from cell to cell and gathered the nectar that is sweeter than honey and edifies the soul. Much of what they saw and heard is recorded in *The Spiritual Meadow*.

Soon the Persian Army approached Antioch, and the two saints escaped to Alexandria. While in Egypt they again recorded the deeds and teachings of the holy fathers, to the benefit of all Christians. From the sixty-ninth chapter of *The Spiritual Meadow* it is evident that Sophronius was not yet a monk when he arrived in Alexandria, for his teacher John Eucrates writes, "Before my brother Lord Sophronius was tonsured, he and I traveled to Alexandria, where we met Abba Palladius, a man of virtue and devoted servant of God." Likewise, he says in the one hundred and ninth chapter, "My Lord Sophronius and I went to the Lavra of Oktokaidekaton[5] to see a distinguished Egyptian elder. I said to the old man, 'Tell us, Abba, how we should live with each other. My master Sophronius the Sophist wants to renounce the world and become a monk.' The elder said, 'Children, you do well to abandon the world in order to save your souls. Remain in the stillness of your cells, keep watch over your thoughts, and pray without ceasing. If you trust in God, He will illumine your souls with divine knowledge.'"

So earnestly did the pure, virtuous, and blessed Sophronius exert himself, visiting hermitages and coenobitic communities in search of guidance on the path to salvation, that by the time he was tonsured, he had already attained monastic perfection. Saint Sophronius was gravely ill at his profession and was not expected to recover. In the one hundred and second chapter of *The Spiritual Meadow*, his teacher relates, "When my brother the wise Sophronius was at death's doorstep, Abba John the Scholastic and I were standing beside him. Suddenly, he exclaimed, 'I just saw myself walking on a road, and a company of maidens danced up to me and cried, 'Sophronius has come! Sophronius has been crowned!'" Thus the choir of virgins

---

[5]The Greek word for eighteen is *oktokaideka*, and this community was eighteen stadia (about ten miles) from Alexandria. (Tr.)

rejoiced at the tonsure of the namesake of chastity. Before long Sophronius recovered his health and, now as a monk, redoubled his labors on behalf of his own salvation and that of others.

In those days the heresy of Severus[6] spread throughout Egypt. Being learned and well versed in the divine Scriptures, both Sophronius and his teacher contended against the miscreants, repeatedly besting them in debate. They won the love of the Most Holy Patriarch of Alexandria John the Almsgiver,[7] who regarded them as close friends, allies in the struggle against the heretics, and open-hearted consolers. In his Life, written by Leontius, Bishop of Neapolis, it says that the blessed John would sit at the doors of his cathedral every Wednesday and Friday and permit anyone who wished to speak with him. He received petitions, rendered assistance, settled disputes, and reconciled those at enmity. If no one came, he would return home shedding tears and lamenting, "The lowly John has nothing to offer God in compensation for his sins."

On these occasions the blessed Sophronius, desiring to comfort him, would say, "Truly, you ought to rejoice today, Father. The members of your flock live in peace, like the angels in heaven."

Saint Sophronius and his elder had it in purpose to see or hear or learn something new and spiritually profitable every day. John Moschus writes, "Once, my lord Sophronius and I went to the house of Stephen the Philosopher, who lived on the way to the Church of the All-holy Theotokos, which was built by Patriarch Eulogius to the east of the Great Tetrapylon.[8] It was noon when we arrived at the home of the philosopher and knocked at the door. The porter told us, 'My master is still resting; wait a little while.' I suggested to my lord Sophronius, 'We should go to the Tetrapylon and wait there.' Now the local population greatly reveres that place, because it is said that the Emperor Alexander of Macedon brought the relics of the holy prophet Jeremiah from Egypt[9] and enshrined them there when

---

[6]Monophysitism (Tr.)   [7]Commemorated on November 12

[8]Tetrapylon: an edifice having four gates or portals, usually erected at the intersection of two streets (Tr.)

[9]Ancient writers often designated only the Nile valley as Egypt, excluding the desert or the delta. (Tr.)

he founded Alexandria. We found there no one except three blind men, beside whom we quietly sat with our books. They were conversing and one asked another, 'Friend, how did you go blind?' This was the reply: 'As a young man I was captain of a ship that plied the African coast. From staring at the sea I got webeye and lost my sight.' Then the second man asked the first the same question and was told: 'I used to be a glass-blower. One day I was careless and burned my eyes.' Finally, the first two men asked the third man how he lost his vision. The third man explained, 'When I was young, I was lazy and detested work. I lived freely until lack of money drove me to theft. Once I saw a richly attired corpse being taken to burial. I followed it to the Church of Saint John, where it was interred. That night I opened the sepulcher and stripped the body, leaving it clad only in its shroud. As I was departing, my wicked thoughts urged me, 'Take the shroud, too; it is an excellent one!' Wretch that I am, I went back and was removing the shroud, when suddenly the dead man sat up, clawed my face, and gouged out both my eyes. I screamed with pain and stumbled out of the crypt.' At this my master Sophronius beckoned to me and we left. As we were walking, he commented, 'It would seem, Abba John, our lesson for today is that no evildoer can escape God's notice.'"

While living in Alexandria, the blessed Sophronius recorded the miracles of the holy martyrs Cyrus and John. He did this out of gratitude, because the unmercenary physicians healed his eyes when he prayed with faith in their church in Alexandria. Afterwards, Sophronius always regarded these saints with particular devotion.

Several years passed and Egypt was threatened by Persian invasion. Fear of the enemy compelled the Most Holy Patriarch John the Almsgiver to take flight, and our blessed fathers John and Sophronius fled with him. Not wishing to be parted, they sailed for Constantinople together, but on the way the Patriarch took ill and died in his native city of Amathus.[10] The wise Sophronius wrote a eulogy praising Saint John's celestial life and countless deeds of mercy.

After the Patriarch's funeral, Sophronius went to Rome with

[10]In Cyprus (Tr.)

his teacher John and twelve men who had joined them as monastic brethren. Having lived in the old capital for several years, the venerable John departed to the Lord at an advanced age. On his deathbed he requested his beloved disciple and spiritual son Sophronius not to bury his corpse in Rome, but to take it in a wooden coffin to Mount Sinai. If it was impossible to reach Sinai because of barbarians, he was to lay the body to rest in the coenobium of Saint Theodosius the Great in Palestine, where the venerable John became a monk. Emulating the Old Testament patriarch Joseph, who took the remains of Jacob to Canaan for burial with his ancestors, Sophronius left Rome for the Greek lands with the body of his spiritual father John. Upon arrival in Ascalon, he learned that the barbarians had made Mount Sinai inaccessible, so he went to Jerusalem (which was still under Persian control) and buried the corpse at the coenobium of Saint Theodosius. Afterwards, he and the brotherhood took up their dwelling in the Holy City.

While the Wood of the Cross and Patriarch Zachariah were captive in Persia, the see of Jerusalem was administered by Modestus. Shortly after Saint Sophronius' arrival in Palestine, however, God deigned to return the honored Cross and Patriarch Zachariah to the Holy City. This took place in the following manner. The Exarch Heraclius revolted against Phocas, put the tyrant to death, and became Emperor of the Greeks. He then carried the struggle to Persian territory, won many victories over Chosroes' armies, and ravaged Persia for seven years. As a result, Prince Kavadh-Shiruya deposed and murdered his father Chosroes. As soon as he was crowned Shah, Kavadh-Shiruya came to terms with the Greek Emperor. Heraclius' first conditions for peace were that the Persians evacuate Jerusalem and return the holy Wood of the honored Cross and Patriarch Zachariah. Thus, after fourteen years of captivity, the Wood of the Cross was given back by the Persians and taken with much ceremony to Jerusalem. Emperor Heraclius himself carried it on his shoulders into the Holy City, as is told in the entry for September 14, and Patriarch Zachariah returned to his cathedra. Several years later Heraclius took the precious Wood of the Lord's Cross to Constantinople, to prevent it from being seized again by enemies. In fact, Jerusalem soon fell to new foes, as we shall explain.

Patriarch Zachariah did not remain long on his throne after returning from captivity, but departed to the Lord. His successor was Modestus, who had earlier administered the Church; however, he survived Zachariah only by two years. After Modestus' death, Saint Sophronius was elected patriarch. In those days the Monothelite heresy made its appearance. The Monothelites confessed that Christ has a divine nature and a human nature, but a single will and a single operation; therefore, the natures are deprived of their characteristic activity and will. Those who profess this mock Christ as imperfect in both natures. The heresy of Monotheletism is described at length in the Life of the venerable Maximus the Confessor, who is commemorated on January 21. Chief among the divisors and disseminators of this error was Cyrus, Patriarch of Alexandria, who convened a local synod and commanded it to endorse the false teaching. His followers included the Patriarch of Constantinople, Sergius; Pyrrhus, Sergius' successor; and others. Many of the Orthodox suffered for refusing to accept the heresy. The opposition was led by Saint Sophronius of Jerusalem, who convoked his own local council and anathematized Monotheletism. The Most Holy Patriarch widely circulated the acts of this synod, and they were subsequently read at the Sixth Ecumenical Council and approved as Orthodox by the fathers. It should be noted that Saint Sophronius was the author of a number of treatises, homilies, and hymns that greatly edified the Church of Christ. He also wrote several Lives of saints, notably the Life of Saint Mary of Egypt, the desert-dweller who by unrivaled asceticism became like an angel. Moreover, he was a good pastor of God's Church, shutting the mouths of heretics and driving the wolves far from the reason-endowed flock.

Before too long, God permitted another barbarian attack on Syria and Palestine. This time the invaders were not the Persians, but the Mohammedans, who began by taking Damascus. The Greek army in Syria was routed, its commander Sergius was slain, and Patriarch Sophronius was besieged in the Holy City with the Palestinian Christians for two years. In a homily for the Nativity of Christ delivered while Jerusalem was encircled, our saint, like a second Jeremiah, laments the destruction and desolation of the Holy Places permitted by God because of the sins of the people. Most of all he regrets that it was impossible to celebrate the Nativity in Bethlehem, which had already fallen to the Hagarenes. At the end of the second year of blockade, hunger forced the Christians to capitulate, but only after Sophronius had secured terms from Omar, Caliph of the Hagarenes, guaranteeing that the Christian faith be tolerated and God's holy churches remain inviolate. After Omar had sworn to these and other conditions, the Christians opened the gates. Clad in tattered sackcloth made of camel's hair, the wicked, deceitful Caliph entered the city on foot. He pretended to be a meek and gentle lamb, but was inwardly a ravenous wolf. "Where is the temple of Solomon?" he asked, intending to perform his loathsome devotions there. The Most Holy Patriarch went to meet him, and seeing the hypocrite clothed in the garb of a penitent, he sighed, "Lo, the abomination of desolation stands in the holy place, as Daniel prophesied!" He and the other Christians wept bitterly and convinced the tyrant to remove the hair shirt and clothe himself in princely robes.

Thus the Hagarenes conquered Jerusalem and the Christians were enslaved. The godless Caliph violated every point of the treaty and repeatedly wronged the Christians. Seeing this, the Most Holy Patriarch lamented continuously and begged God to remove his soul from the land of the living, as he did not want to witness further injustice against the faithful or the continued defilement of the Holy Places by the abomination of desolation. The Almighty quickly hearkened unto him, and the blessed Sophronius departed this world of tribulations and attained the Jerusalem on high and the mansions of those who rejoice in Jesus Christ our Lord, unto Whom be glory forever. Amen.

On the Same Day

The Passion of the Holy Hieromartyr Pionius, Presbyter of Smyrna, and Those with Him[1]

The Apostle exhorts us to honor the saints, urging, *Remember your instructors, who have spoken unto you the word of God.*[2] Calling to mind their faith, life, and blessed end, we yearn to emulate the Lord's favorites, of whom one of the most illustrious is the holy martyr Pionius. We are greatly profited by commemorating this peer of the apostles, who converted many from demonic deception to God, then was summoned to the Lord and adorned with the crown of martyrdom, leaving us his edifying teaching and wondrous example of virtue.

The presbyter Pionius; Sabina, a zealot of piety; Asclepiades; Macedonia; and Lemnus, presbyter of the cathedral of Smyrna, were seized by the heathen on February 23, the feast of the holy hieromartyr Polycarp. At that time Decius was emperor and persecution was raging, especially in Smyrna, a town with a very large Jewish population. Pionius learned beforehand that he would be apprehended on the feast of Saint Polycarp; therefore, he, Sabina, and Asclepiades undertook a fast, and each bound himself with a chain. The martyrs remained in a house awaiting arrest. On the feast, after the saints had prayed, they partook of a little bread and water. Then Polemonus, the magistrate responsible for overseeing religious ceremonies, arrived with his soldiers, searching for the Christians and intending to compel them to offer vile oblations to demons. Polemonus asked Pionius, "Are you aware of the imperial edict requiring that you sacrifice to the gods?"

"We know the commandment of our God requiring that we worship Him alone," answered Pionius.

---

[1]From Metaphrastes and *The Great Collection of Readings*
[2]Heb., Ch. 13

"You must submit, whether you wish to or not. Come, join the worshippers of the gods," advised the magistrate.

Sabina and Asclepiades cried, "We submit to the living God!"

At this point no force was employed, because the saints went willingly with Polemonus, bound only with the chains they had wrapped around themselves. Puzzled by this, the crowd that had assembled trailed close behind. The saints were taken to the city councillors, who were surrounded by a vast throng of pagans and an even larger number of Jews. Onlookers pressed through the doorways and hung out of the windows. As the saints were presented to the council, Polemonus commanded, "Pionius, obey the imperial decree, as have others. Offer oblations to the gods, and avoid brutal torture."

His face radiant, Pionius addressed the crowd, "Hearken, O Smyrnaeans, and give heed, O Jews! I am told that a number of Christians have sacrificed, and that you find this amusing. You heathen take pride in the fact that your teacher Homer lived in this beautiful city. Be guided by his words, for he says that no one should rejoice over the perdition of another. And remember, O Jews, what Moses commands: *If thou see thine enemy's ass fallen under its burden, thou shalt not pass by it, but shalt help to raise it with him.*[3] You should follow the advice of Solomon, who says, *If thine enemy should fall, rejoice not over him, neither be elated at his sorrow.*[4] As for me, I shall do as my Master bids. It is better to die than disobey Him. With all my might I strive to fulfill His statutes, which I learned long ago and since then have taught to others. Why, O Jews, do you laugh at the fallen Christians? Even if, as you maintain, we are enemies, we are still all men. You allege that we insult you when we speak the truth. Wherein is the offense? Whom have we driven into exile? Whom have we forced to worship idols? Do you think that those who out of fear broke God's commandment and worshipped idols are greater sinners than you?[5] No one compelled you to become *initiates of*

---

[3]Ex., Ch. 23   [4]Prov., Ch. 24

[5]The Jews were known to be a peculiar people and generally exempted by the Romans from sacrificing to pagan gods. No such exception was made for Christians; hence, the Jews could mock Christian apostates without

Baal-phegor and to eat *the sacrifices of the dead.*[6] No one forced you to couple with women of foreign tribes, to sacrifice your sons and daughters to demons, to murmur against God, to curse Moses, or to clamor for Egypt. Time fails me to list all your crimes, yet you pretend that no one can lead you astray! Have you never read your own Scriptures: Exodus, Judges, the books of Kings, and the others? All these condemn you. A few Christians under threat of death offer oblations to idols, and on their account you ridicule all of us. But consider, O Jews: the world is like a threshing-floor, on which there is a large stack of wheat and chaff. When the laborer comes with his fan to purge the floor,[7] the chaff is carried away and the wheat remains. Likewise, a net lowered into the water catches fish of all kinds, but the good are separated from the bad. It is the same with life itself. Shall we, in your opinion, suffer deservedly, or undeservedly? If deservedly, then you too shall suffer, for your iniquitous deeds accuse you as malefactors. But if we are righteous and shall suffer undeservedly, then what hope for salvation have you wrongdoers? *If the righteous scarcely shall be saved, where shall the ungodly and sinner appear?*[8]

"The world shall be judged; of this the signs are evident. I have traveled through the land of the Hebrews on both sides of the Jordan and seen how the country bears the marks of God's wrath against its wicked inhabitants, who are notorious for robbing and murdering travelers. Columns of smoke rose from its dry, barren fields and orchards. I saw the Dead Sea,[9] in which fish cannot survive. Its waters, blighted by the Lord, are undrinkable and no one can long remain in them. So buoyant are they that whatever is thrown into them immediately rises to the surface. Closer by, Decapolis in Lydia was devastated by fire because of the sins of its evil citizens, as you know very well. To this day it remains a ruin. Consider Mount Etna in Sicily and the nearby springs that gush hot water. Whence do they derive

having to apologize for their own. To dispel their false sense of superiority, Pionius reminds the Jews of instances in their earlier history when they betrayed God voluntarily. (Tr.)
[6]Ps. 105   [7]Matt., Ch. 3   [8]I Pet., Ch. 4
[9]Also known as the Asphalt Sea, because of the asphalt seepage along its shores and the pieces of asphalt that float on its surface

their heat, if not from the fire within the earth prepared for transgressors? They prove that God will judge sinners and punish them in flames, as said His incarnate Word, our Lord Jesus Christ. Knowing this, we will never serve the Greek gods or worship golden idols."

Polemonus, the city councillors, and the crowd remained silent while Pionius spoke. Afterwards, the magistrate and others said to the martyr, "Give heed, Pionius. You have won our esteem by your modesty and integrity. We do not want you to perish. Remain alive and continue to enjoy the present existence."

"I do enjoy the present life," admitted Pionius, "but yearn for another, which awaits Christians. Incomparably more pleasant than the sunshine is the true light for which we long. We do not demean God's visible creation, much less do we hate it, for it is extremely beautiful; but we much prefer the splendor of the invisible realm."

Then a wicked blasphemer named Alexander shouted, "Hear me, Pionius!"

"You would do better to hear me," the saint advised him. "I know everything you know, but you are ignorant of much that I know."

"If you know so much, explain why you are wearing chains," laughed Alexander.

"We wear chains to make you understand that we have not come to worship your idols, but to be imprisoned and die for our God," answered the saint.

Following this rebuff, Alexander heaped flattery on Pionius, in the hope of winning him over, but without success. Finally, he muttered, "Why waste words? These people are determined to die."

The crowd clamored for Pionius to be taken to the arena so that the entire city could hear him, but Polemonus, fearing disorders, would not allow this. Instead, he pressed the martyr, "If you will not sacrifice to the gods, then at least agree to enter their temple."

"What good will it do the idols for to me to enter their temple?" asked the saint.

"Agree, Pionius," insisted the magistrate.

"If only you would agree to become Christians!" sighed Pionius.

The heathen burst out laughing, "We beg you to refrain from converting us. We have no desire to be burned alive!"

"It is far worse to burn forever after death in the unquenchable fire," said the saint.

Then the blessed Sabina smiled. Polemonus and the others demanded, "What do you find so humorous?"

"I am smiling because I am a Christian," replied Sabina. "Those who stand firm in the faith of Christ rejoice eternally."

The impious said, "Soon you will be on your way to a place you never thought you would call home. They will give you something to smile about there, for women who refuse to adore the gods are taken to a brothel."

"The true and holy God will protect me," answered Sabina.

At this point scribes began recording the exact words used by the martyrs to confess Christ and ridicule the idols. When Polemonus asked Sabina her name, Saint Pionius whispered to her that she should say it was Theodotia. This, because he did not want information about Sabina to reach her former mistress. Sabina had been the slave of a pagan noblewoman who, during the reign of Gordian, had tried to force the blessed one to renounce Christ. Failing in this, she fettered Sabina and drove her into the wilderness. Christians found her in the mountains and secretly provided her with food. With great difficulty Saint Pionius removed her shackles. Pionius feared that if Sabina's former mistress learned about her, the Lord's handmaiden would be enslaved again. Sabina told Polemonus that she was called Theodotia, upon which the magistrate asked, "Are you a Christian?"

"I am," she affirmed.

"What God do you worship?" Polemonus inquired.

The saint confessed, "I worship the almighty God Who created heaven, the earth, and all of us. He is known through His Word, our Lord Jesus Christ, incarnate of the immaculate Virgin Theotokos."

The scribes departed and the saints were taken to a dungeon. Many of the onlookers followed the martyrs, and some commented regarding Pionius, "This man was always pallid, but today his face is full of color." Others shouted, "If these people will not sacrifice to the gods, they must be tortured!"

"Then torture us," Pionius goaded them. "Nothing hinders you. No guard or soldier will protect us. We are in your hands, torment us!"

One of the heathen thrust his finger at Saint Asclepiades and cried, "This man wants to offer oblations to the gods!"

"Liar!" said Saint Pionius. "None of us would do such a thing."

Then the pagans recited the names of Christians who had betrayed Christ: "So-and-so offered oblations; why do you refuse?"

"What is that to me? Every person has free will," countered Saint Pionius, whose words infuriated the mob to such an extent that it almost tore him and his companions to pieces.

In the dungeon, the martyrs found two Christians: Lemnus, presbyter of the cathedral, who was in bonds, and Macedonia, a woman from the village of Karina. The faithful visited the martyrs and provided them with the necessities of life, which the saints reluctantly accepted and distributed among the guards. Pagans also came and attempted to convert the saints to impiety, but left astonished by the martyrs' bold replies. The Lord's prisoners were also visited by Christians who had succumbed to force or fear of torture and sacrificed to idols. These wretches would remain for hours, even days, weeping bitterly. Saint Pionius shed copious tears for them, especially those who led an upright life but had shrunk before torments and offered oblations to statues. With tears in his eyes, he exhorted the fallen, "My heart suffers unrelenting pain and my spirit is broken when I see the Church's pearls trampled by swine, the stars pulled down from heaven by the serpent's tail, and the vineyard planted by God's right hand devoured by wild boars and ravaged by passers-by. *My little children, of whom I travail in birth again until Christ be formed in you;*[10] my beloved nurslings, whom I fed the Bread of Heaven: why have you wandered onto the path of perdition? Again wicked elders sully the reputation of the chaste Susanna, to wit, the Church of Christ; again Haman boasts, and Esther and her

---

[10]Gal., Ch. 4

nation are disheartened. Again there is *a famine in the land, not a famine of bread, nor a thirst for water, but of hearing the words of the Lord;* [11]again, as in the Gospel, the virgins have fallen asleep. The Lord foresaw the apostasy of our generation and asked, *When the Son of man cometh, will He find faith on the earth?*[12] He knew that men would betray their neighbors, as it is now reported, and He prophesied, *The brother shall deliver up the brother to death.*[13] Truly, *Satan hath desired to have* us, *that he may sift* us *as wheat.*[14] The *fan is in* the *hand* of God the Word, *and He will thoroughly purge His floor;*[15] *the salt* has *lost his savor,* so it is *cast out*[16] *to be trodden under foot of men.*[17] Children, let no one imagine that the Lord is enfeebled; not the Lord, but we have failed. 'Is it possible that My arm should lack strength to deliver you, or that My ears should fail to hear you?' asks the Saviour. 'Your own sins have sundered you from God.' We have transgressed, brethren; we have violated the Lord's commandments. Our iniquities have angered God and sorrowed our neighbor. Our *righteousness* should *exceed* that *of the scribes and Pharisees,* but instead, we lie; we revile, slander, and devour one another. I hear that the Jews have invited some of you to their synagogues. Take heed, lest you fall into an even deadlier trap and commit the unforgivable sin, blasphemy against the Holy Spirit. Beware, lest you be numbered with the princes of Sodom or the citizens of Gomorrah, like the Jews, whose hands are stained with blood. It is not we who slew the prophets or betrayed Christ or put Him to death. What more need I say? Remember what I constantly repeat to you. As you know well, the Jews allege Christ to have been a mere man and his death no different than that of any mortal. Let them say what they wish. If He was a mere mortal, how is the whole world filled with His disciples? How are so many willing to undergo grievous sufferings for Him? How are demons expelled by His name? The all-powerful name of Christ works miracles of every kind in the Church of the faithful. The depraved Jews fail to understand that Christ our Lord suffered voluntarily, died for our sake, and rose on the third day in glory. Those evildoers maintain that Christ

---

[11]Amos, Ch. 8   [12]Luke, Ch. 18   [13]Matt., Ch. 10
[14]Luke, Ch. 22   [15]Matt., Ch. 3; Luke, Ch. 3
[16]Luke, Ch. 14   [17]Matt., Ch. 5

was a warlock and rose from the dead by means of sorcery. Let them show us where their Scriptures or ours teach this about Christ, or prove that any righteous man of the past taught it. Slander! And those who spread it are depraved scoundrels. Why believe such persons, rather than the just? Since childhood, I have been hearing their lies. To prove their blasphemous charges, the Jews adduce the story of the witch of Endor. Saul entreated this woman, *'Bring me up* the prophet *Samuel* from the dead.'[18] By means of the black art, the witch brought up *an old man covered with a mantle. And Saul perceived that it was Samuel, and Samuel said to Saul, Why hast thou disquieted me, to bring me up?* Is it possible that the woman really could have brought back Samuel from the dead? If the Jews say that she indeed accomplished this, then they admit iniquity to be more powerful than righteousness, and sorcery mightier than holiness, since the holy prophet was forced to obey the witch. Whoever affirms this is deluded and accursed. If, however, the Jews admit that the woman with a familiar spirit could not actually have raised up Samuel through witchcraft, then they cannot say that Christ our Lord rose from the grave by means of sorcery. Now, children, hear the correct interpretation of this story. The soul of the holy prophet was resting in the bosom of Abraham; therefore, it was impossible for the enchantress to return it to this life. The lesser has no power over the greater, and the devil cannot order about a saint. However, fallen angels do hearken unto persons who have forsaken God. They serve witches and sorcerers, coming when invoked and carrying out requests. The witch called upon the familiar spirit, and the demon assumed the form of the prophet. If it is *no marvel* that *Satan himself is transformed into an angel of light*[19] (as the Apostle writes), then Satan's minions can certainly appear in the form of God's servants. We know that Antichrist will pretend to be Christ Himself. The woman with a familiar spirit did not bring up Samuel; rather, the devil appeared in the form of Samuel to Saul, who had fallen away from God. This is clear from the text of the Scripture in which the demon that appeared as Samuel tells Saul, *Tomorrow thou shalt be with me.* How could Saul, God's enemy, be with Samuel? Saul's place was with the devil, whom he served

---

[18]Kings, Ch. 28   [19]II Cor., Ch. 11

after rejecting God. Thus, let the deceitful Jews know that it is impossible by means of the black art truly to return someone from the dead. Neither was Samuel brought back by means of sorcery, nor did Christ arise by it. Our Lord destroyed the strength of death by His divine might. He willingly suffered and died, and as God willingly rose from the dead by His own power. Tell the unbelievers this: 'Although we sacrificed to idols, we are still better than you. We were coerced; you act willingly.' Do not despair, brethren. It is a terrible offense to sacrifice to idols; but repent sincerely and again cleave to Christ with your whole heart. Our God is merciful and receives all who repent. He will gladly accept you, for you are his children." Hearing this, the fallen Christians bitterly lamented their sin and returned to Christ God.

Shortly afterwards, Polemonus and another magistrate, Theophilus, came to the prison with soldiers and a crowd of unbelievers. The saints were brought out and informed, "Your bishop Eutychianus has worshipped our deities and offered them oblations. You should do the same. Otherwise, you will be tried by Lepidonus the priest and Euchtymonus in the temple of the gods."

Pionius responded, "Bishop Eutychianus will answer for himself. If he sacrificed to idols, what is that to us? We have no intention of following his example. Neither you, nor Lepidonus, nor Euchtymonus have any right to judge us: only the Proconsul can do so. You must await his arrival; otherwise, you will be guilty of usurping authority."

After heaping reproach on the saints, the pagans departed. Later the magistrates returned with troops and a mob and falsely announced, "The Proconsul has sent word that you are to be taken to Ephesus and tried."

"So let his messenger come and take us there," said Pionius.

"Why do you doubt me?" Theophilus asked. "I am a prince; my words can be trusted."

The soldiers slipped a noose around Pionius' neck and hauled him and the others away to the heathen temple. "We are Christians," protested the martyrs, "what have we to do with idols!" The soldiers paid them no heed and continued dragging them to their destination, almost strangling Pionius. When they reached the middle of the marketplace, not far from the temple,

Saint Pionius dropped to the ground and, repeating that he was a Christian, insisted that he would not be taken to the pagan sanctuary. Six servants hit and kicked him and thrust their knees into his ribs, but he refused to go any further; whereupon, they picked him up and carried him to the vile altar. Before it stood the piteous Bishop Eutychianus, offering oblations to idols. Lepidonus asked, "Why do you refuse to sacrifice to the gods, Pionius?"

"Because we are Christians," all the saints answered.

"Whom do you revere as God?" asked Lepidonus.

Pionius replied, "We revere Him *Who hath made heaven and the earth, the sea and all that is therein.*"[20]

"And Who is the Crucified One?" Lepidonus asked.

"He Whom God the Father sent to save the world," replied Pionius. The princes burst into laughter at this reply, and Lepidonus railed against the blessed one. Then the soldiers crowned the saints with the garlands worn by idolaters when they sacrificed, and attempted to force them to taste the contemptible offerings. The martyrs tore the wreaths from their heads, threw them to the floor, trampled them, and spat on the defiled meat. Outraged, the godless dragged the saints back to prison, reviling and pummeling them the whole way. As Pionius was entering the dungeon, one of the soldiers laid an especially powerful blow on him. Straightway, searing pain shot through the brute's every member, especially his arms. Scabs appeared on his flesh, his whole body swelled up, and his breathing became labored.

By and by the Proconsul Quintilianus visited Smyrna. Mounting his tribunal, he ordered that Pionius alone be brought to him for questioning. Interrogation made it clear that the martyr would not submit; therefore, Quintilianus commanded that Pionius be stripped naked and his flesh ripped with iron claws. While the saint was being tortured, the heathen asked him, "Why do you so wish to die?"

"I do not so much wish to die as to inherit eternal life," answered the martyr.

Following this, the saint was condemned to death. In accor-

---

[20]Ps. 145

dance with Roman custom, a herald announced the sentence: "Pionius, who has admitted he is a Christian, is to be crucified and burned alive." The martyr was taken to the place of execution, where he removed his own robes. Looking at his body, he rejoiced at his physical purity, then gazed into heaven and thanked God for helping him to remain chaste throughout his life. He was nailed to a cross-shaped tree lying on the ground, after which the heathen said, "Pionius, submit to the imperial decree and we shall remove the nails. Physicians can still heal you."

A brief silence followed; then the saint answered, "I want to fall asleep and arise to a better life in the Common Resurrection."

Pionius' crucifiers raised the tree and firmly planted it in the ground. Around it they heaped firewood. When they lit the pyre, roaring flames surrounded the martyr, who closed his eyes and silently prayed. God prolonged his life, but the onlookers, seeing his eyes shut, thought he had expired. Pionius continued praying for a long time in the secret chambers of his heart. Eventually the flames died down and he opened his eyes. Seeing this, everyone was astonished. The saint's face was radiant as he said a final prayer. After the "Amen," he added, "O Lord, receive my spirit," then reposed. His body was completely unharmed by the fire, and not even a hair of his head was singed. Saint Pionius' countenance remained luminous, shining with divine grace: a plain token that his blessed soul had inherited the joy of heaven and received the crown of victory from Christ's right hand.

The holy martyr Pionius reposed in Smyrna during the reign of Decius, while Quintilianus was proconsul, on the fifth day of the ides of March according to the Roman calendar. According to the Asiatic reckoning, his death occurred on the eleventh day of the seventh month (counting from September), a Saturday, at the tenth hour.

Here ends Symeon Metaphrastes' account of the passion of Saint Pionius. How the other prisoners died is not explained, but doubtless they endured additional sufferings for Christ and inherited eternal life with Saint Pionius.

The blessed presbyter Pionius wrote the Life and Passion of

the holy hieromartyr Polycarp, Bishop of Smyrna.[21] Like Saint Polycarp, he was deemed worthy of the Kingdom of our Lord Jesus Christ, Who with the Father and the Holy Spirit reigns forever. Amen.

❧❧❧

In the twenty-eighth chapter of the First Book of Kings it is written that the prophet Samuel told Saul, *Tomorrow thou and thy sons with thee shall fall*; but another version has the prophet say, *Tomorrow shalt thou and thy sons be with me.* In his Life of Saint Pionius, Symeon Metaphrastes quotes the passage thus: *Tomorrow thou shalt be with me. The Great Collection of Readings* follows Metaphrastes' variant. It was Saint Pionius' opinion that the devil appeared in the form of Samuel and laid claim to Saul's soul after the King died. Others believe that Samuel's soul (without his body) truly appeared to Saul by the command of God, before the witch could utter incantations. They find support for their view in the forty-sixth chapter of the book of Jesus, son of Sirach,[22] which says that *after his death* Samuel *prophesied, and showed the King his end, and lifted up his voice from the earth in prophecy.*

❧❧❧

On this same day we commemorate the translation of the relics of the holy martyr Epimachus to Constantinople. The saint's Life may be found under October 31.

On this same day we commemorate our father among the saints Euthymius, Bishop of Great Novgorod, whose Life is in *The Prologue.*

---

[21]According to the Life of Saint Polycarp, Pionius was not actually the author, but corrected the epistle of the Church of Smyrna relating the holy Bishop's passion. (Tr.)

[22]The book of Ecclesiasticus (Tr.)

The Twelfth Day of the Month of March

The Life of Our Venerable Father Theophanes, Abbot of the Monastery of Megas Agros on Mount Sigriane[1]

The venerable Theophanes was born in the Imperial City to noble parents, Isaac and Theodotia. Isaac was called "the Isaurian" because he came from Isauria and was related to the Emperor Leo the Isaurian. During the reign of Leo's son Constantine Copronymus, Isaac held high office in the palace and served as a military commander.

At that time the heresy of iconoclasm was raging and the pious were being fiercely persecuted. Isaac and his wife were devout adherents of Orthodoxy, but out of fear kept their beliefs secret. It came to pass that Theodotia bore a son, the future beacon of the Church of Christ, and the parents named him Theophanes, which means "revealed by God." The child was called thus because he was born on the feast of Holy Theophany. Such a name betokened that the Lord had chosen and sanctified him, like the Prophet Jeremiah, while he was still in his mother's womb. According to Anastasius the Librarian, the parents also called the mighty luminary of Christ's Church Isaac, but after his tonsure, Theophanes no longer used that name.

This is how the saint, who had loved the angelic life since

---

childhood, came to be a monk: Three years after the birth of his blessed child, Isaac inherited life eternal. On his deathbed he wrote a will entrusting his wife and divinely revealed son to the care of his kinsman, the Emperor Constantine Copronymus. The child *increased in wisdom and stature*,[2] immersed himself in the divine Scriptures, and was instructed in proper conduct. Since he became a handsome youth and was intelligent, very wealthy, and related to the Emperor, a match with him was regarded as extremely desirable. When Theophanes was only twelve years old, a senator approached Theodotia, offering to betroth his ten-year old daughter to him. Theodotia was agreeable, but nothing could be done without the Emperor's consent; therefore, the senator petitioned Copronymus to allow the marriage. With the ruler's permission, the children were betrothed, but the wedding was deferred until bride and groom reached the canonical age.

When Copronymus died, his son Leo IV became emperor. Leo was called "the Khazar" because his mother was the daughter of the Khan of the Khazars. Her pagan name was Khazara, but in Baptism she was called Irene. Several years after Copronymus' death, but prior to Theophanes' wedding, Theodotia reposed, leaving the saint immense wealth. Now in Theophanes' house there lived a chaste and God-fearing slave. Theophanes had the deepest affection for this virtuous man and regarded him more as an advisor than a servant. As a result of their edifying conversations and, still more, the all-powerful operation of the Holy Spirit, Theophanes came to love purity. Hoping to preserve his virginity and burning with desire for tonsure and monastic life, he began distributing his possessions to the needy.

This did not escape the notice of Theophanes' father-in-law, who advanced the date of the nuptials, contrary to the young man's wishes. On the appointed day the Crowning was celebrated and a banquet held, but the divinely revealed youth Theophanes cleaved in his thoughts to God and silently prayed that the Lord send down His grace and assist him in keeping his virginity. When they were in the wedding chamber alone, the

---

[2]Luke, Ch. 2

young man sat on the bed, sighed deeply, and revealed his secret thoughts to his bride. "Beloved," he said, "this life is brief and the hour of our death uncertain. A harsh judgment awaits those who waste time enjoying pleasures and wealth, always angering God. Although matrimony was instituted by the Lord Himself, worldly cares distance the mind from God, undermining devout thoughts and dimming spiritual vision so that one cannot behold the celestial realm. Lazarus endured temporal sufferings and *was carried by the angels into Abraham's bosom.*[3] But the rich man lived sumptuously and was cast down to the pit of hell, where he could not find a drop of water to cool his tongue amid the flames. To whom do the Gospels promise blessedness? Not to the rich, who enjoy all the blessings of this life, but to the poor, those that mourn, those that hunger and thirst, and those that endure persecution and revilement for Christ's sake. In a word, *strait is the gate, and narrow is the way, which leadeth unto life,* but *wide is the gate, and broad is the way, that leadeth to destruction.*[4] There is no escaping it: he who wallows in luxury and vain pleasures in this life must endure tribulation and anguish in the next. Beloved bride, if you wish, we shall not consummate our marriage, but keep our virginity. Your father is a stern man, so let us remain together for a time and pretend to share a bed as man and wife, while secretly living as brother and sister. Later, when the Lord wills, we shall each retire to a monastery and devote the remainder of our days to Him, so that in the world to come we may inherit a portion with the saints."

Theophanes' edifying words fell like seed on the rich loam of his holy bride's heart and immediately took root. She joyously responded, "Beloved master, I know well the words of our Saviour recorded in the Gospel: '*If any man hate not his father, and mother, and wife, and children, and brethren, and sisters,*[5] and houses, and fields, *and take not his cross, and follow after Me,* he *is not worthy of Me.*'[6] Let us make ourselves worthy of Christ. Let us renounce all vanities, if you are willing. If you are, so am I; if you agree to remain a virgin, I agree also. We shall present ourselves to the Heavenly Bridegroom as unblemished offerings, chaste in

---

[3]Luke, Ch. 16   [4]Matt., Ch. 17
[5]Luke, Ch. 14   [6]Matt., Ch. 10

soul and body. Why waste this life in worthless pursuits, only to be deprived of eternity's blessings? If we have children, we shall add to our burden, for we must provide for them and concern ourselves day and night with their upbringing, thus falling into many worldly snares. When the hour of death unexpectedly overtakes us, what shall be our destination? We do not know. Therefore, let us secretly preserve our virginity until the Lord deems us worthy of the monastic habit."

The blessed youth Theophanes was amazed at the prudence of his chaste bride. Falling prostrate, he thanked God, Who by His Holy Spirit had guided the maiden to complete accord with his own desire. The couple spent the whole night beseeching Heaven's assistance in completing the course. At daybreak they fell asleep briefly, and both had the same dream of a young man whose face shone brilliantly. The youth smiled at them and said in a kind voice, "The Lord has accepted your intention and sent me to bless you to lead the life upon which you have agreed. May your virginity still be intact when you enter His presence." With this, he traced the Cross over their bodies and disappeared. A moment later Theophanes and his bride awoke and told each other of their dreams. Astonished that they could still smell the angel's ineffable fragrance, the couple fell prostrate before God, offering heartfelt praise. The celestial fragrance lingered for a long time, not just in the room, but throughout the house.

Living together as angels in the flesh, the heavenly couple like two candles burned before God with the flame of divine love. They were like fruitful olive trees producing the oil of compassion, for every day they distributed abundant alms, thereby considerably reducing their wealth.

Eventually Theophanes' father-in-law learned that his daughter and her husband had kept their virginity and were giving away their money to the poor. Greatly distraught, he lamented to the Emperor, "Woe is me, born under an evil star! Bitter is my old age, for my worthless son-in-law is squandering his fortune and bringing my young daughter to ruin. He refuses to share her bed and has robbed me of the consolation of grandchildren. Why did he marry her? Why did he not break the vows of betrothal before the wedding was performed? He should have rejected her, rather than entrap her at such a tender age and bring me to despair in my last years. Twofold is my complaint against him, because my daughter, though married, has no husband and cannot become a mother; and because Theophanes has wasted the greater portion of her dowry." The old man persuaded the Emperor to command that his son-in-law live according to the law of marriage and stop misspending his wealth, and before long the blessed Theophanes was summoned to court. The tyrant threatened to blind and exile him if he failed to alter his way of life, but such intimidation could not frighten the God-fearing youth, who was steadfast in his intent and preferred the favor of the King of heaven to the good graces of a temporal ruler.

Shortly afterwards, the Emperor sent Theophanes to attend to government affairs in Cyzicus and the surrounding region. He did this at the behest of the saint's father-in-law, who had been made trustee of Theophanes' fortune and wanted the blessed one gone in order to prevent him from giving away more money. At the same time, the father-in-law hoped that responsibilities would occupy so much of the saint's time that he would discontinue his prayers and fasting. Unable to endure the thought of his daughter being separated from her husband even briefly, he also persuaded the Emperor to order her to accompany Theophanes to Cyzicus. During their travels, the devout couple had to cross the river which separates Olympus from Sigriane. Once called Rhyndakos, it later came to be known by the local peasants simply as "The Great River." It could be forded at the point the road to Cyzicus reached it; however, a physical infirmity prevented the blessed one from entering the water, and he crossed in a ferry. This happened in accordance with providence. Theophanes sent ahead his friends and most of the slaves with the horses and wagons; then he drifted down the river with his wife and a few servants, admiring the beautiful mountains of Sigriane. Soon they reached a place where a broad valley was visible, nestled between the peaks. The whole area was thickly forested and greatly pleased the saint who, eager to lead a life of stillness there, ordered the boat moored. While the others waited, he explored the valley. Smitten with compunction, Theophanes stopped in the middle of the forest, lifted his hands to heaven, and prayed fervently. Then he made numerous prostrations, watered the earth with tears, and entreated God, *Cause me to know, O Lord, the way wherein I should walk.*[7]

Aflame with longing for life in the wilderness, the blessed one yearned to forsake the world and remain there. He prayed until exhausted, and when he sat down, went into ecstasy and saw the same radiant angel who had appeared in the wedding chamber. The angel assured Theophanes, "You will have this place as your dwelling, but you must be patient. Soon those who obstruct your path will be removed from the land of the living, and you will be free to go wherever you desire."

Cheered by the vision, Saint Theophanes returned to the boat and resumed his journey. In the mountains of Sigriane there were monasteries and the huts of anchorites, which he visited with his chaste wife. One of the cells at a place called Polychronion was the abode of a clairvoyant elder named Gregory Strategios. Theophanes revealed his yearnings to the elder, who confirmed what the angel had revealed. The old man, gifted by God with foreknowledge because of his angelic life, explained, "Noble youth, neither the Emperor nor your father-in-law are long for this earth. After they die, you will be free to carry out your good intention." Then the elder whispered into the ear of Theophanes' virtuous spouse, saying that her beloved brother and lord would in time receive the crown of martyrdom.

Upon arrival at Cyzicus, Theophanes occupied himself with the duties assigned him by the Emperor. Whenever he had the opportunity, he and his servants would visit the holy fathers living in the nearby mountains of Sigriane, receive their blessing, request their prayers, and hearken unto their divinely inspired, edifying discourses. Theophanes visited most frequently the clairvoyant elder Gregory Strategios and Christopher, abbot of the Monastery of Mikros Agros.

Once during harvest time, the saint was going from one hermit's cell to another, deep in the mountains of Sigriane. He, his companions, and their donkeys were tormented by thirst

---

[7]Ps., 142

under the blazing sun, but no water was to be found. Exhausted, the men decided they must stop for the night. The blessed one prayed, and then sat down at the foot of a hill, hoping to fall asleep and forget his thirst. No sooner than he had drowsed off than a spring burst out of the ground beneath his head, drenching him. The Lord, Who caused water to pour from a rock for the thankless Hebrews, had hearkened unto His ever-grateful servant in time of need. Awakened by the surging stream, Theophanes rose and called the others. All were amazed by the timely miracle and glorified God. Men and beasts drank their fill, after which they bedded down. The next morning the spring had disappeared and the ground was completely dry. This astonished the men even more than had the first miracle and they praised the wondrous power of God, Who called forth a spring out of parched earth, and made it vanish when need for it had passed. By this the Lord showed that, *in every place of His dominion,*[8] He provides for those who *seek first the Kingdom of God, and His righteousness.*[9]

After accomplishing the tasks entrusted him by the Emperor, Saint Theophanes left Cyzicus and returned to the Imperial City. At that time the prophecy of the venerable Gregory was fulfilled: Emperor Leo the Khazar, son of Copronymus and grandson of Leo the Isaurian, died, as did Theophanes' father-in-law. This allowed the saint and his holy spouse to resume their almsgiving. A short time passed and Theophanes had his wife tonsured with the name of Irene in one of the convents of Bithynia. The blessed couple richly endowed that community. As a nun, Irene greatly pleased God, Who granted her power to heal every illness and expel demons from the possessed. The Most Holy Methodius, Patriarch of Constantinople and author of her Life (and a Life of Saint Theophanes), recorded a number of her miracles.

Following the tonsure of the blessed maiden Irene, Saint Theophanes gave to the poor most of what money remained to him, and then was clothed in the schema at the hands of his spiritual father Gregory Strategios. With the small quantity of gold he kept, Theophanes built a monastery at Polychronion on

---

[8]Ps. 102   [9]Matt., Ch. 6

Mount Sigriane. The blessed one struggled in asceticism there until his elder advised him to take up his dwelling on Kalonymos. There was a small farm on that island which Theophanes had inherited from his parents but had not been sold to benefit the poor. A monastery was built on the property and, at Theophanes' invitation, it was populated by brethren from the community of Saint Theodore at Monocherarius. Theophanes appointed a virtuous, experienced abbot for them and lived in the community as a recluse, copying books. The saint was a skilled calligrapher and provided for himself and others with his earnings.

A space of several years elapsed, the abbot passed away, and the brethren entreated the venerable Theophanes to become the superior. Their pleas drove him back to Mount Sigriane, and he settled at the place in the forest where he had seen the angel. His God-pleasing life drew many solitaries there. The wilderness became a city, and it was evident that God willed a monastery be erected. A portion of the valley was called Megas Agros[10]and belonged to a farmer. With money borrowed from friends, Theophanes bought the parcel and built a monastery on it. God, Who by His providence supplies all our needs, enabled the saint to pay off his debts and furnished everything required by the new brotherhood. All the desert-dwellers insisted that Theophanes became abbot, and this time he could not refuse. As hegumen, Theophanes was guided by Christ's words recorded in the Gospel: *Whosoever will be great among you, let him be your minister; and whosoever will be chief among you, let him be your servant.*[11] The venerable one did not shun toil, but served the brethren with his own hands. God had given him considerable physical strength, and he performed every monastic obedience. No one could rival him for manual labor, and his virtue and industry provided an example for all.

In those days, while Constantine, son of Leo and grandson of Copronymus, was emperor, the devout Empress-mother and regent Irene and the Patriarch of the Imperial City, the Most Holy Tarasius, convened the Seventh Ecumenical Synod at Nicaea. The council anathematized the heresy of iconoclasm

---

[10]Megas Agros means "Great Field." (Tr.)
[11]Matt., Ch. 20

and decreed the sacred icons worthy of veneration. The godly Theophanes shone like a brilliant star among the holy fathers at the synod and affirmed the doctrines of Orthodoxy. Everyone was amazed to see the formerly wealthy, illustrious nobleman— whom they remembered clad in sumptuous robes and parading in a chariot or on a stallion—now wearing an old, tattered, and patched habit and riding a broken-down donkey. Those who had known him personally as a friend and advisor of the Emperor were especially moved and edified by his lowliness and poverty. From Theophanes' example they learned that it is possible for the most exalted to humble themselves, embrace privation, and regard the whole world as of no account.

After the holy council had confirmed the dogmas of the true faith, the saint returned to his monastery and announced to the fathers the great victory of Orthodoxy. Then he resumed his ascetical feats, illumining not only the brotherhood, but the whole surrounding region. The fame of his virtue spread every-where, and all who heard about him glorified the Heavenly Father. Because of his pure life, Theophanes received from God grace to work miracles, and he began to heal diseases and to expel devils from the possessed by a mere word. His wonder-working commenced following a demonic attack on him one night while he was asleep. Assuming the form of a wild boar, the fiend almost gnawed through Saint Theophanes' thumb. Woken by the pain, the venerable one anointed the teeth marks with myrrh taken from the life-giving Wood of the Cross. Straightway the throbbing ceased and the wound healed.

Saint Theophanes generously provided bread and other food to the many pilgrims and paupers who came to the mon-astery, yet the brethren never suffered lack. In this he was like Elijah, who ensured that the widow's barrel of meal remained full. Once, the cellarer murmured against the saint for giving food to visitors when the monastery's supplies were low. The Lord's favorite sent him to the storeroom with orders to count and weigh the provisions. When he found the pantry fully stocked, the complainer fell to his knees begging forgiveness, and the brethren glorified God.

At the age of fifty, the venerable one developed stones and spent the remainder of his life in bed, suffering terribly.

Although he had cured others, he would not ask the Lord to cure this affliction, but endured it thankfully. During his illness the man of God underwent the tribulations foretold by the clairvoyant elder Gregory, who long before had whispered into the ear of Theophanes' holy spouse, saying that her brother would receive the crown of martyrdom.

After the previously mentioned Constantine and his mother Irene, Nicephorus and his son Stauracius ruled the Greek Empire, then Michael Curopalates.[12] Next the scepter fell to Leo the Armenian, by which time the godly Theophanes was an old man. Leo revived the iconoclast heresy and disturbed the peace of Christ's Church. He drove the holy Orthodox Patriarch Nicephorus from his see and Saint Theodore and his disciples from the Monastery of the Studium. Many were the Christians whom he tortured and put to death for venerating icons. George Kedrinus relates in *The Synopsis* that the ship carrying into exile Nicephorus, Patriarch of Constantinople, sailed along the shore near Theophanes' monastery. With clairvoyant inner eyes the venerable one saw this and commanded a disciple to bring him a burning coal in a censer, on which he placed incense. Then, having lit candles, he prostrated himself and spoke as if to someone passing by. The disciple asked, "Father, with whom are you talking? Why are you lying on the floor?"

The godly one answered, "Lo, the Most Holy Patriarch Nicephorus is sailing by on his way into exile for Orthodoxy. I am burning the candles and incense to honor him."

As he sailed by, Patriarch Nicephorus perceived what Theophanes was doing. He suddenly fell to his knees, returning the elder's prostration, after which he lifted his hands and blessed our father. One of his fellow-exiles asked, "Whom are you blessing, Most Holy Father? To whom are you bending the knee?"

"Theophanes the Confessor, abbot of Megas Agros, is saluting us with incense and candles. I am returning the greeting,"

---

[12]Michael Rangabe, who held the rank of curopalates under Emperor Nicephorus, his father-in-law. The title of curopalates was at this time conferred primarily on members of the imperial family and foreign princes. (Tr.)

explained the Patriarch. "Soon he will share our tribulation." Shortly afterwards Saint Nicephorus' words came to pass.

Before too long the Emperor Leo the Armenian decided to lure the godly Theophanes into agreement with his heretical beliefs. He sent messengers to the saint, begging him to come to the Imperial City. In his letter to Theophanes, the deceiver wrote, "I plan to make war on the infidels; however, I must first arm myself with your holy prayers. I entreat you, honored Father: do not refuse my request, but come to me."

Although he knew the Emperor's wickedness and was gravely ill, Theophanes obeyed the summons, because he wanted to suffer for the true faith. The Lord's favorite sailed to Constantinople, but was not permitted to see the Emperor, who was ashamed to confront such a holy man and feared his rebukes. Instead, Leo sent nobles to entice Theophanes into heresy by means of various promises. "If you agree to our beliefs, I will reconstruct your monastery with lofty stone buildings," he offered through his courtiers. "I will enrich it and hold you in higher esteem than any other. All your close relatives will be advanced to exalted rank." To the promises, however, the ruler added the threat: "If you oppose us, you will be responsible for your own downfall."

Through the noblemen, the saint answered thus: "I have no need for the riches of this world. As a young man I renounced gold, silver, and numerous possessions out of love for Christ. I do not long for these now that I am old. God, Who is greater than the kings and princes of this world, will provide for my monastery and relations. Why, O Emperor, do you attempt to frighten me, as you would frighten a young boy with a rod? Prepare the tortures, light the fire! Even though, as you see, I cannot walk unassisted, I am ready to cast myself into the flames for Orthodoxy."

The nobles returned to the Emperor and reported the bold reply. Astonished at the elder's courage, Leo sent John the Sophist, a glib and sly man, a heretic and sorcerer, to debate the venerable one. Our father's divinely inspired discourse silenced the warlock and sent him running back in shame to the Emperor. Thereafter the enraged tyrant imprisoned the godly Theophanes in a small, dark cell of the dungeon in the Palace of Eleutherius.

The sick elder remained there under guard for two years. Every day heretics were sent by the Emperor to flatter or threaten the saint. When pleas failed to incline Theophanes to iconoclasm, the oppressor's lackeys mocked and insulted him.

One day Leo sent a message expressing the highest regard for the venerable one and begging him to sign a document rejecting the icons. The saint answered with this letter:

"Submit, O Emperor, to Him Who gave you the throne. Only by His permission do kings rule and tyrants exercise authority upon the earth. Know that God, being uncircumscribable, deigned to be circumscribed. He assumed our nature, becoming like us in everything except sin. In this nature, divinized in Himself, He raised the dead, gave sight to the blind, cleansed lepers, and performed many other miracles. In this nature He voluntarily submitted to death at the hands of the malicious Jews, rose on the third day, and ascended in glory to heaven, where He remains, inseparable from the Father. We devoutly accept everything that the Gospel teaches about Christ God's human nature and his wondrous deeds in the flesh; therefore, having complete faith in this book, we reverence it and through it, Christ Himself. If we are not condemned for accepting and revering the works of Christ recorded in the words of the Gospel, then how can we be condemned for accepting and revering the Gospel history depicted on icons? Thanks to the icons, even barbarians learn about the life of Christ on earth among men and His marvelous deeds, and they convert to our faith. How many illiterates, gazing upon the miracles of Christ and His voluntary Passion depicted on icons, glorify the Lord Who suffered for them! Doing away with the icons, you would deny them salvation. What council ever condemned the veneration of holy icons as sinful and blasphemous? Christ Himself imprinted the image of His face on the Holy Napkin which He sent to heal Abgar, Prince of Edessa. The holy Apostle Luke painted an icon of the immaculate Virgin Theotokos. There is nothing in the practice of icon-veneration contrary to the tradition and doctrine of the Holy Fathers. The great Basil, initiate of mysteries transcending description, teaches that the honor shown an icon passes on to its prototype. And John Chrysostom acknowledges, 'I love the holy icon depicted in encaustic.' Likewise Cyril, the harp of the Holy Spirit, admits, 'As often as I pass by the icon of Christ's Passion, I am moved to tears.' Not one of the first six ecumenical synods forbade or denounced the veneration of holy icons or their use in honoring the persons and events depicted on them. Do you consider yourself wiser than the fathers of the ecumenical councils? It is your responsibility, O Emperor, to wage war against barbarians. To define ecclesiastical dogmas and enact canons is the task of the holy fathers, not of rulers."

Infuriated by this letter, the persecutor immediately dispatched a brutal officer to Megas Agros in Sigriane with orders to reduce Theophanes' monastery to ashes, beat the saint's disciples mercilessly, and disperse them. The Emperor sent a second officer, as cruel as the first, to the Palace of Eleutherius, where the godly one had been imprisoned for two years. This man removed the holy elder from his dark cell; tore the garments from his body, much wasted by fasting and prolonged illness; and laid three hundred lashes on the saint's back and belly. Leo commanded him to return to the prison the next morning, and the officer flogged Theophanes as mercilessly as he had the day before. Following this, Saint Theophanes was exiled to Samothrace. Several days beforehand, the man of God foresaw with clairvoyant inner eyes his banishment to the island and told the novice that served him to make preparations.

Theophanes' stay on Samothrace lasted only twenty-three days. The elder departed to the heavenly homeland wearing a confessor's crown, and God glorified him in death as during his lifetime, bestowing a healing virtue on his relics. The saint's honored remains were placed in a wooden coffin, which the ill had merely to touch in order to be cured.

After the godless Emperor Leo the Armenian was slain, the venerable one's disciples returned to Mount Sigriane and rebuilt their monastery. The sacred relics of their father Theophanes were brought from Samothrace to Megas Agros and enshrined in the church, where they worked innumerable miracles, unto the glory of Christ our God, Who is praised forever with the Father and the Holy Spirit. Amen.

On the Same Day

The Life of Our Father Among the Saints Gregory the Dialogist, Pope of Rome

Saint Gregory, Pope of Rome, called "the Dialogist" because he wrote the beautiful book *The Dialogues*, was born in the old capital. His father, Gordian, and his mother, the blessed Sylvia, belonged to wealthy, esteemed senatorial families of the first rank. Yet although Gregory came from patrician stock, his family's chief claim to nobility lay in the number of his relatives who led a God-pleasing life. Saint Felix III, Pope of Rome, was Gregory's grandfather. Saint Tarsilla, who on her deathbed saw the Lord Jesus Christ coming to her, and the blessed Aemeliana, who inherited eternal life with Tarsilla, were Gregory's aunts. Sylvia, Gregory's mother, is also honored as a saint by the Church of Rome. The most splendid adornment of this holy family, however, was the blessed Gregory himself, who from childhood pleased God and excelled in virtue. Gregory was a studious youth and at an early age won fame as a master of philosophy and rhetoric. On account of his intelligence and wisdom, he was appointed *praetor urbis*,[1] but his true aspirations were spiritual, not secular. Wishing to become a monk, he kept his virginity and led an ascetic life while still a layman. After his father reposed, Gregory renounced the world.

From his father Gregory inherited a fortune which he used for charitable purposes, especially the building of monasteries. In Sicily he erected and endowed six monasteries. In Rome he founded the Monastery of the Holy Apostle Andrew, which was at first quartered in his ancestral mansion near the Church of the Holy Martyrs John and Paul on Mount Scauri. It was there that Gregory laid aside his golden robes, put on a hair shirt, and was tonsured, submitting to the spiritual direction of the experienced elders Hilarion and Maximian. Later, the saint became abbot of this monastery.

---

[1]The highest judiciary official of the city of Rome (Tr.)

At that time Gregory's widowed mother Sylvia was living near the Gates of the Holy Apostle Paul. She served the Lord by prayer and fasting and attended services in God's house day and night. Her food was raw vegetables, a portion of which she sent daily to her son, the blessed Gregory. She gave everything she owned to paupers and other poor folk. Following her example, Saint Gregory was also very generous to those in need. Once he was in his cell writing a book, and an angel appeared to him in the form of a pauper, saying, "Have mercy on me, servant of the Most High God! I was captain of a merchantman, but my ship sunk with a cargo belonging to me and others."

The true servant of Christ and lover of the needy took pity on the suppliant, called for the brother that served him, and ordered him to give the petitioner six gold pieces. The beggar took the money and left.

A few hours later the captain returned, saying, "Forgive me, servant of God, but I lost so much and you gave me so little."

Again the blessed one called the monk who served him and commanded, "Brother, give this man another six pieces of gold."

A little later the poor man was back, pleading, "Have compassion, Father; give me more! I lost so much merchandise and am deeply in debt to the owners."

The blessed Gregory instructed his servant, "Brother, get six more gold coins for the man."

"Trust me, Father; there is nothing left in the safe," answered the brother.

"Is there nothing at all we can give him: no robe, or vessel of some sort?" asked Gregory.

"Only the silver dish on which our lady your mother sends you vegetables," the monk replied.

"Give the man the dish, so that he will have some consolation in his misery," said God's favorite. "I do not want to disappoint him." The beggar happily took the plate and went his way. He never returned, except as the angel that invisibly guarded and helped Gregory in everything. With His angel the Lord sent down the marvelous power of His grace, enabling Gregory to work amazing miracles.

After the death of Pope Pelagius, the holy superior of the

Monastery of Saint Andrew was elected Bishop of Rome. Fleeing this high office and the adulation of men, Gregory hid in the wilderness. All efforts to find the saint came to nought, and the downcast citizens fervently prayed that God would reveal His servant. Suddenly a pillar of fire, visible at a great distance, descended from heaven and stood over the mountain on which Gregory had taken refuge. Everyone understood the meaning of this and rushed there. Indescribable was the joy of the people, who took the saint back to the city against his will. Maurice was emperor when Gregory became Bishop of old Rome.

As pope, Saint Gregory provided for the needs of countless widows, orphans, and other poor folk. He built numerous hostels and almshouses in Rome and distant cities. He sent Abba Probus to Jerusalem with a substantial quantity of gold and instructions to erect a guesthouse for pilgrims. The monks of Mount Sinai were largely supported by his yearly donation. At his command the names of all the needy and ill people of Rome were recorded, and these unfortunates became eligible for a daily food ration. Often he invited pilgrims and the poor to his own table and served them himself. One day he ordered his treasurer to invite twelve paupers to have supper with him. When he came to the table, the holy Pope saw thirteen men seated. "I told you to invite twelve," he whispered to the bursar.

Unable to see the thirteenth man, the treasurer protested, "There are twelve, Most Reverend Master!"

While eating, Pope Gregory kept glancing at the beggar sitting at the opposite end of the table. The appearance of the man changed every time the saint looked at him: now his hair was gray and he seemed old, now he had the face of a youth. At the end of the meal, the Pope dismissed them all, except the one whose appearance changed. He led the man by the hand to his cell and said to him, "I enjoin you by the infinite power of Almighty God to reveal who you are and what is your name."

"Wondrous is my name; why do you ask it? Do you remember the destitute sea-captain who came begging at the Monastery of Saint Andrew while you were writing in your cell? You gave him twelve coins and the silver dish on which your mother Sylvia sent you vegetables. That man was me. On the day when you showed me such generosity and heartfelt love, the Lord chose you to become archpastor of His Holy Church, for which His blood was shed; He made you the successor of the holy chief Apostle Peter, whose virtuous life you emulate," said the wondrous stranger.

"How do you know that the Lord chose me to become pope that day?" asked Gregory.

"Because I am an angel of the Lord Almighty," replied the stranger. "God sent me to determine whether you gave alms out of compassion or out of vainglory."

Hearing this, the blessed one was terrified. In so far as he knew, he had never before conversed with an angel, and was discomfited at the thought that he had spoken to the celestial messenger as though he were a mortal. Then the angel said, "Do not be afraid. The Lord has appointed me to remain with you the rest of your life and present to Him your petitions, so that you may receive everything you request."

Falling to his knees, Saint Gregory worshipped the Lord and cried, "If Almighty God made me pope of His Holy Church and appointed an angel to protect me, merely because I gave a little charity to a beggar, what shall be the reward of those who do *not weary in well-doing*[2] and the keeping of His commandments!" At this the angel disappeared. The saint offered fervent thanks to the Lord and became even more ardent in striving to please God and help others.

Some time later Pope Gregory held another dinner for the poor. At these meals, he always poured water on the hands of the guests, out of humility. On this occasion, when he turned around to pick up the jug to wash the hands of one of the beggars, the man vanished. Since the beggar could not be found, Gregory was quite puzzled. The following night the Lord appeared to Saint Gregory in a dream and informed him, "On previous occasions you nourished My members, the poor; yesterday you fed Me."

In *The Spiritual Meadow*, the Most Holy Patriarch Sophronius of Jerusalem testifies to the profound humility of Saint Gregory. He writes:

---

[2]Gal., Ch. 9; II Thes., Ch. 3

"At that time we visited Abba John the Persian, who related this about the blessed Gregory the Great, Pope of Rome: 'Because I wanted to venerate the graves of the holy chief apostles Peter and Paul, I went to Rome. While standing in the middle of the city, I heard people say that the Pope would be coming by. I waited to see him and had it in mind to prostrate myself before him. God is my witness, brethren, that before I could carry out my intention, he prostrated himself before me. When I fell to the ground also, he would not rise until I did so first. Having embraced me warmly, he pressed three gold coins into my hand and ordered that I be provided my meals as long as I was in Rome. For this I glorified God, Who had instilled in the saint such humility, compassion, and love for all.'"

We must not remain silent about the fearful transformation of the immaculate Mysteries of Christ accomplished by the prayers of God's great hierarch. One day, before the Most Holy Pope served the Divine Liturgy, a Roman noblewoman brought to the altar prosphora she had baked. When the time came for the laity to commune, the woman approached the Holy Mysteries. Hearing Gregory's words, "The life-giving Body of our Lord Jesus Christ," she laughed. The Pope withdrew his hand and asked, "Why are you laughing?"

"Master, it is ridiculous that bread I kneaded and baked you call the Body of Christ," said the woman.

On account of her unbelief, the saint prayed and immediately the appearance of the Eucharist changed, so that it no longer had the form of bread, but of bloody human flesh. Seeing this, the woman and the entire congregation glorified God and were strengthened in the faith. All believed with certainty that in the immaculate Mysteries, the true Body of Christ is given us under the appearance of bread, and the true Blood of Christ under the appearance of wine. Afterwards, the saint prayed again, and the Body of Christ regained the form of bread. The woman communed with fear and certain conviction, receiving the bread as Christ's Body and the wine as Christ's Blood.

The Most Holy Gregory was a brilliant luminary shining upon the whole world. His life, which equaled that of the angels, and his astonishing miracles are the glory of Christ's Church. The saint was author of many books elucidating the

Orthodox faith. Sometimes when he wrote, the Holy Spirit could be seen over him in the form of a dove, as his archdeacon Peter frequently witnessed. Saint Gregory recorded in four books his dialogues with this virtuous man. The text includes brief Lives of the saints of Italy and various edifying stories.

Saint Gregory shepherded the Church of God for thirteen years, six months, and ten days. He reposed during the reign of the tyrant Phocas. The rest of the illustrious Pope's miracles and righteous deeds, as well as a description of his administration of the Church, and his wondrous, holy way of life may be found in the four books written by John, deacon of the great Church of Rome. In all, there are 260 chapters in the volumes. We have related only a small portion of their contents, but sufficient to benefit the souls of the faithful, who ever praise Christ our God, glorious in His saints and extolled with the Father and the Holy Spirit forever. Amen.

ૐ૱ૐ૱ૐ

The following edifying stories recorded by Saint Gregory the Dialogist may be found in *The Prologue*:

January 25, about the death of a certain righteous man;

January 29, about how a monk who hoarded gold was punished;

February 2, about how three sisters undertook to please God, but one did not persevere in asceticism until her death;

February 12, about a young monk who led a heedless life and on his deathbed was about to be devoured by the serpent, but was delivered through the prayers of the brethren;

February 29, about preaching the word of God;

May 16, about a maiden who saw the immaculate Theotokos and was summoned by her to join the choir of holy virgins;

May 23, about a dead soldier who returned to life after seeing how a cruel man was punished;

June 27, about a presbyter who raised a man who had died without Confession;

July 10, about liturgies offered on behalf of captives and those in danger of death;

August 15, about a bishop who daily celebrated the holy Liturgy;

August 17, about the prosphoron offered for the reposed.

These are just a few of the many profitable accounts included in the four books of Saint Gregory's dialogues with Archdeacon Peter.

The Thirteenth Day of the Month of March

The Translation of the Honored Relics of Our Father Among the Saints Nicephorus, Patriarch of Constantinople

God's great hierarch Saint Nicephorus, Patriarch of Constantinople, was deposed for devoutly venerating the holy icons. The impious Emperor Leo the Armenian exiled him to the island of Proconnesus, where the saint was imprisoned and maltreated for thirteen years. Saint Nicephorus reposed in the Lord, and was buried in the Church of the Holy Martyr Theodore, which he had founded.[1]

Following the murder of the godless tyrant Leo the Armenian, Michael the Stammerer became emperor. He was succeeded on the throne by his son Theophilus. After Theophilus died, the Greek Empire was ruled by his wife, the righteous Empress Theodora, as regent for their son Michael, who was still in his minority. During these years, the false patriarchs of Constantinople were Theodotus Kassiteras, Theodore Spatharocandilates, Anthony Kassimatas, and the sorcerer John Annias. When the last of these was deposed as uncanonically

---

[1]Saint Nicephorus died on June 10.

consecrated, Saint Methodius[2] became patriarch, the holy churches again were adorned with icons, and the honored relics of Christ's confessor Saint Nicephorus were brought to Constantinople.

At that time the Most Holy Patriarch Methodius told the God-fearing Empress Theodora, "It is a disgrace that Nicephorus, the most eminent of hierarchs, should remain in banishment so many years after his repose. He was driven from his cathedra and died in exile because he was steadfast in Orthodoxy. His holy remains should be brought back to this see. We sin if we leave his relics in Proconnesus, for this would signify our consent to his unjust expulsion. Were not Joseph's descendants blessed because they took the bones of their ancestor from Egypt to Canaan, though four hundred years had passed since his death? We are children of piety and can no longer endure to be separated from our father. It was Nicephorus who reared us in the divine statutes of Orthodoxy. Constantinople, the capital of the world and the greatest city under the sun, yearns for the honored relics of its holy guide and pastor and wishes to provide them a final resting-place, where they will be shown due reverence. Let the Church like a bride welcome her bridegroom! An unjust emperor deprived the Church of Saint Nicephorus while he was living; let the righteous Empress who loves the holy shepherd return his sacred corpse to the flock. Your Majesty has restored Orthodoxy and peace to the realm, and the people now desire to be mystically guided by their departed pastor. His mere shadow will suffice to convince them that he is in their midst again. They will receive him as alive and regard his relics as the most valuable of treasures."

The Christ-loving Empress Theodora eagerly agreed, saying, "If we do as you recommend, our souls will benefit greatly and future generations will honor our memory."

Without delay, Saint Methodius sailed to Proconnesus with presbyters, monks, and numerous layfolk. Upon arriving at the Monastery of the Holy Martyr Theodore, the Patriarch opened Saint Nicephorus' grave. Although nineteen years had passed since its burial, the honored body was fragrant and intact.

---

[2]Commemorated on June 14

After serving an All-night Vigil and the Divine Liturgy, Methodius entered the tomb, embraced the precious remains of Saint Nicephorus, and addressed the holy Patriarch as though he were still alive, saying, "O most blessed one, thou didst emulate Saint John Chrysostom in labours and enduring tribulations! Like him, thou didst boldly denounce iniquity and wast sentenced to unjust banishment. For more than thirty years, in both life and death, thou hast remained in exile. The time hath come to go back to thy see with thy loving children, that thy people, still devoted to thee, may greet thee joyfully. The godless tyrant who wickedly drove thee from thy Church hath been punished as his deeds merited, for he lost both throne and life. Now our pious rulers are returning thy Church to thee as to one still alive. Being children of the Gospel, they have, with mine assistance, cleansed the Church of heretical defilement. They have restored the Church to the beautiful and unsullied state it had attained through thy labours. Lift up thine eyes and behold the assembly of thine offspring. Many who live nearby have come to thee, while others, having journeyed from afar, eagerly await thine arrival in the Imperial City. Leave them not to grieve as orphans. End thy separation from them, and let thy city have thy sacred relics as a priceless gift, an adornment more glorious than a royal crown."

With this, the Most Holy Patriarch Methodius put the sacred relics in a new coffer. Chanting psalms, he and the presbyters hoisted the remains on their shoulders and carried them to their ship which, with the other vessels, raised sail and quickly reached the Queen of Cities. The devout Empress Theodora, her son Michael, the entire senate, the clergy, and a vast crowd jubilantly greeted the relics as they came ashore. Bearing candles and censers, and singing hymns, they took Patriarch Nicephorus to the Cathedral of Holy Wisdom, whence he had been expelled. The translation of the sacred relics occurred on March 13, the date on which the impious Emperor had banished Saint Nicephorus.

At sunset an All-night Vigil began in the presence of the honored remains. The next morning the relics were taken from the Cathedral of Holy Wisdom to the Church of the Holy Apostles, where they were enshrined with much ceremony.

Ever since then, the memory of the Lord's confessor Nicephorus has been observed on the thirteenth day of March, unto the glory of Christ our God, Who is praised with the Father and the Holy Spirit. Amen.

❧❧❧❧❧

On this same day we commemorate the holy martyr Alexander, who was beheaded for Christ in the city of Pindus during the reign of Maximian. We also commemorate the holy martyr Christina, who was beaten to death in Persia.

The Fourteenth Day of the Month Of March

The Life of Our
Holy Monastic Father Benedict[1]

The name Benedict means "blessed" and this saint was richly blessed with the grace of God. From childhood he possessed mature understanding, for his heart was detached from every carnal, temporal pleasure. Even in the bloom of youth he rejected all worldly allurements, regarding them as of no more value than wild flowers that quickly wither.

Benedict was born in the Italian town of Nursia, but his parents sent him to Rome for a liberal education. Seeing that many of his fellow students were straying into debauchery and perishing in the abyss of iniquity, he stepped back from the threshold he was crossing, because he feared to ruin his soul and understanding for the sake of a little book-learning. Shortly after abandoning the academy, the unlettered sage (who preferred inner chastity to outer philosophy) also renounced an immense fortune he had inherited from his recently deceased parents. So doing, Benedict was preparing to embrace the monastic life and take up his abode in the wilderness. Then he left home with his former nurse, a virtuous, elderly woman, and went to Enfide,[2] where friends provided them lodging at the Church of Saint Peter. The devout townspeople came to love the blessed youth and treated him with much respect.

One day, the nurse borrowed a winnowing fan from neighbors and left it on the edge of a table. Upon return, she found it

---

[1]Abbreviated from Book Two of Saint Gregory's *Dialogues*
[2]Now Affile (Tr.)

had slipped off and broken in two. The poor woman burst into tears, because the fan was not hers. Seeing his nurse weeping, Benedict took both halves, went off by himself, fell prostrate before God, and prayed for a full hour. Upon rising, he noticed that the two pieces were joined together, without even a mark to show where the winnow was broken. Soon word of the miracle spread among the people. They hung the fan at the entrance to their church, so that everyone who saw it would glorify God and His grace and praise the Lord's favorite, Benedict. The godly one, however, could not endure to be acclaimed by men; therefore, he stole away from his nurse and hid in the wilderness called Subiaco. That place is twenty-three miles from Rome[3] and a clear, cold river runs through it. On the way, Providence arranged for Benedict to meet a monk named Romanus, who was on an errand for his abbot Deodatus, superior of a nearby monastery. While conversing with Romanus about the soul's salvation, Benedict disclosed his longings and intentions. Romanus clothed Benedict in the habit and settled him in a cave deep in a thicket. For three years he told no one about the saint, but would set aside bread from his portion and take it to Benedict. Because a cliff rose directly over it, the cave could be reached from the monastery only by completely circling the mountain; hence, to deliver the bread to Benedict, Romanus lowered it on a long rope from a crag. A little bell at the end of the rope let Benedict know when his food had arrived. Viewing this with anger, the devil, enemy of saints, plotted to put an end to Romanus' labor of love, torment Benedict with hunger, and cast the saint into despair. One day in a rage he threw a stone and broke the bell;[4] however, Romanus continued his faithful service until God granted him rest from his toil and revealed His servant Benedict for the edification of many.

After three years, the time came for the shining lamp to be removed from beneath the bushel. On Pascha the Lord appeared in a vision to a presbyter who was preparing his festal meal. He

---

[3]The distance is actually greater. (Tr.)
[4]Evidently, the cave was so close to the monastery that Romanus feared to shout. (Tr.)

said, "You intend to stuff yourself, while my servant Benedict is wasting away with hunger in a cave out of love for Me!" The Lord explained where to find the grotto, and the presbyter, taking food, set out at once in search of the man of God. Having traversed mountains, ravines, and torrents, the priest found Benedict in his cave. The men exchanged a kiss in the Lord, then sat down and nourished their souls with spiritual conversation. Finally the presbyter told the saint, "Father, it is time to thank God and eat. Today is Pascha."

"Indeed it is Pascha for me, because the Lord has brought you here," replied the man of God, not realizing after his long seclusion that it really was the feast of the Resurrection.

"Truly, Father, it is the day of the Lord's Resurrection," insisted the presbyter. "You should not be fasting on such a joyous occasion. God sent me here so that we could share His gifts." Following this they prayed, the presbyter thanking God for revealing His servant. Not many days later, shepherds discovered the cave, and visitors began coming in number, bringing the saint food. For his part, Benedict provided spiritual nurture for the Christians.

Maddened by Benedict's holy life, the devil tried to lay a snare for the godly one. Assuming the form of a blackbird, he fluttered so close to Benedict's face the saint easily could have grabbed him. The man of God realized this was a demonic temptation and crossed himself. The evil spirit vanished, but in the same instant, Benedict was assaulted by his most violent carnal temptation ever. The demon of fornication brought to mind a woman the venerable one had seen while still in the world, enkindling such a fire of lust in his emaciated flesh that our saint was almost brought to despair. Benedict was on the verge of abandoning the wilderness when, by the grace of God, he came to himself. Noticing a thick patch of nettles and briars, he threw aside his robes and cast himself into it, rolling and tossing until his whole body was stung by thorns and covered in blood. This put an end to his vile thoughts, for which he thanked the Lord. By God's grace, so utter was the victory that the demon of fornication never again troubled him, as Benedict told his disciples.

While report of the saint was spreading, the abbot of a nearby monastery died. The monks asked Benedict to become their guide and pastor, but he refused on the grounds that he was a sinner and unworthy; moreover, he insisted, "My way of life and yours can never be reconciled." Eventually, however, Benedict yielded and against his will became their abbot. He governed the community strictly, instituting a severe regime of fasting and tolerating none of the former disobedience. As a result, the wayward monks regretted having chosen him, and the most evil of them poisoned his wine. When they offered him the deadly glass at the common meal in the refectory, our venerable father traced the sign of the Cross over it. Immediately the glass shattered, as if struck by a rock. The man of God realized that the holy cross had this effect because the wine was poisoned. Calm and smiling, he assembled the brethren and asked them, "Children, why did you do this? I told you from the start that my way of life and yours could never be reconciled. Find another abbot. I can stay here no longer." With this he blessed them and returned to the cave, where he resumed his struggles unseen except by God, from Whom nothing is hidden.

Nonetheless, it was the Lord's will that Benedict should guide others to heaven, rather than tread the path of salvation alone. He Who arranges all things for the best entrusted to the saint a much larger flock than before. Whereas previously He had committed one monastery to Benedict's care, now He appointed the saint overseer of twelve. Word of the venerable one's angelic life spread ever further, and again visitors began coming, some for prayers and a blessing; others to hear his edifying, divinely inspired teaching; others because they wanted to become disciples. Many forsook the world and built huts near the cave. They grew their own food, and in a few years had so greatly increased in number that the thicket was full of them. Consequently, the saint divided the monks into twelve groups of twelve, each with an experienced superior. The brotherhoods erected separate monasteries; the novices, however, remained with Benedict, since he felt they needed his personal guidance. It happened about the same time that several nobles from Rome brought their children to Benedict for schooling in God's service. Euthicius, a man of renowned lineage, brought his boy Maurus, and Senator Tertullus, his son Placidus. Maurus was older and proved very helpful to the saint. Placidus was so young that Benedict's teaching was almost his first food after he was weaned.

In one of Saint Benedict's monasteries, there was a heedless brother who would leave the church during services. Despite frequent reprimands by the abbot, he did not correct himself. Learning of this, Benedict summoned the monk and exhorted him at length, but the transgressor failed to mend his ways. Then our venerable father went to the offender's monastery, attended a service, and saw a black boy pulling the misdoer out of church by the edge of his habit. The godly one asked the monks standing nearby, "Do you see who is dragging that brother out of the chapel?"

"No, Father," they answered. The saint prayed, and God opened the inner eyes of the brethren. The next day the others could see the little Ethiopian tugging at the monk, and they informed the man of God. After the service, Benedict again spoke with the offender, this time harshly. Not only did the Lord's favorite, ordinarily so meek, upbraid the monk; but he gave him a good thrashing with his staff, too. So doing, he drove off the demon. It was almost as if the imp had received the blows and was afraid of more if he returned. Following this, the brother rectified himself.

One of the monasteries stood on bare rocky heights, and it was a hardship for the brethren to haul up water. The monks requested our venerable father's permission to move to another site. The godly one told them to be patient, and that night he and Placidus scaled the cliff. After praying for a long time on bended knees, the saint called forth a stream, like Moses for thirsting Israel in the desert.[5] The water sufficed for all the monastery's needs and rushed down to the ravine below.

At another of Benedict's monasteries, a brother was digging a garden on the riverbank, and the head of his spade flew into the middle of the stream. The poor man was very downcast, because the river was in full flood and there seemed to be no

[5]Ex., Ch. 13

way to recover the iron blade from the deep, rushing water. Then Saint Benedict happened by and, seeing the downcast brother, worked a miracle like that wrought by Elisha.[6] Taking the wooden handle, he thrust it into the water. When he brought it up, the head had reattached itself. Handing the spade back to the monk, the godly one told him, "Get on with your work; there is no need to be upset."

One day, the blessed Benedict was keeping to himself and sent Placidus to fetch water. While filling the jug, the boy lost his balance and was carried away by the river. Seeing this with his inner eyes, Benedict called out, "Run, Brother Maurus, run! Placidus has fallen into the river and it has swept him away." Maurus ran to the bank and saw Placidus drowning. He continued running on the surface of the water, pulled the lad out of the river, and dragged him to land. Only then did he realize what he had done. Terrified, he returned with Placidus to our father. Benedict would not take any credit for the deed, but ascribed it to his disciple's unhesitating obedience. Maurus insisted that the miracle was due solely to his elder's prayers. The dispute was settled by Placidus, who testified, "Father, I saw your mantle over my head as you dragged me to land. Only when I reached the bank did I see Maurus."

Because the fame of Benedict's astounding miracles and the number of his disciples continued to increase, a local presbyter named Florentius became jealous of the saint. Incited by a demon, the priest bitterly slandered and publicly condemned the man of God. In spite of this, Benedict's reputation for holiness grew daily and, with it, the devotion of the people. Infuriated because no one paid him the least heed, the wretch poisoned a prosphoron and sent it to Saint Benedict. Although the treacherous deed could not be hidden from his inner eyes, the clairvoyant elder thankfully accepted the loaf.

At mealtime a raven always came and took bread from our godly father's hand. This time Benedict offered it the loaf given him by the presbyter Florentius, saying, "In the name of Jesus Christ, Son of the living God, drop this bread somewhere neither man nor bird will find it." Flapping its wings and cawing,

---

[6] IV Kings, Ch. 6

the raven circled the loaf as if to indicate it wanted to obey but could not, because of the poison. "Take it," insisted the man of God; "do not be afraid. It will do you no harm. Just drop it where it cannot be found." After much hesitation the raven obeyed, flying away with the loaf in its beak. Three hours later it came back for its meal.

Our father prayed for Florentius more than for himself, begging God not to count the presbyter's resentment and hatred as sin, but to correct him. Florentius, however, was incorrigible. Having failed to poison the master, he devised an infernal plan to corrupt the disciples. One day, while young monks were at work in the garden, Florentius sent seven beautiful girls there. The hussies stripped naked, danced, clapped their hands, sang, and performed every shameless contortion, in order to inflame the brethren with degrading lust. Seeing this, Saint Benedict understood that the attack was aimed at him alone and decided to let envy have its way. He assembled all his abbots and monks, appointed a new elder, and committed the brethren to God's care, then humbly departed with a few of his youngest disciples. Florentius was overjoyed to be rid of Benedict, but the Lord God of vengeance quickly requited the evil presbyter for harassing His guileless servant. While Florentius was sitting on his balcony congratulating himself, it collapsed and he was instantly killed. No one else in the house was injured. Word of this soon reached Benedict's monasteries, and the saint's beloved disciple, the blessed Maurus (one of those left behind), sent this message to the Lord's favorite: "Return, Father; the presbyter who caused you so much trouble has perished!" The venerable one wept bitterly for Florentius and, extremely displeased with Maurus for rejoicing over the presbyter's death, he imposed a penance on his disciple. Although Florentius was no more, Benedict did not return to the cave, but settled near the town of Cassino in Campania. Yet however much the saint changed his habitation, his true enemy remained the same. If anything, the devil's assaults became even fiercer; but no matter how violent the struggle, God's favorite, having the help of Christ, ever prevailed.

There was a heathen temple dedicated to Apollo in a grove on the mountain where Benedict took up his dwelling. After smashing the idol, destroying the temple, and cutting down the grove, the venerable one built a chapel dedicated to Saint John the Baptist. He also founded a monastery, which grew quickly. When he arrived, there were still many idolaters in the countryside, but the peer of the apostles, mighty in word and deed, won them for Christ with his zealous preaching, which was confirmed by miracles. Enraged because of their losses, the demons attacked the saint visibly, breathing fire and screeching, "Benedict, Benedict!" When the man of God would not answer, the demons howled, "Maledictus, Maledictus, non Benedictus!" which means, "Accursed! Accursed, not 'blessed'! What have we to do with you? Why do you persecute us?" But their protests were in vain, for with prayer and the sign of the Cross the blessed Benedict swept them away like dust.

It happened that while the brethren were building the upper level of the monastery, the saint was alone in his cell praying and saw a demon passing by. "Where are you going, enemy?" Benedict asked.

"I am on my way to visit the monks at their work," answered the devil. Immediately, the saint sent word to the brethren to be on guard against temptation, as a demon was approaching. Just as they received the message, the whole wall under construction collapsed, killing a young monk. In their grief over the brother's death, the others hardly noticed the extent of the damage. Weeping bitterly, they told their father about the terrible accident. Benedict commanded them to bring him the corpse. So badly crushed was the dead man that the monks did not carry him in their arms, but on a hair shirt. The venerable one had them put the body on his rush prayer-mat; then he sent everyone out and closed the door. God heard his fervent entreaties and raised the dead as though from sleep, so that the young monk, without a trace of injury, was back to work with the brethren before the day was done.

It was a strictly observed custom of the house, instituted by Benedict himself, that brethren away on errands did not eat or drink outside the monastery. Once, a few of the monks were sent so far they were out until late in the evening. On the way back, they stopped for a meal at the home of a devout consecrated virgin. Upon return, they presented themselves to their father for a blessing. He asked, "Where did you eat?"

"Nowhere, Father," they answered.

"Why are you lying? You entered the house of the pious maiden so-and-so, ate this food and that, and drank such-and-such a quantity of wine," he said.

Hearing this, the monks were amazed that their father knew what they had done far away. They fell prostrate, confessing their misdeed and begging forgiveness. When another monk fell into the same sin on a different occasion, Benedict confronted him in the same manner. Because of the saint's clairvoyance, his monks were afraid to do or say anything indiscreet, wherever they were. They learned that their father was always with them in spirit, listening to their conversations and observing their actions, and that they could not escape accounting to him.

About that time Totila, King of the Goths, was in Campania. He heard tell of the venerable one and decided to visit Benedict and test his clairvoyance. To this end he sent to the Lord's favorite his sword-bearer Riggo, dressed in royal apparel as if he were really the King. When Riggo and his enormous escort of chieftains and warriors were still some distance from Benedict, the godly one shouted, "My son, lay aside the robes! They are not yours, but belong to him who sent you." Terror-stricken, Riggo sank to his knees. After receiving report of what had happened, King Totila humbly came to prostrate himself before God's clairvoyant elder. Saint Benedict rebuked the King for his innumerable crimes and foretold what would happen to him. "With God's permission you will capture Rome, cross the sea, reign for nine years, and die in the tenth," he said. And so it happened.

God also granted power over demons to Saint Benedict. A cleric of the Church of Aquino was tormented by a devil and had been sent by his bishop, Constantius, to the shrines of various martyrs, but the holy martyrs did not grant him the favor of a cure. When he was brought to Benedict, however, the man of God healed him by prayer. After driving out the wicked spirit, Saint Benedict charged the cleric, "Never again eat meat, and never accept the priesthood. The day you are ordained priest, you will find yourself in Satan's power again." The man returned home completely cured. As long as his suffering was fresh in his mind, he obeyed the saint's command. Years passed, however, and he watched his juniors being advanced to the priesthood as older men died. Jealousy stirred in him and he began seeking ordination. On the very day he attained his desire, a ferocious devil gained control of him and mercilessly tortured him to death.

A nobleman from Cassino named Theoprobus was converted from idolatry to the true faith by the divinely wise Benedict. Because of his virtuous life, he enjoyed his spiritual father's love and favor. One day, Theoprobus entered the godly one's room and found Benedict weeping and lamenting. What especially worried the nobleman was that these were not Benedict's usual tears of compunction during prayer, but tears of distress. When this continued for a long time, Theoprobus asked what it meant. The saint, sobbing and moaning, explained, "God Almighty has decreed that barbarians shall destroy this monastery and plunder everything I have, with His assistance, provided for the brotherhood. Only with the greatest difficulty did I prevail upon Him to safeguard the lives of the monks." While Saint Benedict lived, the monastery prospered, but after his death, the prediction was fulfilled. One night Lombards attacked while the community was asleep. They pillaged the monastery and destroyed the buildings, but all the brethren escaped, by the prayers of our holy father Benedict.

A devout man sent two jars of wine to the venerable one, but his servant brought only one to Benedict, hiding the other on the way. When he dismissed the slave, our clairvoyant father warned him, "Child, do not drink from the jar you concealed by the wayside, but tip it and see what is inside." Put to shame by the reproof, the servant bowed and departed. Wishing to test the saint's words, he tilted the jar before carrying it away. A snake slithered out and the horrified slave repented of his transgression.

Not far from the saint's monastery, there was a community of virgins living in a village of former idolaters converted by Benedict. From time to time the venerable one sent experienced brethren to instruct the nuns in the word of God. Once, the monk sent was about to leave the convent and the sisters pressed him to take a few handkerchiefs. The brother put the gift in his bosom and left. When he returned to the monastery, the saint rebuked him, saying, "How is it, Brother, that the evil one has found a way into your heart?" The monk had no idea why he was being reproached, because he had completely forgotten about the handkerchiefs. "Do you think I was absent when you hid the nuns' present?" asked Benedict. At this the offender fell at the saint's feet and begged forgiveness.

Late one evening, the man of God was having his supper, and a young monk, the son of a wealthy, high-ranking official, was holding a lamp for him. Arrogant thoughts whispered to the brother, "Why should I have to stand here like a slave, holding a lamp for a commoner?"

Such thoughts could not be hidden from the clairvoyant elder. Straightway, Benedict asked him meekly, as would a father, "Child, why do you allow proud thoughts to needle you? Trace the sign of the Cross over your heart, and be attentive to yourself." The saint had one of the novices take the lamp, and the erring monk left the cell to weep. When the brethren inquired why their father had asked him to leave, the monk replied that it was on account of his pride. Everyone was astonished at how Benedict knew even the most secret thoughts of the heart.

There was a famine in Campania, and the venerable one's monastery was not spared the terrible shortage of bread. At one point only five loaves remained, insufficient even for a single meal. Seeing the brethren in despair, Benedict scolded them, "Why are you downcast about our lack of bread, *O ye of little faith?*[7] Put your trust in God, Who never forsakes those who labor for Him. Have you forgotten the Saviour's words in the Gospel, *Seek ye first the Kingdom of God, and all these things shall be added unto you? Your Father knoweth what things ye have need of, before ye ask Him.* Do not be fainthearted. Today you lack; tomorrow you shall have more than you need." The next morning the brethren found two hundred measures of flour in sacks at the monastery gates. No one could say who had delivered them or whence they came, but it was clear that God had provided them, by the prayers of our father Benedict.

---

[7]Matt., Ch. 6

A devout layman requested the venerable one to erect a monastery on his estate near Tarracina, to which the man of God agreed. Having selected monks for the task, Benedict told them to clear the land and prepare the necessary materials, adding, "I will come on such-and-such a day and show you the exact site for each building." The monks did as instructed and awaited their father's coming. Before dawn on the appointed day, Saint Benedict appeared to the brethren in a dream, showing them where to put the church, refectory, infirmary, cells, and other buildings. Upon awakening, the monks were amazed to discover that all had the same dream, but wonder turned to disappointment when their father did not arrive that day or the next. Finally, they went to him and protested, "Reverend Father, we were expecting you to show us where to build. Why did you fail to come?"

"What are you saying, brethren!" objected the saint. "I did come."

"Father, you did not," insisted the monks.

"Have you forgotten that I appeared in a dream and pointed out the sites?" asked the saint. "Go back and begin construction according to my orders." The monks returned to the estate and did as commanded.

Not far from Cassino two maidens of noble birth were leading the ascetic life in their own home. Although chaste, they were overcritical, and often judged, disparaged, and upbraided others. The godly Benedict sent them this message: "If you do not curb your sharp tongues, I shall have to excommunicate you."

Before long, both virgins died without even acknowledging our father's letter, much less showing any signs of amendment. They were buried side by side in a church. Whenever the Divine Liturgy was celebrated there and the deacon commanded the catechumens to depart,[8] members of the congregation saw the maidens leave their graves and go outside for the rest of the service. This was reported to Saint Benedict, who took pity on the virgins and sent a prosphoron to that church with instructions that it be offered for their souls at the Liturgy. After this

---

[8]Catechumens are not allowed to partake of the Eucharist.

was done, no one ever again beheld the maidens departing. Evidently, God had forgiven them, through the holy sacrifice and the prayers of the venerable one.

A young monk living in Saint Benedict's monastery was too attached to his parents according to the flesh and often visited their home without our father's blessing. One day he secretly left the monastery, and as soon as he entered his parents' house, he died. Learning this, the brethren retrieved his body and committed it to the earth. The next day they found the corpse lying outside the grave. They buried it again, only to find it a day later in the same place. The parents threw themselves in tears at Saint Benedict's feet, pleading that he take pity on their son and, by the power of the grace within him, command the ground to accept the corpse. Moved by their grief, the godly one placed a small portion of the Holy Mysteries on the chest of the dead monk as he was returned to the grave. After this his body remained undisturbed in the earth.

The man of God was very kind and merciful. He loved the poor and was generous to them. Whatever money God sent to his monastery, Benedict gave away as alms, such that the brethren lived in poverty. One day a pious layman who had fallen into debt came and begged the saint for twelve pieces of gold, the amount he owed a stern creditor insisting on payment. At that time there was not a penny in the monastery, so the saint replied, "Forgive me, brother; I cannot give you that much now. Come back the day after tomorrow." The saint resorted to prayer, entreating God to deliver the man from his plight. On the third day the debtor returned, bowed before the saint, and asked to be given the promised assistance. At that very moment the monks found thirteen gold coins on the lid of a pot of vegetable soup. Our compassionate father gave the money to the debtor, saying, "Child, pay your creditor the twelve pieces of gold and keep the thirteenth for your own needs."

It happened that once the man of God was working in the fields with the brethren, and a peasant came to the monastery carrying his son's lifeless body. Brokenhearted at his loss, the rustic begged to see our venerable father. On learning that the saint was in the fields, he left his child at the entrance to the monastery and hurried off to find Benedict. As it happened,

Benedict was already returning when the peasant caught sight of him. With tears streaming down his cheeks, the man cried, "Father, give me back my son! Give me back my son!"

"Have I taken your son?" asked the Lord's favorite.

"My son is dead; bring him back to life!" the father implored.

Although truly sorry for the man, the venerable one told his monks, "We must flee, brethren; we must flee! Such a miracle is beyond our power. Only the holy apostles can raise the dead."

At this the father, overcome by grief, vowed, "I will not leave until you raise my son!"

When Saint Benedict reached the entrance to the monastery, he fell prostrate beside the corpse, as did the other monks, and he prayed, "O Lord, regard not my sins, but the faith of this man, who asketh Thee to bring back his son from the dead. I entreat Thee to return the boy's soul to its body." Before the saint could complete his supplication, the child stirred. Benedict took the lad by the hand and presented him alive and well to his father.

In the second book of his *Dialogues*, Saint Gregory, Pope of Rome, relates many other astonishing miracles worked by our father Benedict; however, since we cannot relate all of them, we shall limit ourselves to a few more and bring our account to its conclusion.

Benedict had a sister named Scholastica, who was consecrated to God in infancy by her parents. She had kept her virginity and spent her whole life pleasing the Lord by ascetical labors. Once a year, Scholastica visited her holy brother. Benedict received her in a house belonging to the community, a short distance from the monastery, and the saints spent the time together conversing about edifying topics. The last time the blessed Scholastica visited him, Benedict brought several disciples to the house. As usual, the saints talked about the devout life and told edifying stories. After sunset they ate, then continued the discussion until quite late. The holy virgin said to the godly one, "Brother, please remain here the rest of the night, and we will speak until morning about the joys of heaven and everlasting life."

"Sister, what are you saying?" marveled Benedict. "You know I cannot spend the night away from the monastery."

Seeing that her brother was not about to yield, the holy virgin folded her hands on the table, rested her head on them, and in the secret chamber of her heart offered fervent prayer to Almighty God. Although it had been a clear, cloudless night, when she lifted her head, fearsome thunder roared, bolts of lightning fell, and rain poured out of the sky. So powerful were his sister's entreaties that Benedict and his disciples could not even open the doors, much less return to the monastery. Realizing that Scholastica's prayers had brought about the storm, Benedict asked, "Why did you do this, sister?"

"I appealed to you, brother, but you would not listen, so I turned to God and He heard me," replied Scholastica. "Go to your monastery now, if you think it possible." This Benedict could not do, so he was forced to stay. The saints talked the whole night about eternal life, and at dawn parted, having said their farewells. Three days later Saint Benedict was praying and happened to look into the sky. The soul of his blessed sister in the form of a radiant dove was flying to heaven, where it was received into the celestial mansions. Benedict was overjoyed that Scholastica had been accounted worthy of such honor, gave thanks to God, and informed the brethren of her repose. He ordered his monks to bring her holy body to his monastery, and he buried the precious treasure in his own tomb.

Not many days afterwards, the deacon Servandus came to visit Benedict. He was a man full of divine grace and abbot of a Campanian monastery built by a patrician named Liberius. While engaged in edifying conversation about the celestial inheritance which was not yet fully theirs to enjoy, the two holy men groaned contritely and by reflection on God tasted in part that sweetest of all sustenance. At supper they sighed repeatedly and could think only of the incorruptible food. That night our venerable father Benedict slept in his cell on the uppermost story, and his blessed guest was given the room immediately below. After resting a little, Benedict awoke and began to pray. Shortly before midnight, the godly one looked out of the window and saw a light shine down from heaven, so brilliant that the night became brighter than day. It seemed as though he could see the whole world contained in that beam. Gazing at the dazzling display, the saint beheld the soul of the blessed Germanus, Bishop of Capua, being carried by angels to heaven in a ball of fire. Wishing for someone else to witness the marvel, the venerable Benedict called out two or three times in a loud voice for his guest. Servandus was startled at hearing Benedict shout for him at such an hour, and rushed to the upper room just in time to glimpse the last of the ineffable light. The man of God related what had happened, then immediately sent his beloved disciple Theoprobus to Cassino with instructions to dispatch a rider to Capua to learn what had happened to the holy Bishop Germanus. Word soon came that Saint Germanus had died at the very hour the godly Benedict had seen the angels taking his soul to heaven.

Before long Saint Benedict announced that he would also be leaving the body and going to the Lord. Six days before his death, he ordered his tomb opened. Straightway, he fell ill and took to his bed, but he continued teaching the brethren. At this time Benedict dictated his *Rule for Monks*. On the day of his repose he had the monks take him into the chapel of Saint John the Baptist which he had built on the site of the temple of Apollo. After partaking of the divine Mysteries, he lifted his hands to God, prayed, and breathed his last. Benedict's soul flew to the splendid mansions of heaven to dwell with the Lord, upon Whom the man of God had always fixed his gaze.

At the moment when Benedict's soul was departing the body, two monks, one on an errand, the other praying in his cell, saw the same vision. Both beheld a path leading from earth to heaven, strewn with costly robes and illumined on either side by torches. Above the path stood a man who shone brilliantly and whose appearance was indescribably majestic. The monks heard him say that Benedict, the Lord's beloved, had just taken that path to heaven. Although the monks were located far from each other, in the vision they were standing together. Both rushed to the funeral of their holy father and related to the brethren what they had seen. Weeping and lamenting, layfolk from town and country, and monks from all the communities founded by the venerable one, as well as from other monasteries in the region, came to bury Saint Benedict. They laid the saint's body to rest in the Church of the Baptist, praising Father, Son, and Holy Spirit, the one God in Trinity, glorified by all creation forever. Amen.

ᘒᕼᘒᕼ

On this same day we commemorate our father among the saints Euschemon the Confessor, Bishop of Lampsacus. He was fettered and exiled for the holy icons during the reign of Leo the Isaurian.

The Fifteenth Day
of the Month of March

The Passion of the Holy Martyrs Agapius, Paisius, Timolaus, Romulus, Alexander, Alexander, Dionysius, and Dionysius

These holy, much-suffering martyrs were put to death by Governor Urban in Caesarea of Palestine during the reign of Diocletian. Agapius was from Gaza, Timolaus was from Pontus on the Black Sea, both Saints Dionysius were from Tripolis in Phoenicia, Romulus was a subdeacon from Diospolis, and Paisius and both Saints Alexander were from Egypt.

During the second year of the Great Persecution, an imperial edict was published in every city and land, ordering that Christians worship idols and offer sacrifice to them. On a certain feast of the godless, it was announced that several Christian prisoners would be put to death; therefore, all the villagers who had come to Caesarea to participate in the impious rites crowded into the arena. First the holy martyr Timothy[1] was subjected to numerous tortures; then he was burned alive. Afterwards, the

---

[1]Commemorated on August 19 and September 19

holy martyrs Thecla and Agapius[2] (a different saint than his namesake commemorated on this day) were fed to wild animals. During this bloody spectacle, six brave Christian youths stepped forward. These were Paisius, Timolaus, Romulus, both Alexanders, and one Dionysius. Aflame with zeal and love for Christ and eager for martyrdom, they had bound their hands behind their backs. Fearing neither fire nor wild beasts, they rushed to the center of the arena and shouted, "We are Christians!"

The Governor saw how young and handsome the martyrs were, so he heaped flattery on them and for a long time urged them to worship idols and escape destruction. When this failed, he cast them into his dungeon. Several days later the holy band increased in number to eight, as the Lord's prisoners were joined by Saint Agapius and the other Dionysius. Agapius, a man held in high regard by the faithful, had already contended well, confessing the Savior boldly and several times undergoing dreadful torments. Dionysius, an Egyptian, was his slave.

The martyrs were kept in the dungeon for a long time and were repeatedly interrogated and tortured. They courageously endured every torment and were finally beheaded on the same day for Christ the Lord, Head of the Church. Having surrendered their holy souls into the hands of the Master, they were crowned by Him with garlands of victory in the Church Triumphant.

---

[2]Both these saints are commemorated with Saint Timothy on August 19.

On the Same Day

The Passion of the Holy Hieromartyr Alexander, Priest of Side[1]

While Aurelian was emperor and a persecution of the Christians was raging, Antoninus, Governor of Pamphylia, was in the town of Side and took into custody the priest Alexander. Having mounted his tribunal, Antoninus demanded that Christ's servitor identify himself.

"I am a Christian, a priest by rank and a pastor of Christ's flock," declared the saint.

"Where is Christ's flock?" inquired the Governor.

The saint replied, "The flock of Christ is scattered throughout the world which He made. It consists of all who believe in Him; but you who have fallen away from the Creator and serve lifeless idols, *the work of the hands of men*,[2] are aliens to the fold of the saved. At the Dread Judgment, God shall assign you a place, not on His right hand with the sheep, but on the left with the goats."

"I have two reasons to torture you: so that you will sacrifice to our gods and worship them, and reveal where the Christians are hiding," stated the Governor. "Now tell me: Who is Christ?"

The saint answered, "Christ is the Saviour of the world, the Light and Life of them that hope in Him."

"How can a man who perished miserably on a cross be the Saviour?" the Governor sneered.

"He Who in the flesh voluntarily endured the Cross and death as God demolished Hades, freed its captives from their fetters, put death to death, and rose from the grave. No less marvelous, He raised others, as it is written: '*Many bodies of the saints which slept arose, and came out of the graves after His Resurrection, and went into the holy city* of Jerusalem, *and appeared*

---

[1]Abbreviated from *The Great Collection of Readings*
[2]Ps. 134

unto many.[3] By His Resurrection, Christ raised all mankind and restored it to life," Alexander proclaimed.

"You are a blathering fool. How can Christ help others, if He could not help Himself when the Jews were tormenting Him?" scoffed the Governor.

"Not I, but you are a blind fool," retorted the saint. "Your inner eyes are sightless; therefore, you cannot behold the mystery of our salvation wrought by Christ the Lord." At this, the Governor commanded that Saint Alexander's torture begin. The martyr was flogged with rawhide straps, spun on a wheel over knives that sliced his flesh, thrown into a cauldron of boiling pitch and oil, and thrust into a blazing furnace. By the grace of Christ, none of the torments harmed him. While Alexander was in the furnace, the heathen saw two wondrous youths glorifying God with the holy martyr. These were angels, and they cooled the flames for the saint. The crowd was astonished to see three men in the furnace when only one had been put in, but the Governor and his lackeys, unwilling to admit the power of Christ, our omnipotent God, ascribed the miracle to sorcery. Only one of the persecutor's servants believed. Falling at the saint's feet, he begged the martyr to pray that Christ accept him. The Governor at once commanded that the servant be put to the sword.

Presently Saint Alexander was removed from the furnace, suspended, and raked with iron claws until his whole body was shredded. The torturers exclaimed, "How can this man endure such torments? There is nothing left of him except bare bones!" Again they shoved the martyr into the furnace, but he was not burned. Then they ripped out his entrails with a hook and offered him as food to wild animals, which refused to do him any harm. No matter what torture they employed, Christ's sufferer proved invincible. His patience surpassed human understanding and amazed everyone. Finally, the holy hieromartyr Alexander was beheaded. His remains were buried by Eustathius, a devout Christian.

At the moment of Saint Alexander's death, the Governor was sitting on his tribunal, and his gods, the demons, entered

---

[3]Matt., Ch. 27

him and began torturing him cruelly. As servants carried him home, Antoninus wept and bitterly lamented his fate. Before reaching the house, he vomited his wretched soul. Now he dwells in eternal darkness with Satan and his minions, but Saint Alexander rejoices in heaven with Christ the Lord and the holy angels.

On the Same Day

The Passion of the
Holy Martyr Nicander

Saint Nicander lived in Egypt during the reign of Diocletian. A devout physician, he frequently visited the holy martyrs imprisoned for Christ, treated their wounds, provided them food, and buried them when they finished the contest.

Prior to his call to martyrdom, Nicander was a somewhat timid man, but God strengthened him in the hour of tribulation. Once, Nicander came upon the corpses of martyrs lying in a field, where they had been left as food for dogs, wild animals, and birds. Fearing arrest and brutal tortures, he waited until nightfall to remove the bodies, then carried them away on his shoulders one by one, wrapped them in clean shrouds, and secretly buried them. An idolater saw this and reported it to the Governor, who seized Nicander and tormented him long and cruelly. Made strong by heavenly grace, he who once feared tortures now gladly endured them for the sake of the Lord. Nothing could compel him to renounce Christ; instead, he urged the Governor to employ every punishment he knew.

Seeing that the martyr's faith was as steadfast as an unshakable pillar or an immovable mountain, the persecutor commanded that Nicander be flayed and beheaded. Thus the holy passion-bearer *put off the old*, earthly *man, and put on the new*, heavenly *man*,[1] and was joined as an honored member to Christ his Lord, the most honored Head of the Church. His sufferings having come to an end, he reigns eternally with the Master and glorifies the Holy Trinity in the choir of the martyrs.

---

[1]Eph., Ch. 4

The Sixteenth Day
of the Month of March

The Commemoration of the
Holy Apostle Aristobulus,
Bishop of Britain

Saint Aristobulus was one of Christ's Seventy Apostles. He was born on Cyprus and was the brother of the holy Apostle Barnabas, also of the Seventy. After the Lord's Ascension, Aristobulus accompanied the teacher of the whole world, the holy Apostle Paul, and with him preached Christ in many countries. In the Epistle to the Romans, it says; *Salute them which are of Aristobulus' household.*[1] This, because relatives of Aristobulus and Barnabas were living in Rome. At the time Paul wrote the Epistle to the Romans, our saint was with him; therefore, he greeted Aristobulus' kin on Aristobulus' behalf as well as his own.

The Apostle Paul consecrated numerous bishops, assigning some to fixed sees in towns and sending others to travel through various countries proclaiming the word of truth. He appointed Aristobulus Bishop of Britain, commissioning him to preach to its fierce, unbelieving people. In the course of his evangelic labors, Aristobulus suffered greatly at the hands of the brutish tribesmen. Sometimes they beat him savagely; sometimes they dragged him on trails, mocking him. The saint was continuously mistreated by them, until the grace of Christ finally illumined their hearts and the Britons accepted his teaching about the Saviour. After christening the barbarians, erecting a church

---

[1]Rom., Ch. 16

for them, and ordaining presbyters and deacons, Saint Aristobulus reposed in Britain.

ε👤ε👤ε👤

Some believe that Saint Aristobulus was surnamed Zebedee
and was the father of the holy apostles James and John, but this
is doubtful. It is more likely that he was born on Cyprus and
was the brother of Saint Barnabas. The father of James and John
was from Jerusalem, not Cyprus, and Zebedee was his first
name, not a surname.

On the Same Day

The Commemoration of the Holy Martyr Sabine

$\mathcal{T}$he holy martyr Sabine was born in Hermopolis, a city of Egypt. He was well-known throughout the land and was prince of his native town.

During the reign of Diocletian, the Christians of Egypt were relentlessly persecuted. Because many were being seized, tortured, and put to death, the blessed Sabine forsook his house, duties, riches, and family and secretly fled Hermopolis. He hid with other Christians in a remote village, finding shelter in a hut, and spent his days and nights in prayer and fasting. The idolaters searched for him without success until he was betrayed by a beggar whom he provided the necessities of life. This second Judas asked the pagans, "What will you give me if I tell you where to find Sabine?" The heathen paid him two gold coins and followed him to the village. Having surrounded the hut, they knocked, and Sabine, who was inside with six other Christians, unlocked the door, thinking that one of the faithful wished to see him. The idolaters rushed in and bound the Christians, fettering Saint Sabine with two heavy chains. Sabine was taken to Governor Arianus, who attempted to persuade him to offer oblations to idols. When this failed, Arianus resorted to torture, raking the blessed one with iron claws, burning him, and finally drowning him in the Nile. As he finished the course of suffering, the martyr received a diadem of victory from the Lord Jesus, Ruler of the contest. The six other Christians also underwent torture and were glorified by Christ in heaven with Saint Sabine.

On the Same Day

The Passion of the
Holy Hieromartyrs
Trophimus and Thalus

Saints Trophimus and Thalus were brothers according to the flesh and presbyters of Laodicea.[1] Born in Stratonicea, a town in Caria, they were strong in the faith, zealots for Christ and the preaching of the word of God. While guiding the lost to the path of salvation, they frequently disputed with the pagans and denounced them for worshipping demons.

One day the heathen were so infuriated by the saints' reproofs that they clapped both presbyters in irons. At that time the emperors were Diocletian and Maximian, and the Governor of Caria was Asclepiodotes, who resided in the town of Bophorus, not far from Laodicea. The prison warden and the other city councillors sent word to the Governor, informing him about the Christian presbyters and inquiring what to do with them. Asclepiodotes' reply was that the prisoners should be stoned.

The holy martyrs were taken to the place of execution, but God intervened to protect them, for the rocks that the pagans cast returned to strike the throwers. The stoning continued for some time, but the only effect was the wounding and exhaustion of the heathen. The prison warden and those with him were amazed, and the warden set free the saints. Again the holy martyrs fearlessly taught the faith of Christ and condemned heathen unbelief.

By and by the city councillors had Trophimus and Thalus seized again. The martyrs were sent to the Governor in Bophorus, as was this message: "These men were stoned, according to your command, but the throwers failed to strike them even once. For this reason, we thought it best to deliver them to you."

---

[1]Not Laodicea of Syria, but of Caria, a province of Asia Minor between the Lycus and Meander rivers

The Governor had the saints suspended and raked mercilessly with iron claws. As they were being tortured, the martyrs shouted, "We are Christians and will not worship idols! We refuse to obey the impious edict of earthly rulers."

After shredding their flesh, Asclepiodotes condemned the martyrs to death, saying, "Let them be crucified, like the sorcerer in whom they believe." The saints were led out of the city to the place of execution. On the way, they sent up praise to Christ God for deeming them worthy to suffer and die by crucifixion, as He had. An enormous crowd followed them, wishing to see their death. When the saints reached their destination, some of the Christians offered them food. As they did not wish to grieve their well-wishers, the holy presbyters ate a little, handing out the rest to the onlookers. Then the martyrs were crucified in imitation of Christ. Hanging in the air, they exhorted the crowd to belief in God and the holy faith. Some of the people reviled the Governor for his cruelty to innocent men; others shouted, "Glory to Thee, O God, for manifesting Jesus' power in our times!" A Jewess fell prostrate before the crosses and exclaimed, "Blessed is the mother who gave you birth!" The saints' mother was present, bravely watching her sons' passion. Many onlookers caught the blood of the martyrs in handkerchiefs or their palms and saved it for healing spiritual and physical infirmities. Finally, the holy martyrs Trophimus and Thalus prayed to God and surrendered their blessed souls into His hands. The saints completed the course on the sixteenth day of March. Shortly after Christ's martyrs expired, the prison warden came and prostrated himself before them, confessing to everyone that he had seen the saints ascend to heaven escorted by three angels, who were talking with them.

The faithful, having prepared shrouds and sweet spices, went to the Governor and asked leave to remove the bodies from the crosses and bury them. Asclepiodotes was infuriated by this and had his troops beat the suppliants, but when his anger cooled, he relented and allowed the Christians to take the remains. After putting the bodies into a single, new coffin, the faithful began to quarrel about where the corpses should be buried. The believers kept vigil that night beside the relics, holding candles and chanting psalms. At dawn the Governor's wife came and poured fragrant oil on the saints, then covered them with a valuable embroidery. She reviled Asclepiodotes for his cruelty and declared, "Last night I dreamed these men were sent by God with hosts of angels to take revenge on my husband for unjustly putting them to death." The quarrel about where the saints would be buried was resolved when their mother and two noblemen, Zosimas and Artemius, neighbors of the martyrs, took the coffin and committed it to the earth near Stratonicea.

Not many days later, the impious held a celebration in Laodicea to honor the birthday of their vile Emperor Diocletian. The Governor was present, and during the festivities God's vengeance requited him for shedding the martyrs' blood. Asclepiodotes collapsed, thrashed about on the ground, and trembled as though possessed, appalling the onlookers. "Where is Zeus? Where is Heracles? Where is Hermes? Where are the other gods and goddesses? I need their help!" he cried. Then he murmured, "I gained nothing by worshipping our deities. The God of heaven and His servants Trophimus and Thalus are about to commit me to eternal fire." With this he uttered a piercing cry, bit his tongue and flesh, and lamented piteously. A few moments later, he spat out his wretched soul, which joined his loathsome gods in the everlasting fires of hell. As for the holy martyrs Trophimus and Thalus, they are united to Christ in His eternal kingdom and stand before the radiant throne of the one God: Father, Son, and Holy Spirit, unto Whom be glory forever. Amen.

❧❧❧

On this same day we commemorate our father among the saints Serapion, Archbishop of Great Novgorod. His Life may be found in *The Prologue*.

The Seventeenth Day
of the Month of March

The Life of the
Venerable Alexis, Man of God[1]

During the reign of the devout emperors Arcadius and Honorius, a wealthy, pious nobleman named Euphemianus lived in old Rome. Although he had three thousand servants and wore bright silk robes and golden belts, his life was unhappy, for he had no children. The righteous Euphemianus strictly observed God's commandments. He fasted every day until the ninth hour, then supped with monks on pilgrimage in Rome. He provided three meals daily in his home for orphans, widows, the poor, travellers, and the ill. Whenever there were fewer needy folk at a meal than usual, Euphemianus would fall prostrate before the Lord and lament, "I am unworthy to dwell upon the earth fashioned by my God!" His wife Aglais was a devout woman, also very generous and compassionate to the poor. In her sorrow at having no children, she prayed to God, "Lord, remember me, Thine unworthy handmaiden, and loose the bonds of my barrenness. Deem me worthy to be called a mother and grant us a son, that my husband may know happiness in this life and we may have someone to care for us in old age."

The merciful God heard Aglais, who conceived and bore a son. The child brought much joy to his father and was given the name Alexis in Holy Baptism. At the age of six, Alexis commenced his studies, and he was soon familiar with grammar,

---

[1]An abbreviated account, taken from Symeon Metaphrastes and *The Great Collection of Readings*

rhetoric, the divine Scriptures, and various ecclesiastical texts. A perceptive lad, Alexis early understood the vanity of the world and decided to renounce the fleeting pleasures of the present life in order to inherit future blessings. He began to mortify his flesh and secretly wore a hair shirt.

When Alexis reached a marriageable age, Euphemianus told his wife, "We should find a bride for our son."

Aglais was delighted by the suggestion, fell to her knees before her husband, and cried, "May God bless our son to marry, and may I see his children! If the Lord grants me this joy, I shall redouble my almsgiving and other assistance to the poor."

Alexis was betrothed to a maiden of imperial lineage and wedded in the Church of Saint Boniface by esteemed hierarchs. A banquet followed the ceremony, with music and dancing that lasted the rest of the day and into the night. In the evening, Euphemianus told Alexis, "Enter the bridal chamber, my son, and consummate your marriage."

Alexis opened the door and found his bride sitting in a gilded armchair. He removed his golden ring and costly belt, wrapped them in purple cloth, and gave them to her, saying, "Keep these. May the Lord be with us both and by His grace guide us to what is best." With this, he retired to another room, removed his gold-embroidered robes, and donned humble clothing. Then he took some gold coins, jewels, and other items of value; slipped out of the family mansion and the city; and boarded a ship about to sail for Laodicea. As the vessel left harbor, Alexis paid his fare and prayed, "O God, Who hast nurtured me since I was in my mother's womb, do Thou save me from this vain world and deem me worthy on Judgment Day to stand at Thy right hand with all who have pleased Thee." When the ship reached Laodicea, Saint Alexis disembarked and attached himself to a group of travellers who were on their way to Edessa, the town in Mesopotamia where the "Image not Made by Hands" of Our Lord Jesus Christ was kept. The Lord Himself had sent this image to Prince Abgar of Edessa before His Passion. Alexis venerated the Holy Napkin and rejoiced greatly. He sold the valuables he had brought from Rome and gave all his money to the poor; then, clothed in rags, he began living as a beggar.

He found shelter on the porch of the Church of Our Immaculate Lady the Theotokos and fasted continuously, subsisting on a meager ration of bread and water. Every Sunday he partook of the divine and most pure Mysteries of Christ. From time to time a devout Christian would give him money, but he always passed it on to poor old folk. Saint Alexis kept his head bowed and his mind uplifted, exercising himself in the recollection of God. Because of the blessed one's rigorous discipline, his face withered, his eyes became sunken and lost their gleam, and his body was reduced to skin and bones.

The day after the wedding, Alexis' parents discovered that their son had gone missing and found his bride heartbroken. Bewildered by this turn of events, they commanded their servants to search for the man of God. When the servants could not find him, Euphemianus and Aglaïs were overwhelmed by sorrow and wept bitterly. Aglaïs retired to her chamber, shuttered the window, clothed herself in sackcloth, and threw ashes on her head. Collapsing to the floor, she prayed to God and vowed, "I will not leave this room until we learn what has become of my only son."

Alexis' bride lamented with her mother-in-law and assured her, "The faithful dove that loses its mate searches hill and dale and calls mournfully to find it, but I shall remain patiently at your side until I am certain of my husband's fate."

The blessed one's father was no less downcast and again dispatched servants to find Alexis. Several went to Edessa and saw the man of God, but took him for a beggar and gave him alms. Saint Alexis, however, recognized them and thanked the Lord for deeming him worthy to receive charity from his own slaves. Upon return, the servants informed Euphemianus of their failure. Thus, Saint Alexis remained at the Church of the Immaculate Theotokos for seventeen years, pleasing God by his labors. Then, through her icon, the most pure Theotokos spoke to the psalmist of the church, saying, "Bring into my house the man of God who is worthy of the Kingdom of heaven. His prayer rises like fragrant incense to the Lord, and the Holy Spirit rests upon him."

The cantor prayed before the icon, begging the Theotokos to reveal the Lord's favorite, and again the Most Pure One spoke, saying, "The beggar on the porch is the man of God." The psalmist compelled Alexis to live inside the church, and soon the saint's virtue became known to many. Therefore, the man of God forsook Edessa, made his way to the coast, and took ship to Cilicia, reckoning, "I will go to Tarsus, where I am a stranger to all, and find shelter near the Church of the Holy Apostle Paul." Providence, however, ordained otherwise, and a storm arose, carrying the ship on its waves for many days. The vessel came to land near Rome, and Alexis said to himself, "As the Lord God lives, I shall burden no one, but take up my dwelling as a stranger outside my father's house."

Alexis set out for his father's mansion, reaching it at suppertime. A moment later, his father appeared, riding home from the imperial palace and escorted by an enormous retinue of slaves. Falling prostrate, the saint cried, "Servant of God, have mercy on me, a beggar! Permit me to live on a corner of your property and eat the crumbs that fall from your slaves' table. If you allow this, the Lord will bless you and grant you the Kingdom of heaven. If someone from your household has been wandering in a foreign land, I daresay the Master will grant you to see him again."

The beggar's words reminded Euphemianus of his beloved son Alexis and, moved to tears, he mercifully consented. "Whoever agrees to take care of this man will be set free and given a generous reward," Euphemianus announced to the slaves. "Build the poor fellow a hut at the entrance to my property, so that when I come and go, I may see how he is faring. Feed him from my table, and make certain that no one offends him."

The hut was built and Saint Alexis took up his dwelling in it. Every day Euphemianus sent him food, but the man of God gave most of it to the needy and subsisted on just enough bread and water to keep soul and body together. Every night Alexis prayed from dusk to dawn. On Sundays he partook of the divine Mysteries in church. The servants tormented Alexis mercilessly, but his patience was wondrous. After dark they would come to the hut, slap him, pull his hair, lay blows on the back of his neck, pour slops on his head, and mock him. The unconquerable sufferer endured everything without murmur. Knowing that the devil was inciting the servants, he took up arms against the evil one and by prayer prevailed over all his schemes.

Besides these temptations, there was another far more oppressive, for like a second Ruth, Alexis' bride had remained with her mother-in-law. From the hut the man of God could see her window and through it, his bride and mother weeping: one lamenting the loss of her husband, the other of her son. His heart was smitten by pity; nevertheless, love for God prevailed over love for family, and the sweetness of compunction over feelings of sympathy. Alexis lived on his father's property for seventeen years without anyone recognizing him. All that time the son and heir of the household's master was taken for a stranger and beggar and continually ridiculed by the slaves. At length the Lord deigned to translate him from cruel suffering and poverty unto eternal rest, and revealed to him the day and hour of his departure. Alexis asked the servant who attended to his needs to bring him paper, ink, and a pen, and he wrote the whole story of his life. To convince his parents that he was their son, he included details that only they or his bride would know. He told about his conversation in the bridal chamber and mentioned that he had wrapped his ring and belt in purple cloth and given them to his wife. In conclusion, he wrote, "I beg you, beloved parents and chaste spouse, to forgive me the pain I have caused you. Never have I ceased grieving because of your distress or praying that God grant you patience and deem you worthy of His Kingdom. I trust that in His compassion, the Lord will hearken unto my supplication. It was for His sake that I treated you so harshly, and myself harsher still. Knowing that it is better to obey God than one's parents, I saddened you; but I believe that you will be rewarded richly in heaven." Upon completing the letter, Saint Alexis devoted himself to prayer until the hour of his repose.

Not many days later, the Most Holy Pope Innocent was celebrating the Divine Liturgy at the Cathedral of the Holy Apostles in the presence of the Emperor Honorius. At the end of the service, a wondrous voice in the sanctuary thundered, *Come unto Me, all ye that labour and are heavy laden, and I will give you rest!*[2]

---

[2]Matt., Ch. 11

The astonished congregation was seized with trembling. Falling prostrate, everyone cried, "Lord, have mercy!"

Then the voice commanded, "Find the man of God who is departing this life. He will pray for Rome and protect its inhabitants." Every corner of the city was searched for a dying or newly reposed holy man, but no such person was found. That Thursday evening the Emperor, the Pope, and all the people returned to the Cathedral of the Holy Apostles and held an All-night Vigil, beseeching Christ God to reveal His favorite. On Friday morning, the soul of Saint Alexis the Man of God departed the body and went to the Lord. Again a voice was heard coming from the cathedral sanctuary. This time it said, "You will find the man of God at the house of Euphemianus."

The Emperor turned to Euphemianus and asked, "Why have you kept your treasure hidden? You should have revealed it to us."

"As the Lord God lives, I know nothing about this," protested Euphemianus. Then Euphemianus asked his steward, "Is there anyone among the servants particularly remarkable for his virtue and zeal to please God?"

"As the Lord God lives, I believe there is no one like that," replied the steward. "Your slaves are an impious lot, without exception strangers to virtue."

Despite this, the Emperor and the Pope decided to go to Euphemianus' house, in the hope of finding the man of God. Euphemianus hurried home and prepared thrones for the Emperor and Pope and seats for the princes accompanying them; he also ordered servants to meet them on the way with candles and censers. His wife heard commotion outside and asked the reason for it. She was amazed to learn that the Emperor and the Patriarch were coming. From her window, Alexis' bride saw the rulers of state and Church approaching with enormous retinues and, no less astonished, asked herself, "What can this mean?"

When the Emperor, Pope, and princes were seated and there was silence, the servant who attended to Alexis' needs said to Euphemianus, "Master, could the man of God be the pauper you entrusted to my care? I have observed that he leads a life of wondrous virtue. He fasts almost every day, and if he eats, he does so late in the evening. He subsists on bread and water, and every Sunday partakes of the divine Mysteries. At night he keeps vigil, praying rather than sleeping. The slaves torment him constantly, slapping him on the face, pulling his hair, and pouring slops on him. He endures it all with joy and meekness."

Euphemianus rushed to the hut and thrice called through the window, but there was no reply, so he entered. The man of God was dead, laid out as though someone had prepared his body for burial. His face was covered, and the letter was rolled up in his right hand. Euphemianus uncovered his face, which shone like an angel's with the light of grace, but he could not remove the letter from Alexis' hand. Without delay Euphemianus returned to the Emperor and Pope and exclaimed, "Come, see the man for whom we were searching! He is already dead and is holding a letter which I could not pry from his hand."

The Emperor and Patriarch ordered a splendidly adorned bier taken to the hut and reverently placed the sacred corpse of the man of God upon it. Then they fell prostrate before the holy relics and kissed them, addressing the saint as though he were alive: "Servant of Christ, we beg you to give us the letter so that we may read it and learn who you are."

At these words the saint surrendered the letter. The Emperor and Pope commanded that there be silence, and Aetius, the archivist of the Great Church, read the text in a loud voice. After hearing the lines about Alexis' parents, and about how the saint gave his ring and belt to his bride in their chamber, Euphemianus was convinced that the man of God was his son. He cast himself on Alexis' breast, flooded the coffin with tears, and cried, "Alas, sweetest child! Why did you cause us such grief? Woe is me! For years you remained at our door, hearing your parents' lamentations, but never revealing who you were and assuaging our sadness in old age. Your love is bitter, beloved son and consolation of my soul. I know not whether to mourn your death or celebrate your finding." So saying, Euphemianus wept inconsolably and tore out his gray hair by the root.

Hearing Euphemianus' lamentation and learning that the dead pauper was her son, Aglaïs threw open her doors and ran to the bier. Ripping out her hair and tearing her robes, her eyes full of tears and raised to heaven, she pushed through the crowd, crying, "Let me through, that I may see the beloved hope of my life! Let me through, that I may see my only son!" She hurled herself on the corpse and, embracing and kissing it, sobbed, "Woe is me, sweetest child! Why have you done this? Why have you caused us such sorrow? Woe is me, light of my eyes! You lived here for so many years. Why did you not tell us who you were? Did you feel no pity when you heard us grieving for you?"

Behind Aglais ran her daughter-in-law, who for thirty-four years had worn black mourning garb, but had never given up hope for Alexis' return. She also threw herself upon the holy relics, covered them with loving tears, and wailed inconsolably, "Woe is me!" So piteous were her laments that she moved the entire crowd to join her and the parents in weeping for the deceased. Amid the tumult, the Emperor and Pope announced, "Lo, we have found that for which we were searching!" and ordered that the relics be taken to the Forum, so that everyone could see and touch them.

The entire population of the city came to the Forum and kissed the sacred remains, and numerous miracles occurred. The blind received sight, lepers were cleansed, and demons were expelled from the possessed. Seeing that God's favorite could heal every affliction, the Emperor and Pope also yearned to be sanctified by the relics. When the time came to carry the remains into the church, they hoisted the bier onto their own shoulders. The saint's parents and bride followed, still weeping bitterly, but such was the press and so eager to touch the honored body that little progress could be made. Hoping to clear a way, the Emperor ordered that gold and silver coins be thrown into the crowd, but no one bothered to take the money. Instead, the people surged forward to glimpse, or handle and kiss the man of God. Finally the Pope addressed the throng, promising not to bury the holy remains until everyone had venerated and been sanctified. The crowd gave way a little, and the relics reached the cathedral, where they remained for seven days. During that time Saint Alexis' parents and bride stayed beside the corpse, weeping continuously. The Emperor ordered that a sepulcher be made of marble and decorated with gold and pearls, and that the body of the man of God be placed in it. As soon as this was done, the holy relics gushed myrrh, which filled the tomb. The fragrant oil was distributed to the people, who anointed themselves with it to cure every disease. After this the Romans buried Saint Alexis, glorifying God.

Saint Alexis the Man of God reposed on the sixteenth of the calends of April, that is, on March 17, in the year 5919 from the creation of the world and 411 from the Incarnation of God the Word.[3] Honorius was Emperor of Rome, Innocent was Pope, and Theodosius the Lesser was Emperor of Constantinople. Over them all ruled our Lord Jesus Christ, unto Whom, with the Father and the Holy Spirit, be glory forever. Amen.

෴

On this same day the holy martyr Marinus died by the sword for Christ.

On this same day we commemorate our holy monastic father Macarius, the new wonderworker and abbot of the Monastery of Kolyazin. His Life is in *The Prologue*.

---

[3]The paschal letter was D and the column six that year. March 17 was a Friday.

The Eighteenth Day
of the Month Of March

The Commemoration of
Our Father Among the Saints Cyril,
Archbishop of Jerusalem

Saint Cyril, the son of devout, Orthodox parents, became a monk while Constantine the Great ruled. During the reign of Constantine's son Constantius, the blessed Maximus, Archbishop of Jerusalem, inherited life eternal. Saint Cyril was elected successor and as archbishop zealously battled the heresies of Arius, Macedonius, and Manes. His ardor for the apostolic dogmas won him the enmity of the bishops who were inclined to misbelief, especially Acacius, Archbishop of Caesarea of Palestine, who secured Cyril's banishment.

Soon after the Most Holy Cyril became archbishop, a wondrous sign was revealed in the heavens over Jerusalem. At the third hour of the day of Pentecost, the honored Cross appeared, shining more brilliantly than the sun and stretching from holy Golgotha to the Mount of Olives. Because the Emperor Constantius had strayed from the path of piety into the delusion of Arius, and was aiding the renegades while oppressing the Orthodox, Cyril sent him a letter relating the miracle and urging him to return to the true faith. Meanwhile Acacius, who enjoyed the ruler's favor, began undermining Cyril, accusing him of heresy and insubordination. After the heathen Roman emperors had devastated Jerusalem, its archiepiscopal see was greatly reduced in standing and made subject to the Metropolitan of Caesarea of Palestine. Because Acacius was a heretic, had been deposed by the holy fathers at the local council of Sardica, and held the rank of metropolitan uncanonically and only because the Emperor supported him, Cyril refused to acknowledge his authority. Our saint censured the Metropolitan's evil deeds, for Acacius was no pastor, but a persecutor. Moreover, the Council of Sardica, which had deposed Acacius, had also transferred his primacy to the blessed Maximus, Cyril's predecessor as Archbishop of Jerusalem. On these grounds, and because he rightly considered the see of Jerusalem, as the mother of all churches, to have precedence over Caesarea, Cyril would not be subject to Acacius.

Full of malice and hatred, Acacius cast about for a pretext to bring down Cyril. He found it when a famine befell Jerusalem and the poor of the city turned for help to their Most Holy Archbishop. Saint Cyril was very merciful and expended all his money feeding the hungry. Since the famine continued and there was no other way to provide for the needy, he sold costly hangings and the gold and silver things of the Church, and bought wheat for the people. A rumor spread that a woman was dancing through the streets lewdly, clad in sacred vestments. When asked where she had gotten this attire, she said it was from the stall of a certain merchant. The merchant said that he had bought it from the Archbishop. Whether or not the story was true, it reached the ears of Metropolitan Acacius, who now had an excuse for raising formal charges against the saint. Acacius convoked a synod in order to depose Cyril on the grounds that he had trafficked in the Church's holy things and permitted them to be ridiculed and defiled. With the aid of bishops who looked lightly on heresy, that heretic unjustly dethroned the righteous Orthodox hierarch Cyril and expelled him from Jerusalem. The saint first took refuge in Antioch, then in Tarsus with the blessed Bishop Silvanus. Realizing that Silvanus did not fully understand certain dogmas of the faith, Cyril corrected him and firmly established him in Orthodoxy. Hearing about this, Acacius wrote to Silvanus concerning Cyril's deposition and insisted that he expel the saint or at least forbid him to celebrate the divine services. Silvanus paid no heed to Acacius, because he was thankful to the devout Cyril, whose teaching had strengthened the faith of all the Orthodox in the province. Silvanus was sure Cyril was a holy man and that Acacius had acted out of jealousy and hatred.

After this a local council was held in Seleucia, attended by 150 bishops. Acacius demanded that before the synod begin, Cyril be ejected as an excommunicate. When many of the hierarchs refused, Acacius quit the assembly and went to the Imperial City where, in the presence of the Emperor and Patriarch Eudoxius (who was an Arian), he slandered the bishops gathered at Seleucia, calling them a mob of evildoers bent on the Church's ruin. Alleging that Cyril had sold in the market the gold-embroidered phelonion Constantine the Great of blessed memory had given to Archbishop Macarius of Jerusalem for use at baptisms, and that the vestment had been worn by a dancer at the theater, Acacius aroused Constantius' wrath against the saint and obtained his banishment.

Some time later Constantius died and the wicked Julian became emperor. At first Julian feigned piety and virtue. He rescinded the decrees issued by Constantius and released the Orthodox bishops exiled by him, including Cyril, who returned to his see. When, however, he had established himself firmly on the throne, Julian renounced Christ and gave the Jews freedom to do whatever they wished. He allowed them to erect a new temple on the site of the one built by Solomon, allocating public funds to aid them in the God-accursed enterprise. At the commencement of the work, Saint Cyril declared that Christ's words would certainly be fulfilled and that not one stone would be left upon another.[1] He also prayed to the Master, begging that God's enemies not be permitted to complete the building, but that their intention come to nought. The Lord heard His servant's entreaty and quickly brought to pass the prophetic saying. One night a mighty earthquake threw up the foundation stones of Solomon's Temple and brought down the walls the Jews were building. God's invisible power reduced everything to rubble. At daybreak a crowd assembled at the site and marveled at the miracle, but the Jews were undeterred and resumed work. Suddenly fire fell out of heaven and consumed the tools of the

---

[1]Matt., Ch. 24; Mark, Ch. 13; Luke, Ch. 21

laborers, terrifying the Jews. That night the sign of the Cross appeared on the clothing of the Jews, who could not remove it, no matter how hard they tried.

After this Cyril was exiled again and Cyriacus, it would seem, served as guardian of the archiepiscopal throne. Before his baptism, Saint Cyriacus was a Jew known as Judas. It was he who revealed to the holy Empress Helen where the honored Cross was buried. He occupied the cathedra very briefly, then suffered for Christ at the hands of Julian the Apostate, as it says in our entry about him under October 28. After Julian's death, Cyril recovered his throne. When the Arians gained ascendancy during the reign of Valens, the saint was exiled a third time for his devotion to piety and steadfast opposition to heresy. The godless Valens perished miserably; and his successor Theodosius the Great allowed Saint Cyril to return in triumph to Jerusalem. Cyril spent the last eight years of his life there, shepherding the flock of Christ undisturbed. Leaving his edifying writings as a legacy to the Church, the saint fell asleep in the Lord.

On the Same Day

The Life of
Our Holy Monastic Father Aninas
the Wonderworker[1]

$\mathcal{T}$he venerable Aninas was born in Chalcedon. His parents were Orthodox. *He was little of stature,*[2] like Zachaeus of old, but a capacious vessel of the Holy Spirit. From childhood Aninas was remarkable for meekness and silence, virtues which he acquired on his own, because he had no spiritual guide.

At the age of fifteen, our saint was orphaned. Straightway, he forsook the world, entered a monastery, and received the angelic tonsure. By and by longing for stillness drew him into the desert. He settled in the region where the Euphrates River separates Syria from Persia, and there met a cave-dweller named Maiumas. The saint became Maiumas' disciple and emulated his fasting and night-long vigils. So harsh was the asceticism of the two monks that they ate nothing at all during Great Lent; nevertheless, their countenances remained bright, as though they had been fed at a king's table. Before long the blessed Aninas' austerities surpassed those of his elder. To Maiumas' astonishment, even outside of Great Lent Aninas would keep forty-day fasts, during which time the young monk prayed continuously.

Since there was no nearer source, Aninas would fetch water from the Euphrates, three miles away. He carried the water in a little pot, refusing to use a larger one because he wanted to increase his labor and the frequency of the errand. Once Aninas was on his way to the river and, about a mile from the cave, an angel appeared and filled the vessel. Maiumas was amazed at how quickly the blessed one returned. Realizing that a miracle had occurred and that the grace of God was with his disciple, he begged Aninas to become his elder and teacher. Wishing to remain under obedience, Aninas refused. As a result, Maiumas abandoned the cave, for he was unwilling to be the guide of

---

[1]Abbreviated from *The Great Collection of Readings*
[2]Luke, Ch. 19

such a God-pleasing man. Maiumas entered a monastery on the Euphrates and told the brethren about Aninas, after which they began visiting the saint.

Despite his elder's departure, Saint Aninas remained in the cave, saying, "God brought me here; here shall I remain until I die." Nonetheless, he would frequently leave the cave for twenty or thirty days at a time and retire into more remote parts of the desert. He mortified every carnal passion and subjugated his flesh to the spirit; therefore, God subjected wild animals to him and they became his servants. Whenever he left the cave, he was followed by a lion on either side. One of these beasts had hurt its paw, and Saint Aninas healed the wound.

Aninas was an unmercenary physician not only for animals, but for people as well. God gave him power to cure every disease and ailment, and his fame spread throughout the land. Both men and women began flocking to him, bringing their sick. Aninas cured them all, by the grace of God which dwelt in him. Because the people were disappointed when they came and he was absent, the venerable one stopped leaving the cave. The Lord granted Aninas as a healing fountain to the villagers, some of whom were made whole physically, and others spiritually, by his teaching.

The crowds were always thirsty and there was no water at the cave, so the saint dug a little cistern. On a hot day a group of visitors came, and Aninas sent one of his six disciples to fetch a drink for the guests. The disciple, hurrying back, announced that the cistern was dry. In a quiet voice, the venerable one told him, "I put my trust in the wondrous name of the Lord and am certain that if you go back, you will find enough water for these people." Retracing his steps, the astonished disciple found the cistern filled to the brim. Glorifying God and rejoicing, he took water to our father. The cistern remained full for many days, though water was drawn for every need. This miracle took place seventeen years after Aninas began leading the ascetical life. The disciple proclaimed it to everyone, ascribing it to the saint's prayers. Now the weather remained hot and dry, and the cistern eventually was emptied, but Aninas did not wish to ask God to repeat the miracle, so he humbled himself and began bringing water from the Euphrates every night to meet the needs of the visitors. From sunset to sunrise he carried water, glorifying God and repeating the words of the Gospel, "*Whosoever shall give to drink unto one of these little ones a cup of cold water only in* My *name, he shall in no wise lose his reward.*"[3]

Once, the cistern was empty and brethren arrived from the nearby monastery, worn out and thirsty. The godly one took jugs and went to the river for water. He returned so quickly everyone thought that he had become exhausted and turned back before reaching the Euphrates. Seeing him approach, the visiting monks went out to meet him. They were going to relieve him of the jugs and fetch the water themselves, but as they were removing the pots from the godly one's shoulders, they realized the vessels were full. An angel of the Lord had provided water, as when the elder Maiumas was living with the saint. "Glory to God!" exclaimed the monks. "Our holy father's shoulders gush cool, living, delicious water."

"Forgive me, brethren. I am a sinner," said Aninas in his humility. "The jugs were filled by an unseen hand, not for my sake, but for yours. You would have collapsed from thirst by the time I returned from the river."

Patricius, Bishop of Neocaesarea, frequently visited the man of God. He deeply loved and revered Aninas for his holy life and the miracles worked through him by divine grace. Against the saint's will, Patricius ordained Aninas presbyter. Hearing that the venerable one was exhausting himself by his trips for water, he sent Aninas a donkey for transporting the jugs. Only for a few days did the saint have rest from the labor, because a poor man came asking help in paying a debt. Being poor in spirit and material possessions, the godly one had nothing else to give the man, so he told him, "Take this ass, brother: sell it and pay what you owe."

Word of this reached the Bishop, who sent another donkey and this message: "I am not giving you this animal, but only lending it. Use it to carry water. When I need it again, I will take it back."

It was not long before a second poor man came to the venerable one, requesting assistance. Since he had no money or pos-

---

[3]Matt., Ch. 10

sessions of value, Saint Aninas gave him the Bishop's donkey. A few days later, Patricius came for a visit and, not finding the animal, ordered an enormous cistern dug. Then he had a train of donkeys fill it with water from the river.[4] He took the beasts back to Neocaesarea and afterwards lent them to the saint for short periods of time, but only when the cistern was empty.

Not far from Apameia there lived a stylite named Pionius, a man of angelic life. Some evil neighbors broke through the wall of his monastery, but finding nothing worth taking, departed empty-handed. Before leaving, one of them threw a rock at the stylite and badly hurt his head. The stylite considered coming down from his pillar and pressing charges against the thieves. Being clairvoyant, the godly Aninas learned about this. Aninas summoned the lion that served him, gave it food, and commanded it, "Eat until you are full, because you have a long trip to make." Then he wrote this message to the stylite: "Venerable Father! It has come to my attention that you were injured by malefactors and are thinking of descending from your column to obtain temporal justice. Please abandon this notion. If you will follow it through, you will lose the eternal reward for patience that awaits you in the Kingdom of heaven."

Saint Aninas hung the note on a cord around the lion's neck. He gave the beast instructions as if to a person, sending it to Apameia and forbidding it to harm anyone on the way. The lion hurried to its destination and knocked on the monastery doors with its paws. The porter opened the little window and, seeing an enormous lion, rushed to tell the stylite. After praying, the stylite calmed the gatekeeper and had him let in the beast, which made straight for the pillar and dropped the note. Reading it, the stylite marveled at how Saint Aninas, although far away, knew his thoughts and at how God made wild animals serve His favorite. He decided not to trust in human justice, but to put his hope in the Lord.

A certain devout woman was troubled by an infirmity and, having faith in Aninas' ability to heal, was on her way to the

---

[4]In desert lands, water is difficult to find in the earth. The inhabitants dig cisterns which are filled by rainwater or runoff from snow, or by water brought from elsewhere.

saint's cave when a barbarian armed with a spear confronted her. The barbarian was planning to rob her, but since she was carrying nothing except a little bread, decided instead upon rape. He thrust the spear into the ground and grabbed the woman, but she fought to get loose and cried, "Saint Aninas, help me!" Somehow, the sound of the venerable one's name threw the fierce barbarian into a panic. Trembling violently, he released the woman and tried to pull up the spear, but could not. A demon entered the terror-stricken man, and his victim made good her escape. She related everything to the saint, was healed, and safely returned home. The barbarian followed her to the godly one's cave and, after he repented of his crimes, Aninas expelled the demon that had him in its power. Saint Aninas instructed the man in the holy faith, baptized him, and clothed him in the angelic schema. The robber became a virtuous monk and, by the power of God, his spear grew into a mighty oak.

God's great favorite cured many illnesses, enabled paralytics to walk, and drove devils out of the possessed. He was also famous for healing animals, and worked other miracles of every kind. One cloudless day when the sun was blazing, a huge crowd came to see the man of God, but because there was no water, everyone was wilting with thirst until the saint prayed. Suddenly the sky became black, a downpour filled to overflowing every hole and crevice in the earth, and the people drank their fill.

The venerable one frequently prophesied, predicting barbarian invasions and the repose of a number of his disciples. Whenever he foresaw with clairvoyant inner eyes the death of one of the brethren, he would summon him and tell him privately, "Child, look to your soul, for the hour of death is at hand."

Finally, when Aninas was 110 years old, his own death drew near. Knowing beforehand the day of departure, he gathered his rational sheep (now a large flock) and instructed them for a long time. Then, pointing to the worthy presbyter Veronicianus, he announced, "This man will succeed me as abbot." Saint Aninas' last hour followed an illness of seven days. On the seventh day the venerable one became uneasy and wanted to rise from his bed, but fear subsided as quickly as it had manifested itself. Bowing his head, Saint Aninas said, "Peace be to you, my lords." After brief silence, he inquired, "Who are you, my lords?" Another moment of silence followed; then he said, "God's will be done. I will go with you, as the Lord commands." Everyone was frightened and fell prostrate.

The saintly presbyter Veronicianus, who had been chosen abbot, asked the man of God, "Master, are you about to inherit the reward for which you labored throughout your life? What do you see?"

"The *Jerusalem which is above*[5] has been revealed to me," replied the saint. "A bright cloud came down bearing three radiant men, who announced, 'Aninas, the Lord is calling you. Come with us.' I inquired, 'Who are you, my lords?' They said, 'We are Moses, Aaron, and Hur.'"[6] Hearing this, the monks became even more terrified. The venerable one requested, "Brethren, pray that I not be put to shame before the dread throne of judgment." Then he said, "Receive, O *Lord, my spirit*,"[7] and reposed. The day of his death was the eighteenth of March. The brethren buried Saint Aninas reverently, praising Father, Son, and Holy Spirit, the one God glorified by all unto the ages. Amen.

                          ❧❧❧❧

On this same day we commemorate the holy martyrs Trophimus and Eucarpion, who were burned alive for Christ in Nicomedia.

---

[5]Gal., Ch. 4
[6]Aaron and Hur (Or) held up Moses' arms in the form of a cross while the Israelites were battling Amalek. See Ex., Ch. 17. (Tr.)
[7]Acts, Ch. 7

The Nineteenth Day of the Month of March

The Passion of the Holy Martyrs Chrysanthus and Daria, and Those with Them

There once lived a man of princely origins named Polemius, who moved from Alexandria to Rome, where he was welcomed by the nobility and admitted to the Senate by the Emperor. Wishing to give his only son Chrysanthus a good education, Polemius enrolled him in a school of philosophy. The youth was inquisitive, wise, and intelligent (as will become evident in our story), and while exploring the writings of the ancients, he came upon the Gospels and Epistles. After reading them through attentively and immersing his mind in their meaning, he reflected, "Chrysanthus, as long as you were studying heathen writings, which are full of darkness, you could not find the light of truth. Now that you have found it, you must cleave to it, for it would be senseless to return to darkness from the light. Your labor will be wasted if you destroy its fruit. You have read God's promise: *Seek and ye shall find.*[1] God rewards our toil with fruit. If you discard what you have sought and found, you will prove yourself aimless and senseless. Hold fast to it with your whole mind, and do not foolishly deprive yourself of it. You have discovered gold and silver; you have turned up a precious jewel.

---

[1]Luke, Ch. 11

You searched in order to find; you have found, that you might inherit the promise. Take heed, lest the treasure you have unearthed be snatched from you."

Reasoning thus, Chrysanthus sought for a teacher of the divine Scriptures. Formerly he had devoted himself to the study of rhetoric and philosophy and was a pupil of the foremost scholars; now he inquired where to find teachers like the simple fishermen who drew the whole world into the net of the knowledge of Christ. The wise youth sought such teachers because he had read the Apostle's words: *Where is the wise? Where is the scribe? Where is the disputer of this age? Hath not God made foolish the wisdom of this world? For after that the world by wisdom knew not God, it pleased God by the foolishness of preaching to save them that believe.*[2] Chrysanthus remembered this passage and day after day continued his search. At length someone told him about a Christian named Carpophorus who was learned in Holy Scripture and because of the persecution raging at that time had his dwelling in a remote grotto in the mountains. Overjoyed, Chrysanthus clasped the feet of the man telling him this and begged to learn exactly where the servant of God lived. As soon as he was told, the youth hurried to the cave. The blessed Carpophorus, who was a presbyter, explained to Chrysanthus the word of God and the mystery of the Christian faith. For several months Chrysanthus returned often for guidance on the path to salvation. The young man attained a sound understanding of the divine Scriptures, and Carpophorus baptized him. Being perfectly established in the holy faith and the love of Christ, Chrysanthus began preaching the Son of God to all only seven days after his Baptism. Several of his noble relatives took word of this to his father, saying, "Your son is blaspheming our gods and proclaiming that a man named Jesus Christ is the true God. If this reaches the Emperor, you will be blamed and we shall lose his favor. Whoever reviles the gods is considered a criminal and punished without mercy."

Polemius flew into a rage. He locked his son in a gloomy dungeon and tortured him with hunger, feeding him only a few miserable crumbs every evening. The blessed Chrysanthus,

---

[2]I Cor., Ch. 1

however, regarded imprisonment and starvation not as punishment, but as an introduction to the difficult Christian life of stillness and fasting. He rejoiced more in the dark, fetid cell than another would in a bright, spacious palace. Understanding this, his relatives and the members of the household advised Polemius, "The Christians consider prisons, fetters, hunger, and torture to be glory and honor, not misery. If you want your son to abandon the Christian faith, then free him and allow him to enjoy every pleasure. Wed him to a beautiful, intelligent maiden. Once he has experienced conjugal pleasure, he will gladly renounce the Christian religion."

So Polemius removed his son from the dungeon and took him to a specially prepared mansion, where the walls were adorned with magnificent tapestries and the bedcovers were of softest silk. Everything was splendid and cheerful in the building, which was stocked with the finest foods and wines. Polemius locked Chrysanthus in the mansion with the most beautiful of the maidservants, who were alluringly dressed and instructed to seduce the young man by any and all means, and to turn him away from Christ. A banquet was prepared at which the girls sang licentious songs, danced and frolicked lasciviously, whispered shameless words to Chrysanthus, and urged him to surrender to fornication and other carnal pleasures. The saint, however, remained unmeshed by their nets, and thereby proved that he was no raw recruit, but a brave and invincible hoplite of Christ. He refused to taste the delectable food and drink, recoiled from the wenches' touch as from the fangs of an adder, and prayed continuously. When necessity compelled him to sleep, he shunned the bed for the floor. With the shield of faith he fended off the arrows of the girls' wanton coaxing, and he cried to God, "*Arise, O Lord, unto my help; say to my soul: I am thy salvation.*[3] How can I prevail in this struggle against the devil, unless Thou assist me with Thy right hand? If a man strives to conquer carnal passion and preserve his chastity by his own strength, he is deceived. The flame of fleshly lusts can only be quenched by the rain of Thy compassion; the soul cannot attain Thy mansions unless Thou leadest it thither.

---

[3]Ps. 34

Carnal pleasure is a ravening beast lurking in the wilderness of earthly vanity and waiting to destroy souls. Whoever escapes its maw must render heartfelt thanks unto Thee, O God the Saviour, our Deliverer from perdition. Jacob lamented, *'An evil beast hath devoured*[4] my son,'* Thy blessed favourite, Joseph, who fled to Thee and was delivered from the hands of the adulter-ess as from the jaws of a vicious wild animal. Verily, Potiphar's wife like a ferocious beast fell upon Joseph: like a lioness she sank her claws into the innocent lamb and dragged him toward the pit of sin. What animal is more vicious than the devil, more relentless than a woman? The Egyptian temptress stirred Joseph's flesh and blood with flirtatious eyes, beautiful robes, a lovely face, and deceitful promises of wealth and power, draw-ing the chaste youth toward perdition and death. What a mar-vel that he escaped the clutches of the savage beast! With good reason did Jacob exclaim, *It is a great thing for me that my son is yet alive.*[5] The Egyptian woman put Joseph in greater peril than had his brothers; but he escaped death, for Thou wast with him, O God Almighty, and he had Thine unfailing help. Now, O Lord, I humbly implore Thee: grant me aid, for my father has entrapped me with beasts and serpents. As charmers lull to sleep poisonous snakes, so do Thou lull to sleep these dissolute maidens by the sound of my prayer, lest they arouse warfare in my young flesh. Help me, O Saviour, for I know Thee to be the true God, Who rescuest those who believe in Thee and grantest them invincible help." At this the wenches fell into a deep sleep, from which they could not be awakened. Only when they were removed from the house did they rouse and eat; but when taken back, they fell asleep again. This went on for several days.

Polemius was told what was happening and mourned Chrysanthus as one dead. "Your son has been initiated into sor-cery by the Christians," alleged his friends, "and easily cast a spell on the ignorant servant-girls. You must marry him to an intelligent, well-educated maiden, even if he is unwilling. Sooner or later they will consummate the nuptials, and he will abandon the Christian religion."

---

[4]Gen., Ch. 37   [5]Gen., Ch. 45

"And where shall I find a maiden capable of softening the hard heart of my son and returning him to our beliefs?" wondered Polemius.

His relatives said, "One of the maidens serving in the temple of Athena[6] is named Daria. She is an exquisite beauty, has read all the books of the ancients, and has mastered the art of rhetoric. You must act quickly, for she is of a marriageable age. Arrange her betrothal to your son before someone else takes her."

Polemius agreed and requested his relatives to tell the maiden about Chrysanthus. They proposed to Daria that she marry Chrysanthus and turn him away from the Christian faith, to which she agreed. After rehearsing the words she would use to seduce Chrysanthus and persuade him to worship the gods, she dressed in her finest robes, adorned herself in dazzling jewelry, and was led into the saint's bedroom. The two were left alone, and she began her attempts to lead the chaste youth into fornication. What endearments she whispered into his ears! What deceptive promises she uttered! Nevertheless, vanquishing carnal love by love for God, Christ's soldier remained as firm as adamant, as unshakable as a pillar, as unmovable as a mountain. With the Cross as his defense, he deflected all the fiery arrows of the evil one. Sighing to God from the bottom of his heart and calling upon the Holy Spirit for assistance, he told Daria, "O beautiful maiden, you have adorned yourself splendidly and rehearsed your words carefully in order to dissuade me from my good intention, corrupt my soul (which is enthralled by divine love), and change my convictions. If you have done all this for the sake of a brief union with a mortal, should you not exert yourself far more to win the love of the Son of God and immortal King? You can easily achieve this, if you wish. Preserve your soul and flesh unsullied, and as you have adorned your body with costly jewelry, adorn your heart with virtues. Think: you will have angels as friends, apostles as companions, and martyrs as intimates. Through their mediation, Christ will accept you as His bride. He will prepare for you a bridechamber in heaven incomparably superior to any on earth. He will grant you the everlast-

[6]Minerva

ing joy of paradise, preserve the bloom of your youth forever, and enter your dowry into the book of eternal life."

Daria was moved by the holy youth's words and said, "It was not carnal lust that brought me here in this attire, but your father's tears and love for you and his desire to return you to the worship of our gods."

"If you can provide clear proof and irrefutable arguments demonstrating the truth of polytheism, I will change my beliefs accordingly. Let us discuss the matter for our common benefit," suggested Saint Chrysanthus.

"Unless we worship the gods and placate them with offerings, they will be roused to anger and we shall lose their protection," Daria asserted.

"What are you saying, wise virgin!" cried the saint. "How can the gods protect us, when they themselves require protection? Dogs are tied to them at night, so they are not stolen; and they are fastened down with metal pins and weighted with lead to prevent their falling and being shattered."

"If the rabble could do without them, we would not make statues of the gods," said Daria. "We cast figures of gold, silver, and bronze, sculpt them of marble, and carve them of wood so that when the people see with their eyes what they should envision with their minds, they will worship and fear our deities."

"Then let us consider whether those whom the idols depict merit divine honor," the blessed one continued. "Anything that lacks the totality of holiness, righteousness, and divine glory cannot be called divine. Which of these qualities does the scythe-wielder Cronus[7] possess? He swallowed his children the moment they were born, as his own worshippers admit! And what do you find worthy of praise in Zeus,[8] for whom murder and fornication were daily pastimes? He made war against his father, destroyed his own offspring, committed adultery, perpetuated sorcery, slaughtered mortals, and was guilty of other foul deeds too shameless and numerous to relate. Do you really believe such an evil person is a god? Your own heathen authors testify that he was merely a man. They admit that foolish people ascribed divinity to mortals, especially to kings who were victo-

[7]Saturn [8]Jupiter

rious in battle. Tell me a single virtue that Zeus possessed. Until the day of his death he was enemy of everything pure and honorable. He defiled the air when he snatched up to heaven the youth Ganymede, whom he wanted as his lover; he polluted the earth by violating his own sisters. And what is divine in Hermes,[9] whose head is winged like a monster's? By means of sorcery he found gold hidden in the earth, and by wizardry and a magic wand rendered harmless the venom of snakes. He did this with the help of demons, to which he daily sacrificed a hog or a cock. What holiness is there in wretched Heracles,[10] who exhausted himself murdering his neighbors, and by the will of God was immolated with his club and the pelt he wore? What do you find admirable in Apollo, or in the secret rites of Dionysus,[11] with their drunkenness and immorality? Call to mind how the sister and wife of Zeus and queen of goddesses Hera,[12] the foolish Pallas,[13] and the lewd Venus envied and hated one another, argued about who was fairest, and submitted their dispute for judgment to a shepherd boy.[14] None of these are worthy of divine honor, for they are devoid of holiness and righteousness. There is no point even in mentioning the lesser gods, for what is true of the head applies to the other members. Which of the minor deities can be considered divine when Cronus, Zeus, and Venus, whom the ignorant regard as the chief divinities, are not gods at all? If your gods are so vain and loathsome, then their worshippers are pitiable in the extreme."

Daria listened attentively to Chrysanthus and responded, "It is true that the poets relate many senseless myths. This is why we must study the philosophers, who reject these immoral tales and teach us virtue. In their explanations of the world's origins, they interpret the gods' names symbolically. Cronus they understand as a representation of time, which consumes all things and reduces them to nothingness; Zeus as heat; Hera as the air; Aphrodite as fire; Poseidon as the sea; and Ceres as the earth. They understand all the gods as personifications of components of the natural world."

---

[9]Mercury   [10]Hercules   [11]Bacchus
[12]Juno   [13]Athena (Tr.)   [14]Paris of Troy (Tr.)

To this Chrysanthus replied, "Usually, men make images of what is impermanent to preserve its memory, but everyone knows that the earth, the sea, fire, and air exist throughout the generations. What need is there to depict such things as idols having human form? This is completely senseless. Moreover, why reverence depictions of personifications of nature's components more than nature itself? Why not simply worship the earth, air, and the sea? No king or prince commands that his image be adored while forbidding honor to his own person. Clearly, the idols cannot represent either nature or deities. They depict ordinary mortals."

"Your arguments confirm my own speculations," said Daria. "The worship of statues is best left to simple, ignorant people. We should directly adore nature, which is merely represented by the images of the gods."

"If you believe this to be so, let us further examine the matter," Chrysanthus proposed. "Consider the implications of nature-worship. Whoever adores the earth ought to treat it as a goddess and scrupulously avoid doing anything to dishonor it. He should not dig or till, but leave the ground free of cultivation. The farmer who worships the earth as a goddess must not apply to it plow or spade, because this would be treatment unworthy of a divinity. But whose fields and vineyards produce more: he who adores the earth as a deity, and refrains from tilling; or he who proffers the earth no worship, but diligently cultivates it? If the earth is truly a divinity, as you say, it should provide you, its devotees, all its fruits without being tilled or sown. Likewise, if the sea is a god, then set out on it without oars, and it will carry you wherever you desire. If you want fish, do not cast nets, but simply worship the sea as divine and pray to it. Understand, O maiden, that neither the earth nor the sea nor any of the lifeless components of nature have a soul or reason. They have no cognizance of their worshippers, but serve the needs of man in accordance with Providence. But by the command of the Creator, rain and dew water the ground, and the sun warms the earth, so that seed germinates and plants grow and produce fruit in due season. Therefore, we should not adore what the one God has created, set in order, and provided for our sustenance: we should worship the Lord Himself. Schoolchildren do not honor their books, slates, and papers, but their teachers; likewise, those healed of illness do not thank their medicines, but their physician."

By means of these and many other proofs, Saint Chrysanthus convinced Daria to believe in the one true God, our Lord Jesus Christ. The saints married, but kept their virginity intact and lived in the fear of God. Polemius was delighted that his son had wed and, unaware of the couple's secret, gave Chrysanthus full freedom and made him, as his only child, his sole heir.

Before long, Polemius died, for God wished the married virgins Chrysanthus and Daria to toil for Him unimpeded. In the privacy of his home Chrysanthus baptized his blessed spouse, who applied herself to the divine Scriptures and all the Christian writings. Daria led a holy life and became a perfect handmaiden and bride of Christ. Moreover, Chrysanthus and Daria labored not only for their own salvation, but for that of others as well. He converted many men to Christ and exhorted youths to preserve their virginity, while she betrothed to Christ a multitude of women and maidens. Each organized a community similar to a monastery. Chrysanthus began living with young men who had rejected the pleasures of this world and vowed before God to remain pure, and Daria the same with virgins betrothed to Christ.

Several years passed and both houses grew quickly. Then unexpected turmoil broke out. A mob appeared before Celerinus, Prefect of Rome, clamoring against the Lord's servants Chrysanthus and Daria. The men cried out, "Our wives have fled us!" and the youths, "Because of Daria, we have lost the maidens espoused to us!" The women shouted, "Our husbands have abandoned us!" and the maidens, "Chrysanthus has stolen our bridegrooms!" The whole crowd exclaimed, "If marriage is rejected, how will the human race survive? The population will dwindle if Chrysanthus and Daria continue to bewitch men and prevent them from sharing their bed with women!"

Without delay the Eparch commanded that Chrysanthus and Daria be seized and subjected to tortures unless they sacrificed to the gods. Chrysanthus was handed over to a tribune named Claudius, who in turn delivered the saint to his troops, saying, "Take this man to the temple of Zeus outside the city. Torture him until he worships the invincible Heracles."

The soldiers bound Chrysanthus with rough rawhide thongs, tying them so tightly they bit through his flesh to the bone. When the straps ripped apart, the soldiers tried to tie him up again, but were unable. After a long time they exhausted their patience, flew into a rage, and cast him into a dismal prison. There they fastened three shackles on him and put him in stocks. When the soldiers began to mock Chrysanthus, the shackles and stocks crumbled to dust. Then the tormentors poured human urine on the martyr, saying, "This will render your magic useless," but the ill-smelling liquid changed into a strong and fragrant perfume. Next they killed a calf, wrapped the naked martyr in its hide, and left him in the blazing sun so that the raw pelt would dry tight on his body. When the hide did not shrink, the tormenters returned Chrysanthus to prison. They shackled the martyr with the same result as before, only this time the dungeon was illumined by a celestial light more brilliant than countless burning candles. The soldiers reported this to Claudius, who hastened to the prison and himself saw the light. The tribune took Chrysanthus to his quarters and asked him, "How do you work these miracles? I have dealt with numerous warlocks, but none possessed such power. You are clearly an intelligent person and of noble birth; therefore, I make no demand of you but that you renounce Christian teaching, which is disturbing the tranquility of Rome. Act as befits your lineage, and offer the almighty gods the oblations that are their due."

Claudius then ordered that the martyr be tied to a tree and flailed with branches, which were firm and heavy in the hands of the soldiers, but weak as twigs when they struck Chrysanthus' body. Witnessing this, the tribune halted the thrashing, untied the martyr, clothed him, and said to the troops, "I have seen every kind of sorcery, but this is not the working of the black art. Leather straps burst, shackles and stocks crumble to dust, a fresh skin open to blazing sun all day fails to dry, again iron shackles dissolve, a dungeon is illumined, and heavy branches become light twigs when they touch this man's body! What else can this be, than the power of God Himself? No choice remains for us, but to fall at the feet of the servant of God. There is no denying the divine power that works in him. Let us beg forgiveness for our cruelty; let us entreat him to reconcile us with his almighty God. We have seen how this God strengthens His servants and makes them invincible in the face of every danger. The Lord's servant has vanquished us and surely will prevail over our princes and emperors, putting them to shame by the irresistible might of the God of heaven."

Then Claudius and his soldiers fell prostrate before Saint Chrysanthus and exclaimed, "Yours is the true God! Lead us to Him and make us His servants."

"If you desire to approach my God, draw near to Him with your heart, not your feet. God is close to all who seek Him with faith and offer Him their heart," said the blessed one. Chrysanthus discoursed at length about the true God, converting not only Claudius, but also his wife Hilaria, his sons Jason and Maurus, his relatives and friends, and his entire household, as well as the soldiers and their families. All were baptized together and remained with Chrysanthus day and night, hearkening attentively unto his teaching and yearning to suffer for Christ the Lord.

At that time the Emperor of Rome was Numerian. When he learned that Claudius had accepted our Lord Jesus Christ and been baptized with his household and troops, he ordered that the tribune be cast into the sea with an enormous stone tied to his neck. He also commanded that the soldiers and both of Claudius' sons be decapitated. Near the site where the martyrs were beheaded, there was an old tomb. After clearing it out, Christians took the saints' bodies there by night and buried them. Hilaria frequently visited the sepulcher and prayed by the relics and at the place where her sons were executed. Once, while so doing, she was seized by unbelievers, who began dragging her away for torture. "Let me finish my prayers!" she pleaded. "Then take me wherever you wish."

The pagans released her, and she bent the knee and lifted her hands and eyes to heaven, saying, "O Master, Lord Jesus Christ, Whom I confess with my whole heart! Permit me to dwell with my sons, who answered Thy call to suffering and laid down their lives for Thee, their Lord." With these words Hilaria surrendered her soul into God's hands. The heathen, moved to pity, allowed Hilaria's two handmaidens to lay her to rest in the tomb with the holy martyrs.

Meanwhile, the Emperor turned his attention to Saints Chrysanthus and Daria, commanding that they be subjected to various torments. Chrysanthus was loaded with chains and imprisoned in the *Cloaca Maxima*, the great sewer of Rome, which drained all the filth of the city. Daria was carried away to a brothel. God sent his invincible aid to both martyrs. A heavenly light shone upon Chrysanthus in the dark sewer, and the stench of human waste was transformed into a wondrous fragrance. At the same time a lion escaped from captivity and ran straight to the room where Daria was on her knees praying to God. Unaware that the beast was guarding Daria, a mob assembled outside and goaded a shameless youth to defile the saint; but when he entered the room, the lion threw him to the floor and pinned him with its paws. Like a human servant, the animal looked to its mistress for a sign, and the young man's life hung in the balance until Daria said, "In the name of the Son of God, I command you to release your prey. I want to tell him the word of the Lord." The lion obeyed at once and went to the door to prevent anyone else from entering. Daria then said to the youth, "You see, wretch, how the name of Christ tames even the fiercest of beasts. The lion knows the true God, and fears and honors Him. You, however, a rational being, have no fear of God. You are a reprobate, wallowing in filth and boasting about things of which you should be ashamed and repent."

Falling to his knees before Saint Daria, the young man begged, "Handmaiden of the Lord, permit me to escape unharmed, and I will proclaim to all that Christ, Whom you serve, is the only true God!" Daria ordered the lion to let him pass, and the youth exclaimed throughout the city, "Daria is a goddess!"

Shortly afterwards gladiators came to the brothel to take away the lion, but these fearless men proved no match for the beast, which was strengthened by God. The lion threw them all to the floor at Saint Daria's feet and would not let them move, although it killed or harmed no one. As the animal awaited her command, Daria told the gladiators, "Believe in Christ, and you will leave unscathed. Refuse, and you will have to depend on your gods' protection."

"Death to him who does not believe that Christ is the true

and living God!" shouted the men as with one voice. Daria ordered the lion to release the gladiators, who ran through the streets shouting, "Romans! There is no God other than Christ, Whom Daria preaches."

Word of events reached Celerinus, who had the house of ill repute set afire. Frightened by the flames, the lion roared wildly, but the saint calmed it, saying, "Have no fear. You will not be harmed or captured or killed. Your death will be peaceful and natural. Return to the wilderness and God, Whose presence you sensed in me, shall defend you." The lion bowed its head and departed, walking through the city without harming anyone and taking up its dwelling in the wilds. All those who had narrowly escaped becoming its food were baptized.

Numerianus learned what had happened and ordered the Eparch to destroy Chrysanthus and Daria by means of cruel tortures. Saint Chrysanthus was stripped naked and suspended from a tree, but when candles were brought to burn him, the tree snapped, the flames were extinguished, and the martyr was miraculously loosed. Those who tried to touch Saint Daria were stricken with such violent pain in their hands and muscles that they shrieked in anguish. The Prefect became frightened and hurried to relate everything to Numerianus. The Emperor ascribed the miracles to sorcery and commanded that the martyrs be buried alive outside the city alongside the Salarian Way. As they were being led to the deep pit that had been dug for them, the holy martyrs Chrysanthus and Daria chanted and prayed. When they had descended into this tomb, the saints were covered with earth and stones, in accordance with the Emperor's command. Together they had lived in spiritual wedlock, and together they died and were crowned with imperishable garlands by God, Who accepted them as living, fragrant oblations. Many healings and other miracles occurred at that site. On the anniversary of their martyrdom, a large crowd of Christian men, women, and children assembled at a nearby cave, joyfully commemorated the death of the saints, and partook of the divine Mysteries. Learning about this, the tyrant had the mouth of the cavern sealed with earth, interring the worshippers alive. Among the Christians martyred were Diodorus the presbyter, Marianus the deacon, and several clerics.

I, Varinus, have written these things with the help of my brother Armenius, at the command of the Most Holy Pope of Rome Stephen. We are sending copies of the text to every city, so that all may know that the blessed martyrs Chrysanthus and Daria received crowns of martyrdom in the Kingdom of heaven from our Lord Jesus Christ. Unto Him be glory and dominion, now and ever and unto the ages of ages. Amen.

ه‌ه‌ه‌ه‌ه‌

On this same day, while Diocletian and Maximian ruled, the holy martyr Pancharius was beheaded with a sickle for Christ in the city of Nicomedia.

The Twentieth Day of the Month of March

The Passion of Our Holy Monastic Fathers John, Sergius, and Patricius, and the Other Holy Monks Slain at the Monastery of Saint Sabbas by the Saracens[1]

While Constantine and Irene ruled in the Imperial City, the Most Holy Elias II was Patriarch of Jerusalem. At that time the Holy City was already under Hagarene rule, and a war broke out between Saracen tribes. As they fought one another, the barbarians devastated not only villages, but Eleutheropolis, Ascalon, Gaza, Scarithius, and other cities. Attacking unexpectedly, they would loot everything of value and murder whoever resisted. They lay in wait near roads and set upon travelers, beating them and stripping them to their underclothing. The victims were fortunate to escape alive. Jerusalem was in terror and full of people fleeing from nearby towns and hamlets. The inhabitants of the Holy City manned their ramparts and prepared to fend off the barbarian robber bands. In those days the glorious Monastery of Saint Chariton was destroyed, and it was never rebuilt.

Meanwhile, the brotherhood of the Lavra of the venerable Sabbas (which consisted of monks from many lands) held firm under the guidance of Abba Basil. The brethren could have

---

[1]An abbreviated account, derived from Greek manuscripts

taken refuge in Jerusalem, but refused to forsake the holy lavra, where they had taken up the yoke of Christ and pleased God by ascetical labors. They did not fear the sword, for they were dead to the world and had put all their trust in Christ. "If He so deigns, our Master can deliver us," they reminded one another. "If, however, it is His will that we fall into the hands of the barbarians and be slaughtered, then may He hasten our death, as being to our benefit. Let us accept the excellent gift offered by the Master. Let us not exchange the stillness of the desert for the tumult of the city out of fear of the barbarians, lest we be taken for cowards, too craven to heed the commandment of the Lord: *Fear not them which kill the body, but are not able to kill the soul.*[2] It is delightful to see men fleeing the world and following Christ's footsteps in the desert, but pitiful to behold monks abandoning the wilderness and seeking safety in the world. With the help of Christ our King, we have often defeated the devil, putting that cur to flight. May our foe not drive us out of the wilderness and into the city now; may he not deprive us of our stillness nor reduce us to a laughing-stock! We have no need of stone walls for defense, because our unbreachable bulwark is Christ, to Whom the holy David has taught us to chant, *Be Thou unto me a God to defend me and a house of refuge to save me.*[3] Though we have no iron armor, nor helmets, nor shields to turn the arrows of our enemies, we possess the weaponry of spiritual love, the armor of hope, *the shield of faith, and the helmet of salvation.*[4] We do not rely on soldiers for defense, for *the angel of the Lord will encamp round about them that fear Him, and will deliver them.*[5] For us *to live is Christ, and to die is gain.*[6] If we wished to cling to this fleeting life, we would never have taken up our abode in the desert. Love for Christ brought us to this lonely place, and if we fall here, our death will be for Christ's sake." Having thus comforted and reassured one another, the monks committed their souls to God and remained in the lavra.

The brethren also knew that the neighboring Bedouin hated the holy place and would have liked nothing better than to see it laid to waste. If they had left even for a short season, the

---

[2]Matt., Ch. 10   [3]Ps. 30   [4]Eph., Ch. 6
[5]Ps. 33   [6]Phil., Ch. 1

tribesmen would have torched the church and cells, and leveled the ruins. To forestall this, the holy fathers had steeled themselves to remain. Yet the brotherhood stayed not so much to guard buildings as to glorify Christ the Lord, Who had long been glorified and was soon to be glorified there again. By remaining, the monks proved themselves to be pillars set on a foundation of solid rock and unmovable in every storm, and not reeds *shaken in the wind.*[7]

By the prayers of our venerable father Sabbas, the holy fathers continued living in the lavra, unharmed by the barbarians until the time came for the will of the Protector on high to be done. Although bands of Hagarenes from Arabia and other lands often appeared at the monastery, they only demanded food and did not harm the brethren. The barbarians glared fiercely and gnashed their teeth; they took all the provisions without thanking the monks and boasted that they would come back to devastate the lavra; but contrary to the will of God they could not harm His servants. Once, Saracens were on their way to loot and destroy the lavra, but outside of holy Bethlehem encountered troops sent from Jerusalem to defend the city where Christ was born. A battle ensued, the barbarians were defeated, and few of them escaped death. On another occasion a different band was headed from its camp to the lavra with the same wicked intent. In a village not far from the lavra the Ishmaelites found a large stock of wine hidden beneath brushwood. They drank themselves into a frenzy, began arguing, and before long were killing one another. Their plan was forgotten and the survivors scattered in every direction.

After learning how those raids had come to nought, the holy brethren were relieved in mind and spent Great Lent at their usual strict labors. Then God deigned that the time had come for his servants to be tested like the righteous Job. The devil enticed sixty Ethiopians armed with bows, arrows, and swords to raid and plunder the lavra. Having prepared martyric crowns for the monks, the Lord permitted the bandits to put His favorites to death so that, purified like gold in a furnace, they might be found worthy of Him. On the thirteenth day of March, dur-

---

[7]Matt., Ch. 11; Luke, Ch. 7

ing the last week of holy Lent, the barbarians approached the lavra. Hearing that the Ethiopians were near, many monks abandoned their desert cells and took refuge in the monastery and its church. With swords bared and arrows nocked, the barbarians rushed toward the lavra, shouting war-cries. Some of the fathers went out to calm them, saying, "Why, men, have you come to do battle with us peaceful, unarmed monks, as though we were enemies who had wronged you? We have not injured you or anyone else. We have forsaken the world and everything in it, hoping to live out our days in peace, weeping for our sins and escaping hatred and strife. We have done you no harm, and whenever any of your people come here, we provide them food and a place to rest. You should thank us for our kindness and not return evil for good."

"We did not come to beg food, but to take your silver and gold!" cried the Ethiopians. "Unless you give us your treasure, we shall put you to the sword."

"We are poor men," said the fathers. "Not even in our dreams do we see silver or gold. Our needs are simple, yet our poverty is such that we can hardly feed and clothe ourselves."

The barbarians were infuriated and loosed a hail of arrows on the monks. They did not stop firing until they had emptied their quivers, killing thirteen of the holy fathers and wounding others. Then the Ethiopians broke down the doors of the cells with large rocks and removed the meager possessions of the monks. They put many of the cells to the torch. They wanted to burn the church also, but Providence had decided otherwise. While collecting kindling, they thought they saw men approaching from afar. Fearing that troops from the Jerusalem garrison were coming to the monks' rescue, they took their plunder and rode off.

One of the monks, Abba Thomas, was a skilled physician. He removed the arrows from the wounded brethren and treated their injuries. The fathers were a gruesome sight, worthy of pity. Some had taken arrows in the chest or back, others in the face or head; some had their skulls crushed by rocks; all were covered with blood.

During the All-night Vigil for Palm Sunday, word reached the holy fathers that the barbarians had been heavily reinforced and were planning another attack on the lavra. The blessed fathers were terrified, but did not abandon the monastery; rather, they resigned themselves to God's will and prepared to meet their end. As the Master's Passion drew near, so did their suffering. In the early morning on March 20, Great Thursday, the Ethiopians attacked the lavra a second time, in larger number than before. They mercilessly slew the fathers by various means, filling the bodies of some with arrows; stoning others; slicing others in half; and hacking off arms, legs, and heads. Those whom they did not kill at once the bandits herded into the church, intending to torture them until they revealed where the sacred vessels and the monastery's treasures were kept. Although a number of monks fled, few escaped their enemies, who had posted sentries on the surrounding hills and mountains. Blessed John, the guest-master, attempted to flee, being young and quick; however, he was caught and tortured in the mountains. After cutting the tendons of his arms and legs, the barbarians dragged him over the rocky ground to the church, serating the skin on his back. Seeing the vicious torments being inflicted on the holy fathers and fearing that the Ethiopians would extract from him the location of the ecclesiastical vessels, the venerable Sergius, sacristan of the lavra, also fled. He was quite far from the lavra when sentries caught him. Because he resisted their attempts to take him back to the monastery, the barbarians decapitated Sergius. Several fathers hid in a grotto outside the monastery, but a guard on a hill spotted them, with shouts caught the attention of a fearsome Ethiopian patrolling the area, and pointed out the cave to him. The Ethiopian ran to the entrance and, brandishing his sword, commanded the monks to come out. Himself quaking with fear, the godly Patricius whispered to his brethren, "Do not be afraid: I shall go out alone. You sit here quietly until it is safe, then make your escape."

He crawled out of the cave, prepared to lay down his life for his friends. "Are others in there?" the Ethiopian demanded. When Patricius assured him that he was alone, the barbarian dragged him to the church, where the bandits presented this ultimatum to the fathers: "Four thousand gold coins or we shall put you to the sword and burn the building."

"For God's sake, do not shed innocent blood," begged the holy fathers. "Such a sum we have never had, nor do we have it now. The truth is that there is not a single piece of gold in the lavra. Take our clothes and whatever else you wish, but spare our lives."

The enraged barbarians pressed their blades against the monks' necks and howled, "Hand over the gold and silver vessels and the treasures of the monastery!" but the holy fathers denied that they had anything of value. "Tell us who are the superior and the trustees!" the Ethiopians shouted.

"Our father the abbot is in the Holy City attending to the lavra's affairs," answered the monks. "We are all equals."

The barbarians led the holy fathers into the cave of the venerable Sabbas and made a fire of brushwood and dung at the entrance. Their hope was that the stench and smoke would compel the monks to reveal the location of the church's treasures and who were the seniors. Frustrated in this, they again threatened to torture the saints to death; but they learned nothing. The fathers resorted to prayer, one crying, *Lord, receive my spirit*[8] *in peace!* and another, *Lord, remember me when Thou comest into Thy kingdom!*[9] Then the bandits flung them back into the cave and tormented them again with the dung-fire. Eighteen of the fathers were overcome by the smoke and perished, including the previously mentioned John and the blessed Patricius. The names of the others (whether they died of the smoke, or by the sword, or from torture) are known only to God, Who has written them in the Book of Life. Those they did not kill, the heartless tribesmen threw to the ground, beat, trampled, and wounded gravely. In all this they achieved nothing but to exhaust themselves. Finally, having loaded their camels with whatever they found in the church and remaining cells, they rode away.

The wounded brethren and those who had hid beforehand in the mountains and caves took the dead bodies to the church, which God had preserved intact. They spent the night of our Lord's salvific Passion weeping inconsolably, and in the morning gave them reverent burial. With the help of other survivors,

---

[8]Acts, Ch. 7   [9]Luke, Ch. 23

the blessed physician Thomas treated those severely wounded. Later Thomas became abbot of the Old Lavra.

The barbarians had not ridden far when the wrath of God overtook them. Smitten by the Lord's invisible sword, they all collapsed lifeless from the backs of their camels and became food for the beasts and birds of the desert. Not one escaped. Their souls were cast down to the bottomless pit, *where their worm dieth not, and the fire is not quenched.*[10] As for the holy fathers who were put to death in the Monastery of Saint Sabbas, they are in the Lord's hands and have been glorified as martyrs by Christ, our Saviour and God. Unto Him, with the Father and the Holy Spirit, be praise and honor forever. Amen.

❧❧❧❧

The full Passion of the holy fathers slain in the Monastery of Saint Sabbas was written by the blessed Stephen the Sabbaite. This is not the Stephen the Sabbaite commemorated on July 15, but another, a hymnographer who penned his account shortly after the saints were put to death. We could not find his complete text, but only fragments in several Greek manuscripts. At the end of his narrative, Stephen writes the following:

"I wish to relate what I was told by a trustworthy presbyter of great virtue, a Syrian who knew only his native tongue, but very much wanted to learn Greek. He tried his best to master the Greek Psalter, but found it difficult to pronounce the words and phrases. This caused him much grief. Then Anastasius the Protodeacon, one of the holy martyrs and a friend of the presbyter, appeared to him in a dream and asked why he was so downcast. The presbyter explained that he could make no progress in learning Greek, upon which the venerable Anastasius laughed, saying, 'Open your mouth and show me your tongue.' When the presbyter did so, Saint Anastasius wiped clean his tongue with a fresh handkerchief. Straightway, the presbyter awoke and realized that he now understood Greek. Thenceforth he could both speak and read Greek as though it were his native language, for which he thanked God and the Lord's holy favorites."

---

[10]Is., Ch. 66; Mark, Ch. 9

આ•આ•આ•

On this same day we commemorate the holy martyr Photina, the Samaritan woman who spoke with Christ at the well. Her Life may be found in *The Prologue*.

On this same day we commemorate the seven holy women Alexandra, Claudia, Euphrasia, Matrona, Juliana, Euphemia, and Theodosia of Amisus, a city in Pontus on the Black Sea. They were burned alive for Christ in a furnace.

The Twenty-First Day of the Month of March

The Commemoration of Our Venerable Father James the Bishop and Confessor

The only Life of this Saint James we could find was the account in *The Prologue*. According to it, James devoted himself to asceticism at an early age, becoming a monk and mortifying his flesh by fasting and vigils. His obedience was to copy holy books, and before beginning this work he always cleansed his mind and heart by prayer. Eventually he became a bishop. During the reign of Copronymus, the iconoclasts urged him to denounce the sacred icons. Because James would not agree, he was deposed, exiled, deprived of food and water, and subjected to various tortures. As a result of this ill-treatment, he surrendered his blessed soul into the hands of God, for Whom he labored until his end. Now Saint James is with the Lord in the Kingdom of heaven, rejoicing forever.

On the Same Day

The Commemoration of Our Father Among the Saints Cyril, Bishop of Catania

Saint Cyril was born in Antioch and was a disciple of the holy Apostle Peter, who appointed him Bishop of Catania in Sicily. He pastored his flock in a God-pleasing manner, led many unbelievers to faith in Christ, and worked numerous miracles, one of which we shall relate. In Catania there was a spring of brackish water. By prayer, God's hierarch Cyril sweetened the spring and thereby converted the chief heathen priest and many other people. Having reached great old age, the man of God fell asleep in the Lord. His remains were buried reverently in Sicily and are a source of healing for those who honor them with faith.

❧❧❧❧

In the Greek *Menologion,* written at the command of the Emperor Basil Porphyrogenitus, this saint is not called Cyril, but Beryllus.

On the Same Day

The Commemoration of Our Father Among the Saints Thomas, Patriarch of Constantinople

On account of his many virtues and perfect understanding and piety, our father among the saints Thomas was ordained deacon of the Great Church of Constantinople during the reign of Maurice by the mighty wonderworker, our venerable father Patriarch John the Faster. Later, Patriarch John made Thomas his *sakellarios* or comptroller. After the repose of the Most Holy John and his successor, the blessed Cyriacus, and during the reign of the tyrant Phocas, Saint Thomas was consecrated Patriarch of Constantinople. He governed his see well, vigilantly keeping watch over Christ's reason-endowed flock.

While Saint Thomas was patriarch, a miracle occurred in Galatia. In several cities of this province, there was a custom of carrying large crosses in processions. One day, moved by a wondrous and unrestrainable power, the crosses began to strike one another with such force that they broke apart. Word of this spread everywhere, and the Most Holy Patriarch Thomas summoned Theodore of Sykeon,[1] a clairvoyant and wonderworker, to inquire about its meaning. Saint Theodore confirmed that the miracle indeed had taken place, but would say no more, pleading ignorance. The Patriarch fell at the feet of Saint Theodore and by his humble entreaties finally persuaded the elder to explain the mystery. The elder declared that the swaying of the crosses meant that enemies from within and without would devastate the Church of God and the Greek Empire. From without there would be barbarian invasions; within, a schism over the faith would divide the Christians. There would be persecutions soon, and many churches of God would be reduced to ruins. Aghast, the Patriarch begged the venerable one to pray that God take his soul from the body before these ordeals, as he did not wish to behold the Church in tribulation.

---

[1]Commemorated on April 22

Thereafter, the godly Theodore remained in the Imperial City at the Church of Saint Stephen, living in reclusion and observing a fast. The Patriarch fell ill and sent word of his condition to the venerable one, again requesting Saint Theodore to beseech God to hasten his repose. When Theodore refused, the blessed Thomas appealed to him a third time, reminding him of his wish to depart the body before the Church's trials began. Saint Theodore finally agreed to the Most Holy Patriarch's desire and, after praying for Saint Thomas, sent him this message: "Will you rather see me now, or yonder, when we are in God's presence?"

Saint Thomas, through a messenger, answered thus: "Do not interrupt your silence, Father. It will suffice if we see each other in God's presence." That same day, shortly before sunset, the Most Holy Patriarch Thomas joyfully departed the body and joined the Lord. Phocas was still emperor at the time.

After Saint Thomas' repose, Sergius, a deacon of the Great Church of Constantinople, became Patriarch. At first he was Orthodox, but later he was corrupted and became one of the founders of the Monothelite heresy, the impious teaching that there is but one will in Christ the Lord. This error is described at length in the Life of Saint Maximus the Confessor.[2] In those days the Church underwent numerous tribulations: schisms arose, the temples of God were destroyed, and the faithful were persecuted and tortured. At the same time, God uplifted the hand of the Persians over the Greeks, on account of the increase of heresy. The Persians devastated the Greek lands by fire and the sword, and conquered whole provinces. When Jerusalem fell to them, they gained the honored Wood of the Cross and took it to Persia. In this way, then, the disasters foretokened by the miracle of the crosses and foreseen by Saint Theodore of Sykeon came to pass. Having served as shepherd of the Church of Christ for three years and two months, the Most Holy Patriarch Thomas was granted his request and fell asleep in the Lord before the catastrophes occurred. He struggled valiantly against heretics and by his way of life truly honored Christ our God, unto Whom, with the Father and the Holy Spirit, is due praise forever. Amen.

---

[2]Commemorated on January 21

The Twenty-Second Day of the Month of March

The Passion of the Holy Hieromartyr Basil, Presbyter of Ancyra[1]

Saint Basil was a presbyter of the Church of Ancyra, a town in Galatia, and was most diligent in teaching the people the truths of the Christian faith and turning them away from the wicked works of the devil. Always he proclaimed that the times were evil and warned of fierce assault by the princes of hell and their regiments. "Some of the devil's slaves are ravening wolves disguised as sheep," he explained. "They linger on the wayside of this temporal life until opportunity presents itself for them to capture their prey. But I point out to everyone the path leading to salvation in Christ God and expose the error of the impious. Whoever forsakes the living God and turns to blind, deaf, and dumb idols shall inherit the unquenchable fire that emanates from the heathen gods. Knowing this, we the faithful must offer all our love to Christ our Guide. We must scorn and deride the heathen feasts and the devil's attempts to deceive us; we must flee our loathsome adversaries and safeguard in our hearts incorruptible treasure. Christ, the Giver of eternal rewards, will be our protector." Every day the saint walked through the city, encouraging the Christians to remain steadfast in the truth and avoid everlasting torments. Because he cleaved to the true faith, Basil was forbidden to celebrate the divine services by a council of Arian bishops held in Constantinople, presided over by Eudoxius, heretical patriarch of the Imperial City. Later, a synod

---

[1]An abbreviated account, derived from Greek manuscripts

of 230 hierarchs met in Palestine and annulled the suspension. Holding to true piety and leading an upright life, Basil continued to declare the word of faith and convert many from error to Orthodoxy.

At that time persecution threatened every devout Christian. Slanderers reported to the Emperor Constantius, son of Constantine the Great, that our saint was inciting turmoil by his preaching. Basil was put to torture, but remained steadfast in his devout confession. Many were converted to the true faith by his firmness. Then Julian the Apostate became ruler and began destroying men's souls, legislating that everyone taste the loathsome offerings made to idols. In Galatia, the people were compelled to worship idols for a period of a year and three months, in accordance with the imperial command. Because numerous souls were being brought to perdition in Ancyra, Basil prayed for his city, saying, "O Christ, Redeemer of the world, unwaning Light, Chamber of everlasting treasure: by the will of the Father Thou dispellest darkness and by the Spirit settest in order all things! Look down, holy and dread Overseer of all creation, and bring to nought the incantations of those who defy Thee. May all the devices of the heathen be thwarted. May they fail to harm the souls of them that ever strive to remain loyal to Thee."

Hearing this, the idolaters became angry with Saint Basil, and one of them, Macarius by name, laid hold of him. "Why do you wander through the city, disturbing the people and flouting the Emperor's excellent law regarding worship of the gods?" the pagan demanded.

"May God shatter your jaw, slave of the devil!" replied the saint. "I defy the unjust decree, but by His invisible power He Who dwells in heaven shall abolish it altogether. He shall overturn your counsel and bring you pagans to your knees, then punish you in the life to come with eternal death."

The enraged mob dragged Saint Basil before Saturninus the Governor and shouted, "This man is causing an uproar in our city and has led many into error! Now he is openly urging the overthrow of altars and fulminating against the Emperor."

The Governor asked Saint Basil, "Who are you to challenge our gods and ruler?"

"I am a Christian," answered Saint Basil. "The name 'Christian' I regard as the most illustrious of all."

"If you are a Christian, you ought to conduct yourself as a Christian should," said Saturninus.

"Excellent advice, Governor!" exclaimed the saint. "A Christian's good deeds should be seen by all. The holy Gospel teaches, *Let your light so shine before men, that they may see your good works, and glorify your Father which is in heaven.*"[2]

Saturninus asked, "Why are you disturbing our city, demeaning the Emperor, and impugning his justice?"

"I am not demeaning your emperor; however, I do exalt the true King living in heaven," Saint Basil replied. "Our fathers proved themselves devoted servants of the celestial King, Who is everywhere worshipped by pure hearts. He can quickly do away with your ruler's impious, senseless edict."

"So it is true you condemn our emperor's decree," charged Saturninus.

"How can I approve a law that commands men to carry flesh in their mouths like mad dogs, to devour it as they circle the altar of foul spirits, and to bark before the sacrificial table?" asked the presbyter. "How can I praise an edict that orders worshippers to offer oblations of their own flesh and blood: to slaughter children as gifts to devils?"

"Enough of this nonsense. Submit to the Emperor!" Saturninus demanded.

Saint Basil responded, "I have always submitted and will continue to submit to the King of heaven. Never will I renounce holy faith in Him."

"Who is this King of heaven to Whom you submit?" asked Saturninus.

"My King is enthroned on high and has dominion over all creation," Basil said. "He shall break the power of the earthly, mortal ruler whose favor you curry." At this, the Governor lost his temper and had the martyr stripped naked and suspended. While his flesh was being shredded by instruments of torture, the saint prayed, "I thank Thee, O Lord God of the ages, for deeming me worthy to suffer for Thee and to find the path to

---

[2]Matt., Ch. 5

life. As I tread Thy way, I can see those who have already inherited Thy promises."

Meanwhile, the Governor advised, "Basil, you have suffered enough. It is time to submit to the Emperor."

"Brutish man, are you so ignorant of our Christian hope? How many times must I explain that I believe in God, the true King, obey Him, and will never renounce Him!" exclaimed the martyr.

At length the torturers exhausted themselves, and Saturninus ordered them to halt. He commanded the martyr, "Believe as we do and sacrifice to our gods."

"I will not sacrifice to your loathsome gods. I will not partake of oblations that poison the soul," insisted the martyr.

Then the Governor ordered that Saint Basil be taken to prison. As the Lord's favorite was entering the dungeon, a pagan named Felix asked him, "Why, Basil, are you so eager for your own destruction? Why not win the favor of the gods and the gifts of the Emperor? Unless you submit, your ordeal will be ghastly and drawn out, and justly so, because you have freely chosen torments."

"Away from me, impious, debased man!" cried the saint. "You know nothing of the certain promises of Christ, the eternal King of heaven, and are unworthy to learn them. Utterly blinded, you cannot see the light of truth. Worse, you do not even understand that you are enshrouded in darkness."

Governor Saturninus wrote a letter to the Emperor about the presbyter Basil, and upon receiving it, Julian immediately sent to Ancyra the pagan teacher Elpidius and a companion, Pegasius, both formerly Christians. At Nicomedia the apostates were joined by the heathen priest Asclepius. Arriving in Ancyra, the three warlords of the demonic hosts found Saint Basil still in the dungeon, where he had been praising and glorifying God unceasingly. On their second day in Ancyra, Pegasius went to the prison and greeted the saint, "Hail, Basil!"

"Why greet me thus when there is nothing hail about you? You are a deceiver and an evildoer and have lost the salvation you once drank from the Fountain which is Christ," replied the martyr. "You have become a putrid cesspool swallowing victims of sacrifice. Before, you were a communicant of the divine

Mysteries; now you preside over the banquet of devils. Before, you were a teacher of truth; now you are a guide to perdition. Before, you celebrated feast days with the saints; now you dance with Satan's puppets. Before, you guided to the light those who had gone astray; now you are yourself utterly benighted. How was it that you lost your hope and spiritual treasure? How will you reply when the Lord demands a reckoning from you?" Then Saint Basil prayed, "O God, Who art known by Thy servants and guidest unto the light those that desire to behold Thee; Who glorifiest those that hope in Thee and puttest to shame those that hate Thy law; Who art praised on high by the citizens of heaven and worshipped on earth by men! Do Thou cast off all diabolical bonds from the soul of Thy slave, that I may escape the haters of truth who boast they will overcome me."

Confounded by the saint's words, Pegasius returned to his friends and related everything. Elpidius and Asclepius were roused to anger and told the Governor what Basil had said. Saturninus ordered that the saint be tortured again. When he was brought to the tribunal, the holy martyr fearlessly told Saturninus, "Do with me as you wish."

Elpidius said to the judge, "This criminal has lost his mind. He should be tortured until he worships the gods, then set free. If he refuses to submit, send him to the Emperor for further punishment."

Enraged by the martyr's boldness, Saturninus ordered that Basil be suspended naked and his ribs raked for a long time. Afterwards the saint, wearing heavy shackles, was returned to prison. At that time the Emperor Julian was traveling through the eastern provinces and within a few days arrived in Ancyra. He was greeted by the devil's servants carrying an idol of Hecate,[3] and he went directly to his palace where all the heathen priests were summoned and given much gold. The next morning games were held in the arena. While the Emperor was watching them, Elpidius reminded him about Basil; whereupon, Julian arose, returned to the palace, and had the saint

---

[3]The three-headed or three-bodied goddess of the underworld, connected with black magic. (Tr.)

brought to him. Despite his sufferings, Basil was as handsome as ever and his countenance was radiant. "What is your name?" Julian asked him.

The saint replied, "My chief name is 'Christian,' derived from 'Christ,' the name eternal and beyond human understanding. I am also called Basil. If I do not disgrace His holy name and mine, Christ will grant me an everlasting reward on the Day of Judgment."

"Do not deceive yourself, Basil," said the Emperor. "I know all the secrets of your faith. The Man in Whom you trust was crucified under Pontius Pilate."

"I do not deceive myself, O Emperor; rather, it is you who are deceived," Basil retorted. "You have apostatized and lost the Kingdom of heaven, but I continue to believe in Christ, Whom you denied although He made you ruler on earth. Soon you will lose both your throne and your life, and then will understand how much you have angered God."

"You are a madman and false prophet, possessed by a devil!" shouted Julian.

The martyr said, "You have forgotten how Christ rewards His servants; you are unashamed to dishonor the altar that sheltered you when, as a boy of eight, your life was in danger and you found refuge in the sanctuary;[4] you have failed to keep the law that, as a cleric, you often proclaimed.[5] Because of this, Christ, the mighty Potentate, will quickly deprive you of temporal authority; moreover, He will judge you harshly when he comes in His eternal kingdom. Know also that the earth will refuse to accept your carcass and that your wretched soul will be cast into hell and subjected to grievous torments."[6]

"Godless man," said Julian, "I was about to release you, but because you prefer talking nonsense and insulting me to accept-

---

[4]Upon the death of Constantine the Great, there was a general massacre of the junior line of the Flavian family, descended from the saint's father Constantius Chlorus and his second wife Theodora. Julian owed his life to the intervention of Mark, Bishop of Arethusa, who sheltered him in a church. (Tr.)

[5]While a Christian, Julian was admitted to the office of reader. (Tr.)

[6]Here the saint predicts Julian's immanent death and that the earth would throw up the apostate's corpse after its burial.

ing good advice, I command that until further notice seven strips of skin be cut daily from your body."

Julian assigned to Count Frumentinus, the commander of his bodyguard, the task of flaying the martyr. Every day Basil manfully endured the knife for Christ's sake, until no skin remained to be cut: it was all hanging from his body. When things had reached this state, Basil informed the Count, "I wish to speak to the Emperor."

Thinking that the saint intended to worship idols, the Count was overjoyed. He announced to the Emperor, "Your Majesty! Basil cannot endure more suffering and is willing to submit."

At this Julian went to the temple of Asclepius and had the martyr brought to him there. "Priests and soothsayers are ever at your side. Where are they now?" Saint Basil asked the tyrant. "Did they inform you of my request?"

"It has been announced," Julian replied. "Being a wise person and understanding that further resistance is hopeless, you have decided to sacrifice to the gods."

"Know, O Emperor: the deaf and blind idols you call gods are nothing of the sort. Those who worship them are doomed to hell," Basil asserted. With this he tore from his body a strip of flesh and threw it in the Emperor's face, crying, "Eat your favorite food, Julian! I live for Christ and count it gain to die for Him. He is my Helper; in Him I believe, and for Him I suffer."

Word of Saint Basil's defiance spread quickly among the Christians, and all praised Him for bravely confessing Christ. Along with the flesh, Basil hurled many insults at the Emperor, and Frumentinus became terrified as he saw Julian's face blaze with anger. The Count realized that because he had assured Julian of the saint's willingness to sacrifice, the ruler was more enraged at him than at Basil. Frumentinus spirited away the martyr to the praetorium and had him tortured even more cruelly than before. This time Basil was not merely flayed: his flesh was gouged away, exposing his inwards. As Saint Basil endured this torture, he prayed, "Blessed art Thou, O Lord, Hope of the Christians, Who raisest the fallen, liftest those who are cast down, and deliverest from corruption them that hope in Thee. Thou knowest my distress, O good, compassionate, merciful, and long-suffering God. Look down from the lofty throne of

Thy glory, enable me to complete the course successfully, and deem me worthy of Thine eternal Kingdom."

At nightfall the saint was returned to prison. Very early the next morning Julian left for Antioch without bidding the Count farewell. The Emperor was still furious at him. Frumentinus decided he must destroy the saint in order to protect himself. He had the martyr brought to him and demanded, "O most foolish of men, will you sacrifice to the gods, as the Emperor commands, or not? Have you chosen to submit to the imperial edict or to perish in agony?"

The holy martyr Basil replied, "Wicked blasphemer, for days you have been paring away my flesh and reducing crowds of onlookers to tears of sympathy, yet now I stand before you healed by the grace of Christ.[7] Brutal henchman of the devil, are you prepared to report to the persecutor Julian how great is the power of Christ God, Whom he renounced? Your emperor is deceived by Satan and has ensured his own perdition. There is no point in recounting how Christ God, through His priests, saved your ruler from execution, hiding him beneath the altar of the holy temple. Julian has forsaken the Church and forgotten her assistance, and for this Christ shall soon punish the wretch with a much-deserved and miserable death."

"Fool, you are possessed by a devil," said the Count. "Our invincible master Julian showed himself compassionate to you as he has to all others, commanding that you celebrate with us by offering incense and feasting on sacrificial meat. You thanked His Majesty with disobedience and insults, thereby putting me in the gravest danger. For this I will now punish you with tortures certain to end your life quickly." So saying, Frumentinus ordered heated iron rods driven into the martyr's back and belly.

Saint Basil collapsed in pain, but found strength to cry, "O Christ my light, O Jesus my hope, Thou art the calm haven of the tempest-tossed! I thank Thee, O Lord God of my fathers, for Thou hast snatched my soul from the bottomless pit. Having Thy help, I have not disgraced Thy name. May I complete the

---

[7]Evidently, the saint's wounds were miraculously healed the night before, in prison. (Tr.)

course triumphantly and inherit eternal rest according to the promise made to my fathers by Thee, the great High Priest, our Lord Jesus Christ. Assist me in holding fast to a good confession, and receive my spirit in peace, for Thou art compassionate and plenteous in mercy, our God Who abidest forever. Amen." Having completed this prayer, the martyr fell as it were into a deep sleep and, with his belly full of punctures made by the heated rods, he surrendered his soul into God's hands. Saint Basil finished the course of martyric confession on January 28. The next year Julian was slain, and on March 22 of the year following the Apostate's death, the Christians held festive services to honor Saint Basil's much-suffering body. This became the date of the martyr's commemoration. By his courage the holy hieromartyr Basil strengthened all Christians in the faith of our Lord Jesus Christ, unto Whom be glory and dominion for endless ages. Amen.

On this same day we commemorate the holy martyr Drosis, daughter of the Emperor Trajan. Her Life may be found in *The Prologue.*

The Twenty-Third Day of the Month of March

The Life and Passion of the Holy Hieromartyr Nicon and His 199 Disciples[1]

ℐn Neapolis,[2] a city of Campania, there once lived a brave, handsome soldier named Nicon. Although raised as a heathen by his impious father, Nicon knew about Christ, because his mother was a Christian. Showing him the Lord's cross, she would tell Nicon, "Beloved son, when you are in battle, make the sign of the Cross and you will never be captured or wounded. Neither arrow nor sword nor spear shall harm you, even at the moment of utmost peril."

Once, Nicon's regiment and other units of the Roman Army were engaged in bloody combat with barbarians. Surrounded by numberless armies, Nicon was trapped. All around his comrades were falling, and he waited to be struck down at any moment. Suddenly, Nicon remembered his mother's admonitions. He lifted his eyes to heaven, sighed from the bottom of his heart, and traced the cross upon himself, saying, "O Christ, God Almighty, manifest the power of Thy Cross in me, and I will evermore be Thy servant, honouring Thee and Thy Mother." After praying, Nicon was filled with courage. One hundred and eighty of the bravest adversaries fell victim to his spear, and the rest ran for their lives. No one could withstand him, for his right hand was strengthened by the power of the Cross of Christ. The

---

[1]An abbreviation of the account written by Cheromenus, a disciple of the saint
[2]Now Naples (Tr.)

other Roman soldiers were amazed and shouted, "What a miracle Providence has worked! Never have we seen or heard of anyone fighting as the brave Nicon has today."

At the end of the campaign, Nicon and the other troops returned home. Praising God, the saint related to his mother the feats of valor that Christ had enabled him to accomplish by the power of the Cross. She was overjoyed and cried, "I extol Thy holy name, O Lord, for Thou wilt *have all men to be saved, and come unto the knowledge of the truth.*[3] Now hearken unto the prayer of Thy handmaiden and deem my son worthy of the laver of regeneration granted us for the remission of sins. Teach him to do Thy will, so that he may please Thee and inherit Thy promised blessings."

Nicon asked, "How, mother, do I become a Christian?"

"You must fast forty days and study the faith with a Christian presbyter; you must renounce Satan and all his works and receive Holy Baptism. After this you will be a true Christian, a perfect servant of Christ," she explained.

"As the Lord lives, I shall become His slave!" cried Nicon. "No longer do I wish to be an idolater, a pagan, and a soldier, or to worship idols made of stone. No longer shall I adore anything created, but only the one God, *Who hath made heaven and the earth, the sea and all that is therein.*"[4] Then Nicon prostrated himself before his mother and begged, "Pray for me, your servant, and ask God to entrust me to the care of a holy angel, a guide and guardian of my soul and body. May my angelic protector lead me to a servant of the Lord who will baptize me and teach me to do the will of Christ our true God, that I may be numbered among the Saviour's reason-endowed sheep. O esteemed mother, had you not instilled in me knowledge of the true God, I would still be trapped in heathen error, facing the fires of Gehenna and bound for Hades, where those ignorant of God are suffering. Again, I beg you, mother: pray for me." With this Nicon turned towards the door, but his mother seized his hands and would not let him leave. Reckoning that at her age death must be near, she enjoined him to return after his Baptism and bury her. Then she prayed for Nicon, gave him a large

---

[3] I Tim., Ch. 2   [4] Ps. 145

quantity of gold, and bestowed on him her maternal blessing. Only after this did she allow him to begin his search for a Christian priest: no small undertaking at this time of fierce persecution. All the presbyters had fled into the deserts and mountains, leaving no one to instruct and baptize those wishing to become Christians.

Nicon went directly from his house to the docks, where he boarded a ship about to sail for Byzantium. In the meantime, troops came to Nicon's house, looking for the valiant soldier. They asked his mother, "Where is your son?" but she did not know where he had gone.

Sped by the Lord's grace, the servant of God reached the island of Chios. There he disembarked and prayed for eight days at the summit of a high mountain, begging the Master to guide him to someone who could baptize him and instruct him in the mysteries of the holy faith. That night an angel appeared to Nicon in the guise of a bishop, gave him a staff topped by a cross, and commanded him to descend at once to the shore. Reaching the seaside at daybreak, the saint found that a ship was awaiting him. The angel had also appeared to its captain, telling him where to find Nicon, who would be carrying the cross mounted on a staff. Nicon entered the ship, which favorable winds carried to Mount Ganos[5] in two days. There the saint was met at the wharf by Theodosius, Bishop of Cyzicus, and a multitude of monks who had hidden with him in a cavern because of the persecution. The Bishop was the abba and superior of the monks, and God had revealed to him Nicon's coming. Theodosius took Nicon to the cave, catechized him, baptized him in the name of the Holy Trinity, and imparted to him the immaculate Mysteries.

After his Baptism, the blessed Nicon remained in the cave, reading the divine Scriptures and observing how the brethren lived. By and by he was deemed worthy of the habit, on account of his extreme humility. So meek and mild was he, so rigorous were his fasting and other forms of self-denial, that the monks likened him to an angel. His every vigil was night-long, his patience in labors extreme, his asceticism unrivalled,

---

[5] In Thrace, on the Sea of Marmara (Tr.)

his zeal to study edifying books unquenchable, and his life spotless, amazing both the holy hierarch Theodosius and the brotherhood.

After the blessed Nicon had dwelt on the mountain for three years, the Bishop was granted a divine revelation. An angel of the Lord appeared to him in a dream, saying, "Before you depart this life, consecrate Nicon as your successor. Earlier you baptized and tonsured him; now commit your flock to his care and instruct him to take it to Sicily. Otherwise, the monks will perish at the hands of the barbarians who will shortly devastate this region."

Theodosius promptly ordained the blessed one deacon and later presbyter. Following Nicon's consecration to the episcopacy, Theodosius entrusted to the saint authority over the brotherhood, then fell asleep in the Lord. Nicon buried Theodosius and sailed to Lesbos with the monks, who numbered 190. Having spent two days in the town of Mytilene, the saint and the brotherhood continued on to Naxos. From there they proceeded directly to Italy, by God's permission reaching Neapolis in twenty-two days. While in Neapolis, the saint visited his mother, who embraced and kissed him and shed tears of joy. "I bless Thy most holy name, O Lord," she cried, falling to her knees, "for Thou hast vouchsafed me to behold my son in episcopal rank and clothed in the angelic habit. Now, O Master, hearken unto Thy handmaiden and receive my soul." No sooner had that blessed woman completed the prayer than she delivered up her spirit into the Lord's hands. Seeing this, everyone glorified God. Saint Nicon's mother was reverently laid to rest with the customary chanting of psalms.

Word that Nicon had returned spread through the town, and nine of his former comrades came to visit him. Taking the saint aside, they enjoined him, "By the power of Heaven, tell us: was it the black art or some other force that gave you such might and bravery in combat? Share with us your secret."

"Believe me, brethren," answered the saint, "it was not sorcery or anything else of the kind that gave me courage, but the honored Cross of the Lord. Armed with it, I am undefeatable. The power of God, working through the Cross, vanquishes every foe."

Hearing this, the soldiers fell at the feet of the holy Bishop Nicon, imploring: "Have mercy on us, hierarch of God, and take us with you! As you rescued us from visible foes, so deliver us from invisible enemies. We wish to be near you in the Kingdom of heaven." Leaving wives, comrades, and homes, the soldiers became followers of Saint Nicon.

Shortly afterwards the godly one, his monks, and the soldiers took ship to Sicily. Having come ashore near Mount Taormina, they walked a considerable distance and reached the Asinus River. Alongside it, in the wilderness of Gugias, they found a large, old, stone bathhouse. Since the area was quiet and beautiful and the soil fertile, they took up their dwelling there and planted fruit trees of every kind, as well as a vineyard. The holy Bishop baptized his nine former comrades-in-arms and tonsured them.

A long time passed, but the persecution of the Christians continued. During the reign of Decius, heathen living near the brotherhood informed the Governor of Sicily, Quintianus, "On the river Asinus there live men who worship the God of heaven. Their bishop, Nicon, teaches them to disdain our laws and reject our deities."

His anger aroused, the Governor straightway dispatched a company of soldiers to arrest the saints and bring them for interrogation. When they reached Gugias, the soldiers found the martyrs and asked, "Are you Nicon and his friends, the flouters of our laws and mockers of our gods?"

The blessed Nicon said, "Children, it is good that you have come; good indeed, for through you, Christ the Master is summoning me and my companions." After this the brethren prayed, beseeching God to strengthen them for the contest by His grace. They could not, however, complete their supplication, because the soldiers wanted to return quickly to the Governor.

As the martyrs were being led like sheep to the slaughter, our blessed father Nicon exhorted them, saying, "Take courage, brethren, and do not fear the persecutor. We are near the end of our course and the open gates of heaven. Let us remain steadfast in the Christian faith. Let us defy the oppressor and boldly reprove him. Let us hearken unto the voice of our Good

Shepherd, Who urges, *Fear not them which kill the body, but are not able to kill the soul.*"[6]

The saints were presented at the tribunal, and the Governor glared at them and asked, "Is it true that you have been put under a spell by the warlock Nicon, that he has deceived you with vain and foolish promises, and that you refuse to worship the immortal gods or obey their laws?"

With one voice the holy brotherhood replied, "We are Christians and will never renounce our faith! We put our trust not in vain promises, but in *the Lord God, Who hath made heaven and the earth, the sea, and all that is therein.*[7] Your gods are deaf and dumb; they are lifeless stone, *the works of the hands of men. Let all they that put their trust in them become like unto them.*"[8]

Realizing that the saints were steadfast in the faith, Quintianus declared, "If I do not execute these men quickly, they will lead many into error." He then had the martyrs stripped naked, stretched out on the ground, and lashed with rawhide for a long time. The flogging stopped only when he commanded that all the passion-bearers except Saint Nicon be taken to the bathhouse by the river and be decapitated. As they bent their necks beneath the sword, the holy martyrs prayed, "O Lord, into Thy hands do we commit our souls. *For Thy sake are we slain all the day long, we are counted as sheep for the slaughter.*"[9] With this, the 199 disciples of Saint Nicon (or rather, of Christ Himself) were beheaded. By order of the persecutor, a fire was made in the bathhouse that had served as a monastery, and the bodies were thrown into it.

Meanwhile, the godly Nicon was chained and imprisoned, and the Governor pondered the cruelest way to put him to death. That night an angel appeared to the saint in a dream, exhorting, "Be strong in God, O Nicon, champion of Christ. Be glad that Christ God has accepted your 199 disciples as a sweet fragrance. They are now resting in heaven with the celestial Bridegroom." After this Saint Nicon beheld a maiden clothed in gold and sapphire and shining more brilliantly than the sun. She was holding a lion that was white as snow,[10] and she was

---

[6]Matt., Ch. 10   [7]Ps. 145   [8]Ps. 134   [9]Ps. 43
[10]The maiden was probably the holy martyr Agatha, who was tortured by Quintianus. The lion represented her courageous confession and unsullied virginity.

standing in a field on the east side of the Psimiphus River. On the west side stood two giants whose heads touched the sky. They held fiery spears and asked the virgin, "Why must we remain idle? The King of heaven sent us to do battle with Quintianus. We have been waiting for him, but he has not ventured forth."

"Yesterday Quintianus executed 199 of Christ's servants," said the radiant virgin. "Now he is plotting a cruel death for their teacher Nicon, who has evaded all the snares of the devil. Be patient, for Quintianus will soon appear at the appointed place." Then she released the lion and told the giants, "Take the beast, for he will aid you in the struggle against the persecutor."

The holy Bishop Nicon awoke and joyfully praised and glorified God. He told the dream to his servant, Cheromenus, who later wrote his Life and Passion. So doing, Nicon predicted that the Governor would perish quickly and miserably.

The next morning Saint Nicon was again presented at the tribunal. "Who are you and what is your religion? How is it you have destroyed so many persons by sorcery?" asked the Governor. "Because you made them lose their minds, your victims will never again enjoy the brilliance of the sun or the luster of the moon."

Saint Nicon answered, "You are a godless liar, claiming that I bewitched my monks and am therefore responsible for their death. Who I am and what my beliefs are, you know very well. My every word has been confirmed by others, and especially by the saints you slaughtered yesterday because you are blinded by idolatry. Now I repeat that I am a steadfast, devoted Christian. I put my hope in God, the Creator of heaven and earth. He shall deliver you to the unbearable torments which are your punishment for inhuman cruelty and wicked impiety."

At this the persecutor roared like a lion and commanded that the saint be disrobed, tied hand and foot to four wheels, and stretched over blazing coals. As though lying upon a flowery field, the saint chanted happily, "Thou, Lord, art *my foundation, and my refuge, and my deliverer*[11] from enemies that rage against me."

---

[11]Ps. 17

After some time the servants told the persecutor, "Your Excellency, we are exhausted. No matter how much we feed the fire or how long we burn the criminal, we cannot harm him." Next Quintianus ordered the saint dragged behind unbroken stallions, but Nicon made the sign of the Cross over them, and they became placid as sheep. It seemed the animals were being held with bit and bridle, for they refused to run even when the servants whipped them furiously. Seeing this, the persecutor flew into a rage and ordered that the tendons of the horses' legs be cut. By the command of God, the stallions spoke with a human voice, as once did Balaam's ass. They cried, *"Our God is in heaven and on earth; all things soever He hath willed, He hath done.*[12] We are fellow-sufferers with Saint Nicon!"

Presently Quintianus had the martyr wrapped in chains and hurled from a high mountain into a deep ravine. This time an angel preserved the Lord's favorite, releasing him from bonds, leading him out of the chasm, and returning him to the tribunal completely unharmed. The astonished Governor exclaimed, "Nicon, our gods' concern for you is amazing! Do you see how they care for you and prevent your destruction? Acknowledge their compassion by reconciling yourself to them and offering sacrifices."

"Anathema to you, your gods, and all who hope in them!" retorted the saint. As punishment for this, the Governor had Nicon's face smashed with rocks and his tongue pulled out with tongs and sliced off. Finally, Quintianus had the saint beheaded under a pine tree at Gugias, where the brotherhood had lived. The martyr's sacred corpse was left unburied, to serve as food for birds and beasts.

On the day he condemned Nicon to death, Quintianus left for Panormus[13] to confiscate the possessions of Saint Agatha,[14] whom he had tortured and who had died not long before. While crossing the river Psimiphus on a ferry, his men lost control of their horses. One bit Quintianus on the face, disfiguring it; another trampled him and kicked him into the river. The wretch drowned and Saint Nicon's prophecy was fulfilled.

---

[12]Ps. 113   [13]Now Palermo (Tr.)
[14]Commemorated on February 5

A shepherd possessed by a demon happened upon the martyr's unburied remains. Immediately, the foul spirit threw the man to the ground and fled, driven out by the power of the saint. As it departed, the devil screeched, "Woe is me! Where can I go to escape Nicon?" The shepherd, overjoyed at being freed from demonic oppression, told everyone about the miracle. Before long the Bishop of Messina learned of it and had the shepherd guide him and his clergy to the place where the much-suffering body lay. In the nearby bath the Bishop found the corpses of Saint Nicon's holy disciples, which were untouched by the fire. He reverently buried all the remains at a suitable location, praising Christ our God, Who is glorified forever with the Father and the Holy Spirit. Amen.

On the Same Day

The Life of
Our Holy Monastic Father Nicon,
Abbot of the Kiev Caves[1]

Soon after planting in Russia the fruitful vineyard of monasticism, the Lord brought an excellent helper to Saint Anthony of the Caves, His skilled and diligent overseer. This was the godly Nicon, who was nurtured in every monastic virtue by Saint Anthony and soon became guide of those who came to the Kiev Caves to labor in the noetic vineyard of asceticism. After initiating the novices in the mystery of obedience, Saint Anthony would turn them over to his disciple and co-struggler for tonsure in the angelic schema, since Nicon was both a holy priest and a proven monk. Then one could see a new Moses and Aaron leading Israel out of the Egypt of this world and to the promised land of heaven. As Moses brought down the Commandments from Sinai, so the venerable Anthony brought the statutes of monasticism from Holy Mount Athos. As Aaron was honored with the priesthood, so was the venerable Nicon, who toiled under Anthony's watchful eye and with him bore abundant fruits of repentance in the spiritual vineyard.

Nicon's labors brought him sorrow as well as joy; nonetheless, he never despaired, but always remained content and thanked God for everything. He was delighted to tonsure our venerable father Theodosius, who became the wondrous teacher of Russian monasticism, and likewise the blessed Balaam, a boyar of the highest rank, and the blessed Ephraim the eunuch, esteemed steward of Prince Izyaslav. The latter tonsures, however, were the beginning of much grief for Nicon. When Izyaslav learned about them, he was furious at Anthony and Nicon, and ordered his servants to bring our saint to him. As the blessed one was being presented to the Prince, Izyaslav glared at him and demanded, "Was it you who tonsured the noble and my eunuch? I gave no permission for this."

---

[1]From *The Patericon of the Caves*

"The grace of God assisting me, I performed the tonsures," the venerable one answered courageously. "I had the permission of Jesus Christ, the King of heaven, Who called both men to the monastic life."

"Persuade them to return home, or I will exile you and the other monks and destroy your cave," threatened the Prince.

"Do as you think best, master, but I will never encourage soldiers of the Heavenly King to desert," said Nicon.

Izyaslav put Nicon under custody; and Saint Anthony and the brethren, giving place to his wrath, abandoned the cave and made ready to leave the principality. Meanwhile, a servant told the whole story to Izyaslav's consort. The Princess reminded her husband how God had chastised Poland when her father, Boleslaw the Bold, expelled the monks from that land because of the tonsure of Moses the Hungarian. "Hear me, my lord," she appealed to Izyaslav, "and keep your temper. Because of a tonsure that displeased him, my father expelled the monks from Poland, bringing terrible misfortunes upon that land. Do not make the same mistake." Hearing this, the Prince became frightened that God would punish him. He released the blessed Nicon and sent him back to the cave. He also sent word to the other brethren, begging them to return to the monastery. According to the Life of the venerable Anthony, it was only after entreating the brethren for three days that the messengers persuaded them to do as the Prince requested. Having undergone this trial, our holy father Nicon increased his ascetical labors and by prayer and fasting won spectacular victories over the evil spirits. He and his equals in holiness, Saints Anthony and Theodosius, shone like three brilliant lamps in the cave, dispelling demonic gloom.

Gradually the brotherhood grew, and the blessed Nicon conceived a longing for stillness and silence. With the venerable Anthony's consent, Nicon left the cave with a Bulgarian Athonite from the Monastery of Saint Menas. Upon reaching the sea, the monks parted ways. The Bulgarian visited Constantinople and settled on the island known to this day as "Bolgarov." He spent the rest of his days there, enduring cold and hunger. The great Nicon went to the island of Tmutorokan and took up his dwelling at a deserted spot not far from the

town. He multiplied his labors and served God tirelessly in stillness, and before long his fame had spread throughout the
region. Crowds of townsfolk and villagers came to see him and,
knowing little about the faith and nothing about monasticism,
they were amazed by his strange way of life. Many of the visitors were inspired by God to become monks and begged the
venerable one to tonsure them. Our father instructed the aspi-
rants, clothed them in the schema, and built a church there,
which he dedicated to the most holy Theotokos. By the prayers
of the godly Nicon, the brotherhood grew and a glorious monastery was established, patterned in every respect upon the
Monastery of the Caves.

After the death of Rostislav Vladimirovich, Prince of
Tmutorokan, the people of that region sent our venerable father
Nicon to Svyatoslav Yaroslavich, Prince of Chernigov, asking
that he allow his son Gleb to become their ruler. His mission
successfully completed, Nicon visited the Monastery of the
Caves in Kiev. When he and the blessed abbot Theodosius met,
they fell prostrate before each other, embraced, and shed many
tears, because of their lengthy separation. The venerable
Theodosius begged the godly Nicon not to leave again while
they were both still in the flesh, to which our father replied, "I
must put the affairs of my monastery in order. Afterwards, if it
pleases God, I shall return."

The saint went to Tmutorokan with Prince Gleb Svyatoslavich,
and the new ruler was enthroned; then Nicon attended to various matters in his monastery and hurried back to the Kiev
Caves, gladly submitting himself to the godly Theodosius. Saint
Theodosius loved Nicon sincerely and regarded him as his
father. Whenever Theodosius left the premises, he entrusted
Nicon, as the most senior monk, with supervising and teaching
the brethren. When Theodosius himself instructed the brotherhood, he would have the blessed Nicon read aloud apt passages
from holy books. So profound were the humility of the two
saints and their mutual love that while Nicon, an experienced
scribe and bookbinder, was doing his work, the godly Theodosius
would frequently sit nearby and spin thread to use in stitching
the quires of the manuscripts.

About that time Svyatoslav drove his brother Izyaslav from

Kiev and mounted his throne. Because of the quarrels of the Russian princes, there was no peace in the realm, and Nicon decided to return to his island. The venerable Theodosius begged our father to stay with him; however, the blessed hesychast was unwilling to remain in the Monastery of the Caves when affairs were so unfavorable to the guarding of his thoughts. Accustomed to seclusion, he shunned all tumult. After beseeching the venerable Theodosius' forgiveness, Nicon left with two other monks.

For several years the blessed Nicon stayed on his island, performing his usual labors. Then, moved by brotherly love, he decided to visit the godly Theodosius again. As it turned out, Theodosius had already reposed. His successor as abbot was the blessed Stephen. Saint Nicon was grieved not to find his dear friend among the living, but decided to remain the rest of his days in the Monastery of the Caves. He often visited Theodosius' grave and shed joyous tears of compunction there, grieving over the loss of his beloved brother and thanking God for deeming him worthy to clothe in the schema a man whose angelic life was a light for all Russia. Following the expulsion of the blessed Stephen, the brethren chose as their abbot Nicon, because he was senior to them all, had tonsured the godly Theodosius, and was equal in holiness to both Saint Anthony and Saint Theodosius. They gladly submitted to him as their guide and father and considered that in his person his two holy co-strugglers were in their midst. Frequently the enemy, hater of everything good, tried to thwart the saint's care for God's chosen flock, as he had the blessed abbot Stephen's, but with no success. He could not dim the light of the venerable one's good deeds and always was vanquished.

The blessed Nicon pleased the Lord and was an example of wondrous virtue for his flock. During his abbacy, and by his prayers and those of our venerable fathers in heaven, Anthony and Theodosius, the church of the Caves, which was fashioned by God, was beautifully adorned with icons. This occurred after Saints Anthony and Theodosius appeared to certain iconographers in Constantinople, paid them in advance for their work, and sent them to the Caves. When the iconographers arrived at the monastery, Nicon showed them an image of his beloved friends, Saints Anthony and Theodosius.[2] The Greeks immediately recognized their hirers and admitted that they had nearly turned back to Constantinople, but an awesome miracle had prevented them. While they were journeying, they had seen the church of the Caves in a vision and, inside the church, an icon of the most holy Theotokos. A dread voice spoke from the image, forbidding them to return to the Imperial City. When they disobeyed, their boat continued to move upstream, against the current and despite their strenuous rowing. Spurred on by the marvels and the blessed abbot's enthusiasm, the iconographers began work. Through the prayers of our holy fathers Anthony, Theodosius, and Nicon, other miracles followed. For example, a dove flew out of the lips of the lavish mosaic of the most holy Theotokos which adorned the wall of the altar, as we learn from *The Patericon of the Caves.*

After many years of labor, the ever-memorable abbot, peer of the angels and boast of the Monastery of the Caves, fell asleep in the Lord. Our venerable father Nicon died in the year 6596 from the creation of the world and 1088 from the Nativity of Christ, while Vsevolod Yaroslavich was Great Prince of Kiev. His body was laid to rest in the Monastery of the Caves. Incorrupt to this day, the wonderworking remains testify to the holiness of the blessed Nicon, whose spirit has joined our venerable fathers Anthony and Theodosius in the heavenly mansions and enjoys the marvelous vision of God, no longer beholding Him in images, *but face to face.*[3] The three saints shine like a triple lamp before the throne of the triune Godhead and pray that we, their children, may share their grace and glory and please the Lord. Unto Him be praise, honor, and worship, now and ever, and unto the ages of ages. Amen.

ぞ▲ぞ▲ぞ▲

On this same day we commemorate the holy martyr Philetas the Senator, his wife Lydia and sons Macedon and Theoprepius, Cronides, and Duke Amphilochius. They suffered for Christ in Illyria while Hadrian was emperor.

---

[2]This occurred ten years after the death of Saint Theodosius.
[3]I Cor., Ch. 13

The Twenty-Fourth Day of the Month of March

The Commemoration of Our Father Among the Saints Artemon, Bishop of Seleucia[1] in Pisidia

The blessed Artemon was born and reared in Seleucia, a town in Pisidia. During those days the holy apostles were illumining the entire world with the light of the Gospel, and when the Apostle Paul came to Seleucia, he made the acquaintance of Artemon, who was the most virtuous of the citizens. Saint Paul converted Artemon to the Christian faith and initiated him into divine wisdom. Thereafter Artemon shone ever brighter with good deeds. Since *no man, when he hath lighted a candle, putteth it under a bushel,*[2] Saint Paul ordained Artemon as the first Bishop of Seleucia. The blessed Artemon pastured his flock well and was a haven of salvation for all. He provided for widows, orphans, and the poor and was a marvelous healer of souls and bodies. Having lived out his days in a godly manner, he reposed in old age.

꧁꧂

Be it known that Saint Artemas, mentioned by the holy Apostle Paul in the third chapter of the Epistle to Titus, is not the same person as Saint Artemon. Artemas was Bishop of Lystra and one of the Seventy Apostles; Artemon was the first Bishop of Seleucia in Pisidia and was not one of the Seventy.

---

[1]Or Laodicea (Tr.)   [2]Luke, Ch. 11

On the Same Day

The Commemoration of Our Holy Monastic Father James the Confessor[1]

After the holy fathers of the Seventh Ecumenical Council had anathematized iconoclasm, Leo the Armenian, impious Emperor of the Greeks, revived the heresy and tortured many of the Orthodox who devoutly venerated the sacred images. It was during his reign that Saint James the Confessor was subjected to torments. The blessed one was a disciple of Theodore the Studite,[2] who wrote about James' sufferings. Following the exile of Saint Theodore for the holy icons, many of his monks were seized and tortured, including the blessed James. Eventually the godless Emperor Leo the Armenian was assassinated, and Saint James and the rest of Christ's confessors were released. James returned to the Monastery of the Studium, where Hypatius was serving as abbot in Theodore's absence; but our sufferer was so badly injured that he survived for only a few days. While making his way back to the Imperial City and staying at the Monastery of Crescentius, Theodore received a letter from Hypatius about James' death and burial. Here is the venerable Theodore's reply:

"With pain of heart, but with spiritual joy we have received from you, O child, word of the repose of Christ's confessor, our beloved brother James. We mourn him as a son, although I, because of my sins, am unworthy to be called his father. We rejoice that he has attained the everlasting life prepared for him by the Lord, and in this we are not alone. He is one of our holy members, our brotherhood's chief adornment; but also the boast of the entire Church. You know what sort of person he was: a confessor, a martyr, a saint. From his first days as a monk, he contended lawfully and proved his obedience. He struggled manfully against temptation, watched carefully over his chastity, subsisted on the plainest food, and subjugated his flesh to

---

[1]From Theodore the Studite
[2]Commemorated on November 11

the spirit. He scorned even the demands of health in his quest to conquer sleep. His mind he bent at all times toward God, immersing himself in deepest contemplation and often soaring in ecstasy. Coming to himself, he was afire with love divine. Let no one think I am exaggerating. I have as witnesses God and also John, James' spiritual father, who told me what I would not have known otherwise. James trained for the encounter with ascetical exercises; then he entered the arena of confession and began his drawn-out contest, becoming *a spectacle to angels and to men.*[3] Oh, what a steadfast, beloved soul! As the Lord's fearless soldier, James engaged the adversaries, who covered him with wounds. The persecutor's servants lacerated his shoulders and chest and reduced his flesh to shreds; they left his broken body in a pool of his own blood. At no time did a groan escape his lips, even as he completed the God-pleasing course of martyrdom for Christ the Son of God and our true God.

"To suffer for Christ's holy icon is to suffer for Christ Himself. *Let the meek hear and be glad!*[4] Let those who love the martyrs rejoice! Let the devil and the iconoclastic horde be scattered! Besides Saint James, how many confessors of Christ were tortured, starved, or executed: both our monks, and not ours—although they are all truly ours, since we are one body in Christ Jesus, Who is the Head of all!

"After his members had been broken into shivers, Saint James was given over to the care of physicians. Wracked with pain, he died daily[5] and finally breathed his last, humbly thanking the Lord. You write that he foretold the day of his repose. Doubtless, God granted him this knowledge as a reward for sufferings. You also mention that at his burial a multitude was present, including many people of high rank. Here is a plain sign of the Lord's approval. Otherwise, such a throng would never have assembled to honor a person so seemingly insignificant —although James was certainly not insignificant before God.

"Having gone up to the heavens, Saint James has joined his co-sufferers and enlarged the choir of holy confessors and martyrs. Heaven rejoices, receiving the soul of James, by whose prayers may we be saved, brethren. The Lord's favorite received

---

[3]I Cor., Ch. 4   [4]Ps.33   [5]I Cor., Ch. 15

a reward worthy of his labors. Happy are the devout lovers of the martyrs who were present at his burial! May their portion be with him whom they laid to rest. If it be pleasing to God, I shall see to it that the relics receive due honors, in accordance with my own instructions in *The Catacheses. Greet ye one another with a holy kiss.*[6] Read this epistle to all the brethren. Our master the Archbishop[7] greets you, as do his protopresbyter and steward and all the brethren. May the Lord be with you. Amen."

Through the intercessions of Christ's holy confessor James, may the Lord assign us a place with his saints for all eternity. Amen.

---

[6]I Cor., Ch. 16; II Cor., Ch. 13; I Pet., Ch. 5
[7]Saint Nicephorus, Patriarch of Constantinople

On the Same Day

The Commemoration of a Miracle that Occurred at the Monastery of the Kiev Caves[1]

In the city of Kiev there lived two noblemen, John and Sergius, who were good friends. Once, they went together to the church fashioned by God at the Monastery of the Kiev Caves and saw a light brighter than the sun shining from the wonderworking icon of the most holy Theotokos. After this, the men adopted each other as brothers[2] before the icon. Many years later John fell gravely ill. He summoned the blessed Nicon, Abbot of the Kiev Caves, and gave him a portion of his wealth for distribution to the poor. The rest—a thousand pounds of silver and a hundred pounds of gold—he gave over to Sergius, who was to hold it in trust until Zacharias, John's five-year old son, reached adulthood. John also entrusted the care of Zacharias to Sergius, as his spiritual brother and closest friend. Soon after completing these dispositions, John died.

When Zacharias reached the age of fifteen, he asked Sergius for his inheritance. Sergius, however, had been wounded by the devil's arrow of greed, and for money was prepared to forfeit his very salvation. He told the youth, "Your father offered all his property to God. Ask the Lord for silver and gold: He is your debtor. Perhaps He will have pity on you. I owe you and your father nothing. Your father was a fool to have squandered his money on the poor and left you a pauper."

The youth wept bitterly over his loss. Later, he suggested to his guardian, "Give me half of my inheritance, and you take the other half." Sergius replied by again heaping ridicule on Zacharias and his father. Afterwards Zacharias requested a third of his due, then a tenth. When it seemed clear he would lose everything, Zacharias proposed, "If you have indeed taken

---

[1]From *The Patericon of the Kiev Caves*
[2]The adoption of a brother or sister, *adelphopoiia*, created a spiritual relationship between two people, carried with it an obligation of mutual help and support, and was blessed by a ritual of prayer. (Tr.)

nothing that is mine, come testify to it in the church of the Caves before the wonderworking icon of the most holy Theotokos, where you adopted my father as your spiritual brother."

Sergius agreed, went to the church and, standing before the icon of the Theotokos, swore, "I did not take a thousand pounds of silver and a hundred pounds of gold." He tried to kiss the wonderworking icon, but a miraculous force prevented him. Then, as he was leaving the church, he suddenly cried, "O venerable fathers Anthony and Theodosius, do not allow the merciless angel to destroy me! Beseech our most holy Lady the Theotokos to drive away the horde of demons which has gained control of me. Let the evil spirits take the silver and gold hidden in my room." All were stricken with terror, and after this no one was permitted to make an oath before the icon of the most holy Theotokos.

The perjurer's safe was opened, and it was found that the Lord, Who richly rewards almsgivers, had doubled the precious metal. Zacharias gave Abbot John, Nicon's successor, its entire contents: two thousand pounds of silver and two hundred of gold. He received the tonsure and lived out his days in the holy Monastery of the Caves. To honor the donors, John the boyar and his son Zacharias, the gold and silver were used to build a church dedicated to Saint John the Forerunner, adjoining the main church of the community. Everyone glorified Christ God and the immaculate Virgin Theotokos, who is especially venerated in the Monastery of the Kiev Caves. May her wondrous grace be with us forever. Amen.

❧❧❧

On this same day we commemorate our holy monastic father Zacharias the Hospitable, the door of whose cell was ever open to all. This couplet to him survives:

Alike to Christ thy God in might,
Inherit, Father, His true life.

The Twenty-Fifth Day of the Month of March

A Homily on the Annunciation of the Most Holy Theotokos[1]

When the fullness of time had come and the deliverance of mankind through the Incarnation of God was at hand, it was necessary that a pure, holy, faultless virgin provide flesh to the Lord, in order for Him to effect our salvation. Such a virgin was found, who was purer than all purity, holier than all holiness, and more faultless than the angels: the most holy, all-blessed Virgin Mary, offshoot of the barren root of the holy, righteous ancestors of God (Joachim and Anna), the fruit of parental prayer and fasting, and a child of royal and high-priestly lineage. Herself a living temple, she was found in the holy place, Solomon's Temple. She who would bear "the Word, Holiest of all that is,"[2] was seen within the area of the Temple known as the Holy of Holies. There the Lord *looked* down from the height of the glory of His kingdom *upon the lowliness of His handmaiden*[3]

---

[1]Based on the divine Scriptures, and the writings of the Holy Fathers and trustworthy chroniclers
[2]From the Akathist Hymn to the Most Holy Theotokos, Kontakion Thirteen
[3]Luke, Ch. 1

and chose her who from all generations was foreordained to be the Mother of the pre-eternal Word.

From trustworthy accounts written by the saints, we learn that even before the archangel brought his good tidings, the Virgin was mystically apprised of God the Word's Incarnation from her. For about twelve years the immaculate Virgin lived in the Temple, practicing ceaseless noetic prayer, doing handiwork, and immersing herself in the law of the Lord by reading holy books day and night. Saints Epiphanius and Ambrose write that her mind was extraordinarily keen, that she loved to learn, and that she applied herself diligently to study of the divine Scriptures. The ecclesiastical historian George Kedrinus adds that while her parents were still alive, she thoroughly acquainted herself with all the sacred writings of the Hebrews. Mary often read the prophecy of Isaiah, *Behold, a virgin shall conceive, and bear a son, and thou shalt call His name Emmanuel, which being interpreted is, God with us;*[4] therefore, her heart burned with love not only for the expected Messiah, but also for the virgin who would conceive and bear Him. She pondered what a great honor it would be to give birth to Emmanuel, the Son of God, and how ineffable was the mystery of the virgin birth. Knowing from the prophesies that the advent of the Messiah was at hand, because the scepter had been taken from Judah[5] and Daniel's weeks were coming to an end,[6] she concluded that the Virgin foretold by Isaiah had already been born. She frequently sighed from the bottom of her heart and begged God to permit her to see this virgin and, if possible, to become her least servant.

Once, at midnight, the Virgin was fervently supplicating the Lord concerning this matter while praying beyond the second veil[7] in the Temple according to her custom. Suddenly a brilliant light shone from heaven and encompassed her, and she heard a voice say, "You shall give birth to My Son." Who can express the spotless Virgin's joy at this, or her gratitude as she prostrated herself before God the Creator? The Lord had *looked upon the lowliness of His handmaiden;*[8] He had exalted her who out of love for God had hoped to be a handmaiden of the Messiah's Mother,

---

[4]Is., Ch. 7; Matt., Ch. 1   [5]Gen., Ch. 49   [6]Dan., Ch. 9
[7]That is, within the Holy of holies (Tr.)   [8]Luke, Ch. 1

and chosen her to be the Mother herself and the Mistress of all creation. Mary was granted this revelation when she was twelve years old: two years prior to her betrothal. She revealed it to no one before Christ's Ascension. After the revelation, she awaited the time when she would mystically conceive within her virginal womb.

When the eleventh year of her stay in Solomon's Temple had ended and the twelfth year had begun,[9] and while she was fourteen years old,[10] the chief priests and priests ordered Mary to leave the Temple, in accordance with the Law, and to wed— like her companions, the other virgins. She replied that while she was still in swaddling, her parents had dedicated her to God alone, and that she had made a vow to preserve her virginity for the Lord; therefore, it was impossible for her to marry a mortal man. Nothing, she insisted, could force her to enter into wedlock, since she had pledged her virginity to the immortal God.

The high priests were amazed at this, because never yet had a maiden vowed to God perpetual virginity, and they discussed what to do. They did not want Mary to continue living in the Temple or venturing beyond the inner veil; at the same time, they hesitated to betroth to a man a virgin consecrated to God. They were uncertain how to arrange for her to live as an unwedded virgin without angering the Lord. It would be a terrible sin, they reckoned, to compel a virgin to wed when she had already promised her perpetual virginity to God, and as great a sin to allow a maiden who had come of age to continue entering the Holy of Holies. Thus, Saint Gregory of Nyssa writes, "While she was a little girl, the priests kept the Virgin in the Temple of the Lord, as they had Samuel; but when she reached adulthood, they took counsel with one another about what to do with her, in order to avoid angering God." And the ecclesiastical historian Nicephorus Callistus relates, "When the Virgin came of age, the priests met in council to decide how to avoid affronting her purity. Because the maiden had pledged herself once and for all to God, they were afraid of committing sacrilege by forcing her

---

[9]According to Saint Evodus, one of the Seventy Apostles
[10]According to George Kedrinus

to submit to the law of matrimony. At the same time, they said that it was improper and a flagrant violation of the Law to permit a maiden of her age to enter the Holy of Holies. Therefore, having approached the Ark of the Covenant and prayed fervently, they received, as Jerome testifies, an answer from the Lord: God directed them to search for a worthy man who would safeguard the Virgin and her purity under the pretence of marriage. The counsel of the Lord was that unmarried men of the house and tribe of David be chosen and that their staves be placed upon the altar. The Virgin would be entrusted to the man whose staff blossomed."[11]

At that time the feast of the consecration of the Temple, instituted by the Maccabees, was celebrated,[12] and a multitude of people from nearby towns assembled in the house of the Lord. Among them were descendants of David, relatives of the Virgin Mary. George Kedrinus writes: "The great High Priest Zacharias, father of the Forerunner, assembled twelve unmarried men of the house of David. One of them was the righteous elder Saint Joseph. Zacharias left their staves overnight on the altar. 'Reveal, O Lord,' he prayed, 'the man worthy of betrothal to the Virgin.' The next morning the high priest entered the Temple with the twelve men and found that Joseph's rod had budded. On the rod (as Jerome testifies) there sat a dove that had flown down from heaven. From this it was clear that God wished the Virgin to be entrusted to Joseph. Some believe that since the immaculate Maiden shunned betrothal and every embarrassment to purity, God must have granted her a special revelation as well, encouraging her to be espoused to the righteous, God-pleasing, and holy Joseph and to live in his house. Providence ordered matters in this way not to enable Mary to enjoy the carnal pleasures of wedlock, but to guard and preserve her virginity. Following the betrothal, the High Priest Zacharias and the other priests entrusted the Virgin to Saint Joseph, who took her to his home. There the couple lived chastely, and the blossom of Mary's virginity remained fresh.

---

[11]Nicephorus, Bk. 1, Ch. 7
[12]I Mac., Ch. 4. The feast began on November 25; its leave-taking was on December 3.

Saint Joseph merely seemed to be the Virgin's husband; in truth, he was the chaste and holy guardian of her purity."

In the house of her betrothed, the immaculate Virgin continued to live as she had in the Holy of Holies. She spent all her time rapt in mental prayer, reading sacred books, and doing handiwork. For her, Joseph's home was a temple of prayer. She never left it, but remained inside, fasting and keeping silence. If she did speak, it was only to the other members of the household, that is, to Joseph's daughters. As George Kedrinus tells us, "Mary avoided leaving the home of her betrothed and going out among the people. She fasted, and passed the time with Joseph's two daughters. Only now and then, when it was necessary, did she speak briefly even with these companions."

After the Virgin had spent four months in Joseph's house,[13] the time came for the Incarnation of God the Word: the initiation of our salvation, awaited by the whole world from the ages. God sent one of the celestial spirits closest to His throne, the Archangel Gabriel, to announce to the immaculate Virgin "the mystery hidden from eternity and unknown to the angels":[14] the strange conception of the Son of God in a manner surpassing the understanding of every mind. About this, the Evangelist Luke writes, *In the sixth month the angel Gabriel was sent from God.*[15] It had been six months since the conception of Saint John the Forerunner, and the same angel that brought Zacharias word of John's conception brought the glad tidings of Christ's conception to the most pure Virgin. Having been conceived six months earlier, the Forerunner leapt for joy in his mother's womb when, shortly after the Annunciation, the Lord's mother visited Saint Elisabeth.

The angel was sent unto a city of Galilee, named Nazareth. In those days, Galilee was mostly a heathen land, although some of its inhabitants were Israelites. This is why the Scriptures call it *Galilee of the Gentiles.*[16] The Israelites regarded Galilee as the most inglorious province of their land, because it was full of sin-

---

[13]According to Saint Evodus
[14]Theotokion of the Fourth Tone Resurrectional Dismissal Hymn
[15]Luke, Ch. 1   [16]Matt., Ch. 4; Is., Ch. 9

ful, unbelieving foreigners. They spoke of it with disdain, saying, *Shall Christ come out of Galilee?*[17] and, *Search, and look: for out of Galilee ariseth no prophet.* Likewise Nazareth, a town of Galilee, was regarded as the most miserable and insignificant of cities, so that they asked, *Can there any good thing come out of Nazareth?*[18] But observe how the will of God operates. Where did the Lord deign to settle His immaculate Mother? Not in Judea, in the illustrious city of Jerusalem; but in little Nazareth, in sinful Galilee, to make clear that He came to earth for the sake of sinners. *I came not,* He declared, *to call the righteous, but sinners to repentance.*[19] He came, on the one hand, to the unbelieving heathen, to found a faithful Church for Himself and, on the other, to show that He looks favorably not on the proud and distinguished, but on the humble, the rejected, the outcast. When God the Word deigned to bow the heavens and descend to sinners, He looked down from the height of His glory to see where the greatest number of wrongdoers lived. He saw that the Jerusalemites considered themselves righteous and justified themselves *before men,*[20] whereas the Galileans were regarded as the worst transgressors of the Law and were scorned by all. Therefore, passing over supposedly holy Judea, He descended to supposedly sinful Galilee; passing over respected, glorious, and populous Jerusalem, He chose for Himself the lowliest place in this world. He *made Himself of no reputation, and took on Him the form of a servant*[21] and sinner.

Nazareth was small, but how abundant was the grace vouchsafed it! Not one of the larger cities of Israel, *which were exalted unto heaven,*[22] was deemed worthy of the like. In little Nazareth lived the Virgin who is more exalted than all the angels and whose womb is "more spacious than the heavens."[23] There Gabriel was sent, there the Holy Spirit overshadowed, there God the Word assumed flesh; for where there is humility, the light of divine grace shines. Proud cities are not pleasing to Christ, but humble ones are. In despised Nazareth Christ our Lord was conceived; in renowned Jerusalem Christ our Lord

---

[17]John, Ch. 7   [18]John, Ch. 1   [19]Mark, Ch. 2; Luke, Ch. 5
[20]Luke, Ch. 16   [21]Phil., Ch. 2   [22]Matt., Ch. 11; Luke, Ch. 10
[23]From Compline and the Liturgy of Saint Basil the Great

was crucified. God takes up His abode in the humble, but the proud drive Him away.

In one of his letters, Saint Andrew of Crete describes how God dispatched the angel to the humble Virgin living in poor, lowly Nazareth: "Having deigned to send one of His chief angels to proclaim the mystery, God (it seems to me) majestically proclaimed to him, 'Gabriel! Go to Nazareth, a town in Galilee, where the young virgin Mary lives. She is betrothed to a man named Joseph.' 'Go,' commands the Lord, 'to Nazareth.' And why? Because there Gabriel will find the splendid, chosen flower of virginity blooming like a fragrant rose in a field of thorns. 'Go to Nazareth,' says the Lord, 'that the prophecy *might be fulfilled which was spoken, He shall be called a Nazarene.*'[24] Who shall be called a Nazarene? He Whom Nathaniel would call *the Son of God* and *King of Israel.*[25] Gabriel is sent, because he had previously ministered divine mysteries, as we know from the Book of Daniel.[26] 'Go to Nazareth, a town in Galilee,' the Lord charges His archangel, 'and announce to the Virgin tidings of the joy lost to Eve. Take care not to frighten her. Let your proclamation bring joy, not fear; consolation, not alarm.' Indeed, what could be happier than for human nature to be united with the divine nature; than for humanity to become one with God through this union in a single hypostasis? What could be more amazing than the sight of God making Himself so small as to be carried within a womb? Oh, marvel astonishing the whole world! God the Son, Whose throne is heaven and footstool the earth,[27] Whom the heavens cannot contain, Who being one with the Father shares with Him the throne of eternity, is contained in the Virgin's womb! What could be more astounding than to see God in the form of man, without ceasing to be God, or to see human nature united with its Creator: God become perfect man?

"Having heard the divine proclamation, but reckoning the task beyond his powers, Gabriel wavered between dread and elation. Yet although he regarded himself as unworthy, he dared not disobey God's command. He flew to the Virgin and, arriv-

---

[24]Matt., Ch. 2   [25]John, Ch. 1
[26]Dan., Ch. 8   [27]Is., Ch. 66; Matt., Ch. 5

ing in Nazareth, stopped at the entrance to Joseph's house. 'How should I begin the task given me by God? Should I rush into Mary's chamber? If I do so, I may startle the Virgin. Should I enter slowly? This may frighten the Maiden, and she may hide. Should I knock? But why, when it is contrary to the nature of angels? For the bodiless there is nothing that can bar entrance. Should I open the doors? But I can go through them. Should I call out the Virgin's name? Again, this may startle her. I will address her softly, as He Who sent me would wish. But what words shall I use? Shall I first say, *Rejoice*; or, *The Lord is with thee*; or, *The Holy Spirit shall come upon thee, and the power of the Highest shall overshadow thee?*[28] First I shall announce the joy, then the wondrous mystery. I shall approach and say, "Hail! Be glad! Be of good comfort!" These words will serve as a fine beginning to my conversation with the Virgin. She will not be troubled or frightened. When a joyful message is brought to a queen, it should begin with cheerful greetings; and indeed, this is an occasion for joy, a time of happiness, the kingdom of tranquility, the counsel of salvation, and the beginning of consolation.'"

Consider the reverence with which the archangel approaches the Virgin, the fear with which he draws nigh to the Mistress of the whole world, the care with which the herald rehearses his joyful proclamation. Note also that he found Mary not outside her room and house, on the streets of the city, amid crowds engaged in worldly conversations, or even busy at home attending to the cares of life; but keeping silence, praying, and reading, as icons of the Annunciation frequently show. In them, an open book often lies before the Virgin, indicating that she was always reading, or reflecting on God. It is the devout opinion of the divinely inspired Fathers of the Church that when the celestial herald appeared to her, Mary was meditating on those words of Isaiah: *Behold, a virgin shall conceive,*[29] and on how and when that strange conception and birth, so alien to virginity, would occur. George Kedrinus explains that because God had already revealed to her the mystery that she would bear the longed-for Messiah, she was burning with seraphic love for her Creator and pleading that, out of compassion, He quickly fulfill

[28]Luke, Ch. 1   [29]Is., Ch. 7; Matt., Ch. 1

His divine promise and Isaiah's prophecy. "When will the awaited day come?" she wondered. "When will my Maker bow the heavens, descend, take up His dwelling in me, and receive my flesh? When will I experience the blessed joy of becoming the Mother of my God? Until that time comes, *my tears* shall be *my bread by day and by night.*[30] For those eagerly anticipating a happy event, how long even a brief wait can seem!"

While the Virgin was mediating on this and engaged in noetic prayer within the secret chamber of the heart, her ardent love for the Lord of Sabaoth blazed higher and higher. Suddenly Archangel Gabriel, who had quietly approached, became visible to her. The holy teacher Andrew of Crete tells us:

"The archangel entered the house and neared the inner chamber where the Virgin lived. He silently passed through the doors and, when inside the room, addressed the Virgin meekly. *'Rejoice, thou who art full of grace,'* said he, *'the Lord is with thee.*[31] He Who was before you is now with you and shall shortly appear from you. He Who was before all eternity has entered time.' Oh, boundless love for mankind! Oh, indescribable benevolence! The archangel brings salutations, the glad tidings that the Creator is making His abode in the Virgin. The words *The Lord is with thee* demonstrate the presence of the King Who, taking human flesh from her, in no way diminishes His innate glory. Rejoice, recipient of joy, *the Lord is with thee!* Rejoice, all-honored channel of joy, through whom the woeful decree of condemnation becomes a gladsome call to blessedness! Rejoice, truly blessed one! Rejoice, sublime Virgin! Rejoice, splendid temple of celestial glory! Rejoice, sanctified palace of the King! Rejoice, bridal chamber in which Christ was betrothed and united to humanity! *Blessed art thou among women.* You were revealed to the prophet Isaiah as a prophetess, a virgin, and a sealed book. You are truly blessed, so Ezekiel called you the morning star and the closed door through which passed the one God. You alone are blessed, whom Daniel, the man of desires, beheld as a mount, and whom the wondrous Habbakuk saw as *a mountain overshadowed and densely wooded.*[32] The Lord's forefather, King David, hymned you as *the mountain of God, a butter*

---

[30]Ps. 41   [31]Luke, Ch. 1   [32]Hab., Ch. 3

mountain, a curdled mountain, the mountain wherein God is pleased to dwell.[33] *Blessed art thou among women!*[34] Zachariah, the seer of divine mysteries, saw you as *a candlestick all of gold,* with *seven lamps upon it*[35] representing the seven gifts of the Holy Spirit that adorn you. Truly, you are blessed, for within you is paradise and the Garden of Eden, even Christ the almighty, Who springs from your womb and waters the entire earth with four evangelic streams of living water."

The immaculate Virgin was perplexed by the angelic greeting and asked herself what it meant. She was perplexed, but not very frightened, as she might have been were the salutation something altogether new or unexpected. Angels did not terrify the Maiden, for they were her usual visitors in the Holy of Holies where, according to Saint Germanus, an angel fed her daily. Nevertheless, she was perplexed, because she had never seen an angel shine so brilliantly with celestial glory. She had never seen an angel whose face was so joyous or voice so cheering. Even more perplexing were his words, *Blessed art thou among women,*[36] since from this it might be construed that Mary's virginity would be sacrificed. As one perfectly chaste, the Maiden was perplexed; as indomitable, she was unafraid; as wise and prudent, she *cast in her mind what manner of salutation this should be.* "What does this greeting mean?" she asked herself. "Will the angel lead me back to the Temple, or has he brought me some unknown food from heaven? Will he announce a new revelation from God? Or will he teach me the meaning of the words, *A virgin shall conceive, and bear a son,* on which I meditate so much, but cannot understand? And what will follow his greeting?"

Then the angel continued, *"Fear not, Mary.* Do not doubt Isaiah's prophecy about the Virgin. You are the Virgin deemed worthy of the grace to conceive Emmanuel seedlessly and to bear Him in a manner comprehensible only to God. You have found favor with the Lord on account of your innumerable virtues, of which three are chief. Firstly, you have obtained grace because of your profound humility. *God giveth grace to the*

---

[33]Ps. 67   [34]Luke, Ch. 1
[35]Zech., Ch. 4   [36]Luke, Ch. 1

humble,[37] and He asks, *Unto whom shall I look down, save upon the meek and humble?*[38] Secondly, you have obtained grace because of your virginal purity. God, Who is supremely pure by nature, wishes to be born of an immaculate virgin. Thirdly, you have obtained grace because of your flaming love for God. The Lord says, *I love them that love Me, and those that seek Me find grace.*[39] Since you have loved and sought Him with your whole heart, you have found favor with Him and shall bear a son: not an ordinary child, but the divine Son of the Most High, God of God, begotten of the Father without a mother before all ages. Now, at the end of the ages, God the Son shall come forth without a father from you, a virgin mother. His name is wondrous and ineffable: *thou shalt call His name Jesus,*[40] which means *Saviour.* He shall save the whole world and reign beyond compare more gloriously than His ancestor David and the other sovereigns of the house of Jacob. His kingdom will not be temporal, but eternal, and shall abide unto endless ages."

Then said Mary to the angel, How shall this be, seeing I know not a man? So saying, the immaculate Virgin did not express disbelief in the angel's words, for by the grace of God, with which she was filled, she knew she would bear the One heralded. The Lord Himself had revealed this to her while she was still in the Temple. What was unknown to the Virgin was how she could give birth without knowing a man; therefore, she asked the angel, *How shall this be?* According to Saint Gregory of Nyssa, she told Gabriel, "O angel, disclose the manner of the birth, and my heart will readily accept God's decision. I greatly desire to bear divine fruit, but only with my virginity intact." Saint Ambrose's interpretation is similar. He writes, "Fittingly did the Virgin ask the angel, *How shall this be?* She had read the prophecy that *a virgin* would *conceive,* but it was only from the angel that she learned how."

The angel therefore revealed to the Virgin the manner of the conception, which would take place not according to the human order, but supernaturally, for "wheresoever God willeth, the order of nature is overcome."[41] This conception shall

---

[37]Jas., Ch. 4; Prov., Ch. 3   [38]Is., Ch. 66
[39]Prov., Ch. 8   [40]Luke, Ch. 1
[41]Dogmatic Theotokion, Tone Seven

come to pass by the operation of the Holy Spirit," declared Gabriel. *"The Holy Spirit shall come upon thee, and the power of the Highest shall overshadow thee.*[42] The Holy Spirit shall enter your womb and bring about the ineffable conception. If God could create Adam from dust, He can easily bring forth an infant from a virgin. If he could fashion a woman from Adam's rib, He can certainly fashion a man in a virgin's womb. Within your seedless womb, O most holy Virgin, the all-accomplishing Spirit shall impart your flesh to the immaterial Word of God. The Lord shall pass through you, 'the door sealed in purity and guarded by virginity,'[43] as a ray of the sun passes through glass or crystal. He shall sanctify and illumine you with His divine glory. You shall become the true Mother of God, giving birth at once to perfect God and perfect man. An undefiled virgin before giving birth, you shall remain a virgin as you give birth and after giving birth. All of this God shall bring to pass by the descent of the Holy Spirit upon you. Let this be a sign of the truth of my words: *Thy cousin Elisabeth, who was called barren* since her youth, *hath also conceived a son in her old age.*[44] When God wishes, the impossible becomes possible. With men it is impossible that an uncorrupted, unmarried virgin or a barren, aged woman should conceive, but nothing is beyond the power of the omnipotent Creator. *With God nothing shall be impossible*: the barren, elderly woman has conceived, and you, a virgin, shall conceive."

Having heard the angel's glad tidings, the Immaculate One gave her assent to the will of the Lord. Her heart filled with love for God, she said with the most profound humility, *Behold the handmaid of the Lord; be it unto me according to thy word.* Straightway, by the operation of the Holy Spirit, the ineffable conception came to pass. At that moment, the Maiden experienced no carnal pleasure, but spiritual bliss. Her virginal heart melted with divine desire, her spirit burned with seraphic love, and her mind exulted in God and delighted in His goodness. As the Maiden immersed herself in the noetic vision of the

---

[42]Luke, Ch. 1
[43]Theotokion of the Second Tone Resurrectional Dismissal Hymn
[44]Luke, Ch. 1

Lord and was overcome by sweet spiritual ardor for Him, the Son of God was conceived. *The Word was made flesh, and dwelt among us.*[45]

Having announced the will of the Master, Gabriel with fear worshipped the Lord Who had become incarnate in the Virgin's womb and venerated her who had given flesh to God. Then he returned to the throne of the Lord of Sabaoth and joined the hosts of heaven in jubilantly magnifying the mystery of the Incarnation unto the ages. Amen.

---

[45]John, Ch. 1

A Homily on the Annunciation of the Most Holy Theotokos

By Our Father Among the Saints John Chrysostom, Archbishop of Constantinople[1]

"The joy of the Annunciation is a token of freedom from slavery," the angel announces to the Virgin. The angel converses with the Virgin so that the serpent might never again sway woman as once in Paradise. *In the sixth month*, I say, *the angel Gabriel was sent from God to a virgin espoused to a man.*[2] Gabriel was sent unto the Virgin to proclaim salvation for the whole world; to deliver the summons recalling Adam; to end womankind's disgrace; to prepare a spotless chamber for the Bridegroom; to betroth the Creator to His creation. Gabriel was sent to the animate palace of the King of angels. *Gabriel was sent to a virgin espoused to Joseph* and whose purity was guarded by the Son of God. The bodiless one was sent to an undefiled maiden; he who was free from sin to her who knew not corruption. The brilliant luminary appeared leading the way for the Sun of righteousness; the morning star preceded the light of day. Gabriel was sent to announce Him Who is in the bosom of the Father and is carried in the arms of His mother; to point out Him Who sits upon the throne and lies in the manger. The guardsman was sent to proclaim the King's secret, a mystery known by faith but undiscoverable by vain curiosity; a mystery worshipped, but beyond human comprehension; a divine mystery surpassing man's intellect.

In the sixth month the angel Gabriel was sent from God: he was sent six months after Elisabeth was told of John's conception. How do we know? Because the angel himself revealed it, telling the Virgin, *Behold, thy cousin Elisabeth, she hath also conceived a son in her old age: and this is the sixth month with her, who was*

---

[1]This homily is included in Symeon Metaphrastes' collection.
[2]Luke, Ch. 1

called barren. John was conceived six months prior to the Annunciation, because a soldier should advance before his commander, a footman before his master, a herald before his ruler. *In the sixth month the angel was sent to a virgin espoused to a man*: espoused, not fully wedded; espoused, but with her virginity intact. Why espoused? So that the mystery might be concealed from the robber, to wit, the devil. The evil one knew that the Master would appear from a virgin, for he had heard Isaiah's words: *Behold, a virgin shall conceive, and bear a son;*[3] therefore, he carefully observed every virgin, with the intent of bringing dishonor on the prophesied one. This is why the Lord chose to appear from an espoused virgin: *from a virgin espoused to a man whose name was Joseph.* Hear what the prophet tells us about that man and that virgin: *A book that is sealed* (which is to say, she whose virginity is truly sealed) *they shall deliver to one that is learned.*[4] By whom shall she be delivered? By the priests. And to whom? To Joseph the carpenter. By his first honorable marriage, brethren, Joseph begat children. After the death of his wife, he did not marry again, but lived chastely and reared his offspring in the fear and instruction of the Lord. When the Apostle Paul went forth to preach the Gospel, he became acquainted with one of Joseph's sons, as he writes: *Other of the apostles saw I none, save James the Lord's brother,*[5] who was Joseph's offspring, but not Mary's. While entrusting the Virgin to the chaste Joseph, some of the priests suggested that the full rites of marriage be performed for the couple; but Joseph understood that this must not be. Rather, his task was to safeguard Mary's purity. The prophet foresaw this long before, when he wrote, *A book that is sealed they shall deliver to one that is learned.*[6] By *learned* he means one who has knowledge of the pleasures of wedlock. But if Joseph is learned, why does he say, *I cannot read this*? Joseph cannot read this *because it is sealed* for the Creator of all.

In the sixth month Gabriel was sent to the Virgin, after God had explained to him his mission. "Hearken, O angel," the Lord said; "I appoint you servitor of a strange and wondrous mystery.

---

[3]Is., Ch. 7; Matt., Ch. 1   [4]Is., Ch. 29
[5]Gal., Ch. 1   [6]Is., Ch. 29

Moved by compassion, I hasten to descend and search for Adam, who has gone astray. He who in the garden was fashioned in My image was disfigured and cast down to the earth. The work of My hands has been defiled, its perfection marred. A wolf has snatched away my charge, the child of Paradise is a wandering exile, the tree of life is guarded by a flaming sword, Eden's delights are hidden. I feel pity for the lost, and will find and capture the foe, but for the present this mystery must remain unknown even to the powers of heaven, save you alone. Go now to the Virgin Mary; go to the animate city, of whom the prophet said, *Glorious things are spoken of thee, O city of God.*[7] Proceed to My living paradise, to *the east gate,*[8] to the palace that shall house the Word. Onward to the second heaven which is upon the earth. Draw near to the light cloud and announce My coming; go to My tabernacle, to the chamber of My divine Incarnation, to the pure couch of My Nativity according to the flesh. Speak into her ear and proclaim My entry into the living ark; but take care not to bewilder or frighten the Virgin. Approach the divine temple reverently and greet the Maiden cheerfully, saying; *'Rejoice, thou who art full of grace!'*[9] I have come to make known the Lord's mercy to Eve, who was once led astray.'"

The angel thought, "This is a strange order, beyond understanding. He Whom the cherubim fear, upon Whom seraphim dare not gaze, Who cannot be upborne by all the angelic hosts, declares that He shall mystically descend, take up His abode in a virgin's womb, and dwell hypostatically therein. He Who condemned Eve has highly exalted her daughter and wishes me to take to her word of His coming, as He says: 'Speak into her ear and proclaim My entry.'"

While the angel was pondering this, the Master inquired, "Why are you troubled by doubt, O Gabriel? Is it because this conception is altogether a new thing? Remember that a short time ago I sent you to the priest Zacharias with word of John's conception. You punished the elder because of his unbelief, sealing his lips so that he cannot speak. On that occasion, did I not bring to pass what you announced? Was there not *a performance*

---

[7]Ps. 85   [8]Ez., Ch. 10 and 11   [9]Luke, Ch.1

of the things spoken? Did not the barren conceive? Did not the womb *well stricken in years* obey? Did not sterility come to an end? Why are you troubled by doubt?"

To this the angel replied, "For Thee, Master, everything is possible. Thou curest natural disorders; Thou dispelest the gloom of maladies; Thou restorest potency to lifeless organs. Thou commandest barren nature to produce children, making fruitful a sterile womb. Thou makest a dry rod leafy; Thou easily renderest wasteland fertile. Sarah and Rebekah, as well as Hannah, are proof of this. All were utterly barren until Thou didst rid them of infirmity. But now Thou revealest a stranger marvel: that Thou shalt take up Thine abode in the Maiden, although it is beyond the laws of nature for a virgin to bear a child. A virginal womb shall hold Him Whom heaven and earth cannot contain!'"

"Since, O Gabriel, you remain so perplexed by the mystery, reflect upon how Abraham's tent accommodated Me, the infinite One," commanded the Lord.

"Because of his hospitality," said the angel, deep in thought, "Thou didst deign to visit Abraham and reveal Thyself to him at the entrance of his tent. But Mary shall carry Thee within her womb, O Lord Who fillest all things. I cannot fathom how she shall endure the fire of the Godhead. How can she not be burned, when Thy throne in heaven is all aflame?"

The Master replied, "The fire burning in the bush was a type of the fire of My divinity. That flame did not consume the bush in the wilderness, and My presence, descending like a gentle rain, will not consume Mary."

After this the angel tarried no longer, but hastened to fulfill God's command. He appeared before the Virgin and with a gladsome voice announced, *"Rejoice,* O august one, *the Lord is with thee!* No longer shall the devil tyrannize your race. The Physician is ready to apply healing salve to the mortal wound inflicted by the ancient foe, whose stab shall become a source of life. A woman brought ruin upon humanity, and a woman shall bestow upon humanity blessings richer than those it lost. *Rejoice, thou who art full of grace!* Do not be ashamed because a woman was the cause of condemnation. You shall be the Mother of the Judge and Redeemer. Rejoice, O august one, bearer of life, through whom death is destroyed. Rejoice, animate church of God, easily accommodating both heaven and earth. Rejoice, most spacious dwelling of the uncontainable nature of God. Rejoice, immaculate Mother of the widowed world's Bridegroom. Rejoice, renewal of the desolate earth. Rejoice, Mary: on account of your purity, you are worthy to shelter the noetic Sun. Rejoice, vessel of heavenly joy. Rejoice, for because of you, joy has shined upon the whole world and the human race is restored to its primal estate. Rejoice, O august one, for you shall hold in your arms the Maker and Master of all!"

"What does this mean?" Mary wondered. "Could these salutations be a deadly ruse, like that which brought about the downfall our foremother Eve?"

Perceiving the Maiden's apprehension, the angel continued, *The Lord is with thee. Fear not, Mary: for thou hast found favour with God. And, behold, thou shalt conceive in thy womb, and bring forth a son, and shalt call His name Jesus. He shall be called the Son of the Highest: and the Lord God shall give unto Him the throne of His father David: and of His Kingdom there shall be no end.*

How shall this be, seeing I know not a man? asked Mary.

And the angel concluded with this explanation: *The Holy Spirit shall come upon thee, and the power of the Highest shall overshadow thee: therefore also that which shall be born of thee shall be called the Son of God.*

After the Annunciation, *Mary arose and went into the hill country with haste* to her cousin Elisabeth, *and entered into the house of Zacharias and saluted Elisabeth. And it came to pass, that, when Elisabeth heard the salutation of Mary, the babe leaped in her womb; and Elisabeth was filled with the Holy Spirit.* Wherever the august one entered, she brought joy; therefore, John leaped and danced in his mother's womb when Mary greeted Elisabeth. *And* Elisabeth *spake out with a loud voice, and said, "Blessed art thou among women, and blessed is the fruit of thy womb. And whence is this to me, that the mother of my Lord should come to me? Blessed art thou among women,* for you are the origin of the Resurrection, our door into Paradise. No longer shall women be disdained; no longer shall Eve's descendants fear the curse, for Christ, the Redeemer of our race and the Creator of heaven and earth, shall come forth from your holy womb."

Hearing this splendid greeting, the mind of the immaculate Virgin was illumined and she confessed divine mysteries, saying, *My soul doth magnify the Lord, and my spirit hath rejoiced in God my Saviour. He hath holpen His servant Israel in remembrance of His mercy, as He spake to our fathers, to Abraham and his seed forever.*

Brethren, the holy Virgin attained perfection surpassing that of righteous Abraham, and she is preeminent among all created beings. From her, Christ appeared: the Physician of the sick, the Sun of righteousness *for those sitting in darkness*,[10] the haven of the storm-tossed, salvation for the perishing, and reconciliation for those at enmity; *for He is our peace.*[11] On this day our sinful race celebrates the revelation of a most glorious mystery; therefore, spur yourselves and be adorned with virtues. Cry out with one voice to the Theotokos: "Rejoice, O august one, for today thou receivest in thy womb the Creator of the whole earth, upon Whom cherubim dare not gaze! Rejoice, O animate heaven, in which the Lord hath come to dwell in the flesh. Rejoice, golden lamp, brimming with the oil of God's ineffable mercy. Rejoice, *beauty of Jacob, which* God *loved*[12] and exalted above the angels. Rejoice, luminous cloud, inexplicably carrying the Master. One of the prophets called thee a door, another a burning bush that was not consumed, another a holy mountain, another a sealed fount, and another a paradise planted by the Lord. All their sayings are fulfilled in thee and through thee. Truly, great and marvelous wonders are wrought in thee, O Lady. Thou, O most holy Virgin, Mother of God, art above all praise. It is impossible to hymn thee worthily, for our God assumed flesh from thee. All creation extolleth thee; wherefore, O Theotokos, visit us paupers and sinners, and deliver us from every misfortune. Deem us worthy of the Kingdom of thy Son and our God, the Lord Jesus Christ: to Whom be glory and dominion, with the Father and the most holy, good, and life-creating Spirit, now and ever and unto the ages of ages. Amen.

---

[10]Is. Ch. 42   [11]Eph., Ch. 2   [12]Ps. 46

The Twenty-Sixth Day of the Month of March

The Synaxis of the Holy Archangel Gabriel

𝔍n accordance with the Jerusalem Typicon and the liturgical observance of the Great Monastery of Saint Sabbas, the Holy Church has, since ancient times, convened her children on the day following the Annunciation of the immaculate Virgin Theotokos to celebrate the Synaxis of the Archangel Gabriel and extol the herald of joy. Verily, the minister of the mystery of our salvation is deserving of particular veneration, for he brought to the blameless Virgin tidings of how God the Word would assume flesh in her pure womb. If subjects of an earthly king honor a noble spokesman sent to announce a royal favor, much more should we honor with a special feast the most eminent and respected prince of angels who was sent by the Heavenly King to proclaim the supreme favor of eternal salvation for the entire human race. Eminent indeed is this messenger, who revealed his greatness to Saint Zacharias, saying, *I am Gabriel, that stand before God,*[1] that is, nearer to the throne of God than the other angels. As in an earthly court the nobles that stand closest to the King rank highest, are the most illustrious, and are the most privy to royal secrets, so in the Kingdom of heaven the holy angels standing closest to God rank highest, shine the most gloriously, and discern divine mysteries the most clearly.

According to Holy Scripture, the seven spirits of the highest rank are the princes of the angels and stand directly in the

---

[1]Luke, Ch. 1

unapproachable, divine light. In the book of Tobit, it says that the companion of young Tobias declared himself to be *one of the seven angels* [2] who stand before God. In the Book of Revelation John the Theologian mentions these same seven angels when he writes, *Grace be unto you, and peace, from Him Which is, and Which was, and Which is to come: and from the seven spirits which are before His throne.* [3] The seven are named Michael, Gabriel, Raphael, Uriel, Salathiel, Jegudiel, and Barachiel. Among them, Gabriel is second in authority, after Michael.

All seven preeminent angels are equal in rank, and Michael is first only in seniority. Because each has different duties, God did not send Archangel Michael, first of the seven, to the immaculate Virgin, but Gabriel, the second. Michael is the conqueror of enemies; Gabriel is the messenger of God's mysteries; Raphael is the healer of human infirmities; Uriel, being the effulgence of the divine fire, is the enlightener of the benighted; Salathiel is an intercessor, praying constantly for men and spurring them to pray; Jegudiel ever glorifies the Lord, imparts strength to those laboring for God, and ensures that they receive their reward; and Barachiel obtains God's blessings for us and bestows them.

Michael, then, was not sent with the joyous proclamation, because his work is to take up arms against foes and to scatter them with his flashing sword. Gabriel was dispatched instead, because his task is to declare God's mysteries. To Daniel he announced the liberation of the Lord's people from Babylonian captivity and also the time of the Messiah's coming; to Zacharias he proclaimed the birth of the holy Forerunner from a barren mother. It is said that Gabriel appeared to Moses in the wilderness and revealed the account of creation and the history of our earliest forebears, which was then recorded in the Book of Genesis. [4] According to pious tradition, Gabriel proclaimed to the holy, righteous Joachim and Anna the conception of the immaculate Theotokos. He was the Virgin's guardian angel and brought her food in the Holy of Holies; therefore, it was fitting that he should announce the glad tidings of the conception of God's Son. Furthermore, Gabriel was sent to the Virgin because

---

[2]Tob., Ch. 12   [3]Rev., Ch. 1   [4]According to *The Prologue*

his very name foretokened the wondrous proclamation: it hinted that the mighty God and Master would become perfect man in the womb of the Virgin. And verily, the perfect God did become perfect man, a child full of strength and wisdom. Other children are powerless and understand nothing when conceived in their mothers' wombs; however, He Who was clothed in flesh within the Virgin's womb was infinitely wise and possessed ineffable might from the moment of His conception. The prophet says, *I went unto the prophetess; and she conceived and bare a son. Then said the Lord to me, Call His name Conquer Quickly, Plunder Speedily. For before the Child shall have knowledge to cry, Father or Mother, He shall take the power of Damascus and the spoils of Samaria.*[5] This means that before the Child begins to talk, He shall possess such power that no enemy can withstand Him, as the name "Gabriel" intimates. Accordingly, Saint Proclus, Patriarch of Constantinople, writes: "The very name of the angel is wondrous, for the herald of good tidings sent to the Virgin Mary is called Gabriel. This name foretold the coming of the God-man into the world. Being derived in part from the word *gever*, which means "mighty man," in its entirety it means 'the mighty man-God.'" While still in His mother's womb, the God-man possessed the strength not of a mere child, but of a mighty man and the mighty God; therefore, Jeremiah says, *The Lord hath wrought a new work upon the earth; a woman shall compass a man,*"[6]

Truly glorious are both the name and the mission of God's messenger to the Virgin! Gabriel was already held in high esteem by the celestial powers while he was disclosing lesser mysteries to the holy prophets. Then "the mystery hidden from eternity and unknown to the angels"[7] was revealed to him before any of the other powers of heaven knew it. After this, all the angels regarded Gabriel with the utmost awe, as the pre-eminent initiate of God's most secret counsels.

The teachers of the Church, especially Dionysius the Aeropagite, explain that the seven chief angels remain before

---

[5]Is., Ch. 8
[6]Jer., Ch. 31, according to Jerome's translation
[7]Theotokion of the Fourth Tone Resurrectional Dismissal Hymn

the throne of God, while the others are dispatched on various tasks. Nevertheless, even the seven are sent to announce foremost mysteries and to effect the greatest manifestations of God's power, in accordance with the Apostle Paul's words: *Are they not all ministering spirits, sent forth to minister?*[8] What mystery could be a greater manifestation of divine might than the ineffable, unfathomable Incarnation of Christ? Because the incomparable mystery required a most eminent servitor, it was fitting that Gabriel, who stands directly before God's throne and is the pre-eminent initiate of the Lord's secret counsels, be chosen as its minister.

Some believe that Saint Gabriel belongs to the rank of archangels, which occupies the middle position in the third and lowest angelic hierarchy, between the principalities and angels, and that as a leader of the archangels he is dispatched to proclaim God's wondrous works. This opinion is derived from the very name *archangel*,[9] and from the words of Saint Dionysius, who states that the chief angels remain before the throne of God and that lower angels are sent on tasks. It is, however, much more likely that Gabriel is a member of the seraphic rank, which is the highest. He is not sent on lesser assignments, but only to proclaim the greatest mysteries, of which God's Incarnation is chief. Gabriel's wondrous salutation to the immaculate Virgin brought joy to her, and through her, to all creation, both here below and on high, as Saint John of Damascus chants, "The heavens rejoiced out of love, and the earth was amazed and trembled when thou didst hear the most pure voice, O Theotokos. A single festival dawned for both as the bodiless one brought thee joy."[10] To every order God has assigned a location closer to or farther from Him, as is explained in the entry for the eighth day of November. Saint Gabriel must belong to the seraphic

---

[8]Heb., Ch. 1

[9]Which means "ruling over the angels." But an archangel can either be an angel of the middle rank in the third angelic hierarchy, ruling over the angels proper, who belong to the very lowest rank; or else one of the seven preeminent seraphim, ruling over all nine angelic ranks. Michael, Gabriel, Raphael, Uriel, Salathiel, Jegudiel, Salathiel, and Barachiel are archangels in the latter sense. (Tr.)

[10]Sessional Hymn of the Third Tone

order, since no other rank stands closer to the unapproachable throne of divine glory, according to the certain testimony of Saint Dionysius the Aeropagite. His teaching about this is borne out by Isaiah's words: *I saw the Lord sitting on a high and exalted throne, and seraphs stood round about Him: each one had six wings.*[11]

Saint Andrew of Crete confirms that Gabriel, as one of the seven angels closest to God, is second among the seraphim. He writes, "God commanded one of the chief angels to announce the mystery. If the messenger is one of the chief angels, then he is one of the seven spirits that always stand before the Lord. If he is one of the seven, then he is a seraph. None of the angels are higher than the seraphim or closer to the divine throne. Therefore, Gabriel is a seraph, a captain of his order."

Saint Gregory the Dialogist agrees that the accomplishment of a mighty work of God calls for the dispatch of a mighty angel, and that since the Incarnation of God the Word is the greatest of God's deeds, it was proper that it be announced by Gabriel, preeminent among the seraphim. He tells us that "the servitor of the exalted mystery was the most illustrious of messengers, a mighty angel of the seraphic order."

As the supreme prince of darkness beguiled Eve, so the foremost prince of celestial light proclaimed the Annunciation to the immaculate Virgin. A seraph was dispatched to Mary, who burned with seraphic love for God. Therefore, let us devoutly venerate the highest prince of angels, one of the seven seraphim closest to God, the universal archangel, the herald of salvation to the whole world, celebrating his synaxis with prayers and hymns, and thanking him for his past and present beneficence to the human race. By the intercessions of the holy archangel Gabriel, who ever prays for us to the incarnate God, may we be granted remission of our sins! Amen.

ತ♠ತ♠ತ♠

It should be noted that in the divine Scriptures only four of the seven chief angels are mentioned by name. In the Book of Daniel, it is written that Saint Michael assists the Hebrews, who

---

[11]Is., Ch. 6

were then still pious worshippers of God.[12] In the Epistle of Jude, it says that *Michael the archangel, when contending with the devil, disputed over the body of Moses and said, The Lord rebuke thee;* and in the Revelation of Saint John the Theologian that he *fought against the dragon.*[13] Saint Gabriel also appears in the Book of Daniel, revealing to the prophet the meaning of God's future, hidden mysteries.[14] The Gospel of Luke relates how Gabriel proclaimed to Saint Zacharias the conception of the Forerunner, and to the immaculate Virgin Theotokos the Incarnation of God the Word.[15] Saint Raphael is mentioned in the Book of Tobit as young Tobias' protector from unexpected danger on his journey,[16] as the expeller and binder of the wicked spirit that cleaved to the maiden,[17] and as the healer of blind Tobit the elder.[18] In the Third Book of Esdras, Saint Uriel challenges the prophet to *weigh fire.*[19]

The names of the other three chief angels are not mentioned in Scripture. Nevertheless, certain divinely inspired exegetes are of the opinion that Saint Salathiel is the angel that appeared to Hagar when she was in the wilderness and cried in desperation to God. The angel said, *"Fear not, for God hath heard*[20] the contrite prayer you uttered after being thrust out by your mistress."* Thus Salathiel the intercessor was sent to reassure her who entreated the Lord's help. The same interpreters believe that Jegudiel was the angel that the Lord offered to send to the Israelites in the desert in order to lead them to the Promised Land, as it were in reward for honoring Him and observing His sacred commandments. Regarding this, the Lord said, *If ye shall indeed hear My voice, and do all the things I shall tell thee, I will send Mine angel to instruct thee, that he may bring thee into the land which I have prepared for thee.*[21] The expounders of Holy Writ consider Saint Barachiel to be one of the three angels that appeared to Abraham at the Oak of Mamre and represented the Holy Trinity: Father, Son, and Holy Spirit. The angels imparted the Lord's blessing to Sarah's aged womb, and the barren woman conceived a child, Isaac.

---

[12]Dan., Ch. 10   [13]Rev., Ch. 12   [14]Dan., Ch. 8
[15]Luke, Ch. 1   [16]Tob., Ch. 5   [17]Tob., Ch. 8
[18]Tob., Ch. 11   [19]III Es., Ch. 4   [20]Gen., Ch. 21
[21]Ex., Ch. 23

Since antiquity the Holy Church has devoutly revered the seven chief angels, among whom Michael is first in seniority and Gabriel second. All seven are depicted on icons, and churches are built in their honor, as we learn from the following story.

The impious persecutor and emperor Diocletian forced thousands of Christian prisoners to erect a stone bath in old Rome. The laborers were afflicted by the guards, and the building was sanctified not only by their sweat, but by their blood, since many were worked to death or tortured and executed for Christ's sake there. Years passed, the heathen tyrants perished, and their religion passed into oblivion. By the grace of Christ, the true faith shone upon the whole world and pious emperors reigned. Since Diocletian's magnificent bath was built by martyrs, the faithful of old Rome cleansed it of pagan defilement and consecrated it as a church named after the seven celestial spirits, the archangels and commanders of the heavenly hosts: Michael, Gabriel, Raphael, Uriel, Salathiel, Jegudiel, and Barachiel. Afterwards, churches were constructed to honor the holy seven chief angels in other cities (including Neapolis[22] in Campania and Panormus[23] in Sicily); moreover, the seven angels were depicted on panel icons and in mosaic, each in a way that mystically hints at the nature of the service he performs. Saint Michael was portrayed trampling Lucifer. In his left hand he held the branch of a date palm; in his right, a spear from which flew a white pennon emblazoned with a red cross. Saint Gabriel held a burning lantern in his right hand, and in his left a green jasper orb speckled with crimson. Saint Raphael carried an alabaster physician's box in his left hand and led the youth Tobias with his right hand. Tobias held the fish that leaped out of the Tigris River.[24] Saint Uriel held in his right hand a sword, which was pressed against his chest. His left hand was lowered and emitted fire. Saint Salathiel looked down with head bowed and arms crossed over his breast, as though he were praying contritely. Saint Jegudiel bore a golden crown in his right hand and a black whip woven of three cords in his left. Saint Barachiel was depicted with white roses embroidered on the upper half of his robe.

---

[22]Now Naples (Tr.)   [23]Now Palermo (Tr.)   [24]Tob., Ch. 6

On the Same Day

The Passion of the Holy Hieromartyr Irenaeus, Bishop of Sirmium[1]

During the reign of the impious Roman emperors Maximian and Diocletian, a fierce persecution of the Christians raged and the faithful, hoping for an eternal reward, gladly contested for Christ and submitted to torture. In those days the Bishop of Sirmium in Pannonia was Irenaeus. Although a young man, Irenaeus had attained perfection in the Catholic faith and the law of the Lord. On account of his love for Christ, he was deemed worthy to undergo numerous torments and wear the garland of a victorious confessor.

Irenaeus was arrested in Sirmium and taken by soldiers to Probus, Governor of Pannonia. The Governor demanded, "Submit to the laws of the Empire and sacrifice to our gods!"

"He who sacrifices to false deities rather than to the true God is excluded from the Lord's people," answered the holy Bishop.

"The all-merciful rulers have commanded their subjects either to offer oblations or to submit to torture," said the Governor.

"If I renounce the true God and sacrifice to demons, I shall certainly undergo the most excruciating torments," the martyr replied.

Probus repeated, "Either sacrifice to the gods or I shall straightway order your punishment."

I shall be delighted if you punish me," said the martyr. "I am eager to share in the Passion of my Lord by suffering for Him." At this the Governor commanded his soldiers to begin their work.

While the saint was being tortured, Probus asked him, "Will you sacrifice now, Irenaeus?"

"As ever, I offer to my God the sacrifice of a pure confession," answered the saint.

---

[1]From Greek manuscripts and *The Great Collection of Readings,* page 1,247

Soon the parents of the holy Bishop arrived with the members of his household. Seeing him endure merciless ill-treatment, they fell at his feet and begged him to pity himself and to remember that he was young and could live many more years if he submitted to the imperial decree. On one side, his father and mother lamented; on the other, his friends and relatives wept and wailed. With a single voice all cried, "Irenaeus, spare the blossom of your youth!"

The saint, however, had fixed his desire on God. Contemplating the divine statutes with the uplifted eyes of his soul, he declared, "This is what my Lord Jesus Christ teaches: *Whosoever shall deny Me before men, him will I also deny before My Father Which is in Heaven.*[2] Know, beloved, that neither your entreaties, nor anything else can come between me and God and His law. With my whole mind I aspire to a heavenly calling."

Then Probus said to the blessed Irenaeus, "Yield to the tears of those who grieve for you and cease playing the fool. Sacrifice to the gods and save yourself from an early death."

"I will save my soul for all eternity by not sacrificing," the saint retorted. The Governor therefore ordered that Irenaeus be imprisoned, while he pondered what to do next.

For many days the saint remained in the foul dungeon, enduring much distress because his wounds received no medical treatment. Then late one night Probus dragged Irenaeus to the tribunal and demanded, "Offer oblations to the gods. You have suffered long enough."

"Do not expect me to yield," said Saint Irenaeus. "I confess the name of Christ steadfastly. Deal with me as you wish."

The enraged Governor ordered his men to beat Saint Irenaeus with staves for a long time. While the soldiers were carrying out the order, Irenaeus cried, "I cleave to the God Whom I learned in childhood to honor! Him alone do I worship and to Him alone do I sacrifice. Never will I worship divinities made by the hands of men."

"You have endured sufficient misery," said Probus. "There is no need for you to die."

"Not death, but life awaits me," affirmed the martyr. "You

---

[2] Matt., Ch. 10

may torture me for my fidelity to the name of the Lord Jesus Christ, but you are powerless to destroy me."

"I see," said the Governor. "Are you married?"

"No," said the saint.

"Are your parents alive?" the Governor asked.

"They are not," answered Irenaeus.

"Have you sons or daughters?" continued the persecutor.

The saint replied, "I do not."

"Who, then, were the people weeping and lamenting for you before my judgment seat?" asked Probus.

Saint Irenaeus explained, "I strive to fulfill the precepts of my Lord Jesus Christ, Who taught that no one can become His disciple without renouncing father, mother, and possessions.[3] He said, *'He that loveth father or mother* or children or brethren or kindred *more than Me is not worthy of Me.'* [4] Whoever truly loves God and hopes in Him alone disdains earthly vanity and acknowledges no parent other than the Lord."

"I know that you have children," said Probus. "If you love them, you should sacrifice to the gods, lest you ruin your family's name."

"My children also acknowledge my God as their Father," replied Saint Irenaeus. "Knowing His power to save us, they share my complete trust in Him. We have committed our souls to His care and are certain He will preserve us. Now, carry on: fulfill the command of your emperors."

"If you have no concern for your children, then have pity on yourself and your parents. Offer oblations to the gods and submit to the imperial decrees, or I will destroy you," Probus threatened.

"Do with me as you wish," said the martyr. "You must realize by now that I will never sacrifice to your vile deities. You and the devil have devised many snares for God's saints, but my Lord Jesus Christ grants me the patience to endure every torment."

"If you do not sacrifice, I shall issue the death sentence at once," Probus warned.

"That is what I have been waiting for all along," laughed the saint. "Is not death the portal to everlasting bliss?"

---

[3]Luke, Ch. 14   [4]Matt., Ch. 10

Upon this the Governor decreed: "Irenaeus, who refuses to submit to the imperial edicts, is to be drowned in the River Sava."

"I was hoping for your most brutal tortures and the chance to show you that Christians, because of their faith in God, are fearless. Now it seems I must be content with an easy death," Irenaeus taunted the Governor. Flying into a rage, Probus commanded that the blessed one first be decapitated, then thrown into the river. The saint was delighted and exclaimed, "I thank Thee, O Lord Jesus, for granting me invincible courage in confessing Thy holy name and beg that Thou vouchsafe me Thine eternal glory!" Presently soldiers led Irenaeus to the Bridge of Artemis, the loathsome goddess. There the martyr removed his clothing, lifted his hands to heaven, and prayed contritely, "O Lord Jesus Christ, Who wast crucified for the redemption of the world, open the heavens to receive the soul of Thy faithful servant Irenaeus. Thou didst choose me from among the members of the Catholic Church of Sirmium to suffer for Thy holy name and hast strengthened me to face death. I beseech Thee, O Lord: in Thine ineffable compassion, protect the citizens of Sirmium from every calamity. Preserve them from enemies visible and invisible, and establish them in Thy holy faith." No sooner had the saint completed the prayer than the sword fell. His remains were discarded in the river Sava. God's servant Irenaeus was martyred on March 26, the seventh day of the calends of April, while Probus was Governor of Sirmium and our Lord was reigning in heaven. Unto Jesus Christ be glory forever. Amen.

ఆఆఆఆ

In *The Prologue*, an entry for this saint appears under August 23 as well as March 26. Since he was beheaded on the latter date, we have included his Passion here. Saint Irenaeus, Bishop of Lyons, a Father of the Church and ecclesiastical author, was put to death on August 23. His martyrdom occurred years before that of Saint Irenaeus of Sirmium.

On the Same Day

The Life of
Our Holy Monastic Father Malchus[1]

$\mathcal{T}$he venerable Malchus hailed from the Syrian village of Maronia, three and a half miles from Antioch. He was of hardy peasant stock and an only child. Both his parents insisted that he take a bride and continue their line, but the pious youth was determined to become a monk. With his father threatening him and his mother nagging him day and night, Malchus decided that he could only avoid wedlock by fleeing home and parents. Escaping to the desert, he was accepted into a monastery in the region between Immae and Beroea. Malchus became an emulator of the devout brethren and devoted himself to mortification of the fleshly passions by means of fasting and other ascetical labors.

Years later Malchus learned that his father had passed away. As a result, he conceived a desire to return to Maronia, console his mother in her widowhood, and sell his inheritance. Malchus wanted to give some of the proceeds to the needy and some to the monastery, and keep a portion for himself. Hearing about the plan, the abbot declared that it was a demonic temptation and that the ancient foe was preparing a trap for Malchus, under the pretext of virtuous intentions. He explained, "This is just what the Scripture means when it says, *The dog is turned to his own vomit again.*"[2] He related to Malchus pertinent accounts from various holy books, including the story of how the devil tricked Adam and Eve by instilling in them a yearning to become equal to God, with the result that they lost Paradise. When he failed to dissuade his disciple, the superior fell on his knees and begged him not to abandon the brotherhood and cause his own perdition by looking back after *having put his hand to the plough.*[3] These warnings did not stop Malchus, and the hegumen escorted the disobedient monk out of the monastery as though he were a corpse being taken to burial. "Child, Satan has marked

---

[1]Abbreviated from the account written by Saint Jerome
[2]II Pet., Ch. 2   [3]Luke, Ch. 9

you with his brand," said the abbot before turning back. "I will not ask you again to explain your reasons for leaving. I do not accept your excuses. Know that a sheep that wanders from the fold is devoured by wolves."

The monastery was not far from the highway connecting Beroea and Edessa. Saracens wandered about the desert through which it passed, and frequently attacked travelers, who joined together in large parties for security. Malchus attached himself to one such group of about seventy persons, including women. But at times not even a company of this size was safe on the road, as Malchus and his companions learned when a band of half-naked Ishmaelites descended and took them prisoner. Only then did the monk realize that he had been deceived and repent of his error. Having abandoned the spiritual brotherhood and attached himself to layfolk, he fell into the hands of barbarians; wishing to claim the inheritance left him by his father, he became the property of Saracens. Now he was sorry, but it was too late to avoid the consequences of his decision. The captives were divided, and the Ethiopian who took Malchus put him on a camel with one of the women. So fast did the beast run that only by holding on tightly to the woman could Malchus avoid falling. In this way the monk traveled through the wilderness with the barbarians, subsisting for days on their food of half-cooked meat and drink of camel's milk.

After crossing a mighty river, the slaves reached the Saracen's homeland. The Ethiopian presented Malchus and the woman to his wife and ordered them to pay homage to her and to his children, in accordance with the custom of the tribe. Both captives prostrated themselves before their mistress; then Malchus was assigned household chores: fetching water, sweeping, and onerous work of every sort. He was further punished for disobedience to his father the hegumen by being deprived of the habit and forced to adopt the scanty dress of the natives who, because of the extreme heat, wore nothing except a loincloth. Eventually he was given the task of tending sheep in the wilderness. Malchus found consolation in this, because it meant he rarely saw his owners or the other slaves. While alone with the flock, he remembered holy Jacob and Moses, both of whom were shepherds. He lived on cheese and milk, prayed without ceasing, and chanted the psalms he had learned in the monastery. Before long he began to enjoy this existence and, realizing that he had regained in the desert the life he had abandoned in his own country, he thanked God for arranging matters thus. Still, the devil's traps are innumerable and found everywhere, and Malchus could not escape them even as a shepherd living in the wilds.

Seeing that Malchus was a devoted and diligent slave and that the flock in his care was growing, the Ethiopian wanted to reward him. He summoned Malchus and offered him as a wife his fellow slave, the woman with whom he had ridden on the camel. Her husband had also been captured, but was the slave of a different master. On the grounds that as a Christian he was not allowed to marry a woman whose husband was alive, Malchus refused her. Enraged by this, the Ethiopian drew his sword and would have driven it into Malchus, had not the monk finally accepted her into his arms.

Night fell and Malchus took the woman to a cave. What happened next the blessed one himself later recounted, saying, "My happiness had turned to sorrow and my joy to bitterness. The woman did not desire me, nor did I want her. We were both at a loss for words. At that hour I felt with full force the pain of my captivity and, throwing myself to the ground, lamented the piteous end of my life as a monk. 'How did I, the wretch, arrive at this?' I wondered. 'Have my sins brought me to the point where I must take another man's wife and lose my virginity at an age when my hair is already turning gray? If I do this, what was the point of renouncing home and parents for the Lord's sake and shunning marriage in my youth? Doubtless I have come to this because I preferred my village to the monastery. What are we to do, O my soul? Shall we perish, or win the victory? Shall we await help from the hand of the Lord, or put an end to this with the sword? Turn the sword upon yourself, my soul! Worse for the soul to perish, than for the body. To preserve one's virginity is a form of martyrdom. Let me die as a martyr and remain unburied in this wilderness! I shall be both a martyr and my own persecutor.' So saying, I rose and unsheathed my sword. It gleamed in the darkness as I placed its point against my chest and told my wife, 'Farewell, woman. It is better that you have me as a dead martyr than a living husband.' But she threw herself at my feet and cried, 'In the name of our Lord Jesus Christ, I beg you to wait! Do not kill yourself on account of me. But if you are determined to die, turn the sword on me first. Finish me off, then dispatch yourself, so that we may be united in death. I had already decided that if my husband were returned to me, I would maintain the chastity that captivity has taught me. I would rather die than lose it, and I would rather die than yield to you. So have me as your partner in chastity, united to you in spiritual, not carnal love. Let our masters think you are my husband: Christ will know you are my spiritual brother. Seeing us bound by mutual affection, our owners will believe that we enjoy a fleshly union.' I was astonished by what that virtuous woman said, and we agreed to live together continently. I came to love and admire her greatly, but was careful never to glimpse her naked or to touch her, lest I lose in peacetime the virginity I had preserved through earlier years of fierce conflict."

The godly Malchus lived with that upright woman for a long time in a state of spiritual wedlock. This union won for them the favor of their owners and allayed all suspicion that they might escape. Sometimes Malchus was away from his master's house for a month at a time, fulfilling his duties in the wilderness as a trusted shepherd.

One day long after being enslaved, the venerable Malchus was alone in the desert with only the earth and sky for companions. Sitting quietly, he called to mind the brethren in his monastery and especially his father the abbot, who had instructed him in the Scriptures and the ascetic life. Absorbed in these thoughts, he noticed a large number of ants marching in and out of their home, with loads larger than their bodies. Some were dragging grass seeds; some were carrying soil out of the nest and banking the anthill against the rain; some were biting apart seed to prevent it from sprouting and to prepare it for use as food in winter; some were removing the bodies of their dead. What most amazed him was how, despite their number, not one of the ants got in the way of another; instead, any that needed assistance quickly received it. Watching this, Malchus remembered the words of Solomon: *Go to the ant, thou sluggard: consider her ways. She gathereth much food in the harvest.*[4] It occurred to him that a monastery is like an ants' nest: all work for the common good, no one claims anything as his own, and everything is held in common. He began to regret his captivity, to long and sigh for his monastery, and to yearn for life in his former cell.

When Malchus returned to his hut, his supposed wife noticed that he was wearing a downcast expression. "Why are you so sad?" she asked. Malchus explained his thoughts, and she urged him to flee and take her to a convent. After discussing plans in whispers, they began preparing their escape. Malchus slew his two largest goats and dried their meat. Then, on a dark night, he and his sister put their trust in God and departed. On reaching the river, a mile from the Ethiopian's house, they inflated the goats' entrails, tied them securely and, climbing on them, entered the water. Paddling with their feet, they reached the opposite bank; but most of the meat was lost in midstream. What remained was sodden and hardly sufficient for three days. Preparing for the thirst to come, they drank until they could swallow no more, then hurried on their way, journeying mostly by night, both to avoid the Saracens and because of the extreme heat. Nevertheless, they did travel some by day, out of fear that their master would catch them.

After three days the fugitives noticed two Saracens approaching rapidly on camels. Realizing that their master had followed their tracks in the sand, they were paralyzed with fear and awaited death at his hands. Then Providence directed their attention to a cave off to their right. It lead deep into the ground, but they took shelter just inside, to the left of the entrance. They were afraid to descend further, lest they be killed while escaping death, as crevices and caverns in the desert are usually infested by scorpions, venomous serpents, and fearsome beasts. Equally terrified of an enraged master and dangerous creatures, the runaways tried to control their violent trembling and stand motionless. "Only if God takes pity on us can we escape," they thought. "If He abandons us sinners, this pit will be our grave."

A few moments later the Ethiopian reached the cave. He

---

[4]Prov., Ch. 6

tied the camels together and flashed his sword at the entrance, then ordered the second man—another of his slaves—into the cavern to retrieve the escapees. The servant stepped into the cave, and Malchus and the woman were just behind him, but since they were out of the sunlight, he did not see them. "Come out, you scoundrels; come out to die!" he shouted. "What are you waiting for? You cannot escape your master. Come out!"

While the slave was shouting, a lioness rushed up from the bottom of the cave. It seized him by the throat, killing him instantly, and dragged his corpse deep into its lair. O all-gracious Lord, how marvelous is Thy concern for Thy servants and quick Thou art to rescue those in peril! When some time passed and his helper did not emerge, the Ethiopian decided that his assistance was needed to overpower two people; therefore, he ran into the cavern, roaring like a wild animal and brandishing his sword. Hearing this, the lioness rushed up again, dispatched him before he could do the fugitives any harm, and dragged him into its den. When they saw God's wondrous and unexpected assistance and protection, the venerable Malchus and the blessed woman thanked the Lord for His extreme compassion. Still, their joy was diminished by fear of being the lioness' next victims, although they preferred to be the wild animal's prey than to have fallen into the hands of savage men. Fortunately, the lioness soon picked up her cub and left. Malchus and the woman remained in the cavern, not making a sound, until they felt certain it was safe to depart. By then the sun was setting. They refreshed themselves with provisions from the camels' packs, then mounted the animals and continued on their way, thanking God. It took them ten days to cross the desert and reach an outpost of the Roman Army, where they told the garrison commander their story. The officer sent them to Sabinus, Duke of Mesopotamia, who showed them every kindness, bought their camels, and gave them permission to return home. The godly Malchus left his wife, or rather, spiritual sister, at a convent and went back to his monastery. He found that his spiritual father the abbot had died, and he related to the brethren everything that had occurred. After this he never again left the monastery, but urged the other monks always to remain on the premises and not to disobey the hegumen in any way.

Malchus lived out his days in a God-pleasing manner and departed to the Lord. The story of his captivity teaches every generation the might of chastity. A person who has dedicated his life to the Lord Jesus may be put to death for righteousness' sake, but his spirit cannot be conquered, for he is strengthened by Christ our God, unto Whom be glory forever. Amen.

On the Same Day

The Life of
Our Holy Monastic Father
Basil the New[1]

During the tenth year of the reign of the devout Greek emperors Leo the Wise and his brother Alexander, the sons of Emperor Basil the Macedonian, several high–ranking officials were sent by the rulers to Asia Minor on affairs of government. While traveling back to the Imperial City, the nobles were passing through the wilderness and sighted on a mountain a man clad in rags. This was the blessed Basil the desert-dweller, and his appearance was strange and awesome. Thinking he could be an enemy scout, they captured him and took him to Constantinople. There they presented him to the Emperor Leo, who entrusted his interrogation to Samonas, a patrician of Saracen birth.[2] Samonas assembled his advisors and called for the man of God, who upon entry made the customary prostration before the noble. Samonas demanded, "Who are you? Where are you from? What is your name?" but the blessed one *gave him no answer*[3] and gazed meekly at his judge. "Tell me where you are from!" Samonas repeated.

"Better that you explain who you are, and where you are from," responded the saint.

"How dare you mock me!" exclaimed the nobleman. "You have no right to ask me anything at all; nonetheless, know that I am Samonas, a patrician and the *Parakoimomenos*[4] or Imperial Chamberlain. Now reply to my questions."

"I am a pilgrim and a stranger upon the earth," answered the blessed one.

---

[1]Written by his disciple Gregory. This version was compiled from the original Life and the version in *The Great Collection of Readings*.

[2]Perhaps the patrician, as an Arab, would know the native language of the suspected scout and more easily than a Greek might uncover his doings. (Tr.)

[3]John, Ch. 19

[4]The rank of *parakoimomenos* or guardian of the Emperor's private quarters was the highest to which a eunuch could attain. (Tr.)

"You are a scout and were spying out our territory!" shouted Samonas. Since Basil remained silent, the Chamberlain's aides also demanded that he reveal his identity, but he would not answer them either. Then Samonas commanded that iron rods, rawhide whips, and other instruments of torture be brought, in the hope that terror would make him speak. When Basil still said nothing, the *Parakoimomenos* had him drawn out and flogged cruelly. While Basil was under the lash, Samonas repeated, "Who are you?" but the blessed one uttered not a word, even though the servants beat him almost to death. Finally, they dragged away the saint like a log (since he could not walk) and cast him into prison.

The next morning merciless Samonas returned to the tribunal and ordered that the man of God be brought to him. The servants found Basil completely healed and waiting for them outside the locked dungeon. "How did you escape?" asked the astounded servants. God's favorite maintained his silence, but went with them to the patrician. Several of the men ran ahead to tell Samonas what had happened, but their master and most of his aides did not believe the amazing report. A few of the advisors conjectured that Basil was a sorcerer and had worked a miracle by means of the black art. Greeting the blessed one with a second interrogation, the Chamberlain threatened additional torture if the prisoner would not reveal his identity. Basil said nothing, and Samonas lost his temper and had the man of God stretched out on the ground and bludgeoned with iron rods. Although six rods cracked, Basil did not speak. Everyone else was amazed by Basil's patience and tenacity, but the patrician was unmoved and vowed, "By the health of the emperors, I will not release this man until he speaks. My tortures shall pry open his mouth and prevent him from boasting that he conquered us by silence." The Imperial Chamberlain commanded the servants to continue beating Saint Basil for an entire week. Every day they laid on him three hundred stripes with the whip and three hundred blows with the rod.

Having attained a state of sublime holiness, the man of God patiently endured his punishment. Because he had become a monk at an early age and for many years had led a harsh life, wandering through the wilderness barefoot and clad in rags, and feeding on wild herbs, he could not be compelled to speak against his will. The Lord's favorite had always concealed his virtues and borne in mind the Master's words: *Let not thy left hand know what thy right hand doeth.*[5] Those who make known to others their good deeds *have their reward*—the praise of men; but they fail to win eternal glory. He who desires an everlasting reward conceals his accomplishments from others. If he is beaten, he keeps silent and thus is counted a martyr.

After belaboring the martyr for a week without the least success, the patrician sat upon his tribunal a third time and had Basil presented to him. Glaring at the saint, he snarled, "Most despicable of men, how long will you hide the truth from us? Reveal who you are and where you are from!"

"The most despicable of men are secret sodomites like you," responded the martyr.

Furious at being exposed, Samonas had the venerable one's hands tied behind his back and his right leg bent backwards and lashed to cord wound tightly around his chest. Then he commanded the saint to be taken to another room and hung upside-down by the left leg from a crossbeam. The prisoner was to remain suspended until he broke. The room was locked and the *Parakoimomenos* sealed the doors with a signet. By now convinced of Basil's innocence, the others were appalled by this inhumanity and muttered condemnation of the detestable patrician.

Three days and nights passed, after which the brute opened the doors. Basil was still hanging, but seemed none the worse for the ordeal. Amazed, Samonas approached him with his usual questions: "Who are you and where are you from? Have you learned your lesson yet?"

No reply was forthcoming, so Samonas ordered that the blessed one be let down and untied. When this was done, the saint at once rose to his feet. The advisors and servants were astonished because the grace of Christ had healed Basil completely, but the patrician exclaimed, "Surely this man is a war-

---

[5]Matt., Ch. 6

lock! By sorcery he has made his wounds vanish, but I will soon destroy his power. Summon the caretaker of the beasts!"

When the keeper of the wild animals arrived, Samonas instructed him, "Give the fiercest lion nothing to eat today. I want him to be ravenous tomorrow. We shall see if this wizard survives an encounter with him."

The next morning the hungry, roaring lion was led into the Hippodrome, where an enormous crowd had assembled. Saint Basil was offered to it as food, but the animal trembled and lay down at the blessed one's feet like a harmless lamb. The people were astounded and cried, "Lord, have mercy!" whereupon, the godly one petted the beast, then took it by the ear and sent it on its way, shouting, "Take back your lamb!" Yet even this miracle failed to convince the impious barbarian that the victim of his cruelty was a man of God. The patrician ordered that Basil be drowned, so the venerable one was bound and at the third watch of the night thrown from a rowboat into the sea. No sooner had the boat turned about than, at the command of God, Who watches over His saints, two dolphins lifted the Lord's favorite upon their backs and carried him to shore at Hebdomon,[6] a suburb of Constantinople. The saint's hands and feet were miraculously loosed and Basil walked back to the city. As the Golden Gate[7] was shut, the blessed one sat outside the portal and rested briefly.

Soon a man with a high fever came along and sat by the gate, shivering and moaning. Saint Basil was moved to compassion, laid his hands on the sufferer, and prayed. Vigor coursed through the man's veins and he fell prostrate, thanking the saint and begging him to come to his house. The venerable one gladly agreed, although the man (whose name was John) belonged to the lower class of citizen.

John's wife Helen feared God and earnestly loved Christ and the poor. She was overjoyed that the venerable one had

---

[6]So-called because it was seven Roman miles from the Milion, the point near the Hippodrome from which distances throughout the Empire were measured. (Tr.)

[7]The monumental portal at the south end of Constantinople's walls. The *Via Egnatia* led directly from Hebdomon to the Golden Gate. (Tr.)

cured her husband by prayer, and she thanked the Lord for deeming her worthy to have Basil as a guest. The three enjoyed a meal together, but when the couple asked the man of God who he was and where he was from, he responded, "It is not time to speak about these things. You will learn them later. Presently I must go to the Monastery of the Icon of the Most Holy Theotokos 'Not Made by Hands.'" The saint arose and, accompanied by John, hastened to the monastery's church, where he prayed. Afterwards, John persuaded the blessed one to return to his house. Again the couple entreated Saint Basil to reveal his identity. Finally, he told them, "I am the man Samonas the patrician threw into the sea yesterday. In a way known to Him alone, the Lord Jesus Christ, whom I have served since my youth, preserved me unharmed." He also let it be known that his name was Basil and related everything the patrician had done to him. John and Helen were astonished, although they and everyone else in the city had already heard that he had been tortured by Samonas and had tamed a lion. The couple begged the man of God to live at their house. He agreed, and they converted one of their rooms into an chapel for him, with a lamp for illumination. Who knows how many tears Basil shed there while praying, how many prostrations he performed, how many night-long vigils he kept? Truly, the saint's virtue was indescribable. An unshakable pillar could more easily be toppled than could the saint be moved to anger, for he was as meek as Moses and David, and as silent as Jacob. He was more compassionate than Abraham, because the patriarch gave alms out of his abundant wealth, while Basil endured poverty for God's sake, yet straightway distributed among the poor whatever he was given by those who loved Christ.

A few days after Basil took up his abode in the house of the God-fearing John, people began visiting him, some seeking edification, some bringing their ill. By the grace of Christ, the venerable one healed the ailing by prayer and the touch of his hands. As a result, his name and way of life became well-known, not only among the common folk, but among the nobles, many of whom were his admirers. The saint possessed the gift of clairvoyance, and no secret, good or evil, could be concealed from him. He would reprove sinners privately, and often persuaded the erring to repent. He also foretold the future, as the following story demonstrates.

The Emperor Leo and his brother Alexander died within approximately a year of each other, leaving the throne to Constantine Porphyrogenitus and his mother Zoe. Since Constantine was still a little boy, a regency was established, headed by Nicholas, Patriarch of Constantinople, and the *Curopalates*[8] John Garidas. Its members were to administer affairs of state until the young Emperor reached adulthood. During those days barbarians[9] were laying waste the Greek lands up to the very walls of the Imperial City and, because no one dared lead the army against them, the whole realm was in turmoil. The citizens of Constantinople accused the Patriarch of misruling the Empire, and discontent reached such proportions that he was forced to convene a special meeting of the nobility. After he had conferred with the nobles, Patriarch Nicholas wrote to Constantine Ducas, commander of the eastern armies, praising him as a brave and skilled general and begging him to come to the Queen of Cities and share the throne with the Emperor Constantine, who was too young to leave the palace and face the adversaries. Indeed, Duke Constantine was a fearless, invincible leader, terrifying to his foes. By their own admission his enemies had more than once been routed by fire blazing from his weapons and the nostrils of his stallion. He did not hide the fact that God had imparted divine grace to him, but avowed, "Once, in my youth, I was sleeping, and a radiant lady clad in imperial purple appeared to me, holding the reins of a fiery steed laden with flaming armor and weapons. I was terrified, but she urged me to don the panoply and mount the horse. When I did so, she said, 'May God's enemies be terrified of you, and may my Son's blasphemers melt like wax before you.' So saying, she departed."

Constantine Ducas received the Patriarch's letter but declined the throne, saying he was unworthy of it. To a second, similar letter from the Patriarch and Senate, Constantine replied thus:

[8]A high dignity, in this period usually conferred upon members of the imperial family and on foreign princes (Tr.)
[9]The Bulgarians (Tr.)

"Although the Emperor is young, he was crowned by Christ the Lord Himself. I refuse to sin against God by accepting imperial rank. Furthermore, I fear that you may turn on me and take my life."

Upon receipt of this answer, the Patriarch and senators dispatched a third letter to the pious General, in which they swore by the Wood of the Life-giving Cross of the Lord that their desire to have him as co-emperor was sincere. Trusting their word, Ducas came to the Imperial City, accompanied by his entire household. He entered the capital on a bright day shortly after dawn and was greeted enthusiastically by people of every station and rank; however, their jubilation turned to horror when a light rain the color of blood began to fall. This was an evil portent, signifying that the Duke would be murdered. Meanwhile, the crowd's enthusiasm had persuaded Nicholas and his counselors to reverse their decision and forbid Ducas to enter the palace or see the Emperor or the Empress-mother. Constantine responded by setting up his marquee in the Hippodrome, where he daily received homage as emperor from nobles and commoners. Certain noblemen who had taken the Duke's part and loved Saint Basil asked him how matters would end for their leader. Weeping bitterly, the blessed one predicted that within three months Ducas and his supporters would be slaughtered. After this the nobles locked themselves in their houses and in silence awaited the certain fulfillment of the prophecy.

Two brothers, both *protospatharioi*,[10] asked the saint, "Should we go to the Hippodrome and pledge allegiance to the new Emperor?"

"Children, by no means go," said Basil with tears in his eyes. "If you do, one of you will be decapitated, the other will lose his ears and nose and will be a laughing-stock for the rest of his life." But the brothers ignored the saint's warning, went to the Hippodrome, and declared their support for Ducas.

For two months the situation in the capital remained unresolved. Ducas could have avenged himself on his deceivers and

---

[10]*Protospatharios*: a title conferring membership in the Senate, granted usually to the commanders of the themes (major military units and territorial divisions of the Empire) (Tr.)

mockers, because he was courageous in battle and had the support of the citizenry and a powerful force of soldiers. He could have either broken into the palace or besieged it, by hunger compelling his adversaries to open to him and throw themselves on his mercy; notwithstanding, he refused to harm his own countrymen, being a devout, God-fearing person. He did not want the throne at the price of bloodshed, so he put his trust in the Lord and hoped that the Patriarch and senators would remember their oath. Finally, having taken counsel with his officers, he commanded that the Chalke Gates[11] of the palace be forced open and his men follow him into the complex unarmed. He explained, "I hope that the Patriarch and senators will receive us graciously, but if they slay us, they will answer to God for murder and oathbreaking." After this Ducas made each of his men swear that he would neither draw the sword nor shoot the bow. "I do not want a single drop of Christian blood shed on my behalf," he insisted. When his men had sworn the oath, they burst through the Chalke Gates and entered the palace grounds. They were met by a volley of archery released by the palatine guard at the order of the Patriarch and his advisors. As the wounded were dropping to the ground, an arrow penetrated deep into Constantine's right side, beneath his armpit. Then a battalion of the guard rushed out and fell upon Ducas' unarmed, unresisting followers, slaughtering many with the sword. Ducas and his son were among the slain. Some of Ducas' men fled, but were captured and sawed in half, hung from trees outside the city gates, or lost their noses and ears and had their tendons severed. In all, three thousand of Constantine Ducas' innocent followers were butchered. As for the *protospatharioi* who had asked the blessed one whether to throw in with the Duke, they suffered exactly as Basil had predicted: one was decapitated, the other lost his nose and ears.

Soldiers hacked off the lifeless heads of Ducas and his son and took them to Patriarch Nicholas and his counselors. The Patriarch generously rewarded Ducas' murderers and ordered that the heads be paraded through the city on spears and the bodies flung into the sea. In this way, then, the Imperial City

---

[11]The main entrance to the Great Palace of Constantinople (Tr.)

was stained with the blood of the guiltless, which cried out against the murderers like that of Abel against Cain. The mighty, brave, glorious, well-loved, God-pleasing General Constantine Ducas, the so-called Emperor, perished not by the sword of foreign enemies, but by that of unscrupulous, oathbreaking fellow-countrymen and fellow-believers. His soul and the souls of his followers were deemed worthy of divine mercy and found a place in the bosom of Abraham. Every night for as long as the corpses of Ducas' men hung from the trees, stars descended and shone brightly over their heads until dawn. The miracle proved that Ducas' partisans had suffered innocently and that their souls were assigned to the dwellings of the saints.

We have related this to demonstrate that our venerable father Basil truly possessed the Spirit of prophecy. Everything he predicted came to pass. Now we shall tell about other examples of his clairvoyance.

Eventually the patrician Romanus[12] was elevated to the throne, which he shared with young Constantine Porphyrogenitus. When Constantine reached a marriageable age, Romanus gave his daughter Helen to him in wedlock. Another son-in-law of Romanus was the patrician Saronitas, a haughty, vain, ambitious, evil man who boasted in his wealth and was constantly plotting to destroy the Emperor Constantine and seize power. Saronitas' house was near that of the previously mentioned John, where our holy father Basil lived. Beholding with clairvoyant eyes Saronitas' intended crimes, Basil said to himself, "Observe this wretch closely, for he is bent on ungodly deeds. I shall reprove him in the hope that he abandon his schemes."

One day while the evildoer was riding from his mansion to the palace, the saint blocked his steed and shouted, "Why are you plotting against Christ's chosen one? It is not yours to rule the Empire. Abandon your designs on the throne, *lest the Lord be angry*[13] with you and you be stripped of patrician rank!"

Saronitas flew into a fury, threw himself on the saint, and mercilessly horsewhipped him, cursing him all the while; then he continued on his way. The blessed Basil endured this ill-

---

[12]Romanus Lecapenus (Tr.)   [13]Ps. 2

treatment manfully. The next morning as Saronitas was leaving his house, the venerable one confronted him again. Saronitas had his slaves drag Basil into the mansion and hold him there while he attended to affairs at court. Upon return from the palace, Saronitas commanded the servants to bring him thorny branches and the man of God. "Tell me, wicked elder, what is the name of the demon that provoked you to revile me?" the nobleman asked our saint. "Are you ignorant of the fact that I am the Emperor's son-in-law and his most eminent courtier? My money is uncountable, like the grains of sand on the seashore; my slaves, estates, villages, and flocks are beyond number. I possess an untold amount of gold and silver. The emperors, all the nobles and, clearly, God Himself hold me in the highest regard. How dare you, an impoverished commoner in your dotage, rail against me in front of all the world? Explain yourself quickly, before I have you put to death!"

The blessed one answered, "Do you think that your traitorous plans can remain hidden? The Lord Himself revealed to me your designs on the throne. Abandon your plottings against Christ the Lord; otherwise, you will move Him to wrath and He will blot out your memory from the earth."

The madman ranted and raved, his face contorted hideously, and he ordered that the saint be stretched out upon the ground and thrashed mercilessly with the thorny branches. "Flail the false prophet until you drive the demon out of him!" Saronitas urged his men. They whipped Basil cruelly, but he remained silent, like a tree that cannot speak and is devoid of feeling. He neither writhed in pain nor sighed, and the only sound to be heard was that of the branches whipping his flesh. As soon as his ordeal was over, he was cast into a small prison cell. The next day the servants removed Basil from the dungeon and brutally flogged him with leather straps, then returned him to confinement and clapped him in irons. On the third day, glutted and intoxicated, they dragged him out again and pummeled him with staves.

While the godly one was being tormented, the gates to Saronitas' mansion were left open and the devout Helen, John's wife, happened by. Seeing the slaves abusing the venerable Basil, she shed hot tears and cried, "Flog me, the sinner! Release my pastor and spiritual father, the light of my life, and permit me to suffer instead."

The brutal patrician was infuriated by this and told the servants, "The wench must be this scoundrel's mistress. Beat her too, if that is what she wants!" The servants flogged Helen until she lost consciousness, then dragged her by the legs into the street like a dead dog. Afterwards, Saronitas had our venerable father strung up by the private parts. Five hundred additional lashes were laid upon him with a rawhide whip. Having God's assistance, the saint bravely endured until he was cut down and shackled again.

That night Saronitas had a dream foretelling his death. He saw a broad, leafy oak in which a raven had made its nest. As the bird spread out its wings to cover its chicks, two men carrying axes approached the tree, intending to fell it. One commented to the other, "The raven's cawing prevents the Emperor from getting a good night's sleep."

"Worse," said the second man, "it annoys Basil, God's favorite." After the two men cut down the tree, the branches were gathered and burned by others, clad in rags. Nearby stood the venerable Basil, who first repeated the Scripture, *Every tree which bringeth not forth good fruit is hewn down, and cast into the fire,*[14] then told Saronitas, "I warned that unless you abandoned your evil schemes, your fall was inevitable."

Saronitas awoke and realized he was ill. Pondering the dream, he became terrified and straightway released the saint. Basil returned to the home of John, who was overjoyed to see him. Shedding tears of jubilation, Basil's admirers thronged the house; but John's wife, the blessed Helen, did not long survive her savage beating. Within a few days Saronitas also died, in accordance with his dream and Saint Basil's prophecy.

Shortly after this, the godly one's devout friend and benefactor John departed to the Lord. Basil remained in the house, healing by prayer the many sick folk who were brought to him. Large numbers of the poor also came to him, because each day he gave away everything he received from his Christ-loving patrons.

---

[14]Matt., Ch. 3

As time went on a God-fearing man named Constantine Barbaros began entreating the saint to come live in his house. Barbaros promised to provide the venerable one a cell so that he could live in stillness, and eventually the man of God accepted the offer. Preparing the cell, Barbaros *put there for* God's favorite *a bed, and a table, and a stool, and a candlestick*[15] as once did the Shunamite woman for the prophet Elisha. The task of attending to the man of God he assigned to the aged, upright maid Theodora. This virtuous, God-pleasing woman, who had been a chaste widow for many years, lived in a room near that of Saint Basil. Theodora served Basil devotedly, as though he were an angel of the Lord. If someone wished to speak with Basil, Theodora would notify him. It was in Theodora's room that the elder received visitors, taught the faithful, healed the sick, and distributed to the needy the necessities of life, which were provided by his admirers. In the evening the blessed one would return to his cell and perform his rule of prayer.

The fame of the venerable Basil continued to spread in Constantinople. Those who esteemed him included both laity and clergy. Many monks, priests, and bishops visited the saint and benefited from his prayer and counsel. Princes and nobles invited Basil to their homes to intercede with God on behalf of their ailing friends and relatives, for whenever the man of God prayed for the ill and laid his hands on them, they were healed. The saint expelled wicked spirits by a mere word. With eloquent discourses he urged the faithful to virtue, and condemned and corrected the vices of sinners. All secrets were revealed to him by the all-seeing God. Once he was summoned to the palace and privately rebuked the Emperor Romanus for his greed and profligacy. The Emperor was not angered in the least, but humbly accepted the reproof and vowed to amend his life. Similarly, the blessed one reproached the *patrikia*[16] Anastasia for her secret transgressions and brought her to repentance. He also predicted the time and manner of her death. To Helen, wife of the Emperor Constantine Porphyrogenitus, Basil foretold that after giving birth to a daughter, she would bear a son who would reach

---

[15]IV Kings, Ch. 4
[16]The spouse or widow of a patrician (Tr.)

manhood and rule. Delighted, Helen offered the saint a large quantity of gold, which he refused. Then the Empress enjoined him, in the name of the All-holy Trinity, to take as much money as he wanted. Picking up three gold coins, the saint gave them to the maid Theodora. Several of the Empress' attendants urged him, "Father, give the old woman more."

"Children," responded the saint, "those who collect thorns are likely to be pricked."

"In truth, venerable Father, you love Christ wholeheartedly!" exclaimed the Empress. "Remember us in your holy prayers." With this she let him depart in peace.

Possessing the divine gift of clairvoyance to the highest degree, Basil knew both future events and the thoughts of men's hearts. About that time, he made the acquaintance of Gregory, a layman who became his disciple, witnessed many of his miracles, and wrote the full Life from which the present account was abbreviated. Although no one had mentioned it to him beforehand, the saint called the future disciple by name at their first meeting, and also brought out into the open Gregory's most private thoughts. In like manner the blessed one knew the hidden iniquities of a certain witch, a false nun, and exactly predicted her miserable death. Again, a presbyter was eating with the saint and tried to remember the cost of the apples he had brought as a gift. "Brother, why are you vexing yourself, trying to recall the price of the fruit?" asked Basil. "The simplest thing would have been to ask me what you spent. They cost ten coppers." Hearing this, the presbyter trembled with amazement at the elder's clairvoyance and thanked God that he lived at a time when such a saint walked the earth.

A wine merchant whom the saint knew was downcast because his business was failing; nevertheless, he was certain that if Basil came to his shop and prayed there, his fortune would be restored. He persuaded the man of God to come to his house and cooked a fine supper for him, to which he invited many of the poor. In the name of Jesus Christ, Saint Basil blessed all the merchant's wine jars, except for one, which held fifteen measures of a superior vintage. "This one must be destroyed," he announced.

"Do not break it, Father; bless it too!" pleaded the merchant.

"Sales are poor and I am deeply in debt. I cannot afford to lose so much wine."

"I know this; nonetheless, I must shatter this vessel in order to deliver you from terrible misfortune," insisted the saint. "This is the main reason I accepted your invitation."

"Shatter my skull rather than the jar!" pleaded the merchant.

A large piece of wood lay nearby, and Basil snatched it and smashed the jar. Wine poured out, the shopkeeper was aghast, and his neighbors became very upset with our blessed father. Perceiving their thoughts, the venerable one probed the bottom of the vessel with a walking-stick. Out of the remaining wine he pulled a rotting snake four-and-a-half feet long. "Why, children," asked Saint Basil, "are you condemning me in your hearts? You see the serpent. If I had not smashed the vessel, many people would have drunk the wine and died. This man would have been held responsible for their deaths. Would you have wanted that? Did I well, or not?" With this, he tossed the serpent to the floor. The merchant fell at the saint's holy feet and begged to be pardoned, and afterwards he enjoyed every abundance, through the prayers of the godly Basil.

On another occasion, a woman named Theodotia brought to the saint her ailing four-year old son (whom she was still nursing) and requested prayers for the boy. All of her other children died when they reached the age of three or four, so she was terrified this one would not survive his illness. As soon as she explained this to Saint Basil, the child began to cry and ask for bread. The holy elder smiled, gave a round of bread to the boy, and asked him, "What is your name? Is it Leo?" Then he told the mother, "Because of your ardent love for the immaculate Virgin Theotokos and because you frequently pray before the icon of the Hodigitria,[17] God will restore the health of this child. You will see him reach manhood, and he will bring you much joy. He will be learned, virtuous, and wise; he will become a monk and a cleric and will enjoy a good reputation, for the Lord will be with him. But any children you bear in the future shall die at

---

[17]The wonderworking icon of the Mother of God in the Blachernae church (Tr.)

an early age, like the others." The woman made a prostration before the saint and departed, and everything he predicted came to pass.

A friend of the elder came to receive a blessing from him before departing on a journey to the eastern lands on behalf of his master. The venerable one carefully studied the man's face and, foreseeing what would befall him, declared, "The river Khelidon is terrifying, but will be calmed by the sinner Basil." What the blessed one meant by this the man did not understand at the time.

In Anatolia the traveler found his path blocked by a rushing river about fifty yards wide. Its name was unknown to him, as he had never before passed through that region. While he was sitting on his mount at the edge of the river, looking for shallows where he could cross to the other side, the water surged and carried horse and rider downstream. In desperation the man cried, "O Lord, by the prayers of our venerable father Basil, help me, a sinner!" No sooner had he shouted this than he saw the elder Basil walking on the river and commanding it to slow. Then the blessed one took the horse by the bridle, guided it to the far bank, and became invisible. The man sincerely thanked God and His favorite, Saint Basil, for saving him. When he reached the next village, he rested and inquired what was the name of the river, and learned that it was called "Khelidon," which means "swallow," for it was swift as a swallow. Many people, he was told, had drowned attempting to cross it. The man recalled the words spoken to him by the venerable one before he left on the journey: "The river Khelidon is terrifying, but will be calmed by the name of the sinner Basil," and he gratefully cried, "Glory to Thee, O Lord! One thing only do I ask of Thee, Master: permit me to see Thy favourite again and to kiss his venerable grey hair." Without further incident he returned to Constantinople and his holy protector. Falling at Basil's feet, he thanked our father and related how God had revealed His mercy.

Although surrounded at home by worldly persons, Gregory, the young layman spoken of earlier, maintained a strict, almost monastic way of life. Because he observed rigorous fasts and carefully guarded his virginity, Basil regarded him highly.

Gregory frequently came to Constantine Barbaros' house in order to hear the venerable one's discourses. Eventually he became one of our father's most devoted disciples.

When his parents died, Gregory inherited everything they owned, including a vineyard near the Thracian town of Randistus. He decided to visit this property at harvest, and before departing obtained the blessing of his holy teacher. He also went to the Church of the Holy Protomartyr Stephen (whom he held in especial esteem and affection) and prayed on bended knees for a long time before the saint's icon. Gregory concluded his supplication with these words: "I am about to undertake a lengthy journey by land and sea; wherefore, O holy protomartyr Stephen, protect me from all evil. I have served thee in this holy temple to the best of mine ability, so help me in every difficulty, through the grace given thee by the Lord."

One night while traveling, Gregory slept at an inn, where he found a valuable belt, worth two *nomismata*.[18] It was lost by the innkeeper's daughter, and when the members of the household began searching for it and questioning the guests, Gregory, swayed by the devil, hid the belt. "This family is well-off," he reasoned. "I will sell the belt, give the money to the poor, and the alms will be accounted to the girl and her parents for their salvation."

Several days later, Gregory lost his own belt, which was also worth two pieces of gold, as well as his moneybag, in which there were four gold coins and a large number of silver ones. Because he had lost all his travel money, Gregory was extremely downcast. Eventually he fell asleep and the godly Basil appeared to him in a dream, holding a cracked earthenware pot. The saint asked, "Do you see this broken vessel?"

"I do, my lord," Gregory replied.

"If someone were to steal this useless pot, he would receive fourfold punishment, now or in the life to come," explained Basil. "If the thief were wealthy, his loss would equal four times its value. If he were poor, he would suffer quadruple chastisement."

---

[18]*Nomisma*: a gold coin, also called the *solidus*. There are seventy-two nomismata to a Roman pound. (Tr.)

"But Father, I have never stolen anything," protested Gregory.

"You hid the belt belonging to the innkeeper's daughter, yet you pretend never to have stolen anything!" marvelled the saint.

"I did not steal it, Father. I found it," said Gregory.

"Child, understand that if someone finds a lost item, he must return it to the owner. Otherwise, he will be condemned as a thief. You should have returned what you found. Because you hid it instead, you lost more than four times what you gained. Now beware, lest something even worse happen to you," warned the saint.

Awakening from sleep, Gregory was very downcast, both because of his sin and because he feared additional punishment. He continued on his way in low spirits and reached the vineyard. As the grapes were being harvested, he underwent a temptation worse than what he had already suffered. Alexander, one of the laborers in the vineyard, was married to a young woman named Meletinia, an adulteress and witch. So dissolute was this hussy that within a short time after her wedding, she had seduced almost every man in the area. No one dared say a word in condemnation of her, because she would straightway put a hex on her accuser, causing him to fall grievously ill. When her husband rightly cuffed her for unfaithfulness, she drained his strength by means of the black art. Afterwards, he could offer no resistance when she set upon him with a stick or a length of rope, but could only crawl away under the blows. Indeed, he was so feeble he could hardly even drive off flies that lit upon him. It was said that the witch's mother could halt flying birds, reverse the flow of rivers, and prevent animals from moving, and that she performed so many hurtful deeds that no one could tell of them all. Meletinia was the infernal offspring of that evil raven, but surpassed her mother in wickedness. The mother was merely hateful; the daughter was also dissolute. Those who criticized Meletinia found themselves paralyzed within two or three months, while those who struck her rarely survived more than a day or two.

Seeing that Gregory was young and handsome, the witch and adulteress was wounded by lust and decided to seduce him. Every day she shamelessly followed him about; every night she appeared in his dreams and aroused him. There was not a moment's peace for Gregory, because the demons were stoking the flames of desire within him while the sorceress did her utmost to corrupt him. Had not the Lord assisted Gregory through the prayers of the holy protomartyr Stephen and the venerable Basil, the young man would certainly have fallen into sin and his soul been cast into Hades. Struggling courageously with carnal thoughts day and night, he occasionally weakened, but never permitted his virginal flesh to be defiled. Frequently he was at the point of driving off that shameless woman with blows, but feared that she would employ her diabolical powers to make him ill, as she had so many others. Then he remembered the prophetic words spoken to him by Saint Basil in the dream: "Beware, lest something even worse happen to you." The ship of virginity was now in peril of sinking; the column of purity was threatened with toppling. What could have been worse for such a chaste person? Determined to die ten thousand deaths rather than ruin the virginity he had preserved out of love for Christ, Gregory finally summoned up the courage to assail Meletinia with a stick and insults. "Shameless daughter of Beelzebub," he shouted as he struck the wench, "if you come near one more time, I shall carve your despicable flesh into little pieces!"

After this the loathsome witch desisted from attempts to seduce Gregory, but revenged herself by causing him to fall gravely ill. Doubtless, she would have made an end of him, had not the holy protomartyr and the venerable Basil appeared and healed him. Gregory himself wrote the following about his sickness and cure:

"One Sunday, not long after thrashing the sorceress, I went to my vineyard chapel dedicated to the holy great-martyr George. It was a hot day and, after praying, I fell asleep outside. In a dream I saw a black, foul-smelling cloud envelop me, and heard a voice saying, 'Come, take what Meletinia has prepared for you.' The cloud, dense and cold, somehow entered my body. I straightway awoke and realized that I was terribly ill and that the adulteress had brought me to this condition because I refused to satisfy her iniquitous desires. With extreme difficulty I arose and, groaning, stumbled to my house and fell into my bed. Daily my plight grew worse, and soon I lay at the gates of death. I burned with a high fever which consumed my members like dry reeds, and my pain was so intense it is impossible to describe. Unable to endure any longer, I took refuge under a stand of shady trees. From there I made my way to a nearby river, hoping to quench the flames of fever in the cool water. Several times I considered drowning myself, because I could not bear it any longer. 'Woe, woe is me!' I moaned. 'If the fire of Gehenna is anything like this, then better for us never to have been born.' I recognized and spoke with no one that day, and the night seemed to last forty years. My strength was gone.

"Then it seemed to me that I was in a deep ravine, over which steep, lofty cliffs towered to the east and west. As I clambered down the western face, I remembered the holy protomartyr Stephen. Tears flowing upon my cheeks, I groaned, 'Is this, O saint, how thou answerest the prayer I uttered in thy temple before I left the Imperial City? I am descending into the abyss, and thou hast turned away thy face from me. No longer shall I serve thee as in the past, for I am nearing the gates of death.'

"At that moment I looked across the ravine and on the eastern side beheld as it were another world, which no human tongue can describe. The holy protomartyr Stephen crossed over to me from there. He was robed in a scarlet sticharion[19] and asked me affectionately, 'What do you need, beloved? What is your ailment? Why are you so anxious? I was busy traveling throughout the world visiting the churches dedicated to me. All the saints frequent their temples thus. But now I have come to help you.' Then, after a moment of silence, he exclaimed, 'Oh, godless witches and sorcerers! See what mischief evildoers work, when the Lord permits.'

"'Saint Stephen,' I asked, 'what are these cliffs, and what is this ravine?'

"'The ravine is death, and those nearing their end traverse it with much difficulty. Reaching the eastern cliff, the dead find a path leading up to another world,' the protomartyr said.

---

[19] A long tunic with sleeves, the primary vestment of deacons (Tr.)

"'Does this mean, my lord, that I am about to breath my last?' I wondered.

"'Why else would you be here?' he replied.

"Sighing from the bottom of my heart, I groaned, 'My lord, I am not ready to die!'

"The saint led me by the hand through the abyss and to the top of the cliff on the east side. 'You have passed beyond Hades, the realm of death,' he assured me. I saw that I was near a beautiful courtyard, but in my weakened state I could walk no further. Thereupon the holy protomartyr, whose breath was redolent with divine fragrance, put me, the most worthless of men, upon his shoulders and said, 'Hold on with both hands, and I will carry you.'

"Entering the courtyard, I saw jars made of stone white as snow. They were full and sealed, and some holding one hundred measures, some two hundred, some three hundred. I asked the saint, 'What is this courtyard, and what are the jars, and what is in them?'

"The protomartyr answered, 'Everything here belongs to your spiritual father, the venerable Basil. The vessels contain the spiritual oil given him by the Lord. Anointing sinners with it, he cleanses them of stains and makes them children of God. He is a new apostle and has rescued many souls from the maw of Satan.'

"'Where to next, my lord?' I asked timidly.

"'We are about to see the godly Basil,' answered the saint.

"Suddenly the elder Basil emerged from an astoundingly beautiful room. The holy protomartyr asked him, 'How is it, Father Basil, that you abandoned your beloved child Gregory in his hour of utmost need? Had I not come to his aid, he would have perished.'

"'I knew that you were with him, blessed martyr. There was no need to come to his rescue,' said the venerable one. 'But now, if it pleases the Lord, we shall grant his desire.' The saints then led me to a very dark place where a dreadful snake nestled. 'This serpent almost took the life of my son Gregory!' cried the godly Basil as he crushed the reptile's head with an enormous stone.

"Next we found ourselves in Constantinople, standing by

the church of the holy protomartyr. Inside, a choir of youths was singing sweetly to the Lord. Saint Stephen told me, 'Lo, the grace of Christ has healed you. Enter the church and chant a hymn of thanksgiving to God the Master, Who has deemed you worthy of His mercy.'

"After making a prostration to my defenders, Saint Stephen and the venerable Basil, I crossed the threshold and sang the entire psalm, *The Lord is my light and my saviour; whom then shall I fear?*[20] As I did so, the handsome youths happily beckoned to me, 'Come, beloved; come share our joy.'

"Thereupon I awoke and, to my amazement, felt much better. I strengthened myself with a little food, then slept peacefully. When I awoke again I could walk without difficulty, and before long completely recovered my health. I sailed back to Constantinople where I told everyone of my cure by the prayers of Saints Stephen and Basil."

Meanwhile the blessed Theodora,[21] who had served Saint Basil for many years, received the tonsure. Her repose followed shortly thereafter. All who loved the venerable Basil mourned Theodora, their intermediary with the holy elder. She received everyone joyfully, fervently loved Christ, was compassionate and chaste, and possessed spiritual discretion. Gregory strongly desired to learn whether Theodora was assigned a place on the Lord's right hand or His left and whether she had been deemed worthy of divine mercy and consolation on account of the unselfish assistance she provided the elder. He asked the venerable one many times to disclose her condition, because he believed firmly that God's favorite knew the state of her soul. Worn out by his disciple's frequent, earnest entreaties and not wishing to grieve his spiritual child, the elder begged the Lord to reveal Theodora's circumstances to Gregory in a vision. The very night Saint Basil prayed for this, Gregory had a dream in which he saw the blessed Theodora in a mansion prepared by God for the holy elder. It was through the intercessions of the Lord's favorite that Theodora had been deemed worthy to dwell in that glorious celestial place of ineffable blessings.

---

[20]Ps. 26
[21]She is commemorated on December 30.

Having faithfully ministered to Saint Basil for many years in this world, Theodora was vouchsafed an abode with him in the blessed life yonder, by his holy prayers. Gregory was overjoyed to see Theodora and spoke with her at length, as though she were still alive. From this conversation Gregory was much comforted. He inquired about how the soul separated from the body, what kind of suffering Theodora endured at the hour of death, what she saw as she died, and how she made her way past the aerial spirits. Theodora related to him the following:

"Gregory, my child, you ask me about things truly terrifying. I saw faces and heard voices unknown to me. How can I describe it? I was confronted with everything shameful, everything sinful I had done but forgotten. It was only by the intercessions of our holy father Basil that I passed through the ordeal. How child, can I describe to you the pain and distress of the dying? As a naked man who falls into a roaring fire melts away, is consumed, and is reduced to ashes, so the dying are brought to destruction by the pangs of death and the bitter separation of soul and body. I can say nothing about what the righteous experience, but truly, death is harrowing for sinners like me.

"When the end of my life drew near and my departure was at hand, a multitude of Ethiopians crowded against my sickbed. Their faces were as black as soot or pitch, their eyes were like glowing coals, and their entire appearance was as dreadful as fiery Gehenna itself. They made an awful din as the sound of every wild and domestic animal: barking like dogs, howling like wolves, and grunting like pigs. They glared menacingly, snarled threats, gnashed their teeth, and snapped their jaws. They were hungry for me. Some were preparing lists, as if waiting for a judge, and were rolling up scrolls on which were written all my evil deeds. Fear and violent trembling seized my miserable soul. I was afraid both of bitter death and the dreadful glare of the Ethiopians, whose wrath seemed worse than death. No matter which way I turned to escape their faces and voices, I could not rid myself of them, for they were numberless.

"I was at the end of my strength and in despair of assistance when two radiant angels in the form of marvelously handsome youths approached. Their faces shone brightly; their eyes were full of love; their hair was white as snow, but glowed with a golden tinge; their garments flashed like lightning; and they wore golden belts strapped over their breasts. The angels stood at the right side of my couch and whispered one to another. Seeing them, my heart rejoiced; but the Ethiopians shuddered and retreated. One of the radiant youths berated the dark fiends, saying, 'Shameless, accursed, black-hearts, embittered foes of the human race! Why do you always rush to be the first at the scene of death? Why do you clamor, hoping to frighten and discomfit every soul departing the body? You have no cause for rejoicing now, for this woman is not yours. God's mercy is with her, and you have no claim on her soul.'

"As the angel spoke, the Ethiopians first became flustered, then raised an outcry and began reciting all the evil deeds I had committed since I was a girl. 'If we have no claim to her, whose sins are these? Did she not do such-and-such?' they protested.

"The demons had only a short wait before I breathed my last. Death came, roaring like a lion, but in the form of a horrifying human skeleton, entirely bereft of flesh and carrying swords, arrows, spears, scythes, sickles, antlers, saws, pole-axes, adzes, mason's hammers, and hooks, as well as other instruments of torture unknown to me. My lowly soul shook with fear. The holy angels beckoned death, 'Why do you tarry? Free this soul from the bonds of the flesh. Do your work quickly and quietly, for its burden of sins is light.' Using a hatchet, death hacked off first my legs, then my arms. Next it cut apart most of what remained of me, using other tools and weapons. Without legs, arms, or inner organs, I felt lifeless, and was unable to move. Then, with an adze, death decapitated me. My head seemed no longer mine, and I could not move it. Lastly, death mixed a potion in a cup and forced me to drink. Shuddering from the bitterness of the draught, my soul took leave of the body and was accepted into the arms of the radiant angels.

"Looking back, I saw my body unmoving, devoid of feeling, and lifeless. I was astonished to be gazing at my own corpse, as one might gaze at clothes he has removed. Meanwhile, the demonic Ethiopians surrounded the blessed angels holding me and shrieked, 'This soul has a multitude of sins for which it must account!'

"As the devils shouted my transgressions, the holy angels

enumerated all the good deeds that I had performed, by the Lord's grace and with His assistance. The angels mentioned every occasion when I gave alms to the poor, fed the hungry, provided drink to the thirsty, clothed the naked, sheltered strangers, served holy men and women, or visited the sick and imprisoned and rendered them assistance. They recounted the instances when I went eagerly to church, prayed with compunction and tears, listened attentively to the reading and chanting of the services, brought incense or candles or some other offering to God's temple, provided olive oil for the lamps illumining the sacred icons, or devoutly kissed the holy images. They spoke of my fasting on Wednesdays and Fridays and during the holy fasts, my numerous prostrations and vigils, and my wholehearted sighing to God. They told how I wept for my sins, confessed my trespasses to God before my spiritual father with heartfelt regret, and attempted to correct my faults. My kindnesses to my neighbors; attempts to restrain my anger when someone reproached or criticized me; refusal to harbor malice or return evil for evil; humbling of myself; grief and lamentation for the suffering; efforts to console the weeping; offers of a helping hand; encouragement of those doing good; attempts to divert those intent on wickedness; averting of my eyes from vanity; unwillingness to lie, slander, or engage in empty talk: all these and every other good deed of mine—regardless how paltry—the angels collected and readied for balancing against my offenses. Seeing this, the Ethiopians gnashed their teeth. They wanted to tear me from the angels' arms and drag me down to the abyss of hell.

"At this point our venerable father Basil unexpectedly appeared and informed the holy angels, 'My lords, this woman conscientiously served me, lightening the burden of my old age; therefore, I have prayed for her, and God has granted me her soul.' With this, he removed from his bosom a pouch full of what I believe was pure gold[22] and gave it to the angels, saying, 'When you pass through the aerial tollhouses and the wicked spirits interrogate this soul, pay its debts with this. By the grace of God I am wealthy, having by the sweat of my brow accumu-

---

[22]The gold represented the saint's holy prayers. (Tr.)

lated vast riches. This purse now belongs to Theodora.' Then he departed. Confounded by the unexpected turn of events, the demons raised a hue and cry and became invisible.

"Shortly afterwards Basil, God's favorite, returned carrying vessels full of pure oil and precious myrrh. He opened these one after another and poured their contents on me, so that I became spiritually fragrant. I sensed a change within me and felt that I was all aglow. Once again the godly one addressed the angels, saying, 'My lords, when you have done everything necessary for this soul, escort it into the house prepared for me by the Lord and allow it to remain there.' Then he became invisible, and the holy angels lifted me through the air towards the east.

The First Tollhouse[23]

"As we rose from the earth to the heights of heaven, we were met by the aerial spirits of the first tollhouse, where souls are interrogated regarding sins of speech: idle talking, quarrelling, and using unseemly or foul language. We halted, and the demons presented a number of scrolls on which was written everything unnecessary or foolish I had uttered since my youth, especially the ribald, obscene, and blasphemous remarks typical of young people. My empty and profane babblings, the shameless worldly songs I sang, and my wild cries and outbursts of laughter were all recorded. The evil spirits reproached me for this and indicated when, where, and with whom I held vain conversations and spoke words that angered God. At the time I did not consider what I was saying to be sinful; therefore, I neither confessed it to my spiritual father, nor did I repent of it.

---

[23]The account of the tollhouses that follows, and other visions in the Lives of the saints revealing heaven, hell, and the cross-examination of the soul are not to be understood in a crude, literal way. By means of imagery they communicate mystical, spiritual reality. The angel that described the tollhouses to Saint Macarius of Alexandria began by cautioning him, "Accept earthly things as the feeblest reflection of the celestial realm." Physical details of the visions may vary, but the calling to account of the soul after death and its preliminary punishment or reward, even before the Universal Judgment, are common to all of them. (Tr.)

"I was silent in the face of the accusations: it was as if I had lost my voice. I knew what the evil spirits were saying was true. It was amazing how they remembered everything, despite the passage of so many years. I had long since forgotten these sins; they never came to mind. But the demons quoted my every word as though I had just said it; they knew every detail with perfect accuracy. Seeing me silent, ashamed, and trembling with fear, the holy angels guiding me proffered some of the good deeds I did in my last years. When these did not suffice, they added to them from the gift of my father, the venerable Basil, thereby settling my debt, and so we proceeded higher.

The Second Tollhouse

"Next we approached the tollhouse of lying, where an account must be rendered for perjury, failure to fulfill vows made to God, misrepresentation of sins during Confession, and similar transgressions, as well as taking the Lord's name in vain. The evil spirits of this customhouse are violent and ruthless, exacting and insolent. However, they accused me of two things only: that I occasionally lied about small matters (something I had not considered sinful), and that out of shame I did not make a full Confession to my spiritual father. By the grace of Christ, the demons had no evidence that I was guilty of oath-breaking, bearing false witness, or other sins of the sort. Nonetheless, they jeered me and tried to snatch me from my guides; but the holy angels laid down some of my good deeds and covered the rest of my debt out of the gift of my father, and I continued on my way unscathed.

The Third Tollhouse

"Then we reached the third tollhouse, that of judging and slander. We were detained here, and I learned how grievous a sin it is to judge one's neighbor; to slander, demean, revile, or mock others; or to ridicule the shortcomings of another while ignoring one's own sins. All who make themselves judges of their neighbors deserve punishment ten thousand times worse than that meted out to those they condemn, for they assume the role of Christ; therefore, the cruel inquisitors torture them brutally as antichrists.

"Throughout my life I was careful not to judge, slander, or mock anyone. If I heard someone else judging, slandering, or mocking others, I usually paid no attention to it. If I did respond to what was said, I was careful not to add to the condemnation and reproached myself for having spoken at all. Nevertheless, I provided sufficient grounds for the toll collectors to revile me for judging and slander. The holy angels paid my dues out of the pouch given them by the godly Basil, and we continued to ascend.

The Fourth Tollhouse

"So doing, we arrived at the next tollhouse, that of gluttony. Eagerly anticipating payment, the despicable toll collectors raced out to meet us. The appearance of these spirits was disgusting and showed how debased are pleasure-loving gluttons and contemptible drunkards. Some of the demons were carrying trays and pots full of various foods, others cups and mugs of drink. The food and drink stunk like pus and vomit. The demons acted like men who had gorged themselves and were intoxicated. Mocking the sinners they detained at their tollhouse, the imps played the fiddle and pretended to be drunken revelers. Circling us like dogs, they produced accounts of all the occasions when I had sinned by gluttony: when I ate secretly, in excess, or without need; or rushed to breakfast like a hog without praying or making the sign of the Cross; or dined during the holy fasts earlier than allowed by the canons of the Church; or ate voraciously between meals; or consumed too large a portion. They did not forget my sins of drunkenness, either, but displayed the goblets and winejars from which I drank and tallied the cups I had quaffed, saying, 'She drained so many mugs at such-and-such a banquet in the company of so-and-so at such-and-such a time. At another time and place she drank so many cups, threw up, and lost consciousness. On still another occasion she danced, clapped her hands, sang, and frolicked, having drained so many glasses of wine and other alcoholic beverages that she scarcely made it home.' They also showed me the cups from which I drank at an early hour when guests came to my house on a fast day, or when I permitted myself wine due to illness, with the result that I became inebriated. They recounted the instances when I got drunk on feasts or Sundays before holy Liturgy, and when I imbibed to excess on other occasions, never considering that I was sinning, and never repenting. Having detailed all this, the demons rejoiced, as though I were already in their clutches. It seemed certain that they would drag me into the abyss of hell. I shuddered at the accusations, because they were impossible to refute. But when the holy angels made a large payment on my behalf from the gift given me by the venerable Basil, the fiends howled, 'Woe, woe! All our labor is in vain; our hopes have come to nothing!' With this they tossed away the scrolls on which my sins were written. I rejoiced, and we continued our ascent unmolested.

"As we rose, the holy angels said to each other, 'Truly, this soul has been greatly assisted by Basil, God's favorite. Were it not for his labors and prayers, it could hardly have gotten this far.'

"Plucking up my courage, I told the holy angels, 'It seems to me, my lords, that the living have no conception of what the sinful soul undergoes after death.'

"'Do not the divine Scriptures read daily in the churches testify to these things?' they asked. 'Are they not confirmed by the preaching of God's holy clergy who minister at the altar? It is because of their passion for worldly vanities that people are heedless of what you have seen. They delight in satiety and drunkenness; they daily glut and inebriate themselves. They have no fear of the Lord, because their stomach is their god. They do not meditate on the life to come, nor do they ponder the words of Scripture, which say, 'Woe to you that are full! For ye shall hunger!'[24] Woe unto you that drink to excess, for ye shall thirst!' Imagining Holy Scripture to be a collection of fables, they live heedlessly and spaciously, dining to the sound of timbrel and dance,[25] like the rich man in the Gospel who fared sumptuously every day.[26] Nevertheless, gluttons and drunkards easily pass by the tollhouses, and their sins are readily forgiven by God, if they

---

[24]Luke, Ch. 6   [25]Ps. 150   [26]Luke, Ch. 16

are merciful and generous to the poor and help those who beg assistance, in accordance with the teaching of Scripture: *Alms deliver from death and cleanse from all sin.*[27] Almsgivers inherit life, but those who do not cleanse their sins by charity cannot escape this tollhouse. Its dark keepers, which you saw, seize them, drag them down to the depths of hell, subject them to infernal tortures, and keep them in bonds until Christ's Dread Judgment. This would have been your lot, if we had not ransomed you with payment from the gift of the venerable Basil.'

The Fifth Tollhouse

"We were still talking when we reached the station of sloth, where transgressors must render an account for all the days and hours they wasted in idleness. Those who take advantage of the generosity of others and refuse to work, as well as those who accept pay without fulfilling their responsibilities are detained here with people who neglect to praise God and are too lazy to attend Matins, the Liturgy, and the other Divine Services on feast days and Sundays. At this stop a meticulous examination is conducted and souls are condemned for laziness, despondency, and disregard for their salvation. As a result, many laypeople and clergy are hurled from here into the bottomless pit. I, too, was questioned at length, and would not have been able to cover my debt had not the angels drawn from the purse I was given by the venerable Basil.

The Sixth Tollhouse

"We were halted next at the tollhouse of theft. My payment here was small, because I had never stolen, except as a child, in ignorance.

The Seventh Tollhouse

"Then we approached the tollhouse of stinginess and love of money. We passed by without stopping, because throughout my lifetime the Lord had sheltered me from these passions, and

---

[27]Tob., Ch. 4

I never accumulated possessions or money. I was content with what God provided and was not tightfisted, but gave willingly to those who asked alms.

The Eighth Tollhouse

"We rose higher and reached the tollhouse of usury, where those who lend money at exorbitant rates, enrich themselves by discreditable means, or swindle others are interrogated. Despite every effort, the toll collectors failed to prove me guilty of these sins, so they gnashed their teeth and we continued on our way, thanking God.

The Ninth Tollhouse

"Next came the tollhouse of injustice, where unrighteous judges who accept bribes, condemn the innocent, and acquit the guilty are called to account, as are people who cheat workers of their wages, merchants who use false weights and measures, and all others who perpetuate similar iniquities. By the grace of Christ we made a small payment and passed by.

The Tenth Tollhouse

"After this came the tollhouse of envy, which cost us nothing at all, since I had never been jealous. Here souls also face accusations of animosity, malevolence, and hatred, but by the mercy of Christ I was proven innocent of these sins. Again the demons gnashed their teeth at me, but this time I was not frightened by them, and we continued on our way rejoicing.

The Eleventh Tollhouse

"Similarly, we passed by the tollhouse of pride, where arrogant devils interrogate the dead regarding vainglory, conceit, obstinacy, and boasting. Here souls must answer for every instance of disrespect for their parents and *the powers ordained of God*;[28]

---

[28]Rom., Ch. 13

for every proud deed and haughty word. Having paid a trifling sum, we resumed our ascent.

The Twelfth Tollhouse

"Then we reached the tollhouse of anger, manned by extremely vicious toll collectors. Fortunately, my debts here were few, and we passed by, thanking the Lord for protecting my sinful soul, on account of the prayers of my holy father, Saint Basil.

The Thirteenth Tollhouse

"Next came the tollhouse of resentment, where those who dare nurture in their heart remembrance of their neighbors' wrongs and return evil for evil are seized by malicious spirits and mercilessly dragged to Tartarus. Again, the Lord's compassion defended me, since I held no grudges and did my best to love those who offended me and to conquer evil by kindness. Unable to charge me with resentment, the demonic toll collectors had no choice but to let me pass freely, and we hurried on our journey, exulting in the Lord. At this point I said to my guides, 'Tell me, my lords: how is it that the dread powers of the air know all the evil deeds of mankind throughout the world? They are aware of what I have done openly and secretly.'

"The angels replied, 'At Holy Baptism, God gives every Christian a guardian angel. This celestial spirit invisibly protects his charge, urges him day and night to do good deeds throughout his life, and records these, so that the Christian may have hope for the Lord's mercy and an eternal reward in the Kingdom of Heaven. But the prince of darkness aspires to destroy the entire human race, so he appoints one of his wicked spirits to shadow the person, observe his wicked deeds from childhood, ensnare him, and record his transgressions. This fiend then visits the customhouses and delivers lists of sins to the toll collectors; hence, the aerial princes know all the sins of every man. When a person's soul is parted from the body and begins the journey to its Creator in heaven, the evil spirits attempt to thwart it, producing the lists. If the soul's good deeds outweigh the sins, the demons fail in their purpose; but if the sins outweigh the good deeds, then the fiends are granted temporary custody of the soul. The demons confine the soul in a dungeon where it cannot see God, and they torment it as much as the Lord allows and until its release is obtained by the prayers of the Church and by alms given on its behalf by relatives. As for the soul which is so sinful and offensive to the Master that it has no hope of salvation, but is bound for eternal damnation, it is straightway cast into the abyss where eternal fire has been prepared for the demons. There it is held captive until the Second Coming of Christ, after which it shall be tormented in the body forever, with the wicked spirits. Know also that these things apply only to those enlightened by faith and Holy Baptism. Unbelieving heathen idolaters, Saracens, and all others who are alien to God do not take this path or undergo this interrogation. While still alive and in the body, their souls are already buried, as it were, in Hades. When they die, their souls are at once, without any examination, claimed by the demons as their property and flung into the bottomless pit of Gehenna.'

The Fourteenth Tollhouse

"As the angels spoke, we reached the tollhouse of murder. At this station highway robbers can expect an especially rigorous interrogation. A careful weighing of deeds is in store here for those who in anger push others or strike them on the back, head, cheek, or neck. We made a small payment and went on.

The Fifteenth Tollhouse

"Next we arrived at the tollhouse of sorcery, bewitchment, poisoning, and communication with devils. The evil spirits assembled here resemble noxious mammals, scorpions, vipers and other serpents, and toads. They are terrifying and disgusting in appearance, but by the Lord's grace, they found nothing to charge me with, and we quickly continued on without making any payment. Enraged by this, the customhouse keepers shouted, 'Next comes the tollbooth of fornication. We shall see whether you escape so easily there.'

"As we rose, I asked the holy angels, 'My lords, must all Christians pass these tollhouses? Do some ascend without undergoing the dread interrogation?'

"'On this path alone do the faithful ascend to heaven,' explained my guides. 'All must come this way, but not all are questioned as you have been. An unsparing examination like yours is reserved for sinners who, out of false shame, have hidden their most disgraceful deeds from their spiritual father. If a person fully confesses all of his transgressions, regrets them, and repents for them, they are invisibly expunged by God's compassion. When they catch sight of his soul approaching, the aerial toll collectors rush for their books, but find the pages blank. They cannot harm or terrify his soul, which joyfully flies past them to the throne of grace. If you had fervently and without omission confessed your sins, and after being absolved attempted to make recompense for them, you would not be undergoing such dire accusations at the tollbooths. Nevertheless, you have been helped by the fact that it has been many years since you ceased committing mortal sins and began living virtuously. More importantly, you have the assistance of the prayers of our venerable father Basil, whom you served earnestly and well.

The Sixteenth Tollhouse

"During this conversation, we reached the tollhouse of fornication, where souls are accused of sins against chastity, including unclean thoughts and fantasies, mental consent to depraved acts, lustful fondling, and passionate embracing. The prince of this tollhouse sat on a throne and was clad in vile, foul-smelling garments, dripping with bloody spittle. He preened in this garb as though it were a robe of imperial purple, and had as his escorts a multitude of wicked spirits. Catching sight of me from afar, the demonic tollhouse keepers were astonished that I had succeeded in reaching their station. They brought out the record of my carnal falls and began their accusations, naming the persons with whom I sinned in my youth, the times of day or night when the transgressions occurred, and the places where they happened. Humiliated and having nothing to say in my defense, I shook with fear. At this point the holy angels told the demons, 'She ceased committing sins of the flesh many years ago and has since led the ascetic life of chastity and abstinence.'

"'We know this, but she failed to confess thoroughly before her spiritual father and has not fulfilled a suitable penance; therefore, she is ours,' replied the demons. 'Abandon her to us and be on your way, or else pay her toll.' The holy angel made a large payment of my good deeds and a larger one from the gift of the venerable Basil. Having barely escaped the gravest calamity, I hurried on with the angels.

The Seventeenth Tollhouse

"Before long we were at the tollhouse of adultery, where the married must give account for failure to keep their bed undefiled and for every lapse in conjugal fidelity. Those who abduct maidens and other rapists must also answer for themselves here, as well as those who are consecrated to God and promise to live chastely for Christ, but fail to keep their vow. The loathsome, merciless toll collectors accused me of being an adulteress and demanded an enormous sum. They were determined to snatch me out of the hands of my guides and drag me down to the abyss of Hades. The holy angels, however, vigorously disputed their claim to my soul, recounting all my efforts in later life to please God. Still, it was only by depositing everything that remained of my good deeds and a large portion of my father Basil's gift that they offset my iniquities.

The Eighteenth Tollhouse

"After this came the tollhouse of sodomy, where men and women are accused of homosexuality, incest, coupling with demons and irrational animals, and other crimes too revolting to mention. The prince of this station was the most abominable of all the despicable fiends and was covered with fetid pus. His servants were, like him, ill-smelling, revolting in appearance, savage, and cruel. They rushed to encircle us, but by the Lord's mercy found nothing of which to accuse me and, put to shame, were forced to retreat. 'You see, Theodora, how horrifying and odious are the tollhouses of the fleshly passions,' said the holy angels. 'Know that few pass by them unscathed, for *the whole world lieth in wickedness*[29] and defilement. Most people love pleasure and sensuality, and from an early age their thoughts incline to wickedness. Very few guard themselves against impure thoughts, words, or deeds; very few mortify their fleshly desires. Therefore, very few freely pass by these tollhouses. If they come this far, they are halted here and straightway sent to perdition. The merciless inquisitors of concupiscence capture the souls of voluptuaries, drag them down to Hades, and torment them viciously. The princes of these tollbooths boast that they, more than all the other demons, fill the fiery pit of hell. And so, Theodora, thank God that, by the prayers of your father, the venerable Basil, you have passed the tollhouse of carnal sins. From this point on you have nothing to fear.'

The Nineteenth Tollhouse

We then proceeded to the tollhouse of heresy, where the demons accuse men of unbelief, blasphemy, doubting Christian truth, reasoning perversely concerning the faith, apostatizing from an Orthodox confession, and similar sins. I was not halted for questioning at this tollhouse and could now see the gates of heaven a short distance away.

The Twentieth Tollhouse

"Before we reached the Kingdom of heaven we were confronted by the wicked spirits of the last tollhouse, that of mercilessness and hard-heartedness. The toll collectors here are grim and their prince is implacable: his face is withered and severe, and he breathes out the fire of anger and ruthlessness. Here the merciless are interrogated without mercy. It matters not whether he has kept strict fasts, prayed frequently, or carefully guarded his chastity: if a man has been callous and shut *up his bowels of compassion*,[30] he is thrust down from this tollhouse, locked in the

---

[29] I John, Ch. 5   [30] I John, Ch. 3

subterranean dungeon of Hades, and never granted forgiveness. But by the grace of Christ, we passed by this tollhouse without being long detained, for I had the help of the prayers of the venerable Basil, whose good works settled so much of my debt.

"Soon we arrived at the gates of heaven, having successfully passed all the dread tollhouses. The celestial gates were as brilliant as crystal and radiant with ineffable light. They were guarded by youths who shone as brightly as the sun. Seeing me in the arms of the angels, the youths rejoiced and affectionately escorted us into the Kingdom, thanking God that He had protected me by His grace and enabled me to escape detention on my way. What marvelous things I saw and heard in heaven, my child Gregory! I could never explain it all to you. I beheld what the *eye hath not seen, nor ear heard, neither* has *entered the heart of* the *man*[31] still living on earth. I was taken before the exalted throne of transcendent glory, which was surrounded by cherubim, seraphim, and a multitude of heavenly hosts that ever sing ineffable odes in praise of the Lord. As I fell prostrate before the invisible, incomprehensible Godhead, the celestial powers chanted sweet hymns glorifying the divine compassion that prevails over men's sins. Then a voice sounded from the resplendent glory, commanding my angelic guides to take me to see the dwellings of the saints and the torments of sinners, and to settle me in the mansion assigned to the blessed Basil. Led by the angels, I beheld the many beautiful, glorious abodes prepared for those who love God. My guides showed me the separate palaces of apostles, prophets, martyrs, holy hierarchs, and other ranks of saints. Each was approximately the same width and length as Constantinople, but incomparably more beautiful, and consisted of numerous resplendent structures not made by the hand of man. Everywhere in the buildings one heard the sound of spiritual celebration and beheld the inhabitants exulting. All were delighted at my salvation, greeted me with a kiss, and praised the Lord Who had delivered me from the snares of the enemy. After being led through the abodes of the righteous, I was taken into the nethermost parts of the earth, where I saw

---

[31]I Cor., Ch. 2

unbearable tortures prepared for sinners in Hades. As they showed me the torments, the holy angels said, 'These, Theodora, are the sufferings from which the Lord has delivered you, by the prayers of His favorite, Basil.' The victims of hell were lamenting, weeping, and wailing piteously. Some cried, 'Woe, woe!' others sobbed, 'How miserable our lot!' and still others groaned, 'Cursed be the day we were born!' but no one came to their aid. Finally, I was brought here, to the mansion of our venerable father Basil, as you see. While settling me in my quarters, the angels informed me, 'At present the venerable Basil is commemorating you in his prayers.' I then learned that, after leaving the body, it had taken my soul forty days to reach its place of repose."

Besides relating this to Gregory in the dream, Theodora showed him the beautiful mansion and the spiritual treasure their blessed father had won by his ascetic labors. Gregory was also permitted to experience the glory and spiritual delight of paradise, and to behold its orchards of golden-leafed trees laden with fruit.

The vision ended and Gregory awoke, marveling at what he had seen and heard. At first light he went, as usual, to receive the godly Basil's blessing. "Where, child, did you go last night?" asked Basil.

"Nowhere, Father," answered Gregory, as though he had not seen the vision. "I was sleeping in my bed."

"Your body was sleeping in the bed, but your spirit was somewhere else," the elder corrected him. "Did you forget what God revealed to you last night in a dream? You saw Theodora, heard what she underwent, and visited the mansion prepared for me by the grace of Christ, as a reward for my paltry labors. You beheld everything you longed to see." Hearing this, Gregory understood that the dream was not fantasy, but a divine revelation granted him through Saint Basil's prayers. He thanked God and made a prostration before the blessed one, who concluded their conversation with a lengthy, edifying discourse.

On another occasion God permitted Gregory to undergo doubts concerning the faith. While engaged in diligent study of the Old Testament, Gregory was troubled by the thought that the Jews believe correctly. The temptation persisted for a long time and could not remain hidden from the clairvoyant elder, who repeatedly upbraided his disciple. When exhortations failed, Saint Basil entreated God to vouchsafe Gregory another revelation. In a wondrous dream, Gregory beheld all of mankind assembled at God's Dread Judgment. The Judge sat upon His throne, with the just at His right hand and sinners at His left. Evildoers were condemned in accordance with their works, and the Jews who failed to believe in Christ were damned with the heathen and sent to the fire of Gehenna. Gregory saw not just the doom of sinners, but how the saints were glorified. His extremely lengthy account of this is included in *The Great Collection of Readings*, but for brevity's sake we have mentioned the revelation only in passing.

Our venerable father Basil was still of middle age when brought to the Imperial City, where he lived about fifty years. After so long a time of punishing himself, but helping others by prophecy and cure, his strength waned. At the age of one hundred or so he was translated to life eternal, where his *years shall not fail*.[32]

Saint Basil foretold the day of his repose to Gregory, his beloved disciple. Gregory had the custom of spending the whole of Great Lent and Passion Week in his room praying, fasting, making numerous prostrations, and keeping nightlong vigils. In the year that Basil died, Gregory came to the elder as usual to receive a blessing before going into seclusion. After speaking at length about various edifying subjects, our father blessed him and said, "Return home in peace, child. You will not see me again in this life." He began to weep, and embraced Gregory and lovingly kissed him. Gregory also wept bitterly, and falling at the elder's holy feet, washed them with tears. After bidding Saint Basil farewell, he began his Lenten labors in solitude.

During the middle week of Lent, on March 25, the feast of the Annunciation of the Most Holy Theotokos, the venerable Basil surrendered his blessed soul into the hands of the Lord.[33] His honored body was laid to rest in the Monastery of Saints Florus and Laurus. Some time later a pious citizen of Constan-

---

[32]Heb., Ch. 1   [33]In the year 944

tinople had a vision in which he saw a fair and spacious building surrounded by blossoming orchards and adorned with gates of gold and precious stone. Over them the inscription read: "The Mansion of the Blessed Basil the New and His Place of Eternal Rest." While the man was marveling at the splendor, lo, a handsome youth came out and asked him, "Why are you so astonished, sir? If you like, I will show you something far more amazing." He thrust open the gates, and within the man saw magnificence beyond imagination and the venerable Basil seated in glory on a royal throne. To the saint's left and right stood many wondrous, radiant men and youths. Afterwards, the man related the vision to all, and they glorified God and blessed the memory of Saint Basil, the Lord's favorite.

May our portion in eternity be with those who love God, by the prayers of His saints and the grace of our Lord Jesus Christ. Unto Him, with the Father and the Holy Spirit, be honor and glory forever. Amen.

ﻬﻬﻬ

On this same day we commemorate the twenty-six holy martyrs who suffered for Christ in Gothia during the reign of Valens and Gratian at the hands of the Gothic chieftain Winguric. They were two presbyters, Bathuses and Wirkas; their two sons and their daughters; Arpylas the monk; the laymen Abippas, Hagnas, Ryax, Egathrax, Eskoes, Silas, Sigetzas, Suerilas, Seimblas, Thermas, and Filgas; and the women Anna, Alla, Larissa, Moiko, Mamika, Wirco, and Animais. The widowed Gothic Queen Gaatha and her daughter Duklida collected the remains of the martyrs and took them to the Greek city of Cyzicus. Later, Queen Gaatha returned to her homeland, and the unbelievers put her to death by stoning. As for Duklida, she died peacefully in Cyzicus.

The Twenty-Seventh Day of the Month of March

The Commemoration of the Holy Martyr Matrona of Thessalonica

Saint Matrona was the slave of a Jewess named Paulita, whose husband was a commander of troops stationed in Thessalonica. Her mistress demanded that she accept the impious teachings of Judaism, but Matrona, a Christian since childhood, would not; therefore, Paulita beat her to obtain her submission. Gladly enduring every mistreatment for the Lord's sake, Matrona secretly continued attending church. Eventually, Paulita learned this and demanded, "Why do you prefer the Christian church to our synagogue?"

"Because God dwells in the Christian church, but has abandoned the synagogue of the Jews," Matrona fearlessly replied. Infuriated, Paulita thrashed her servant mercilessly, bound her, and locked her in a closet. The next day she found the saint loosed by the power of God and glorifying Christ. Paulita in a madness lashed Matrona with leather straps until she was nearly dead. Then she bound Matrona more securely and again locked her in the closet, sealing the door. The saint remained there without food or water for four days, but was strengthened by God. When Paulita broke the seal and opened the door, she found the martyr loosed a second time and praying. Even more enraged than before, she battered Matrona furiously with heavy staves until the saint was scarcely breathing and dragged her back to the closet, whence God translated the martyr's soul to heaven. The hardhearted Paulita took the saint's corpse to the roof of the mansion and threw it off. Christians removed the much-suffering body and gave it an honorable burial. Subsequently Alexander, Bishop of Thessalonica, built a church in honor of the holy martyr and enshrined the relics there.

It was not long before divine retribution overtook Paulita. While standing on the roof at the exact spot where she had thrown down Saint Matrona, the murderess lost her footing and fell to the ground. Her body was shattered and she vomited her wretched soul.

On the Same Day

The Life of
Our Holy Monastic Father
John the Clairvoyant,
Desert-dweller and Recluse of Egypt[1]

𝒥n Lycopolis, a city of Egypt, there once lived a man named John who worked as a carpenter until, at the age of twenty-five, he renounced the world. During his first fifteen years as a monk he lived in various communities, acquainting himself with every ascetical labor; then he departed to Mount Lycus, and on its summit built three huts for himself. One became his oratory, another his workshop, another his cell. He remained there in seclusion until his death fifty years later, receiving provisions and speaking to visitors through a little window.

During the thirty years John lived as an anchorite, the Lord graced him with the power of prophecy. The man of God sent word to the Emperor of the Greeks, Theodosius the Great, fore-telling that he would conquer the usurper Maximus, recover Gaul, defeat the persecutor Eugenius, and then himself repose, leaving the realm to his sons. So it happened, and the fame of this holy man spread everywhere and Theodosius acknowl-edged him as a prophet of God.

Soon after John took up his dwelling in the wilderness, a general came to him and asked whether he would succeed in vanquishing the Ethiopians[2] who had overrun the countryside roundabout the town of Syene,[3] which is on the border of the Thebaid. The venerable one told him, "Do not be afraid to march against the barbarians, for you will subdue them and win the Emperor's favor." This is what exactly happened; moreover, it was from the commander's report that the rulers first learned about John. Afterwards, the emperors unfailingly requested the prayers of Saint John and before setting out to do battle inquired of him what outcome to expect.

---

[1]Abbreviated from the account in Palladius' *Lausiac History*
[2]Bedouin (Tr.)   [3]Now Aswan (Tr.)

The fact that this saint truly possessed an extraordinary gift of clairvoyance was confirmed for us by the fathers living near him (writes Palladius, author of his Life).[4] According to their trustworthy account, the wife of a tribune[5] wanted to visit the man of God and had her husband beg the elder's permission for this. Not once during his years in the desert had the elder seen or been seen by a woman, and indeed, he only conversed with men through the little window in his cell; therefore, he refused to receive the woman. Finally, however, he was swayed by the couple's faith. "I will appear to your wife in a dream tonight," he promised the tribune, "but she must never again try to behold *my face in the flesh.*"[6] This the officer related to his wife.

That night John appeared to the tribune's wife in her sleep and asked, "*Woman, what have I to do with thee?*[7] Why do you wish to see me? Am I a prophet or a righteous man? I am a sinner *of like passions with you;*[8] nevertheless, I have prayed to God for you and your husband, that *it be unto you according to your faith.*"[9] So saying, he disappeared.

When the woman awoke, she repeated to her husband everything the saint had told her, and described his appearance and clothing. The tribune returned to the elder's cell with her message of thanks, but before the officer could speak, Saint John said, "I kept my word and visited your wife. Now she must never again ask to see me."

At another time the wife of a *praepositus*[10] was expecting a child. On the day her husband was visiting the godly one and asking his prayers, the woman gave birth, but so doing, she nearly died. "*If thou knewest the gift of God,*[11] you would thank the Lord," Saint John told the officer. "A son was born to you today; however, your wife almost lost her life in childbirth. The boy will be seven days old when you return home. Name him John and send him to live with the monks in the desert as soon as he reaches the age of seven."

---

[4]This paragraph and much else in the account, is based not on Palladius' *Lausiac History,* but on the anonymous *History of the Monks of Egypt.* (Tr.)
[5]A senior legionary officer (Tr.)
[6]Col., Ch. 2   [7]John, Ch. 2   [8]Acts, Ch. 14
[9]Matt., Ch. 9   [10]The commander of a fort or garrison (Tr.)
[11]John, Ch. 4

Besides the miracles wrought by the saint for those who came from far away, there were others worked for the citizens of Lycopolis, who frequently resorted to him with their needs. The elder foretold what would happen to his supplicants and laid bare their secret deeds; he predicted the rise and fall of the Nile and the annual yield of crops; he warned people when God's wrath was about to overtake them and upbraided those who were at fault. He did not, however, heal the ill publicly. Instead, he gave holy oil to the sick and cured them by this means. For example, a senator's wife developed cataracts and lost her sight. She wanted her husband to take her to the venerable one, but he replied that the elder never saw women or spoke with them. Then she begged that Saint John be told about her, and that he offer a prayer for her. The senator conveyed the request to the Lord's favorite, who sent the woman a little oil. After anointing her eyes thrice for three days, she regained sight and glorified God.

In the desert of Nitria (writes Palladius), there lived seven brethren who were foreigners. I was one of them, and the others included Evagrius and his disciples Albinus and Ammon. We wanted to learn more about Saint John, so Evagrius proposed, "I will go partway to Lycopolis and inquire about him. But unless I find a trustworthy witness to his virtue, I will not go all the way to his cell."

Hearing this, I held my peace and rested for a day; then, entrusting myself to God's care, I set out for the Thebaid. When I arrived at Saint John's cell, I was told by his disciples that the elder spoke with no one on weekdays and that I would have to wait until Saturday to see him. On Saturday at the second hour I drew near and found him sitting at the little window in his cell, waiting to console whoever came to him. After greeting me, he asked through an interpreter,[12] "Where are you from and why did you come here? It would seem to me that you are from Evagrius' brotherhood."

As we spoke, the commander of the local garrison arrived. His name was Alypius. I withdrew a short distance so that the elder and he could speak privately, but because the conversa-

---

[12]Palladius spoke Greek; John, Coptic. (Tr.)

tion lasted a long time, I began to judge the man of God, think-ing he was spurning me and fawning upon the General. Frustrated and perturbed, I was about to leave without bidding him farewell. The venerable one perceived my thoughts, sum-moned Theodore, the interpreter, and instructed him, "Tell that brother to be patient and not to take offense. I am almost fin-ished with the General, and will speak with him in a moment." I marveled that the elder knew what I was thinking and under-stood that he was truly a spiritual man and clairvoyant.

When the commander left, the elder called to me and asked, "My son, why were you angry? What did I do to offend you? The things you imagined are untrue and you disgraced yourself by assuming them. Did you forget the words of Scripture: *They that be whole need not a physician, but they that are sick?*[13] We can visit each other whenever we wish, and if I fail to comfort you, the other fathers and brothers will do so, but the General is chained to the world by many vain cares and in bondage to Satan. Having somewhat come to his senses, he fled the devil as a slave flees a cruel master, and hurried to me seeking edifica-tion. It would have been wrong to ignore him in order to talk with you, for you are always striving for salvation." This com-pletely convinced me that the elder was a holy man, and I begged him to pray for me.

The saint continued speaking with me, now in a joyous, affectionate spirit. Suddenly he tapped my left cheek with his right hand and said, "You are pining to quit the wilderness, but have not yet succumbed to the temptation, even though the devil has suggested an honorable, devout pretext; I mean, con-cern for your father and brother. Lo, I wish you to know that both are alive and well, and have forsaken the world. Your father will live another seven years. Now brace yourself for trials, renew your determination to remain in the desert, and abandon the thought of returning to your homeland and seeing your family. It is written: *No man, having put his hand to the plough, and looking back, is fit for the Kingdom of God.*"[14]

Greatly edified and encouraged by these words, I thanked

---

[13]Matt., Ch. 9; Mark, Ch. 2; Luke, Ch. 5
[14]Luke, Ch. 9

God (says Palladius) that this holy man had made clear the devil's deception and put an end to my warfare.

Then the elder asked me jovially, "Do you wish to become a bishop?"

"I am a bishop already," said I.

"Where?" he asked.

"I oversee wine vats, kitchens, and refectories," I said. "If the vintage has gone sour, I leave it to another; but if it is sweet, I drink it myself. I keep vigil over pots and pans, and if salt or spices are needed, I season to taste. Gluttony has appointed me to my see and made me bishop of my belly."

"Enough of this foolery," the venerable one smiled. "You really shall become a bishop and have your share of troubles and sorrows. But if you wish to avoid them, remain in the desert. No one will consecrate you there."

Upon return to my cell in Nitria, I related to the holy fathers everything about Saint John. Soon, however, I myself forgot what he had told me, wretch that I am. After three years, I fell ill with an ailment of the spleen and stomach, and the brethren insisted I go to Alexandria for medical treatment. When I failed to improve, the physicians there sent me to Palestine, which has a salubrious climate. My health having improved somewhat, I next went to Bithynia where, either by the will of man or God (the Lord alone knows), I was made a bishop. The episcopal rank is far above what I deserve and has brought me much grief. After my consecration I recalled the venerable one's prophecy, but the elder had already reposed. I also remembered that Christ's ascetic, wishing to enlighten my mind and spur me to remain in the desert, told me this about himself: "I have lived forty-eight years in this cell, never seeing a woman's face, nor a single penny, nor anyone eating or drinking; nor has anyone seen me eating or drinking."

Two months after I spoke with Saint John and returned to Nitria (writes Palladius), all seven members of our brotherhood visited the elder. He greeted us cordially and jovially. Our first request was that he pray for us, according to the custom of the Egyptian fathers. He asked, "Are any of you in clerical rank?" When we replied that none was, he studied our faces carefully, and the Lord revealed to him that there was a deacon among us.

This man in his humility reckoned himself as dust compared with the saints and considered that he was unworthy even to be called a Christian, much less a deacon. His rank was known only to one other member of our party; nonetheless, the venerable one pointed at him and announced, "This man is a deacon." Since the brother denied it, Saint John reached through the window, took the deacon's right hand, and kissed it, saying, "Child, do not spurn the grace of God. No Christian should lie about matters great or small. I cannot praise your deceit, for the Saviour teaches that every lie is of the evil one."[15] Realizing he was wrong, the deacon silently accepted the rebuke.

For three days one of the members of our brotherhood was burning with a fever. After we prayed, he begged the venerable John to heal him. Our father pointed out that the illness was to the brother's advantage and had come upon him because of his unbelief.

Nevertheless, John ordered that the sick man be anointed with holy oil. The brother vomited and the fever subsided.

We visited Saint John when he was ninety years old and so wasted by asceticism that his beard had fallen out. He subsisted on nothing more than a little fruit, of which he partook after sunset. Since his youth he had mortified his flesh, and even in extreme old age he never ate bread or cooked food of any kind. When he bade us eat, we thanked God for deeming us worthy to see him and converse with him. For his part, he welcomed us as though we were his own dear sons and, with a smile on his face, inquired, "Where are you from, children? Have you come from afar to visit me, the wretch and pauper?" We told him where we were born and explained that we lived in Nitria, but had been in Jerusalem and come directly from the Holy City to see him for ourselves, since we had heard about him from many others. The blessed John marveled at this and asked, "And what, dearest children, did you expect to find? What induced you to undertake such a long journey? I am a poor outcast and possess nothing worthy of admiring or seeing. Those worthy of admiration and praise are everywhere: the apostles and prophets of God, whose books are read in the churches. Emulate them and

---

[15]Matt., Ch. 5; John, Ch. 8

live as they counsel. I am amazed that you have risked innumerable dangers, thinking I could edify you: I, who am too slothful to go anywhere myself. But even though your intention was noble, do not consider that you have done something admirable. Imitate our fathers, and if you attain their virtues (which is something rare), do not begin to trust in yourself. Some have been confident in this way and, reaching the very summit, ended with a terrible fall. Make certain that your prayers are attentive and fervent, and that your purity of heart is unsullied. Examine yourself and determine whether you have truly turned your back on the world. Ask yourself: are you visiting us because you hope to win admiration, appearing to others as emulators of our works? Be sure not to number yourself among the righteous, to exalt yourself because you have done some good deed, or to dwell upon something temporal while you pray. It is in vain to address the Master with the tongue while the mind is far from Him, as do those who have not altogether renounced the world, but still wish to please it. If a person chases after many things, if he is occupied with bodily and earthly cares of every sort, his thoughts are inevitably scattered. When the mind is dispersed, it cannot gaze upon the Lord; therefore, he who desires to contemplate the Divinity should be free of terrestrial concern, in accordance with the Scripture: *Be still and know that I am God.*[16] Perfect knowledge of God is unattainable; but if a man achieves even partial knowledge of Him, he beholds divine mysteries, foresees the future, works miracles, and obtains from the Lord whatever he asks, as did the saints."

While exhorting and counseling the visiting brethren, the venerable John told them several stories about self-important monks who trusted in themselves. This was one:

In a cave in the nearer desert there lived an ascetic who obtained his daily bread by the work of his own hands. He prayed unceasingly and was making progress in the virtues. As time passed, however, he began thinking he was a holy man, relying upon himself, and imagining that it was impossible that he should take a fall. At this point God permitted the tempter to assume the form of a beautiful woman lost in the

---

[16]Ps. 45

desert. Finding the door open, she entered the cave, threw herself at the monk's feet, and begged for shelter overnight. Certain this posed no danger for him, the anchorite took compassion on the woman and gave her permission to stay. When he asked where she was going and how she had lost her way, the temptress engaged him in a lengthy conversation. Taken in by her lies and flattery, the hermit was smitten by desire for her. The conversation became freer, and there was laughter and touching. By this time the monk was burning with lust and intent on sin. Then, just as he was ready to mount her, the woman shrieked and vanished like a shadow, leaving his hands empty. The air resounded with the laughter of innumerable demons mocking him and saying, "*Whosoever exalteth himself shall be abased.*[17] You exalted yourself to heaven and have now been cast down to hell." Realizing he had made himself a laughingstock, the hermit fell into despair. He abandoned his cell and the desert, and returned to the world. Such was the fall that resulted from his pride!

Saint John counseled us never to lose heart, but to conquer the wicked spirits and cast them into despair by means of humble repentance. As proof he related this account:

A young man in the city was guilty of many sins, but one day the fear of God moved him to compunction and he ran to the local cemetery to lament his evil deeds. Throwing himself on the earth, he dared not pray or even pronounce God's name, for he considered himself unworthy to live. Instead, while still alive, he entombed himself among the dead, weeping and groaning from the bottom of his heart.

A week went by and some of the demons that had earlier incited him to sin appeared, shouting, "A curse on you, loathsome, impious fornicator! Now that you have had enough of our company you suddenly decide that chastity is preferable to carnal pleasures. Get up and follow us to your usual haunts, where whores and drunkards are waiting for you. Come and indulge yourself, for you have no hope of salvation. You have defiled yourself in every way possible and belong to us. Do not imagine that you will slip out of our hands."

---

[17]Luke, Ch. 14

Not answering a word, the youth continued to weep. Because they could not frighten him or drive him from the tomb by screeching the same things over and over again, the demons resorted to blows and would have killed him, had God permitted it. As it was, they left him half dead. When he came to himself a little, the young man resumed his lamentation. Having searched for him everywhere, his relatives finally found him in the cemetery. They begged him to return home, but he refused, saying it was better to die than to go back to his former way of life.

The following night the demons made another assault, shreaking the same things as before. On the third night came their final attempt to conquer the invincible youth. Repulsed again by his patience, they were forced to acknowledge defeat, and withdrew humiliated and shouting, "You have prevailed! You have vanquished us!" Humble repentance and manly patience had brought the demons to despair, and they never again made an open attack on the youth, who led the rest of his life in a God-pleasing manner. His example encouraged many desperate sinners to reform themselves by true repentance.

To show that pride deprives a man of the grace of God and casts him into the abyss, but humility wins divine compassion and exalts, the venerable John told this story as well:

There was a monk who had settled deep in the desert and practiced the virtues for many years. In old age, however, he was tested by the demons and nearly brought to perdition because of pride. This ascetic was particularly devoted to stillness. He spent his days in prayer, and was frequently vouchsafed divine revelations, sometimes while asleep, sometimes while awake. Indeed, his sleep was little and light, and hardly merited the name. So fervently did the anchorite strive to attain an incorporeal life, that he gave no thought to bodily sustenance. He neither tilled the earth, nor cultivated fruit trees; rather, he put all his trust in God from the day he abandoned the world. Dead to everything earthly, he was consumed by longing for God and eagerly awaited his departure to the Lord. His body remained healthy and his spirits high throughout his many years in the wilderness, because he was sustained by *things not seen*[18] and the hope of celestial blessings.

Having attained a sound and exalted inner state, the hermit was approaching angelic holiness while yet in the flesh. God rewarded him with a miraculous gift of bread every second or third day. When he was hungry, the anchorite would pray, then enter his cave and find a loaf of the whitest bread. After saying a prayer and eating, he would return to nourishing his soul by singing hymns, praying, and reflecting on God. Every day he achieved greater perfection in virtue and longed more fervently for eternal blessings.

Meanwhile, however, the ascetic arrived at complete certainty that the better portion was already in his grasp. Once this happened, defeat was certain. He began to think that he was superior to other men and enjoyed God's favor more than they. He also formed the opinion that his recompense in heaven would surpass what others had received and that it was impossible for him to fall. Shortly thereafter he began to feel a little dispirited, but so slightly he hardly realized it. Then he became slothful, and soon was in the grip of listlessness and despondency. Only with great difficulty could he rise from sleep and chant psalms, and he abbreviated his prayers. The thought insinuated itself: "It is time for a respite"; and he consented to the suggestion. His mind became distracted and admitted unseemly notions. For the time being, however, his former efforts kept him from surrendering altogether to laziness and distractions. Then one evening, entering the cave after his usual prayers, he found that the bread sent by God was not of the same quality as before. He ate and strengthened his body, but still entertained his unclean thoughts. He would not acknowledge that by nurturing them he was harming his soul, nor did he seek healing of his original wound; rather, he counted it a matter of small importance to give assent to sinful provocations and to take delight in them.

The next day the hermit prayed and chanted psalms, but with total lack of attention. At sunset he entered the cave for supper, only to find bread disgusting in appearance and taste.

---

[18]Heb., Ch. 11

Although surprised and dismayed, he forced himself to eat it, thereby restoring his strength.

On the third night temptation assailed the monk three times more powerfully than before. Obscene thoughts filled his mind and carnal desire so confused him that he imagined a woman was actually fornicating with him. At dawn the anchorite said his rule of prayer, although much distracted. That evening he entered the cave to eat, but found only a few dirty crusts scattered about and seemingly gnawed by mice or dogs. Seeing this, he groaned and wept, but did not humble his heart sufficiently to check the evil. After collecting the scraps, he made a meal of them and, still hungry, lay down to rest. Straightway, a cloud of vain and indecent thoughts enveloped him. The passions overcame his last, feeble resistance and, taking him prisoner, dragged him back toward the world. Lo, the straits to which he was reduced because of pride!

The solitary stumbled through the night, hoping to find a village. At daybreak he was still pushing forward, and before long the sun was mercilessly beating down on him. He was elderly, he had far to travel, and before long he was scanning the horizon for a monastery where he might find refreshment. Providence did guide him to a monastery, and the brethren received him with love and respect. After saying a prayer, they fed him, and when he had eaten his fill, they asked him to say an instructive word about how to escape the devil's snares and repel unchaste thoughts. Like a father instructing his children, the elder encouraged them to persevere with their ascetic labors and to remember that Christ would soon grant them repose.

Having edified the entire community by his discourse, the elder went off alone to rest. He began to reflect on how he had urged the brethren to struggle while fleeing from it himself, benefited their souls while ruining his own, and guided others on the path to salvation while hurrying to perdition. At last he understood that he had been led astray by sinful thoughts, and he hastened back to the uttermost parts of the desert. He bewailed his fall and repeated, "*Unless the Lord had brought me help, my soul had well nigh sojourned in Hades*:"[19] I would have

---

[19]Ps. 93

fallen into every wickedness." Thus the proverb was fulfilled which says, *A brother helped by a brother is a strong and high city; and is strengthened like a well-founded kingdom.*[20]

The elder stumbled back into his cave, fell to the floor, threw ashes on his head, and wept for days. Not until an angel assured him that his repentance had been accepted did he rise. Even though the anchorite's repentance was pleasing to Him, God no longer sent the elder bread. Having been humbled by pride, the desert-dweller was compelled for the rest of his life to provide his own food.

To the foregoing account the venerable John added this advice: "Be humble, children, in matters great and small. The Savior's first beatitude is: *Blessed are the poor in spirit: for theirs is the Kingdom of* heaven.[21] To be *poor in spirit* is to be humble. Only by humility can you avoid the deception of the evil spirits and the fantasies and specters they devise. Whenever someone arrives at the door—be it your brother, friend, wife, father, teacher, mother, or sister—first stretch forth your hands in prayer. If the person is a diabolic apparition, he will vanish. If either Satan or men praise you, do not exalt yourself. Pay no heed to flattery. Believe me, the devils often tried to lead me astray. They would appear at night and would not let me pray calmly or rest. At sunrise the demons would fall prostrate before me and say, 'Forgive us, Abba, for troubling you all night.' I would answer them, *'Depart from me all ye that work iniquity!*[22] You shall not tempt the Lord's servant.'

"Love stillness, children, and devote yourself to prayer and the remembrance of God, that the Lord may grant you a pure mind. The righteous man who lives in the world and performs good deeds is truly worthy of praise. He practices brotherly love, hospitality, and charity; he provides assistance to others and is always kindly. He fulfills the Lord's commandments and abides in virtue; notwithstanding, he is still concerned about worldly affairs. Better and greater is he whose mind ever cleaves to God, who has transcended the material and risen to the immaterial, leaving temporal concerns to others. Since he denies himself and has forgotten his own needs, such a person experi-

---

[20]Prov., Ch. 18   [21]Matt., Ch. 5   [22]Ps. 6; Matt., Ch. 7

ences heaven. He stands unimpeded in the presence of the Lord, no care drawing him back; he spends his life alone with God, honoring the Creator with ceaseless psalmody."

Speaking about himself as though about another, the elder continued, "I know someone living in the desert who for ten years ate no earthly food. Every third day an angel fed him the food and drink of heaven. Once, demons appeared to this man in the form of legions of angels. Their king sat in a chariot and was surrounded by many bodyguards. The king greeted the monk, 'Truly wondrous and virtuous is your life, O man! Worship me, and I will take you up to heaven like Elijah.'

"'Since I was a child I have worshipped the Lord Jesus Christ,' the monk thought. 'If this were Him, why would He demand adoration now?' Then he said to the devil, 'I worship God, my Master and King. You are no king to me.' At that very moment the demons vanished."

By his exhortations and angelic life the venerable John edified all who visited him. Having pleased God perfectly, he attained the age of ninety. Sensing his end, he told the brethren that they were not to leave for three days. On the third day they found him lying prostrate, as though praying; but his soul had gone to the Lord and was standing with the angels before the throne of God, one in Trinity: Father, Son, and Holy Spirit. To Him be glory forever. Amen.

The Twenty-Eighth Day of the Month of March

The Commemoration of Our Venerable Father Hilarion, the New Wonderworker and Abbot of the Monastery of Pelecete

The godly Hilarion took up the cross of monasticism at an early age. Following the Crucified One, he subdued his fleshly passions by abstinence and quickly became the most virtuous of the brethren in his community. Having led the quiet life of a recluse for many years and attained dispassion, he was deemed worthy of the priesthood and appointed abbot of the Monastery of Pelecete in Asia Minor, near the Hellespont.

Saint Hilarion worked many miracles. By a word he drove vermin out of wheat fields and vineyards; by prayer he ended a drought, soaking the earth with rain. Likewise, the Lord's favorite put a stop to a hailstorm, divided a river like the prophet Elisha, healed a man's withered hand, gave sight to a blind man, healed the lame, cast out demons, and filled the nets of fishermen who for a long time had caught nothing at all.

In the eighth ode of the canon to our saint, the venerable Joseph the Hymnographer calls Hilarion a martyr and says that the godly one was tortured for venerating the holy icon of the Saviour. Certain authorities say that this saint lived during the reign of the iconoclast Emperor Leo the Armenian; others date him much earlier, in the time of Leo the Isaurian and his son Copronymus. According to the latter (who are almost certainly correct), Lachanodracon, one of Copronymus' generals, appeared at the Monastery of Pelecete with a band of soldiers on Great and Holy Thursday. Shamelessly bursting into the altar during the divine services, he ordered the chanting halted and threw the holy, life-giving Mysteries of Christ to the floor.[1] Forty-two of the most revered monks were chained and led away to the utmost borders of the province of Ephesus,[2] where they were locked in an abandoned bathhouse and murdered. The rest of the brethren were tortured. After shredding apart the flesh of some, tarring the beards and faces of others and setting them afire, and cutting off the noses of still others, Lachanodracon torched the church and the other monastery buildings. Most likely it was at this time that the venerable Hilarion suffered, as superior of the brotherhood.

---

[1]Similar crimes committed by the iconoclasts are detailed in the Life of Saint Stephen the New, commemorated on November 28.
[2]Ephesus was the largest city of the Thracesion theme, one of the military divisions and territorial units of Asia Minor. At that time Michael Lachanodracon was *strategus* or commander of that theme. (Tr.)

On the Same Day

The Commemoration of Our Venerable Father Stephen the New, Abbot of the Monastery of Triglia

The godly Stephen, Christ's confessor, lived during the reign of the Emperor Leo the Armenian. He loved ascetic labors from an early age, acquired every virtue, and became abbot of the Monastery of Triglia, accepting this post at the earnest entreaty of all the brethren. His teaching persuaded many to lead a chaste, God-pleasing life.

At that time the godless Emperor Leo was defiling and destroying the holy icons and cruelly persecuting the Orthodox. Having summoned the Lord's favorite, Leo attempted to compel him to renounce holy images and to sign a document condemning them. This the saint refused to do; furthermore, he reviled the Emperor, calling him an impious foe of the true faith. The tyrant replied by torturing and exiling Saint Stephen. Ill-treatment and sickness claimed the body of the elder, but his soul was taken to heaven by Christ, for Whom he had undertaken innumerable feats of asceticism and endured many torments.

On the Same Day

The Life and Passion of Our Holy Monastic Father Eustratius, Faster and Martyr of the Kiev Caves[1]

Saint Eustratius, whose name means "good soldier," was a brave warrior and follower of Christ. Waging war beneath the ensign of the Cross, he endured the same death as did His Champion Leader and could therefore say in truth, *I bear in my body the marks of the Lord Jesus.*[2]

According to the testimony of the holy Bishop Simon, Christ's valiant soldier Eustratius was born in Kiev. Wishing to *put on the whole armour of God,*[3] that is, the monastic habit, and knowing that *no man that warreth entangleth himself with the affairs of this life, that he may please his commander,*[4] he distributed almost all his property to those in need. The small portion that remained he entrusted to his relatives, with instructions to give it away after his death. Once rich, he became poor, taking the schema in the Monastery of the Kiev Caves and contending valorously beneath the standard of Christ his Lord and Master, Who impoverished Himself for our sake. The saint meditated constantly on how Jesus, the Setter of the contest, prayed fervently, fasted forty days, humbled Himself, and was obedient to the Father. This brought him to understand the might of prayer (that sword of the spirit) and of strict fasting, humility, and obedience. Armed with these, he subdued both his flesh and the bodiless foes. He knew that gluttony caused the first defeat of our race; therefore, he regarded abstinence as the foundation of every virtue. So much did he curb the desires of the stomach that he became known to all as "the Faster."

In those days God permitted the Cumans, led by their impious Khan Bonyak, to devastate the Russian land. A large force of pagans attacked the Monastery of the Caves, putting some of the brethren to the sword and capturing others, including the blessed one. The barbarians took Eustratius to Cherson, a pos-

---

[1]From *The Kiev Caves Patericon*
[2]Gal., Ch.6   [3]Eph., Ch.6   [4]II Tim., Ch.4

session of the Greek Empire, and sold him to a Jew, who also purchased fifty other Christian prisoners. Thirty of these were workers from the monastery, twenty were citizens of Kiev. When the God-hating Jew threatened to chain and starve his slaves if they refused to renounce Christ, the brave monk Eustratius exhorted his fellow-captives, "Brethren, you believe in Christ and have been baptized, and must never violate the promises you made before entering the font. Christ begat us by water and the Spirit; Christ redeemed us from the curse of the Law by His blood and made us heirs of His Kingdom. If we live, we live unto the Lord; if we die, let us die for the Lord, and by temporal death gain eternal life. Let us emulate him who said, *For me to live is Christ, and to die is gain.*"[5]

Strengthened by the blessed one's exhortation, the prisoners chose to die of hunger and thirst rather than be separated from Christ, Who is the Bread and Fountain of life everlasting. Soon all fifty had perished, some after three days without food and water, others after four, others after seven, the strongest after ten. Only Eustratius remained alive and strong after fourteen days of thirst and starvation, because he had trained himself in fasting from a young age.

Seeing that all the money he had spent on the captives was wasted because of the monk's teaching, the wretched Jew decided to avenge himself. The day of Christ's Resurrection drew near and he celebrated Passover by reviling Saint Eustratius as his God-slaying forefathers had reviled Jesus Christ, according to the Gospel. As they crucified our Lord, so the miserable Jew and his friends nailed the saint to a cross. While hanging upon the tree, the blessed one thanked God for giving him the strength to survive fifteen days without food or drink, but the Jew and his companions mocked him, saying, "Fool! Taste the Passover of the Law and you shall live and escape the curse. For Moses received the Law from God and gave it to us, and in one of his books it is written: *Everyone that is hanged on a tree is cursed.*"[6]

Eustratius replied, "The Lord has been most gracious to me today, because He has deemed me worthy to suffer for His

---

[5] Phil., Ch.1   [6]Deut. Ch. 21; Gal., Ch.3

name's sake on a cross as He did. May He speak to me the words He spoke to the thief: *Today shalt thou be with Me in paradise.*[7] I do not want your Passover food, and I do not fear the curse, *for even Christ our Passover is sacrificed for us.*[8] He Who is the Life of all abolished death, the curse of the Law, which came from a tree, and by the wood of the Tree on which He was hung He bestowed on us the blessing of life. This is why Moses prophesied, *Thy Life shall be suspended before thine eyes.*[9] Regarding our holy Pascha, David said, *This is the day which the Lord hath made; let us rejoice and be glad therein;*[10] but the Most High hates your sabbaths and has *turned your feasts into mourning.*[11] You, my crucifier, and your Jewish friends shall weep and lament today, because the man who urged you to commit this crime is near to death. Moreover, God will quickly requite you for murdering me and the other Christian slaves."

Hearing this, the Jew was roused to fury and ran a spear through the crucified monk. Christ's champion and trophy-bearer Eustratius met his blessed end, and a flaming chariot pulled by fiery steeds descended and took his joyous soul to heaven. At the same time a voice was heard, saying in Greek, "Behold, the good citizen of the celestial realm!"

The hardhearted Jew removed Saint Eustratius' holy body from the cross and cast it into the sea, where it worked many miracles. At first the faithful could not find the incorrupt relics, but eventually they were discovered in a cave, where they remain to this day, working wonders.

On the very day of his death, the holy sufferer's prophecies were fulfilled. A decree arrived from the Greek Emperor commanding that all Jews be expelled from his domains and their property seized. The Jewish elders were singled out for the harshest punishment as accomplices in the murder of Christians. In accordance with the word of the blessed Eustratius, the first to suffer was the Eparch, who instigated the Jewish atrocities. Once a wealthy, respected Jew, he was baptized and shortly thereafter appointed prefect by the Emperor, who wished to honor him. After attaining this position, he secretly rejected

---

[7]Luke, Ch. 23   [8]I Cor., Ch. 5   [9]Deut. Ch. 28
[10]Ps. 117   [11]Amos, Ch. 8

Christ and His faith and encouraged the Jews living in the Greek Empire to purchase Christian slaves and force them to convert. At last his wicked doings became known, and the Emperor ordered the Jews banished from the realm and the impious Prefect executed.

While the other Jews of Cherson were paying the penalty for their crimes, the contemptible murderer of godly Eustratius was put to death by being hung from a tree. In this way the knave's *toil* returned *upon his own head*,[12] and he inherited a portion with Judas.

The godly one's death was followed by awesome miracles, and many Jews believed in the truth and were baptized. As for the valiant soldier and trophybearer Saint Eustratius, who subjected them to Christ's rule, he reigns forevermore with the Conqueror of death. Standing amid the ranks of the immortal armies of heaven, he chants a song of victory, praising and thanking Christ the Lord, His unoriginate Father, and His life-creating Spirit. Amen.

---

[12]Ps. 7

On the Same Day

The Story of Taxiotes the Soldier, Who Rose from the Dead[1]

$\mathcal{I}$n the African city of Carthage, there once lived a soldier named Taxiotes. This man was a shameless sinner, but when plague struck the city, he was overcome by fear and compunction. With his wife, he left Carthage and settled in a village, where he repented of his sins and led a quiet life.

Some time passed and Taxiotes again heeded the beckoning hand of the devil. He committed adultery with the wife of his neighbor, a peasant, and several days later died in agony from a snakebite.

Taxiotes' wife went to a monastery half a mile from the village and asked that the brethren take her husband's body and entomb it in their church. The monks buried the corpse at the third hour of the day, but at the ninth hour they heard a voice from the sepulcher, crying, "Have mercy! Have mercy on me!" Opening the grave and finding the dead man alive, they were astonished and terrified. They implored him to tell them what had happened to him and how he had returned to life, but he could only weep and wail and beg that he be taken to God's servant, Bishop Tarasius. The monks fulfilled his request, and for three days the Bishop urged Taxiotes to describe what he had seen. Finally, on the fourth day, still hardly able to speak for his bitter tears, Taxiotes related:

"When I was dying, I saw dreadful Ethiopians standing before me, and my soul was gripped by fear. I also saw two very handsome youths. My soul rushed into their hands and began rising into the air. Ascending to heaven, it was blocked by the tollhouses, where the souls of all men are detained. At each tollhouse souls are interrogated about a different sin: lying at one, jealousy at another, pride at another. There are special toll collectors for every transgression. The angels were holding a vessel containing all my good deeds, which they used to offset my iniquities and enable me to pass by the tollhouses. Near the gates of

---

[1]From *The Prologue*

heaven, we reached the tollhouse of fornication, where the toll collectors detained me and produced a record of all the sins of the flesh I had committed since childhood. My angelic guide informed me, 'God has forgiven all the carnal sins you committed while living in the city, because you repented of them.'

"'But after leaving the city, you committed adultery in the village with the peasant's wife,' said my enemies.

"The angels looked to see whether any good deed remained to outweigh the transgression, but the vessel was empty, so they abandoned me. Then the evil spirits laid hold of me and, thrashing me cruelly, dragged me downward. The earth split apart and the devils led me through the foul-smelling cracks to the nethermost dungeons of hell, where the souls of sinners are confined in eternal darkness. Existence there cannot be called life, for it consists of nothing but unending torment, inconsolable weeping, horrible gnashing of teeth, and constant lamentation. It is impossible to describe or enumerate all the tortures and sufferings I saw there. Hades' captives moan piteously, but no mercy is shown them; they mourn, but no one consoles them; they beg to be rescued, but there is none to hear or deliver them. I was abandoned with them in the black holds to grieve and weep bitterly from the third hour of the day until the ninth. Then I noticed a gleam of light, and the two angels approached me. I begged them to rescue me from that miserable place so that I could repent, but they told me, 'Your prayers are useless now. No one leaves these confines until the Common Resurrection.'

"Since, however, I continued to implore them and promise repentance, one angel asked the other, 'This man vows to repent with his whole heart. Are you willing to be his guarantor?'

"'I am,' said the second angel to the first; and they shook hands. Then the angels took my soul back to the grave and commanded it, 'Reenter the body in which you sinned. You cannot repent without it.' At that moment I realized that my soul was glowing like a pearl; but my corpse stank and was black as dirt. Horrified, I pleaded not to be returned to this life. 'Either go back into the body or go back to hell!' the angels threatened. Straightway my soul reentered my flesh and I began crying, 'Have mercy on me!'"

Despite the Bishop's urging, Taxiotes would not eat. Instead, he went from church to church, making prostrations and with tears and sighs confessing to God his iniquities. He told everyone, "Woe to sinners: eternal torments await them! Woe to those who fail to repent while they still have time. Woe to those who defile their flesh!"

Taxiotes lived forty days after returning from the grave, during which time he cleansed himself by repentance. Three days after Heaven apprised him of the hour when he would die a second time, he departed to the compassionate God, Who loves mankind, Who casts men down to Hades and leads them up again, and Who grants salvation to all. Unto Him be glory forever. Amen.

❦❦❦

On this same day we commemorate the holy martyrs Jonah and Barachesius.

The Twenty-Ninth Day of the Month of March

The Passion of
Our Venerable Father Mark,
Bishop of Arethusa,
Cyril the Deacon, and Many Others[1]

$\mathcal{I}$n his first oration against God's vile enemy, Julian the Apostate, Gregory the Theologian writes the following things about the passion of the venerable Mark:

"Who has not heard what happened to the wondrous Mark of Arethusa? Who does not recall the story of his sufferings? Using the benefits which the Christian enjoyed during the reign of Constantine the Great, Mark destroyed a heathen temple and guided many from pagan delusion to the straight path of salvation, as much by the example of his irreproachable life as by his edifying discourses. For a long time the demon-worshippers of Arethusa nurtured enmity toward the saint. When power passed from the Christians back to the Hellenes, impiety flared up and the persecutors attacked the man of God. For when they are permitted, coals kept alive in an oven burst into flames, and a river that is dammed surges forth; likewise, the unbelievers, having restrained their fury for a time, at first opportunity manifested their wrath.

"Immediately he understood the idolaters were about to take revenge, Saint Mark fled, less out of fear than out of obedience to the commandment of the Lord, Who tells us, *When they persecute you in this city, flee ye to another.*[2] However brave and steadfast they

---

[1]From Saint Gregory of Nazianzus, and Theodoretus
[2]Matt., Ch. 10

may be, Christians should not think solely of their own salvation. They should avoid their persecutors and not give them occasion for greater sin. Soon, however, the blessed one learned that because he had escaped and saved himself, many were being seized and dragged to torture, which not all could endure. Therefore, he considered the matter well and returned, voluntarily surrendering himself to the tender mercies of the crowd. He armed his soul for battle since he knew the pagans were capable of any cruelty: boundless was their ingenuity for devising torments. Every one of them was planning his own special torture.

"The saint's fortitude enraged the heathen, and they considered his return less a display of courage than of disdain for them. They dragged the elderly hierarch and voluntary martyr through the city where, on account of his advanced age and, still more, his virtuous life, he enjoyed the respect of all, except his persecutors and tormentors. The mob included men and women, young and old, civic officials and renowned nobles: persons of every age and rank. All were in a fury, all shared the single aspiration of excelling one another in brutality. All considered it a great thing to punish the courageous elder viciously; all were determined to vanquish the athlete who dared contend against them all. The older repeatedly shoved the Lord's favorite into the mud, and the younger mocked him, pulled out his beard, and tore at his flesh. They drove him to the place where criminals were executed; they suspended him and jabbed his body with knives and a sharpened reed. It was a spectacle worthy of tears, but the idolaters thought it was hilarious. They pierced the confessor's shins with metal shards, reaching the very bone, and cut off his ears with fine linen thread. Then they ripped off his clothes, smeared him with honey and lard, and hoisted him in a basket to bake in the midday heat and be stung by bees and wasps. As the sun softened the lard, the bees and wasps attacked the saint's martyric flesh ever more viciously. The sufferer, though old, had all the vigor of youth. His face remained radiant throughout the ordeal; indeed, he experienced a certain delight as he was being tormented. He ridiculed the persecutors and said he felt no pain as he looked down on them from on high. It seemed that another was being afflicted in his body and that he considered the abuse to be proof of God's favor, and not a misfortune.

"The torture was so brutal that anyone who had the least

kindness or human feeling should have tried to stop it. But some of the onlookers feared the saint's tormentors, others the wrath of the Emperor, who had ordered the governors and townships to suppress the Christians. At the time, however, the tyrant's treachery was still not widely known, and many who would later oppose Julian still favored him.

"Saint Mark had not given a single piece of gold to the heathen to pay for having destroyed their temple, and when all was said and done, this was why he was suffering. The Arethusans had demanded that he either pay in full an outrageous price or build them a new temple, but the saint refused, more out of piety than because he did not have the money. As he remained firm, they dropped the price until finally they were asking a mere token sum, which he could have paid easily. They continued to press him, but he would not give them a single penny, even though onlookers were offering him large amounts of money, some out of compassion, others because they admired his invincible courage. From this it is clear that he embraced martyrdom not because he was greedy, but because he loved piety.

"Mark was one of the Christians who hid Julian when the godless Emperor was a youth and his loathsome family was wiped out. Justice, it would seem, demanded that the saint undergo these cruel sufferings as punishment for his act of mercy, although there was no way Mark could have known that his kindness would result in disaster for the whole world.

"Word has it that the Eparch of Arethusa, though an ungodly pagan, was discomfited by the sight of Mark's sufferings. 'O Emperor, we have been put to shame before the Christians,' he fearlessly and forthrightly reported to Julian. 'We could not best a single old man, although we used every cruelty against him. Had we prevailed, it would have been a victory without honor; but the defeat was utter humiliation for us.' Thus did Christian courage bring low the proud Emperor and his prefects.

"In cruelty the Arethusans surpassed Echetus[3] and Phalaris;[4]

---

[3]A king of Epirus who blinded his own daughter, imprisoned her, and forced her to grind grains of bronze. (Tr.)

[4]Ruler of Akragas (now Agrigento) in Sicily, who burned alive his victims in a brazen bull. He made the first experiment of it on its inventor, Perillus. Like Echetus, Phalaris was proverbial for his cruelty. (Tr.)

in malice they equaled the devil himself, the inventor and teacher of every form of wickedness."

Theodoretus writes that the Arethusans finally ceased to rage against the wondrous elder when they saw that his resolve was unshakeable.[5] Astounded by his patience, they untied him and set him free. Afterwards, Saint Mark instructed them in the holy faith, and they became Christians.

As regards the deacon Cyril, Theodoretus writes this: "Who can recount without weeping the crimes committed in Phoenicia by the heathen? In Heliopolis, at the foot of Anti-Libanus, the contemptible pagans remembered that during the reign of Constantine, Deacon Cyril, burning with zeal, had shattered many of the most revered idols of the city. After killing him, they slit open his belly and savagely gnawed his entrails. This could not be hid from the omniscient God, Who punished them in a manner befitting their wickedness. First, the transgressors lost their teeth, one by one. Then their tongues festered, putrefied, and dropped out of their mouths. Last of all, they went blind. By means of these penalties, the power of the true faith was made manifest."

In Ascalon and Gaza, cities of Palestine, the inhuman persecutors disemboweled men in priestly rank, and women and virgins consecrated to God, then filled the bodies with barley and fed them to swine. As a reward for their suffering, the holy martyrs were crowned with garlands in the Kingdom; while the torturers were consigned by the Lord Jesus Christ to unending misery in hell. Unto our true God be glory forever. Amen.

On this same day we commemorate our holy monastic father John the Desert-dweller, who lived in a dry well for ten years.

On this same day we commemorate our venerable father Eustratius the Confessor, a bishop of Bithynia,[6] who was beaten harshly by the iconoclasts and died in exile.

[5]Theodoritus, Bk. 3, Ch. 6   [6]His see was Keaia. (Tr.)

The Thirtieth Day
of the Month of March

The Life of
Our Holy Monastic Father
John of the Ladder[1]

"J cannot say for certain in what country or city the daunt-less ascetic Saint John was born and reared," writes Daniel the monk, author of his Life. "But now he has completed the course of continence, and I do know what place shelters him at present, feeding him celestial ambrosia. That amazing, divine man is surely in the land of which the most eloquent, renowned, and holy Paul speaks, crying, *Our conversation is in heaven.*[2] There he ceaselessly delights in the indescribable sweetness of inexhaustible, immaterial blessings. He enjoys a reward earned by sweat, honor won by afflictions; he has inherited the Kingdom with those whose feet have *stood in uprightness.*[3] Hearken, and I will tell how he labored to attain that immaterial blessedness while in a material body.

"By the time our saint reached the age of sixteen, he had attained such wisdom as most men would fail to achieve were they to live a thousand years. Offering himself as a blameless, well-pleasing sacrifice to God, the Great High Priest, he took up his abode in the body on Mount Sinai and ascended in spirit to

---

[1]Compiled from accounts written by Daniel, monk of Raithu, and Synchronius, monk of Sinai
[2]Phil., Ch. 3   [3]Ps. 25

the heights of heaven. The loftiness of the peak impelled him to the celestial realm and the noetic vision of the immaterial God. Having renounced the world, he embraced meekness, that virtue resplendent with humility, that teacher of every form of moral excellence, that mother of noetic maidens.[4] From the very onset of his monastic training he cut off pride, and with it, idle talk and argumentativeness. By extreme sobriety he put to flight those crafty frauds, self-confidence and self-love. Being in obedience to an experienced spiritual guide, he crossed unharmed the perilous sea of the passions. Dead to the world, he conducted himself as though he were the least of the brethren; as though he were a babe that cannot speak or bring to pass its will. Indeed, it seemed that his soul was actually devoid of reason, volition, and its other natural properties. But what is most remarkable is that although he was well acquainted with secular learning, he fully repudiated the haughtiness that often accompanies it, and instead clung to heavenly simplicity and humility."

According to Synchronius the monk, the venerable John was tonsured at the age of twenty by his elder and teacher, Abba Martyrius. On the day the godly one was clothed in the schema, Abba Strategius foretold that he would become a brilliant luminary for the whole world.

Once Martyrius, accompanied by his disciple John, visited Anastasius the Great of Sinai. Saint Anastasius studied John for a few moments, then asked Martyrius, "Tell me, abba: who is this boy and who tonsured him?"

"He is your servant, Father," replied Martyrius. "I tonsured him."

Anastasius marveled and exclaimed, "It is the abbot of Mount Sinai you have tonsured, Abba Martyrius!"

On another occasion the blessed Martyrius took John to see the renowned elder John the Sabbaite, who was living in the wilderness of Gudda. As soon as the elder saw Martyrius and young John, he rose, poured water on our saint's feet, and kissed his hands; but he did not wash Martyrius' feet. After-

---

[4]Noetic maidens are the virtues that proceed from humility, and also divine thoughts. (Tr.)

wards, Stephen, disciple of Abba John the Sabbaite, asked his elder why he had done that. The old man answered, "Believe me, child, I do not know who the young monk is, but it was the abbot of Mount Sinai that I received and his feet that I washed." In time the words of Abba Strategius and Abba John the Sabbaite were fulfilled.

After he had lived nineteen years with his spiritual father, the venerable John was orphaned. The blessed Martyrius reposed in the Lord and (as Daniel the monk writes) was sent off by his disciple to intercede with the King of heaven for those on earth. Armed with his father's prayers (a weapon effectual for *the pulling down of strongholds*),[5] John went to a solitary place called Thola, half a mile from the monastery church. He spent forty years there, burning with the fire of divine love, yet never being consumed. It is impossible to tell all the labors performed at Thola by the saint, for he lived alone; nevertheless, the little that is known reveals the extraordinary virtue of this holy man. He ate everything permitted by the monastic vow, but in extremely small quantity. By eating all foods, he wisely crushed the horn of pride; by eating very little, he subdued gluttony, the mistress and mother of corporal passions. *Peace, be still,*[6] he commanded his belly as he consumed his meager fare. Solitude and long separation from human society enabled him to quench the furnace of carnal lusts. Covetousness, which is idolatry,[7] according to the holy Apostle Paul, he avoided by almsgiving and depriving himself of even the most basic necessities. Constantly remembering physical death, he spurred himself to rise from that paralysis and death of the soul which is idleness, and to awaken to watchfulness and toil. His tears dissolved the entangling net of attachment to things perceived by the senses. He had already, in his first years as a monk, slain the passion of anger with the sword of obedience. Because he rarely visited anyone, and still more rarely spoke, he easily crushed the leech of vainglory. And how, I wonder, can I find words fitting to praise his victory over pride?

---

[5]II Cor., Ch. 10   [6]Mark, Ch. 4   [7]Eph., Ch. 5

Or how can I describe the supreme purity of heart attained by this new Bezaleel?[8] His work began with obedience, but was completed by the Lord Himself, King of the celestial Jerusalem, without Whose help the devil and his army cannot be put to flight.

As I weave this garland of praise (continues Daniel), I wonder when best to extol the saint's fountain of tears. Few are they in whom such a spring wells up. To this day the retreat where he wept abundant streams is well known. It is a small cave hidden in the desert at the foot of a mountain, far enough from his and every other cell so that the sound of lamentation could not be heard by the brethren and there could be no inducement to vainglory. Saint John often retired to that cave, making it near to heaven by his cries to God, which rent the air like the shrieks of those who are run through by swords or burned with hot iron, or whose eyes are torn out. He slept just enough to avoid losing his mind. Before sleeping he prayed much and wrote books, and the title of one of these, *The Ladder*, became the appellation by which he would be known. Writing was his sole means of driving away despondency. His whole life consisted of unceasing prayer and insatiable longing for God. Day and night he noetically gazed upon the Lord's countenance in that brilliant mirror, purity of soul, but could never have enough of the wondrous vision.

A monk named Moses hoped to imitate the virtuous life of the godly John and learn true wisdom from him. He had others intercede on his behalf with the holy elder, who was persuaded to accept Moses as a disciple. One day, the great father ordered Moses to fetch manure and fertilize the garden. Moses was diligently carrying out the task and by noon was exhausted, since it was August, when the heat in the desert is blistering. Lying in the shade of an enormous rock, he fell asleep and thereby unwittingly put himself in jeopardy of imminent death. He was saved only because the Lord is compassionate and does not wish to grieve His servants in any way.

---

[8]Ex., Ch. 31. Bezeleel was a skillful craftsman whom *the Lord filled with a divine spirit of wisdom, and understanding, and knowledge, and all manner of workmanship.* The Old Testament Bezaleel directed construction of Moses' Tabernacle, but the "new Bezaleel," St. John of the Ladder, skillfully built the tabernacle of his soul. (Tr.)

The godly one was sitting in his cell, engaged in mental prayer, when he fell into a light sleep and a saint appeared to him. The holy man rebuked him thus: "How can you slumber heedlessly, John, when Moses is in peril?"

Rising at once, John took up the weapon of fervent prayer in defense of his disciple. Later, in the evening, when Moses returned, the elder asked him, "Did anything unexpected happen? Did any misfortune occur?"

"I was sleeping beneath a huge rock, and it would have crushed me, had I not woken when you called me. I fled just before it fell," related the disciple. Because he was truly humble, John did not mention the dream, but in his heart he sang a hymn of thanksgiving to our benevolent God.

The venerable one provided all an example of virtue and was a healer of invisible wounds. For example, a brother named Isaacius was violently oppressed by the demon of fornication and was falling into despondency. He made haste to the great father and, weeping and lamenting, confessed his warfare. Saint John told him, "Friend, this calls for ardent entreaty to the Lord." No sooner had His favorite prayed than the Master responded, proving true David's words: *The will of them that fear Him shall He do, and their supplication shall He hear.*[9] Isaacius had not yet risen from the ground when the serpent of fornication slithered away, covered with grievous wounds inflicted by John's supplication. Realizing that the passion had waned and all was well with him, the sufferer was amazed. He glorified God, Who had glorified His servant, and he thanked the venerable John.

Certain people, wounded by jealousy, called Saint John a garrulous deceiver. Not with mere words, but by silence the teacher showed that he could *do all things through Christ Which strengtheneth*[10] all. For a whole year he said nothing whatsoever. Finally, his detractors became his supplicants and admitted, "We have stopped the mighty fountain of edification, to the detriment of everyone's salvation. May the divinely eloquent lips speak again!" Yielding to their pleas, the hater of disputes resumed instructing the brethren.

---

[9] Ps. 144   [10] Phil., Ch. 4

So amazed were the monks at the achievements of the new Moses that they forced him to become abbot of the coenobium, thereby placing the brilliant light upon the candlestand of governance. Having become hegumen of Sinai against his will, John spiritually attained the peak of the mountain of God. Through contemplation he pierced the impenetrable darkness of God's unknowability and climbed the noetic steps of the celestial ladder. The divine law was traced by the Lord's finger on the tablets of his heart. He *opened* his mouth and received the word of God; he *drew in breath*[11] and *poured forth*[12] excellent discourse.

It was forty years after he embraced the monastic life that John became abbot of Mount Sinai. Not many days after his installment (as Synchronius relates), six hundred pilgrims visited the monastery. While they were being fed, a young man dressed in a Jewish tunic was seen, ordering about the provosts, stewards, cooks, and those setting out food and drink. When the pilgrims had finished their meal, the monks who had prepared and served it ate. In the meantime, the others searched everywhere for the man who was issuing orders, but they could not find him. Seeing this, God's servant, our venerable father John, commanded, "Enough! Is it any wonder that the holy prophet and lawgiver Moses was ministering in this place that belongs to him?"

Once there was a terrible drought in the region and the people begged Saint John to pray for rain. When he did so, a downpour quickly followed, soaking the parched earth and rendering it fruitful.

Before he departed from this temporal life, the man of God assembled the spiritual Israelites—the monks of Sinai—and addressed them a last time, as Moses did the Hebrews before his death. In one thing only was he unlike Moses: John attained the *Jerusalem which is above*,[13] whereas Moses for some reason failed to reach even the Jerusalem below.

Saint John's holiness is affirmed by many (writes Daniel the monk), especially by those who have been saved through his divinely inspired counsels and those who even now are being

---

[11]Ps. 118   [12]Ps. 44   [13]Gal., Ch. 4

saved. His admirers include the young David,[14] an illustrious man and inheritor of John's wisdom, and our good pastor John, the holy abbot of Raithu. It was he who persuaded the new God-seer, Saint John of the Ladder, to descend from Mount Sinai with tablets inscribed by God, namely, his book *The Ladder*, which outwardly contains directions for the ascetic life, and inwardly guides us to divine vision.

John of the Ladder had a brother according to the flesh, Abba George, whom he appointed his successor as hegumen of Sinai. Shortly before the saint departed this life, his brother lamented to him, "My lord, you are abandoning me! I had prayed that you would send me to God before you died, because I cannot shepherd this holy flock without your help. Now I see that it is I who shall have to bury you."

"Do not weep or worry. If I obtain favor with the Lord, I shall beg His permission to come back for you," the saint assured Abba George. The blessed one fulfilled his promise, and ten months after John's repose, George also departed to God. Now he stands with his holy brother, the venerable John, in the glory of the saints, praising the Father, Son, and Holy Spirit unto the ages. Amen.

¿▲¿▲¿▲

On this same day we commemorate the holy prophet Joad, who was killed by a lion. His death is recounted in the thirteenth chapter of the Third Book of Kings.

On this day we commemorate our venerable father Zosimas, Bishop of Syracuse, and Saint Eubula, mother of Saint Panteleimon.

On this day we commemorate a certain monk who never judged anyone. Saint Anastasius of Sinai relates this concerning him:

"A certain monk wasted his whole life in heedlessness and idleness. Then he fell gravely ill and his end drew near, but he showed no fear of death. Instead, he was merry, and prepared for his departure from the body by joyfully praising and thank-

---

[14]The identity of this person is unknown. (Tr.)

ing God. Gathering at his bedside, the abbot and the other monks said to him, 'Brother, we are witnesses to your inattentive life. How is it that you are so calm and happy now, when the dread hour is at hand? May our Lord Jesus Christ strengthen you, so that you can rise and explain this mystery, and we may glorify God's greatness.'

"Lifting himself a little, the monk replied, 'Reverend fathers, what you say is true. I have thoughtlessly squandered the days of my life, and a moment ago God's angels appeared to me and read a list of all my evil deeds. "Do you admit to this?" they asked. "Everything is true," I conceded, "but you must take into account that since I renounced the world and was tonsured, I have judged no one and held no grudges. Christ said, *Judge not, that ye be not judged*,[15] and, *If ye forgive men their trespasses, your heavenly Father will also forgive you*.[16] I pray that these passages be applied in my case." No sooner had I spoken these words than the angels tore to pieces the scroll on which my transgressions were recorded. Now you know why I am pleased to be leaving the temporal realm.' With this, the brother peacefully surrendered his soul into the Lord's hands."

---

[15]Matt., Ch. 7   [16]Matt., Ch. 6

The Thirty-First Day of the Month of March

The Commemoration of the Holy Hieromartyr Hypatius the Wonderworker, Bishop of Gangra

God's renowned favorite, Saint Hypatius, Bishop of Gangra in Cappadocia,[1] was one of the 318 holy fathers present at the First Ecumenical Council held at Nicaea during the reign of Constantine the Great. Like the other fathers of the council, Hypatius was filled with zeal for piety by the Holy Spirit and condemned Arius as a heretic, anathematizing him.

God bestowed upon Saint Hypatius the ability to work awesome miracles. The holy Bishop healed every illness and expelled demons from their victims. In a certain village he turned sweet a stream of bitter water running down from the mountains. In another place he bestowed a healing virtue upon hot springs. Once, on a dark night, burning candles suddenly emerged from a river beside which he was walking. They lit his path and prevented him from stumbling into the water.[2] Hypatius also destroyed a fearsome serpent. During the reign of Constantius, son and successor of the great Constantine, the

---

[1]Actually, in Paphlagonia (Tr.)
[2]The third sticheron for Vespers

enormous reptile appeared in the imperial palace, blocking entrance to the room where the Emperor kept his gold and treasures. Knowing the saint's reputation for working miracles in the name of Christ, the horror-stricken ruler wrote to God's hierarch, begging him to come without delay to the Imperial City. Upon arriving in Constantinople, Hypatius was met by the Emperor, who made a prostration before him and took him to the palace. When Constantius lamented that no human power could prevail against the serpent, and that many of the clergy had been hurt trying to drive the monster away by prayer, the saint assured him, "Even if my entreaties achieve nothing, your faith will prove acceptable to God." Hypatius fell to his knees and for a long time begged the Lord for help. Then he rose and told the Emperor, "Prepare a furnace in the Hippodrome, next to the statue of your father. It must be burning fiercely when I arrive there."

Hypatius proceeded to the Emperor's quarters and, battering the serpent with his hierarchal staff, forced his way into the treasure-chamber. The Emperor and a large crowd stood afar off, waiting apprehensively. Hours passed, evening was falling, and neither saint nor serpent emerged. The people thought that the snake had wounded the saint, as it had the priests, but within the room Hypatius, with eyes uplifted to heaven, was calling upon the Lord for assistance. After ending his lengthy prayer, he thrust his staff into the mouth of the serpent and commanded, "In the name of the Lord Jesus Christ, follow me!" The serpent's fangs caught fast in the stave, and it slithered behind Hypatius as though it were a prisoner in shackles; for indeed, the great wonderworker had fettered it by the power of God.

The blessed one led the serpent out of the palace, through the market, and into the Hippodrome. Seeing the horrible creature clinging to the staff, the onlookers were amazed and terrified, for the reptile was ninety feet long. As the Lord's favorite neared the blazing furnace, he shouted, "I command you in the name of Christ, Whom I, the chief among sinners, preach: destroy yourself in fire!" The monster threw itself into the flames and was consumed, and the astonished onlookers glorified God for revealing to the world in their time the mighty luminary and wonderworker Hypatius. The Emperor Constantius was the most thankful of all to God and the saint. Afterwards, he revered the Lord's favorite as his father and had Hypatius' face painted on a panel. He put this portrait in the treasury-room in order to repel the demonic powers. After rewarding the saint with gifts and embracing him affectionately, the ruler bade him warm farewell.

While the saint was traveling back to his see, wicked Novatian heretics,[3] burning with envy toward God's hierarch and armed with swords and cudgels, set an ambush where the road wound under a cliff and through a swamp. Jumping out like wild animals, they beat Hypatius to a pulp and threw him over the edge of the road into the morass. As his life-blood was ebbing, the saint raised his hand slightly, lifted his eyes to heaven and, like the holy protomartyr Stephen, prayed for his assaulters. He was uttering his last words, *Lord, lay not this sin to their charge*,[4] when a wench deceived by the Arian heresy crushed his head with a large rock. Freed from the bonds of the flesh, the martyr's soul flew up to God, but his body was hidden in a barn by the murderers.

God straightway avenged the innocent blood. The woman who shattered Hypatius' skull fell under the power of an unclean spirit. The devil forced her to beat her breast unceasingly with the very stone she used to commit the murder. The other evildoers fled, but demons gained possession of them as well and tortured them cruelly.

Shortly afterwards, the peasant who owned the barn went there for straw, knowing nothing about the murder. He was amazed to hear angels chanting, and even more amazed when, under the straw, he uncovered the mutilated remains of his bishop, Saint Hypatius. He ran to the village and told the other peasants, and they sent report to Gangra. Lamenting bitterly, the townsfolk removed the honored body of their holy father and pastor and took it to burial. The murderess followed the procession, openly confessing her sin and still beating her breast

---

[3]Novatianism was a rigorist sect that denied the forgiveness of serious sin, especially apostasy, after Baptism. (Tr.)
[4]Acts, Ch. 7

with the same rock. As the sacred remains were being committed to the earth, the woman was freed from demonic possession. Her accomplices were also healed at the grave of the martyr, who even after death proved himself free from malice and eager to do good to his enemies. From his sepulcher Saint Hypatius continued to work miracles, by his holy prayers curing many who venerated his relics with faith.

On the Same Day

The Repose of
Our Father Among the Saints Jonah, Metropolitan of Kiev and All Russia, the New Wonderworker[1]

Saint Jonah was the son of a devout man named Theodore and was born in the town of Galich, near the borders of the Khanate of Kazan. At the age of twelve he was tonsured in a monastery near Galich. Later, he took up his dwelling in the Moscow Simonov Monastery, remaining there for many years and laboring at every obedience.

In those days Photius was Metropolitan of Kiev and All Russia and lived in Moscow. Once, he visited the Simonov Monastery, celebrated a Service of Supplication in the Church of the Most Holy Theotokos, and bestowed his blessing on the archimandrite and each of the brethren present. Then he went to see the monks who were at their labors and bless them also. Entering the bakery, he found Jonah, who had fallen asleep after a hard day's work. The Metropolitan forbade the brethren to wake him, and he blessed Jonah as he slept. Seeing that the fingers of our saint's right hand were positioned as if he were bestowing a blessing, the Metropolitan foretold, "This monk will become a renowned hierarch of the Russian lands and guide many to the path of salvation." A few years later the prophecy was fulfilled. By the will of God and with the consent of the Great Prince, an episcopal council elected Jonah Bishop of Ryazan and Murom. While ruling this diocese, the saint converted and baptized many heathen.

Six years after the blessed Metropolitan Photius reposed in the Lord, Great Prince Basil Vasilievich convened a council of Russian hierarchs and ordered them to choose a worthy metropolitan. All agreed that because of his virtue and holiness, the blessed Jonah, Bishop of Ryazan, should occupy the metropolitan

---

[1]An abbreviated account, derived from *The Great Collection of Readings* compiled by Macarius, Metropolitan of Moscow, and *The Prologue*

throne of Russia.[2] But before Saint Jonah could set out for
Constantinople to obtain approval of his election from the
Emperor John Paleologus and the Most Holy Patriarch Joseph,
the ungodly Isidore, a Bulgarian, was consecrated Metropolitan
of Kiev and sent from the Imperial City to Russia.[3] After Isidore
had already left Constantinople, Saint Jonah arrived in the
Queen of Cities and presented to the Emperor and Patriarch his
letter of recommendation from the Great Prince. Both read it
and expressed regret for Isidore's hasty consecration, but told
Saint Jonah, "We can do nothing for you now. You have arrived
too late. Go back to your see and time will tell what God has
prepared for Isidore. If he dies or is deposed, you have the blessing of the patriarchal throne of Constantinople to become
Metropolitan of Kiev and All Russia." Accordingly, Saint Jonah
returned to Ryazan.[4]

Isidore went first to Kiev and then, the following spring, to
Moscow, where he remained until the harvest. In autumn he
departed to the West in order to attend the Council of Florence
and supposedly confess the Orthodox Faith. It was three years
before he returned to Kiev, now as an apostate from the holy
Eastern Church; but he was not accepted there, so he again
went to Moscow, hoping to spread his perfidious beliefs.
Learning that Isidore had changed his loyalties, Great Prince
Basil Vasilievich convened a synod of all the bishops and clergy
of the Metropolia of Russia. Having consulted the canons, they
determined that the teaching Isidore had accepted at the Synod
of Florence was irreconcilable with Orthodoxy and they rejected
him as metropolitan. The Great Prince confined Isidore in a
monastery and sent word of the council's rulings to the Most
Holy Patriarch of Constantinople. Unable to hide his fall into
heresy, Isidore was put to shame and secretly fled to Gregory
Mammes, Patriarch of the Imperial City. When the Patriarch

---

[2]Saint Jonah was actually elected the year following Photius' death. (Tr.)
[3]Hoping to obtain military aid from the West, Emperor John VIII and
Patriarch Joseph II subsequently submitted to the Pope at the Council of
Ferrara-Florence. Isidore, who also signed the decree of union, became a
fervent advocate of the capitulation of the Eastern Church and was
rewarded by the Pope with appointment as cardinal and papal legate. (Tr.)
[4]In the year 1437

would not receive him, Isidore sailed to Rome. His later fate remains unknown.[5]

Meanwhile, Saint Jonah was elected Metropolitan of Russia a second time. Having already obtained the blessing of the Most Holy Patriarch of Constantinople Gregory Mammes,[6] Jonah was enthroned by his own bishops in the cathedral of Moscow. He was the first Metropolitan to be installed directly by the Russian bishops, although still with prior approval from the most holy, apostolic Throne of Constantinople.

After ascending the great cathedra as pastor of all Russia, Saint Jonah increased his labors, striving to confirm piety throughout the land. To this end he unwearyingly instructed the flock and sent epistles to various churches. Being a true shepherd, he zealously defended the Orthodox faith, as is clear from these letters. The saint put no concern above preserving unharmed the reason-endowed sheep entrusted to his care.

God granted to Saint Jonah the power to cure illnesses and foretell the future. For example, Anna, the daughter of the Great Prince, was near death when the man of God healed her. Even though the Princess was cured instantly, a scoffer put it about that the maiden was not helped at all by the Metropolitan's prayers, and that her recovery was natural, not miraculous. The Lord's favorite summoned the disbeliever and reproved him for blaspheming the grace of the Holy Spirit. "Child, let go of your doubts," said the saint. *"The things which are impossible with men are possible with God.*[7] The Lord granted life to the child, on account of the devout parents' faith and hope in Him." When the man not only failed to heed this counsel, but redoubled his fulminations, the blessed one declared, "May your profane tongue be silenced and your irreverent lips sealed. May death

---

[5]From Moscow, Isidore fled not to Constantinople, but to Tver, thence to Novgorod, and finally to Rome. As papal legate, Isidore returned to Constantinople shortly before its fall to the Turks and proclaimed the union with the Papacy. After a brief imprisonment in Turkish hands, Isidore escaped again to Rome and was appointed Latin Patriarch of Constantinople by the Pope. He died in Rome. (Tr.)

[6]During his tenure as patriarch the union with Rome had not yet been publicly proclaimed in Constantinople. (Tr.)

[7]Luke, Ch. 18

claim you, not the maiden, as its victim." Straightway, the blasphemer fell to the ground. He could still see, but was unable to
move or speak. A short time passed and he vomited his soul:
rightful punishment for belittling the great hierarch's gift of the
Holy Spirit.

Our father's cellarer, a monk named Pimen, was responsible
for distributing provisions to the needy. Once, a poor widow
came begging a little mead, which she wanted as a remedy for
an illness from which she was suffering. Pimen drove her away,
bellowing, "Begone, woman! It is too early in the day to be giving out drink to beggars."

Learning about this, God's holy hierarch called for Pimen
and told him, "Brother, you cannot imagine how deeply you
have grieved that devout widow. The Lord has decreed your
death as punishment, so repent of your sins. Not much time
remains for you." The man of God commanded the monk's
spiritual father to clothe the transgressor in the schema. That
same day, after the tonsure, Pimen died, as the Lord's hierarch
had predicted.

On another occasion, the saint gave one of his novices a
quantity of silver, with instructions to distribute the money to
the poor. The novice gave away some and kept the rest for himself. Later, a destitute widow came to the saint, lamenting,
"Hierarch of God, your novice refused to give me any alms!"

The man of God called for the novice and asked him, "Why
did you refuse this widow her due? You have done her a grievous wrong."

"I gave her quite a bit, but she shamelessly demanded
more," answered the novice. When the widow insisted that she
had received nothing, the novice shouted, "Liar! May God punish you with death."

Before the novice could say another word, the saint pronounced this sentence: "No harm shall befall the widow,
because she is telling the truth. You are the liar and a thief as
well. For this you must die." Straightway, the novice became
delirious with fever and gave up the ghost.

The boyar Basil Kutuz distrusted the saint, never visited
him, and did not want to receive his blessing. This continued
until he began suffering from an unbearable toothache which

no human skill could relieve. In his misery, the boyar attended a Liturgy celebrated at the cathedral by God's hierarch Jonah. At the end of the service, the saint called for Basil, blessed him, and gave him a prosphoron. Then, while instructing the noble from the divine Scriptures, Jonah struck him on the cheek so hard that many in the church heard the blow. "Woe is me," cried Basil, "you have put out my last teeth!" Suddenly he realized his pain was gone. He returned home rejoicing, glorifying God, and praising the Lord's favorite, the holy and illustrious hierarch Jonah.

Because of our sins, in the year 6959[8] the Lord permitted the godless Hagarenes to attack the Russian land. A prince of the Horde appeared before Moscow with a large army of Tatars, burned the suburbs, and besieged the city. Carrying holy crosses and icons, Metropolitan Jonah and the clergy walked along the walls chanting a Service of Supplication, weeping, and praying fervently for the town and its folk. During the procession, the Lord's favorite said to the devout elder Anthony of the Chudov Monastery, whom he knew to be a man of virtuous life: "Anthony, my son and brother, pray to the merciful God and the immaculate Theotokos that the city and all Orthodox Christians be delivered from the impious Hagarenes."

"Great hierarch, we must thank God and His most pure Mother, our mighty and speedy intercessor," replied Anthony. "The Theotokos has heard your prayers and begged of her Son, our Lord Jesus Christ, the salvation of this city and all its Orthodox Christians. Soon the Hagarenes will be routed by an invisible power; but the Lord has deigned that first one of their darts must claim my life."

No sooner had the elder said this than the Tatars loosed a hail of archery. Anthony was wounded and shortly afterwards died. He was buried reverently by the holy Metropolitan and the clergy.

On July 2, the feast of the Deposition of the Robe of the Most Holy Theotokos, fear and trembling suddenly gripped the pagans, who were put to flight by God's unseen hand. The grateful Metropolitan commanded that as soon as possible a

---

[8]The year 1450/1451 after the Incarnation of Christ

church be built at his residence and dedicated to the robe of the Theotokos in memory of the city's deliverance from the barbarians on the day of the feast.

Years passed and our blessed father Jonah attained great old age. God revealed the day of his repose in the following manner. Once Maximus, the night-watchman of the cathedral, was making his rounds outside the building. Noticing that the doors were open, he looked in and saw candles burning and heard priests chanting. The perplexed watchman related this to James, the priest who held the keys to the church. James went to see for himself and found the cathedral locked. Light was shining through the windows, and upon entering he saw that candles were indeed burning; the church, however, was empty. His confusion turned to fear when a voice from the sanctuary called to him, "James! James! Tell my servant Jonah that I have hearkened unto his prayer. He asked Me to send him bodily affliction for the salvation of his soul; therefore, on his leg a wound shall appear that will cause his death. He is not long for this world, so let him put in order the affairs of the Church."

The next morning, the holy pastor Jonah summoned the priest and asked him, "James, where were you last night? Why did you not come at once and make known what was revealed to you?"

Trembling violently, James fell at the holy hierarch's feet and begged, "Forgive me, Master! I was afraid to tell you what I learned. In any case, it was not necessary, for God's grace showed it to you directly."

"God forgive you, child," said the saint. "Now I must reveal to you that the Lord will soon take your wife. Hurry home and make ready her soul, so that she may die in a state of repentance." When the Metropolitan called for James, his wife was perfectly healthy; when the priest returned home, he found her gravely ill. Three days later she expired, having partaken of the Holy Mysteries as befits a Christian.

The great hierarch Jonah did not survive long after this. Full of days, good works, and the grace of the divine Spirit, and having perfected *holiness in the fear of God*,[9] he attained his blessed

---

[9] II Cor., Ch. 7

end. The wound appeared on his leg, he fell ill, and he weakened in body but not in spirit. Even in his enfeebled state he continued to attend church. Just before surrendering his soul into God's hands, he pronounced a blessing upon Great Prince Basil, the Prince's family, and all the people. With prayer on his lips, he departed to the Lord on March 31, 6969,[10] having served as pastor of God's Church for twelve years and six months. His honored body was laid to rest in the Cathedral of the Most Holy Theotokos.

After Saint Jonah, Great Prince Basil Vasilievich died. His son John Vasilievich became Great Prince and ruler of the Russian land. It was God's will that this prince erect the new cathedral that stands to the present. Having obtained the blessing of His Grace Metropolitan Gerontius to pull down the old building, the ruler transferred the honored remains of the holy wonderworker Metropolitan Peter to another church until construction was completed. While the foundation of the new cathedral was being laid, the remains of Metropolitans Theognostus, Cyprian, Photius, and Saint Jonah the wonderworker were removed from the earth. A general Memorial Service was chanted, to which Symeon, a seven-year old boy, was brought. The child, born a paralytic, was the son of the presbyter Peter, who served in the bell-tower church of Saint John of the Ladder. Alexius, a presbyter of the cathedral, lifted up the lad, put him at the foot of Saint Jonah's coffin, and told him to ask God for healing. Held upright by the priest, the boy prayed; then he shouted thrice, "It is raining!" In fact, the sun was shining and there was not a cloud in the sky, but after this the boy could stand by himself. He walked home without assistance. Everyone was amazed and glorified God and Saint Jonah, the Lord's favorite.

The great cathedral of the Dormition of the Most Holy Theotokos was completed in the year 6987[11] and consecrated shortly thereafter. First the honored relics of Saint Peter the wonderworker were brought to the church, then those of the holy metropolitans Theognostus, Cyprian, Photius, and Jonah. Since the remains of Saint Jonah were incorrupt, they were

---

[10]In the year 1461 after the Incarnation of Christ
[11]The year 1478/1479 after the Incarnation of Christ

enshrined in the cathedral and left exposed for veneration. To this day they remain in the church, and the prayers of the faithful are frequently answered there. Thus, when a mute named John was kissing the sacred hand of the blessed Metropolitan Jonah, the Lord's hierarch, in a way known to God alone, seized the man's tongue. John shouted for help, and the priests and others in the cathedral came running to see what was the matter. When they reached the reliquary, the saint had already released the man's tongue. John was no longer shouting, but was speaking clearly and proclaiming how the holy Metropolitan had given him the gift of speech. Everyone was astonished by the marvel and, with the healed man, extolled God's greatness and the illustrious wonderworker Saint Jonah.

Besides these healings, the holy relics have worked and continue to work many others for those who venerate them with faith, unto the glory of Christ our God, Who is praised with the Father and the Holy Spirit, now and ever and unto the ages of ages. Amen.

ୈ☙୭☙

On this day we commemorate our holy monastic father Hypatius, abbot of the Monastery of Rufiniana. His Life is found in *The Prologue*. We also commemorate the venerable Apollonius, desert-dweller of the Thebaid in Egypt, and the holy martyrs Audas the Bishop and Benjamin the deacon, who suffered for Christ in Persia during the reign of Theodosius the Lesser.

The Life of the Holy, Righteous Joseph The All-Comely

Included with the Lives of the Month of March[1]

𝒯he blessed Joseph, all-comely in soul and body, was the son of the Old Testament patriarch Jacob, grandson of Isaac, and great-grandson of Abraham. His mother was Jacob's second wife Rachel, who was barren until *God hearkened unto her, and opened her womb, and she conceived, and bare a son.*[2] Joseph was Jacob's eleventh son. Later Rachel bore another child, Benjamin—Israel's twelfth son.[3] But *Rachel travailed* in giving birth to Benjamin: *she had hard labour and died, and was buried in the way to Ephratha, which is Bethlehem.*[4]

Jacob *loved Joseph* and Benjamin, his sons by Rachel, *more than all his children, because* they were the sons *of his old age*[5] and because they reminded him of Rachel, his favorite wife, whose death deeply grieved him. So greatly did he love Rachel that he served his father-in-law Laban fourteen years to win her hand. Both of Rachel's children were deserving of their father's affection, for they were chaste and well-behaved, especially the blessed Joseph. From the time Joseph was a little boy the Holy Spirit rested upon him.

Now *Joseph, being seventeen years old, was feeding the flock of his*

---

[1]Compiled from the divine Scriptures and the writings of the venerable Ephraim the Syrian. The life of the forefather Joseph the All-comely, son of Jacob, who was betrayed by his brothers and sold into Egypt, prefigured the life and Passion of the Saviour. Since it was in March that the Lord assumed flesh for our salvation, and was betrayed and put to death, we have included the blessed Joseph's Life in this volume.
[2]Gen., Ch. 30
[3]Israel was the name given to Jacob in Genesis, chapter thirty-two, after he wrestled with the Lord, Who had appeared in human form. (Tr.)
[4]Gen., Ch. 35   [5]Gen., Ch. 37

father with his stepbrothers. He observed their wicked ways, but since he loved them, he desired their amendment and *brought unto his father their evil report*, hoping that Jacob would chastise them paternally and avert the wrath of God from the family. Pleased by Joseph's intention and his purity and fear of God, Jacob *made* Joseph *a coat of many colours. All the brethren*, however, *hated Joseph*: some because he would not join in their evil deeds and had reported them to Jacob; others because they knew Israel loved Joseph best of all his sons. They never spoke peaceably to Joseph, but mocked him, and slandered him to Israel. Jacob, however, did not believe the accusations, since he knew the excellence of Joseph's character.

At that time, through dreams, the Holy Spirit, Who dwelt in Joseph, began showing to the young prophet what would occur in his life. Joseph did not hide what he saw, but told it to his father and brothers. He said, *Hear, I pray you, this dream which I have dreamed: for behold, we were binding sheaves in the field, and, lo, my sheaf arose, and also stood upright; and, behold, your sheaves stood round about, and made obeisance to my sheaf.*

And his brethren said to him, Shalt thou indeed reign over us? Or shalt thou indeed have dominion over us? And they hated him yet the more for his dream.

And he dreamed yet another dream, and told it to his father and to his brethren, and said, Behold the sun and the moon and the eleven stars made obeisance to me.

And his father rebuked him and said unto him, What is this dream? Shall I and thy mother and thy brethren indeed come to bow down ourselves to thee to the earth?

Jacob upbraided Joseph and forbade him ever to mention his dreams again, since he did not want the lad to incite his brothers' envy. Nevertheless, he asked himself, "What can these things mean except that the Lord will reveal His mercy through this virtuous youth?" And Joseph's words brought joy to his father, but his brothers daily grew more angry and jealous, and they plotted the blessed one's destruction.

And his brethren went to feed their father's flock in Shechem, but Joseph remained with Jacob in *the vale of Hebron*. As a loving father, Jacob wondered how his sons were faring in Shechem, and he bade Joseph, his most beloved son: *Go, I pray thee, see whether it will be well with thy brethren, and well with the flocks; and bring me word again.*

Obedient to his father's command, Joseph departed with Jacob's greeting to his brothers. Benjamin, still a little boy, remained with Jacob. Having searched the wilderness of Shechem, Joseph was downcast because he failed to find his brothers. Then he came upon a certain man who asked him, *What seekest thou?*

And he said, I seek my brethren: tell me, I pray thee, where they feed their flocks.

And the man said, They are departed hence; for I heard them say, Let us go to Dothan. He showed Joseph the way to that place, *and Joseph went after his brethren, and found them in Dothan.*

Catching sight of his brothers, Joseph rejoiced, for he loved them; but *when they saw him afar off, even before he came near unto them, they* became infuriated, like wild animals, and *conspired against him to slay him. And they said one to another, Behold, this dreamer cometh. Come now therefore, and let us slay him, and cast him into some pit, and we will say, Some evil beast hath devoured him: and we shall see what will become of his dreams.*

And Reuben, the eldest brother, *heard it, and* wished to deliver Joseph *out of the* murderous *hands* of his brothers. He *said,* "Do *not kill him or shed* his *blood, but* simply *cast him into this pit that is in the wilderness,* that he perish alone; but *lay no hand upon him."* Reuben hoped to save the innocent youth from death by removing him from the pit and delivering *him to his father again.*

And it came to pass, when Joseph, suspecting nothing, *was come unto his brethren,* that he greeted them lovingly and conveyed their father's regards. But like carnivorous beasts, they threw themselves upon him, and *stripped Joseph of the coat of many colours that was on him.* They gnashed their teeth and threatened to devour him; they pummeled him and heaped insults upon him. Realizing he could expect no mercy from them, Joseph turned to prayer. Then, with tears pouring down his face, he pleaded, "Why are you so angry, brothers? Loose me and hear my entreaty. You know that our father is still lamenting the death of my mother. Do you want to inflict a second wound on him, when the first has not healed? I beg you not to separate me from him, for if you do, his soul will plunge in misery to Sheol. In the name of the God of our fathers, Abraham, Isaac, and Jacob, show mercy! Have pity on me, for the sake of the God Who commanded Abraham to depart from the land and house of his father and come into the good land of promise; the God Who swore to *multiply* Abraham's *seed as the stars of heaven, and as the sand which is upon the sea shore;*[6] the most high God, Who granted Abraham the courage to offer his son Isaac as a sacrifice, then delivered Isaac from death, providing a ram for the oblation; the holy God Who blessed our father Jacob through the mouth of his father Isaac, and protected Jacob when he was at Haran in Mesopotamia, whence came Abraham. Do not separate me from Jacob, as death separated Rachel from him. May Jacob not weep for me as he weeps for Rachel; may death not shut his eyes as he awaits my return. See my tears and reconsider; let me go back to my father!"

Not even by invoking the God of their fathers could Joseph calm his brothers, for they were strangers to the fear of the Lord. As they dragged him away, he held their legs and wept, "Brothers, have compassion!" but they ignored his pleas and *took him, and cast him into*[7] a dry well. Sitting at the bottom of the pit, Joseph wept bitter tears and cried, "See, father, what has become of your child! I am cast into the abyss as one dead. You await my return, but I, like a robber being punished for his crimes, am trapped in this hole. You, father, commanded me, 'Go, visit your brothers, who are with the flock, and hurry back.' Behold, like ravenous wolves they have attacked me and will not let me return. Good father, you will never see me again or hear my voice; you have lost the staff of your old age. Never again shall I see your venerable gray hair, for I am buried alive. No burial can be more grievous than this. Weep for your child, father, as I weep at being parted from you while still a youth. If only a dove could learn human speech and take to you word of my plight! The fountain of my tears is nearly drained; fatigue is silencing my groans; there is no one to help me. O earth, our forefathers told us how you cried to the holy God on behalf of righteous, innocent Abel. As you called out when he was mur-

---

[6]Gen., Ch. 22   [7]Gen. Ch. 37

dered, do the same now, so that my father may know what my brothers have done to me."

Joseph lamented inconsolably in the pit until his strength was gone, but his cruel brothers ate and drank with abandon, like troops who have won a great battle or taken a city from their enemies. While celebrating, *they lifted up their eyes and looked, and, behold, a company of Ishmaelites came from Gilead with their camels bearing spicery and balm and stacte, going to carry it down to Egypt. And Judah,* Jacob's fourth son, *said unto his brethren, "What profit is it if we slay our brother, and conceal his blood? Come, and let us sell him to the Ishmaelites.* Let them take him away, and let him die in a foreign land. *Let not our hand be upon him; for he is our brother and our flesh."*

Joseph's brothers heeded Judah's counsel, *and they drew and lifted up Joseph out of the pit, and sold Joseph to the Ishmaelite* merchants *for twenty pieces of silver;* and the Midianites took Joseph away. Upon this *Reuben,* who had left, *returned unto the pit; and, behold, Joseph was not in the pit; and he rent his clothes. And he returned unto his brethren, and said, "The child is not; and I, whither shall I go?* How shall I endure our father's weeping for him?" And Reuben lamented Joseph's fate.

On the way to Egypt, the Midianites took Joseph to Ephratha, where his mother, returning from Mesopotamia with Jacob, had died. Seeing Rachel's tomb, Joseph rushed to it and fell upon it. In his anguish, he wept bitterly and moaned, "Mother! Rise from the grave and see what has become of Joseph, whom you so loved. Unbeknown to Jacob, my brothers have sold me naked into slavery, as though I were an evildoer. These foreigners, my purchasers, are taking me to Egypt. Open your grave, mother, and let me enter, that we may share it; accept your son, Rachel, and do not let him die in a strange land. Receive the child that was separated from Jacob suddenly and unexpectedly, as he was from you. Hearken, O mother, unto my heartfelt sighs and tears, and allow me into your tomb. I have shed an ocean of tears and can weep no more; I have exhausted myself with lamentation. O Rachel, Rachel, can you not hear the voice of Jacob? Your son is about to be taken from you again, this time by force. Are you unwilling to help him? I called unto Jacob, and he did not hear me; now I call unto you, only to be ignored. I wish to die in your grave, and not perish in a foreign land."

Seeing Joseph throw himself upon the tomb, the Ishmaelites reasoned, "This youth is a wizard and is trying to cast a spell. We must bind him more securely, lest he do us some harm and escape." They drew near to Joseph and shouted angrily, "Enough of your sorcery! On your feet, unless you want us to use this grave as a chopping-board for your flesh. We are not going to lose the money we paid for you."

Joseph rose, and the Ishmaelites saw that his face was swollen from bitter weeping. Their anger cooled and they asked him, "Why did you burst into tears over the gravestone? Do not be afraid: tell us who you are and why you were sold. The shepherds said to us, 'Be forewarned: this youth may attempt to escape while you are traveling. If he flees, we are not accountable.' So, whose slave were you? Did you belong to the shepherds, or someone else? Why did you mourn so bitterly over the grave? Tell us everything honestly, for we are now your masters, you our slave. If not to us, to whom will you reveal your sorrows? We do not know what to make of the shepherds' warning. Calm yourself, and begin by telling us who you are. You do not seem like a slave at all, and we would rather have you as a beloved brother, than as a servant. Your dignity and keen mind are tokens of high birth; your place, we think, is among nobles, standing before a king. Doubtless you will attain a position of authority. We want you as our friend in the land of Egypt. You are a handsome, distinguished youth. Who would not be fond of you?"

Joseph sighed and explained, "Although I was sold to you, I committed no crime. I was not a slave, a robber, or a sorcerer. I was my father's most beloved son, and when my mother was alive, her's as well. The shepherds are my brothers. My father sent me to see how they were faring. They had tarried in the mountains, and my father was concerned for them. My brothers seized me and sold me to you because they could not endure my father's love for me. As for this grave, it is my mother's. She died here while returning home from Haran with my father."

Moved to tears of sympathy, the Midianites consoled Joseph, saying, "Do not fear, young man. Great honors await you in Egypt. Your appearance is proof you are wellborn. Do not be sad, but rejoice that you have escaped your jealous brothers and their hatred."

After selling Joseph, his brothers *took* his *coat, and killed a kid of the goats, and dipped the coat in the blood; and they brought it to their father and said,* "In the mountains we found this *coat of many colours* belonging to our brother Joseph. We are sorry for him and for you, father. Because we could not find him, we brought his coat to you. *Know now whether it be thy son's coat or no.* For our part, we are all certain that it is Joseph's."

Examining the coat, Jacob burst into tears and cried, *It is my son's; an evil beast hath devoured him! And Jacob rent his clothes, and put* on *sackcloth,* and mourned, "Why was I not devoured instead of you, my child! Why did the beast not consume me and leave you untouched? Why did it not tear me to pieces? Why did it not take me for its meal? Woe, woe is me! From the bottom of my heart, I grieve for Joseph. Woe, woe is me! I want to know where my son was killed, that I might tear out my gray hairs there. Without Joseph, I no longer wish to live. I caused your death, fair child! I slew you, my son, by sending you to your brothers and the flocks. Until I join you in Sheol, child, my mourning will never end. Because your corpse is lost, I weep over your coat, Joseph. But because the coat is intact, it throws me deeper into despair. Perhaps you were not destroyed by a wild animal, but murdered. If your brothers' story were true, the coat would be torn in pieces. No beast waits for its victim to disrobe before sinking its teeth into him. And had you taken off the coat beforehand, it would not be bloody. The garment was not ripped by teeth or claws, so whence is the blood? If I could be sure that you had indeed been killed by a beast in the wilds, and not murdered by robbers, my sorrow would be less. But my grief and lamentation are twofold, for I wonder who stripped you of your garment and whether you were slain by an animal or by men. May I die quickly, my child Joseph, my light and my support, and take your coat with me to Sheol. Without you, I do not wish to see another dawn!" Jacob mourned Joseph thus for many days, surrounded by his sons and daughters. They attempted to console him, but he would not be comforted. Weeping bitterly, he said only, "Let me descend to Sheol and lament my son there!"

Meanwhile, the Ishmaelites hurried to Egypt, hoping to sell the comely youth to a noble for a good price. While they were passing through a certain city there, Potiphar, one of Pharaoh's officers, saw Joseph and asked them, "Where is this young man from? He is very handsome and does not resemble you Ishmaelites."

"The youth is of noble birth and a keen mind," said the merchants.

Potiphar gladly paid the Ishmaelites their price and took Joseph to his house, where he tested the youth in various ways, to ascertain what sort of person he was. Living there, the true scion of righteous Abraham, Isaac, and Jacob bloomed with virtue and patience, and the Lord was with him. His conduct was pure and blameless, and his inner chastity and fear of God were evident from his speech and appearance. The all-seeing God of Abraham, Isaac, and Jacob, Who delivered His favorite from the pit of death and the hatred of envious brothers, dwelt in Joseph's heart. Nevertheless, Joseph continued to mourn the fate which took him from his father. *And* Joseph *found grace* in the sight of his master,[8] and Potiphar *saw that the Lord was with him, and that the Lord made all that* Joseph *did to prosper in his hand. And* Potiphar *made* Joseph *overseer over his house, and all that he had:* his villages and field hands and domestic servants. *And* Potiphar *knew not aught he had, save the bread which he did eat. The Lord blessed the Egyptian's house for Joseph's sake,* and all the menservants and maidservants were pleased with Joseph, because he administered the household well and they enjoyed every abundance.

Because Joseph was so handsome, Potiphar's wife was wounded by lust for him. Burning with satanic love for Joseph, she plotted how to cast the chaste youth into the pit of adultery. Every day she set many snares to entrap the young overseer. She changed her clothes hourly, washed and anointed her face, and wore glittering necklaces. By suggestive movements and immodest speech and laughter she tried to destroy Joseph, but harmed herself alone. Shielded by the fear of God, Joseph refused to look at her or think about her, and kept his gaze fixed on the Lord. But failure only stoked the flames of lust in the heart of the woman, and after hesitating briefly, she resorted to

[8]Gen., Ch. 39

direct seduction. Spitting out the venom stored in her heart, she whispered to Joseph, "Throw off fear, handsome youth, and *lie with me*. Abandon all restraint, that I may fully enjoy your comeliness and you, my beauty. Do not be afraid: you have charge over the household, and the servants are in our power. No one will dare to enter the room while we are together; no one will hear our conversation; no one will witness our deeds. Do not fear my husband, for I will poison him, if need be."

The God-fearing, blessed youth doubled the guard on his chastity of soul and body, and remained unharmed by the storm. He turned a deaf ear to everything the woman proposed, and replied to her thus: "My lady, I cannot be your lover, for I fear God. Furthermore, my master *hath committed all that he hath* to me, both in his house and in his villages; *neither hath he kept back anything from me but thee, because thou art his wife*. It would be a terrible iniquity to betray such a kind master and to commit such an outrage in his house. What is more, it would anger God, Who beholds all our secret doings."

That asp in human form was deaf to Joseph's holy admonitions. Burning ever hotter with lust, she waited for the best opportunity to induce Joseph to sin. Knowing his mistress' intention, Joseph often turned his eyes to the Lord and prayed, "O God of my fathers, Abraham, Isaac, and Jacob, deliver me from this plight! As Thou knowest, this madwoman hath secretly devised my destruction. O Master, Who didst rescue me from the hands of my murderous brothers, deliver me from this treacherous adder. Do not allow me to fall into sin and be sundered from the company of my fathers, who loved Thee greatly, O Lord."

Then Joseph cried, "O Jacob, dear father, pray fervently for me to God! Pray, father, for I am locked in bitter combat with an enemy intent on tearing me away from my God. The death of sin devised for me by this woman is worse than the murder planned for me by my brothers. They wished only to kill my body, whereas she is determined to destroy my soul by sundering it from God. I know, father, that the Lord hears your holy prayers, and that they delivered me from death in the pit. Pray again now to the Most High, that your child not fall into the pit of sin to which the lewd, godless woman is dragging me. My brothers attacked me like beasts of prey; like wolves, they tore me away from you. Now I have encountered a creature far more deadly. Holy father, pray for your son, lest he perish spiritually in the eyes of our God."

Although Joseph remained unconquered, his cunning mistress never stopped looking for her opportunity. Then one day it happened that all the servants were either gone or outside. Joseph was attending to his duties in the house, and Potiphar's wife bade him follow her as she was walking toward her bed. Suddenly she slipped off her robe and thrust herself upon the chaste, holy youth in a frenzied attempt to commit adultery with him. Joseph averted his face so as not to see the naked, shameless woman and tore himself from her grasp. He fled, rending the devil's nets; but, so doing, he left his cloak in the woman's hands. As an eagle flies away as quickly as it can when it catches sight of a fowler, so Joseph straightway took flight to escape the woman, whose snares would have yielded him a victim to spiritual death.

Humiliated and frightened because of her failure, the woman considered how to avenge herself on Joseph. She quickly decided it would be best to accuse the righteous youth of trying to have his way with her. This, she hoped, would stir up anger and jealousy on the part of her husband, and he would execute Joseph. "I will not rest until Joseph is put out of the way," she said to herself. "The sight of such a handsome young man ruling my house is unendurable, unless I can satisfy myself with him. His disdain for me is intolerable."

With this the woman cried for her menservants and maidservants. They came running, and she told them, "See, the Hebrew slave my husband made ruler over the house, *he came in unto me to lie with me.* It was not enough for him to have power over the entire household: he also wanted to take me from my husband. He demanded that I commit adultery with him, so I shouted for help. I tried to hold him when he ran away, but he was too strong. I was able to seize his garment, though." All were amazed by this, for they never supposed Joseph capable of such a disgraceful deed.

When Potiphar returned from Pharaoh's palace, the woman showed him Joseph's garment and, playing the innocent victim, she said, *"The Hebrew servant, which thou hast brought unto us, came in unto me to mock me.* Will you permit him to insult and humiliate your wife? Finding me alone in the house, he demanded that I submit to his lusts. Had I not shouted for help, he would have forced me. He is very strong, so there is no doubt that he would have overpowered me. But my cry and the servants rushing to my aid sent him running in fear. See, I snatched his robe as he was fleeing."

Potiphar believed his wife and was furious at Joseph. Without investigating the accusation, he unjustly condemned the innocent, righteous servant. He forgot the blessings God had showered upon his house and villages for Joseph's sake, and ordered that the Lord's favorite be fettered and imprisoned. But the God of Abraham, Isaac, and Jacob, Who searches the hearts of men, *was with Joseph and shewed him mercy, and gave him favour in the sight of the keeper of the prison.* Joseph won the warden's trust as he had Potiphar's, *and the keeper of the prison committed to Joseph's hand all the prisoners that were in the prison.*

And it came to pass after these things that the chief baker of the King of Egypt and the chief cupbearer offended their lord, and Pharaoh was wroth with his eunuchs.[9] *And he put them in ward, into the prison, into the place whereunto Joseph had been led, and they were some days in the prison. And they dreamed a dream both of them, each man his dream in one night,* which signified what would befall them soon. And the godly *Joseph served them,* for they were men of high rank, *and Joseph came in unto them in the morning, and looked upon them, and, behold, they were troubled. And he asked* them, *Why is it that your countenances are sad to-day?*

And they said unto him, We have dreamed a dream, and there is no interpreter of it.

And Joseph said unto them, "Only God, Who knows all things, knows the interpretations of dreams; but He reveals them to those who fear Him. Each of you tell me your dream, and through me, God will disclose its meaning."

And the chief cupbearer told his dream to Joseph, and said to him, In my dream, behold, a vine was before me; and in the vine were three branches: and it budded, and her blossoms shot forth; and the clusters

---

[9]Gen., Ch. 40

thereof brought forth ripe grapes. And the cup of Pharaoh was in my hand; and I took the grapes, and pressed them into the cup, and I gave the cup into Pharaoh's hand.

And Joseph said unto him, "This is the interpretation of the dream: The three branches are three days. In three days Pharaoh shall remember you and take pity on you, and restore thee unto thy place: and thou shalt deliver Pharaoh's cup into his hand, after the former manner. But remember me, my lord, when it shall be well with thee, and shew kindness unto me, and make mention of me unto Pharaoh, and bring me out of this dungeon. For, indeed, I was stolen away out of the land of the Hebrews, and here also have I done nothing evil, that they should put me into this dungeon; but it was malice that brought me here."

When the chief baker heard how clearly Joseph had interpreted the cupbearer's dream, he said unto Joseph, "I also saw a dream, and behold, I had three baskets of loaves upon my head, and the birds did fly down and eat out of the basket on my head."

And Joseph answered and said, This is the interpretation of thy dream: The three baskets are three days. Yet three days, and Pharaoh shall take thy head from thee, and hang thee on a tree, and the birds shall eat thy flesh from off thee.

And it came to pass the third day, which was Pharaoh's birthday, that he made a banquet for all his nobles and servants, and he remembered the chief baker and the chief cupbearer, and brought out both men, and questioned them. And he hanged the baker, but restored the chief cupbearer to his office. Yet did not the chief cupbearer remember Joseph, but forgat him.

And it came to pass at the end of two years that, in accordance with providence, Pharaoh dreamed: and, behold, he thought he stood by the river.[10] And, behold, there came up out of it seven well favoured cows and fatfleshed; and they fed on the bank of the river. And, behold, seven other cows came up after them out of the river, ill favoured and lean-fleshed, and they fed by the other cows on the bank of the river. And the ill favoured and lean-fleshed cows did eat up the seven well favoured and fat cows, but were not filled, and remained as thin as before.

So Pharaoh awoke. And he slept and dreamed the second time: and behold, seven ears of wheat came up upon one stalk, full and good. And

---

[10]Gen., Ch. 41

behold, seven thin ears and blasted with the wind sprang up after them. And the thin ears devoured the full and good ears. And Pharaoh awoke and his spirit was troubled; and he sent and called for all the magicians of Egypt and all the wise men thereof, and he told them this dream; but there was none that could interpret it to Pharaoh. For how, indeed, could sorcerers, servants of demons, penetrate the ineffable mysteries of the God of heaven? Seeing Pharaoh downcast, the chief cupbearer remembered Joseph, who had interpreted his dream in the prison, and he *spake unto Pharaoh, saying, "I do remember my fault this day,* my lord. *Pharaoh was wroth with his servants, and put me in ward, both me and the chief baker: and we dreamed a dream one night, I and he, foreboding things to come. And there was there with us a young man, an Hebrew servant* of Potiphar; *and we told him, and he interpreted to us our dreams. And it came to pass, as he interpreted to us, so it was.* For you had mercy on me, O King, and *I was restored to mine office, but he was hanged."*

Pharaoh was pleased, and *sent and called Joseph, and they brought him hastily out of the dungeon, and shaved him, and changed his raiment,* because his hair had grown long while he was a prisoner, and his clothing was in tatters. And Joseph *came in unto Pharaoh* and his nobles, *and Pharaoh said unto Joseph, "I have heard say that* you are intelligent and wise, and *that thou canst understand a dream. There is none that can interpret* my dream, so I ask you to show its meaning."

And Joseph answered Pharaoh, saying, "When God the Most High wishes, He reveals mysteries to His servants; otherwise, it is impossible to interpret dreams with certainty." *And* in the presence of the entire court, *Pharaoh said unto Joseph* that he had seen seven fat cows and seven thin, and seven full ears of grain and seven thin, and that the thin had devoured the fat and full. Filled with the spirit of prophecy, the righteous Joseph foretold that *there* would *come seven years of great plenty throughout all the land of Egypt,* signified by the seven fat cows and seven full ears of grain. Then a terrible famine would follow, signified by the thin cows that devoured the fat, and the seven ears of wheat blasted by the wind, that devoured the full ears, but were not filled. For seven years the crops would fail, said he, and *the plenty* would be forgotten *by reason of the famine* throughout all the earth.

And Joseph continued: "From the fact that God revealed the same dream to Pharaoh twice, once with cows and once with ears of wheat, it is evident that these *things* will certainly come to pass. *Now therefore let Pharaoh* hearken to the advice of his lowly slave, and *look out a man discreet and wise, and set him over the land of Egypt. And let him take up the fifth part of all the produce of the land of Egypt in the seven plenteous years,* beginning this year. *And let them lay up wheat under the hand of Pharaoh, and let them store* every sort of *food in the cities. And that food shall be for store to the land against the seven years of famine, which shall be in the land of Egypt; that the land perish not through the famine."*

Joseph's prophetic words and wise counsel were amazing *in the eyes of Pharaoh, and in the eyes of all his servants. And Pharaoh said unto his servants, Can we find such a one as this is, a man in whom the Spirit of God is? And Pharaoh said unto Joseph,* "Forasmuch *as God hath shewed thee all this, there is not a wiser or more prudent man than thou. Thou shalt be over my house* and kingdom second after me, *and according unto thy word shall* all the land of Egypt *be ruled: only in the throne will I be greater than thou." And Pharaoh took off his ring from his hand, and put it upon Joseph's hand, and arrayed* Joseph *in a robe of purple, and put a necklace of gold about his neck. And Pharaoh said, "Behold, I have set thee as a second king over all the land of Egypt.* I will not lift my hand without taking counsel with you, *and without thee shall no man* dare to undertake anything whatsoever *in all the land of Egypt." And Pharaoh gave Joseph* an Egyptian *name: Zaphnathpaaneah,*[11] which means *"the saviour of the world"; and he made* Joseph *to ride in the second chariot he had, and heralds to cry* that a second king ruled in Egypt. And all Pharaoh's nobles escorted the chariot wherever it went, according to Joseph the same reverence as to Pharaoh himself.

Oh, what a wondrous change of circumstance, wrought in a single moment for the blessed youth by the right hand of God, *Who raiseth up the poor man from the earth, and from the dunghill lifteth up the pauper,*[12] *to seat him with kings* and *princes!*[13] How marvelous are Thy judgments, O Lord! Thou didst justify Thy righteous servant and splendidly reward him in this life for his

---

[11]The Septuagint renders this name as "Psonthomphanech." (Tr.)
[12]Ps. 112; I Kings, Ch. 2   [13]I Kings, Ch. 2

chastity and patience. Yet how much greater is the recompense prepared for the saints beyond the grave.

When Potiphar, Pharaoh's general and Joseph's imprisoner, saw the blessed one seated majestically in the royal chariot, he was terrified. Hurrying home, he told his wife, "Woman, something strange and difficult to believe has occurred today, and we have reason to fear. Joseph, our former slave, is now our master and the ruler of all Egypt. He is sitting in Pharaoh's chariot receiving worship from all the people. I was too frightened to approach him, and fled the court."

Potiphar's wife told him not to be afraid, and confessed to him, "Today I must reveal my sin. I was hopelessly enamored of Joseph and ever tried to seduce him, but without success. Then I attempted to force myself on him, but he escaped my grasp. I did snatch his cloak, which I showed you to prove he had pressed me to submit to his lusts. Thus, in a manner of speaking, I am responsible for his sudden rise to power. Had I not become obsessed with Joseph, he would not have been imprisoned, but would have remained in our house, and his virtue and wisdom would still be known only to us. He should be grateful to me, the authoress of his good fortune. We should not be afraid of Joseph, for he is a righteous and holy man. I am certain he has told no one what I said and did and that he will forgive us both. Now let us go and prostrate ourselves before him, like the other nobles." Putting aside their fears, Potiphar and his wife did homage to Joseph, who neither reproved them for the evil they had done, nor mentioned it to anyone.

And Pharaoh gave Joseph to wife *Asenath, the daughter of Potipherah, priest of Heliopolis,* that is, the "City of the Sun." *And Joseph was thirty years old* when he began to rule Egypt. *And there were seven years of plenty,* according to his prophecy; *and Joseph went throughout all the land of Egypt, and he laid up all* the grain and all the fruits of the earth, *and laid up the food in the cities. And Joseph gathered very much wheat, as the sand of the sea, until it could not be numbered, for there was no number of it. And unto Joseph there were born two sons before the years of the famine came, and Joseph called the name of the firstborn Manasseh, and the name of the second called he Ephraim.*

And the seven years of plenteousness ended, and the seven years of dearth began. *And the dearth daily grew worse in all lands, and in all the land of Egypt there was no* wheat, except for what was stored in Pharaoh's granaries. *And the people cried to Pharaoh for bread, and Pharaoh sent* them to Joseph. *And Joseph opened all the* royal *storehouses, and sold unto the Egyptians. And all countries came into Egypt to Joseph for to buy bread; because that the famine was so sore in all lands.*

The famine was also severe in the land of Canaan, where Jacob lived; and the elder and his sons grew weak with hunger. *Now when Jacob heard that there was* abundant *wheat in Egypt, he said to his sons, "Why are you idle?*[14] *Behold, I have heard that there is* abundant *grain in Egypt. Get you down thither, and buy* a little *for us from thence, that we may live, and not be consumed with want." And Joseph's ten brethren went down to buy wheat in Egypt. But Benjamin, Joseph's youngest brother,* remained with his father, for *Jacob sent* him not *with his brethren; for he said, "Mischief may befall him,* as it did Joseph."

And the sons of Israel came to buy wheat in Egypt *with those that came* from every land. *And Joseph was the governor in Egypt, and he it was that sold to all the people: and Joseph's brethren came, and bowed themselves before him with their faces to the ground. And Joseph saw his brethren, and he knew them, but they did not know him. And Joseph spake roughly unto them, and said to them, Whence come ye?*

And they said, From the land of Canaan to buy food.

And Joseph remembered the dreams which he had dreamed of them, and understood that what was revealed to him would now come to pass, and in his heart he glorified God. And again he spoke to his brothers, feigning anger and saying, *Ye are spies, and are come to spy out this country.*

And they said unto him, "Nay, my lord, we are peaceable men, to buy food are we come. We are the sons of one man, and *are no spies."*

And Joseph said unto them, "No, you have come to spy out the country."

To show Joseph they were innocent, the frightened brothers told him about their home and father. "Our father is a righteous man and lives in Canaan," they said. "We were twelve brothers,

---

[14]Gen., Ch. 42

but one of our number was devoured by beasts in the wilderness. Our father is still mourning, because he loved that son greatly. The youngest brother remains at home, comforting our father."

And Joseph said to them, "That is it that I spake unto you, saying, Ye are spies. Hereby shall ye be proved: By the life of Pharoah, ye shall not go forth hence, unless your youngest brother come hither. Send one of you, and let him fetch your brother, and ye shall be kept in prison, that your words may be proved, whether there be any truth in you. If you do not bring back your youngest brother, surely ye are spies." So saying, Joseph put them all together into ward for three days.

And the third day Joseph brought them out of prison, and said, "I will not torture you, for I fear God. If you are not spies, but have come in peace, this do and live. Let one of you be detained in prison, and the rest go, and carry back to your father the grain you have purchased. But bring your youngest brother to me, and your words shall be verified, and ye shall not die."

And they said one to another in Hebrew, "Verily, we deserve to suffer these things as punishment for our sins, because we are guilty concerning our brother. We saw the anguish of his soul, and when he besought us, we would not hear; therefore is this distress come upon us."

And Reuben, the eldest brother, answered them, saying, Spake I not unto you, saying, Do not sin against the child; and ye would not hear; and behold, his blood is now required of us. And they knew not that Joseph understood them; for he spake unto them by an interpreter. And he turned himself away from them, and wept; and returned to them again, and took from them Simeon, and bound him before their eyes, for that brother hated Joseph more than the others did, and proved himself the most malicious of all when they threw the blessed one into the pit and sold him to the Ishmaelites.

Having imprisoned Simeon, Joseph commenced to fill the sacks of the other brothers with wheat, and secretly to restore every man's money into his sack; and to give them provisions for the way; and thus did he to them. And they laded their asses with the wheat and departed to the land of Canaan. On the way they stopped to rest, and when one of them opened his sack to give his ass provender, he espied his money; for, behold, it was in his sack's mouth. And their heart failed them, and they were afraid, saying, What is this that God hath done *unto us? And they came unto Jacob their father, and told him all that befell them* in Egypt. *And it came to pass as they emptied their sacks, that, behold, every man's money was in his sack: and when they saw the money, they were afraid.*

And their father said to them mournfully, *Me have ye bereaved of my children: Joseph is not, and Simeon is not, and ye will take Benjamin away. All these evils are fallen upon me.*

And Reuben spake unto Jacob, *saying,* "Give Benjamin *into my hand,* and *slay my two sons, if I bring him not back unto thee."*

And Jacob *answered,* "My son shall not go down with you; for his brother Joseph is dead, and he is left alone to me. If mischief befall him in the way by which ye go,* as it befell Joseph, *then shall ye bring down my grey hairs with sorrow to Hades."*

And the famine was sore in the land[15] of Canaan. *And it came to pass, when they had eaten the corn which they had brought out of Egypt, Jacob said unto his sons,* "Go again to Egypt and *buy us a little food,* lest we perish from hunger."

And Judah spake unto him, saying, The man, the lord of the country, declared unto us with the attestation of an oath, saying, Ye shall not see my face, unless your younger brother be with you.

And Jacob said, Wherefore dealt ye so ill with me, as to tell the lord of Egypt that ye had also another brother?

And his sons said, The man asked us straightly of our kindred, saying, Is your father yet alive? Have ye another brother? And we answered his questions honestly. How could we have known that he would say, Bring your brother?

And Judah said unto his father, "Send the lad with me, and we will arise and go; that we may live, and not die *of starvation, both we, and thou,* and the rest of our household. *I will* take the boy and *be surety for him: if I bring him not unto thee, and restore him to thee, I shall be guilty before thee forever. If we had not tarried* to persuade you to let us take Benjamin, *we should by now have returned twice* with food from Egypt."

And Jacob *said,* "If it must be so, do what you will. Take of the fruits of the land, and carry down to the lord of Egypt a present: balm, honey, frankincense, stacte, turpentine, and nuts. And take double money in your hand, and the money that was brought again in your*

---

[15]Gen., Ch. 43

sacks; take also your brother Benjamin, and arise, go again. And may my God give you favour in the sight of the man, and send back with you Simeon and Benjamin. As for me, I shall be as one desolate without children until you return."

The sons of Jacob *took the presents, and they took double money, and Benjamin, and went down to Egypt, and stood before Joseph. And when Joseph saw Benjamin with them, he said to the steward of his house, Bring these men home, and slay beasts, and make ready a feast; for these men shall dine with me at noon. And the man did as Joseph bade, and brought the men into Joseph's house.*

And the men said, Because of the money that returned in our sacks are we brought in; that he may bring upon us a false accusation and take us for bondmen. And they said to the steward, "Sir, we desire thee to hear us. We came down indeed the first time to buy *wheat. And it came to pass, when we came to the inn, that we opened our sacks, and, behold, every man's money was in his sack;* but *we cannot tell who put our money in our sacks.* Now we have brought double money, to return what we found and to pay for more wheat."

And the steward *said to them, Peace be to you, fear not: your God and the God of your fathers hath given you treasure in your sacks. And he brought Simeon out unto them, and gave them water, and they washed their feet; and he gave their asses provender. And they made ready the gifts, until Joseph came* to the house, *for they heard that they should eat there.*

And when Joseph came home, they bowed themselves to him to the earth, and they offered him the presents they had brought from their home. *And* Joseph *asked them, How are ye? Is your father well, the old man of whom ye spake? Is he yet alive?*

And they answered, Blessed be that man by God. And again the brothers *bowed down before him.*

And Joseph *lifted up his eyes, and saw his brother Benjamin, his mother's son, and said, Is this your younger brother, of whom ye spake unto me?*

And his brothers said, "It is, master."

And Joseph *said unto Benjamin, God be gracious unto thee, my son. And Joseph was troubled, for his bowels did yearn for his brother: and he sought to weep; and he entered into his chamber, and wept there.* He remembered Jacob and sighed, "Blessed are the eyes that ever behold you, my dear, aged father! You are God's favorite, and my kingdom and all its glory are unworthy of you. I want to ask Benjamin whether he remembers me and loves me with his whole heart, as I love you. Understand, father, that I ordered my brothers to bring me Benjamin only because I did not believe them when they said he was alive and you were in good health. I feared that jealousy had driven them to murder Benjamin, since you favored him. We were born of the same mother; therefore, they hated him as they hated me. I know, father, that you are broken-hearted because we are gone. I know that I have added to your misery, depriving you, in old age, of your youngest son. As if your grief for me were not enough, I have doubled your sorrows. I am the cause of your anguish and lamentation, mercilessly demanding that Benjamin be brought here. But I did this because I had to know whether you were indeed still alive, dear father. Oh, if only I could see your angelic face once again!"

Having grieved quietly for a long time in his chamber, *Joseph washed his face,* so that it would not be known that he was weeping, and he *went out and refrained himself.* And he commanded that *they set food for him apart, and for his brethren apart, and for the Egyptians apart: because the Egyptians could not eat bread with the Hebrews, for every shepherd is an abomination unto the Egyptians.*[16] And Joseph assigned to each brother a place according to his age, and called each by name, pretending to divine by means of his silver cup. Holding it in his left hand, he tapped it with the fingers of his right hand. He listened to the sound, then announced, "Reuben is the oldest brother and must sit at the head." Striking the cup again, he declared, "Symeon was born next and shall sit beside him." After the third tap, he commanded the third brother to take his place, and so on until they were all seated. The frightened brothers thought, "Truly, nothing is hidden from this man."

Wishing to calm his brothers a little, Joseph *took and sent portions unto them* from his table, *but Benjamin's portion was five times as much as any of the others. And they ate,* and *drank, and made merry with him.*[17] And Joseph *charged the steward of his house to fill the men's sacks with food, and to put into the mouth* of Benjamin's sack

[16]Gen., Ch. 46   [17]Gen., Ch. 43

the cup with which he pretended to divine, and to send *away the men.*[18] *And the morning dawned, and the men departed out of the city,* rejoicing; *but* before long *the steward overtook them* and accused them of theft. "You cannot be trusted," he berated them. *"Wherefore have ye rewarded evil for good? Ye have stolen the cup out of which the lord* of Egypt *drinketh and in which he divineth."*

"If we brought back the money which we found in our sacks, how then should we steal a cup *from the house of* our *lord?" answered the* brothers. *With whomsoever of thy servants thou shalt find the cup, let him die. The rest of us will be slaves of our lord.*

And Joseph's steward *said, "Now also let it be according to your words.* Put *down every man his sack upon the ground,* and I will search it."

Then they speedily took down every man his sack from his ass, and the steward *searched, and began at the eldest, until he came to the youngest: and the cup was found in Benjamin's sack. And the brothers rent their clothes,* cursed Rachel, and reviled Benjamin, saying, "Joseph wanted to rule over us and deserved to be devoured by wild beasts. Behold, you are of the same ilk, so you filched the royal goblet. Both of you are true sons of Rachel, who stole her father's idols, but denied it."

And Benjamin wept and lifted up his voice, saying, "The God of my father, Who deigned to take Rachel from the living, knows the truth about how Joseph died, and consoles Jacob as he laments the loss of his wife and children. Even now He is invisibly watching us and knows our hearts. He knows that I did not take the cup, and that I did not even consider such a thing. May I never again see Jacob's gray hair or hear his voice, if I stole the goblet! Woe is me, woe is me, Rachel, my mother: what evils have befallen your children! Joseph, so they say, was consumed by wild animals, and I am accused of thievery and am to be enslaved in a foreign land. When the beasts devoured Joseph in the wilderness, no one came to his aid. Now I, your child, plead innocence, but my brothers will not believe me."

The brothers had no choice but to return to the city. Trembling with fear, they fell prostrate before Joseph, who rebuked them, saying, "Is this how you repay me? I shower you

---

[18]Gen., Ch. 44

with favors, and you steal the cup with which I divine! Did I not say that you were spies?"

And Judah said, "What shall we say to my lord? What shall we speak? Or how shall we clear ourselves? God hath found out our sins and is punishing us for them. Behold, we are my lord's servants, both we, and he also with whom the cup was found."

And Joseph replied, "God forbid that I should enslave all of you. But the youth, he shall be my slave; and as for you, get you up in peace unto your father."

Then Judah fell at Joseph's feet and begged, "O my lord, let thy servant, I pray thee, speak a word, and let not thine anger burn against thy servant. My lord asked his servants, saying, Have ye a father, or a brother? And we said, 'Our father, your servant, had two sons whom he loved far more than us. The elder was devoured by a beast in the mountains, and our father weeps for him every day; the younger, whom he always keeps at his side, now takes the place of the elder.' Obedient to your command, master, we brought you our youngest brother; but we do not know how the goblet found its way into his sack. Now therefore, I pray thee, let thy servant abide instead of the lad a bondsman to my lord; and let the lad go up with his brethren to his father. For how will I go up to my father, and the lad be not with me, when I assured my father that I would bring him back safely? I cannot return to my father only to see him die of grief!"

Then Joseph, seeing the brothers disconcerted and apprehensive, and Benjamin, who had torn his raiment out of anguish, prostrate and begging them to intercede on his behalf, was deeply moved and could not refrain himself[19] any longer. He cried out, commanding the Egyptians to leave, and when there stood no man with him, except for his brothers, he wept aloud and said in the Hebrew tongue, "I am Joseph your brother; doth my father yet live?" And his brethren could not answer him; for they were afraid. And Joseph said to his brethren, Come near to me. And they came near. And he said, "I am Joseph your brother, whom ye sold into Egypt. I was not eaten by wild animals, as you told our father, but sold by you to Ishmaelites. I clasped your feet and begged for mercy, but you showed no compassion. Nevertheless, be not grieved, nor

---

[19]Gen., Ch. 45

angry with yourselves, that you sold me hither; for I have become ruler of Egypt. Once you told our father that Joseph was devoured by beasts in the mountains; now proclaim to him glad tidings: 'Your son Joseph is alive, sits upon a royal throne, holds a scepter, and has dominion over Egypt.'"

Hearing Joseph recount their wicked deeds, the brothers were seized with terror. Again Joseph reassured them, *"Be not grieved nor angry with yourselves that ye sold me hither; for God did send me before you to* feed you during the famine and *preserve* your lives. *For these two years hath the famine been in the land: and yet there are five years, in which there shall neither be earing nor harvest. So now it was not you that sent me hither, but God: and He hath made me a father to Pharaoh, and lord of all his house, and ruler throughout all the land of Egypt. Haste ye, and go up to my father; and ye shall tell my father of all my glory in Egypt, and of all that ye have seen; and ye shall haste and bring down my father hither* with his household, that I may feed them." *And* Joseph *fell upon his brother Benjamin's neck, and wept* for joy; *and Benjamin wept upon his neck. Moreover he kissed all his brethren and wept upon them,* for he nurtured no anger or resentment, but truly loved them.

And the fame thereof was heard by Pharaoh and his household, *saying, Joseph's brethren are come. And Pharaoh said unto Joseph,* "This do ye: bring your entire family, *and I will give you the good of the land of Egypt."*

And Joseph gave his brothers many presents: gold, silver, and beautiful robes, as well as wagons and asses for bringing Jacob and his household to Egypt. He also *gave them* abundant *provisions for the way,* and sent rich gifts for his father. As he joyfully sent off his brothers to Jacob, he told them, *"See that ye fall not out by the way,* but go in peace quickly *to my father, and say unto him, 'Thus saith thy son Joseph, God hath made me lord of all Egypt; come down unto me,* father, and fear not. I am eager to behold your angelic, venerable face.'"

And they came into the land of Canaan, and told their father everything about Joseph, *and all the words of Joseph, which he had said unto them.* When Jacob heard Joseph's name, his eyes filled with tears and he moaned, "Why do you remind me of my handsome, beloved son? Do you wish to drown my soul in grief again, or to destroy it in fires of sorrow?" *And* Jacob *believed them not* until Benjamin approached, kissed his knees, and assured him that what the others said was true. Then Jacob believed and marvelled, and his spirit revived. He said, *It is enough; Joseph my son is yet alive: I will go and see him before I die.*

And Jacob happily arose *with all that were his* and hastened to Egypt. Learning that Jacob was coming, Joseph *made ready his royal chariot, and went up to meet his father.*[20] When Jacob caught sight of Joseph, he forgot his years, alighted from his wagon, and hurried on foot to meet his son. The first thing Joseph did when he saw Jacob was to drop his royal staff to the earth, pretending it had slipped out of his hand. He fell to the ground as though bowing before the scepter, then picked it up; but actually he was offering obeisance to his father. He showed respect to Israel in this manner in order not to offend the Egyptians. Had he openly bowed before Jacob, they would have considered it dishonor to the royal purple he was wearing. And Israel *fell on* Joseph's *neck, and wept on his neck a good while,* and Joseph also wept, embracing Israel and kissing his gray hair.

And Joseph led Jacob with much pomp into the Egyptian capital and *brought in Jacob his father, and set him before Pharaoh, and Jacob blessed Pharaoh.*[21] *And Pharaoh said unto Jacob, How old art thou?*

And Jacob said unto Pharaoh, The days of the years of my life are an hundred and thirty years: few and evil have been the days of the years of my life, and have not attained unto the days of the years of the life of my fathers.

And Pharaoh commanded Joseph to settle *his father and brethren in the best of the land, and Jacob lived in the land of Egypt seventeen years,* and died, *and was gathered unto his* fathers. *And Joseph fell upon his father's face, and wept upon him, and kissed him*[22] lovingly. As he lay dying, Jacob enjoined Joseph not to bury him in Egypt, but to take his remains to the land of Canaan and put them into the tomb of his fathers. *And Joseph spake unto the princes of Pharaoh, saying, If I have found favour in your sight, speak in the ears of Pharaoh, saying, My father made me swear, in my grave which I have digged for me in the land of Canaan, there shalt thou bury me. Now therefore let me go up, I pray thee, and bury my father, and I will come again.*

---

[20]Gen., Ch. 46   [21]Gen., Ch. 47   [22]Gen., Ch. 50

And Pharaoh said, Go up. And Joseph went up, and with him went up all the servants of Pharaoh, the elders of his house, and all the elders of the land of Egypt, and all the house of Joseph, and his brethren, and his father's house; and it was a very great company. And they came to the threshing floor of Atad, which is beyond Jordan, and there they mourned with a great and very sore lamentation for seven days. And they buried Israel *in the double cave which Abraham bought for a burying place. And* Joseph returned to his house in Egypt, *he and his brethren, and all that went up with him.*

After Jacob's burial, *Joseph's brethren said* to one another, *Joseph will peradventure remember the evil we have done, and will certainly requite us. And they came to Joseph, and said,* "Thy father did command before he died, saying, Forgive the trespasses of thy brethren, and their sin; for they did unto thee evil. And now forgive our trespasses." *And Joseph wept* bitterly *when they spake unto him. And Joseph's brethren said* to him, "Behold, master, *we be thy servants."*

And Joseph said unto them, Fear not, for I am God's. Ye took counsel against me for evil, but God took counsel for me for good. Fear not: I will nourish you and your families. And he comforted them, and spake kindly unto them.

And Joseph dwelt in Egypt, he and his brethren, and all his father's house: and Joseph lived an hundred and ten years. And Joseph saw Ephraim's children, and the children of Machir, the son of Manasseh. And Joseph said unto his brethren: I die: and God will surely visit you, and bring you out of this land unto the land which He sware to Abraham, to Isaac, and to Jacob. And ye shall carry up my bones from hence. So Joseph died, being an hundred and ten years old.

For all this let us praise Christ our Lord, Who was prefigured by Joseph and is glorified with the Father and the Holy Spirit, now and ever and unto the ages of ages. Amen.

Thus the Month of March
comes to an end,
bringing glory to God
Who is the End of all things.

Translator's Note

In the Slavonic text from which this translation was made, Scriptural references and other pertinent information are provided in the form of notes in the margin of the text. In this English edition the marginal notes have been placed into footnotes, yet retaining as much as possible the format and wording of the original Slavonic. A few changes and additions to these notes have been made by the translator for purposes of clarification and explanation. Also, not all the notes found in the Slavonic have been included: some of these furnish synonyms for Slavonic words used in the main body of the text and are therefore superfluous in an English translation. Occasional minor corrections of an historical nature have been introduced directly into the text.

Quotations from the New Testament in these volumes have been adapted from the King James Version to conform to the Slavonic. For the Old Testament, use has been made both of the King James Version and of Sir Lancelot Brenton's translation of the Septuagint.[1] Quotations from the Psalms, however, are taken from The Psalter According to the Seventy.[2]

Towards the end of the nineteenth century, The Synodal Printshop of the Russian Orthodox Church published a Russian edition of the Lives of the Saints based, for the most part very closely but in some places quite loosely, on the compilation made by Saint Demetrius of Rostov. Reference to this Russian edition has been made on occasion, and the present translation includes several emendations based on it. In addition, a number of saints' Lives from this Russian version have already been translated by the Reader Isaac Lambertsen. When these were available, they were consulted in the preparation of this series.

---

[1] *The Septuagint with Apocrypha: Greek and English,* Sir Lancelot C. L. Brenton, Samuel Bagster and Sons, London, 1851; reprinted, Zondervan Publishing House, Grand Rapids, Michigan, 1988.
[2] *The Psalter According to the Seventy,* Holy Transfiguration Monastery, Boston, Massachusetts, 1987.

Index of Saints and Feasts of March

Names of saints and feasts in bold letters indicate that a Life or Homily is provided. Names in regular type face indicate a commemoration by name only, sometimes with brief information.

(A cumulative index of saints and feasts contained in all the volumes of The Great Collection currently published may be found online at www.chrysostompress.org. This will be updated as each new volume is printed.)